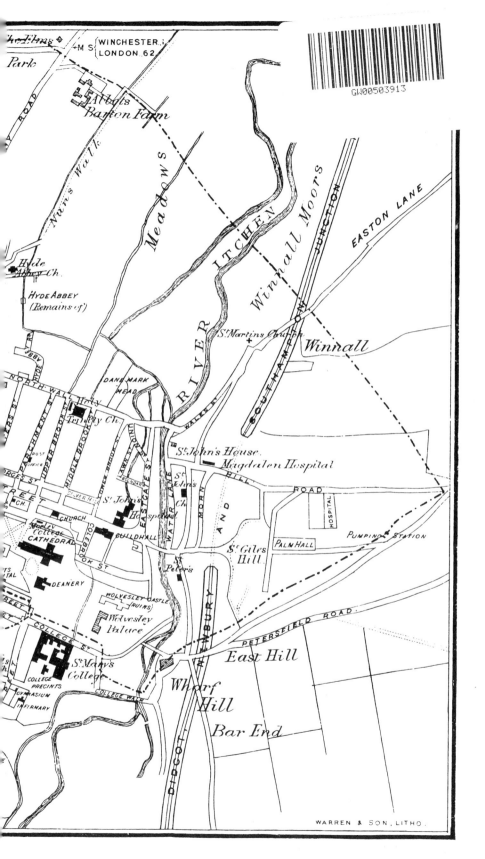

H1998

WARREN & SON, LITHO.

Winchester Notions

College from Black Bridge
(by E. R. D. Thomson, 1855)

WINCHESTER NOTIONS

The English Dialect of Winchester College

CHARLES STEVENS

Edited by Christopher Stray

THE ATHLONE PRESS
London and New Brunswick NJ

First published 1998 by
The Athlone Press
1 Park Drive, London NW11 7SG
and New Brunswick, New Jersey

© The Warden and Scholars of Winchester College 1998
British Library Cataloguing in Publication Data
*A catalogue record for this book is available
from the British Library*

ISBN 0 485 11525 5 hb
0 485 12138 7 pb

Library of Congress Cataloging in Publication Data

Stevens, Charles 1903-1979
  Winchester notions : the English dialect of Winchester College / Charles
Stevens : edited by Christopher Stray.
    p.   cm.
  ISBN 0-485-11525-5 (lib. bdg.), -- ISBN 0-485-12138-7 (pbk.)
  1. English language--Dialects--England--Winchester--Glossaries,
vocabularies, etc.   2. English language--England--Winchester--Slang-
-Dictionaries.   3. Students--England--Winchester--Language-
-Dictionaries.   4. Winchester College.   I. Stray, Christopher.
II. Title.
PE1914.W56S74   1998
427'.2735--dc21   98-23349
                                                                    CIP

Distributed in the United States, Canada and South America by
Transaction Publishers
390 Campus Drive
Somerset, New Jersey 08873

Typeset by Bibloset
Printed and bound in Great Britain by Bookcraft (Bath) Ltd

Charles Stevens in his study at La Grange, Jersey
On his desk are some of the volumes of 'Winton'.

Charles Stevens at Winchester College c 1921.
Stevens is wearing the appropriate school dress of the time (he was Prefect of Chapel).

I. J.

auctor amicus informator

d. d.

C. A. S.

They are for holding their notions, though all other men be against them.
John Bunyan, *Pilgrim's Progress*, 1678

I would not be thought a Reviver of old rites and ceremonies to the Burdening of the people, nor an Abolisher of innocent Customs, which are their Pleasures and Recreations: I aim at nothing but a Regulation of those which are in being amongst them, which they themselves are far from thinking burdensome, and abolishing such only as are sinful and wicked.
H. Bourne, Preface to *Antiquitates Vulgares*, 1775

When I was a boy in College, we were eager for any information about the former manners and customs of the old place.
R. B. Mansfield (Coll. 1836–42), *School Life at Winchester College*, 1866

Contents

Foreword by James Sabben-Clare   ix

Author's Preamble   xi

Author's Preface   xiii

   Notions Examinations   xvi

Preface by Christopher Stray   xxii

Introduction by Christopher Stray   1

   A note on the text   15

   Illustrations   15

THE DICTIONARY **Ablers** to **Zuyder Zee**   21

Index to Introduction   321

Foreword

In the final chapter of A. G. MacDonell's immortal *England their England* (1933) the protagonist Donald Cameron visits Winchester. He walks around the ancient buildings of the College and stops a small black-gowned boy – not so many yards from where I am writing this – to ask him about the tree they are standing beside. It turns out to be Lords Tree, so called, the boy tells him, because only men in Lords can sit under it. Donald is puzzled. Were there that many peers of the realm in the school? Further questioning reveals that 'men in Lords' means boys who play in the school cricket team – and that is called Lords because it used to play matches at Lord's cricket ground until 'quite recently': 1854 in fact. 'Lords' is thus a Notion, a word whose significance at Winchester is quite different from the meaning it bears in the world outside.

The private language of Notions that developed at Winchester College is seen as part of the fabric of Englishness. It finds its way into literature, and even into history. Stories are told of Intelligence Officers during the war, finding they had been at Winchester together, communicating over the radio by means of Notions, confident that no foreign code-breaker would have any idea what they were talking about.

The collection of these Notions into glossaries or 'word-books' was a way of filling the long hours for many a schoolboy in the last century. It also had the practical purpose of providing the new boy with a lexicon of all the special vocabulary he had to learn. That need diminished as the school became a less enclosed society, with less of a wish to parade its distinctiveness by perpetuating peculiarities of speech. From a peak about eighty years ago, the number of current Notions has steadily fallen. In the 1960s several words which had an unbroken pedigree of use going back to the Middle Ages finally fell into obsolescence. Nowadays only the slimmest of notebooks is needed to guide the new boy, and where there is an alternative equivalent, the everyday term is as often used as the Notion.

The language of Notions will not be completely lost, however. The trivial converse of generations of schoolboys provides at least a footnote in social and linguistic history; and so the word-books have become instead a resource for academic study.

None of these compilations is fuller and more detailed than the Notions book of Charles Stevens. The loosely bound typescript was entrusted into my hands by the family about twenty years ago. There was some discussion about having it published; but the technology of printing at the time would have made it prohibitively expensive. And so the original remained on my shelves, within easy reach for providing authoritative answers to all sorts of questions about Wykehamical lore and language.

The most assiduous user of Stevens in recent years has been Dr Christopher Stray, researching into the esoteric mysteries of Mushri (q.v.). He is not himself a Wykehamist, but his knowledge of Winchester history and institutions almost qualifies him for honorary status. Through his initial endeavours, and with the great benefit of his illuminating Introduction, the Stevens Notions book is now to reach a wider audience. Past, present and future Wykehamists will be fascinated; and those whose interest is more scholarly than sentimental will have lasting reasons to be grateful for the light that this book sheds on a small but very special corner of England.

James Sabben-Clare
Winchester College

Author's Preamble

Here you have an attempt at a complete lexicon of the unusual words used, up and down the centuries, by the boys of Winchester College. The extent and status of this local dialect have been recognised by the nation, and the title of 'Notions' has been awarded to it. Many books of Notions have been laboriously copied in manuscript by schoolboys, and from time to time a 'textus receptus' of Notions has appeared in print. This lexicon has gathered together and collated all the Notion books which I have found during the past fifty-three years, and you are sure to find the result surprising, in volume and in content. Whether you will find it interesting depends on you. Modern pressures to cut adrift from the past are strong enough to destroy not only local dialects, but the very institutions that have preserved them for so long. Indeed, this danger has been a stimulus, and sustained me through the 'harmless drudgery' of lexicography.

Some of the Notions you will dislike as much as I do, because they represent the vocabulary of bullies at various stages in the history of the school. Others reflect times when the lives of juniors were controlled by arrogant athlocracies. Both these trends were quite foreign to the ideals of the Founder. He created Praefects, it is true, but never delegated to them the power to thrash. Nor had he any inkling that ball-games, of which he could have but dimly been aware, would one day establish a hierarchy in an institution dedicated to godliness and the studies of good learning. There were, nevertheless, dark periods when the tyrant reigned unchecked, and the phraseology of those times is necessarily preserved in the lexicon. But mercifully a pendulum swings here, and there are intervals, just as long if not longer, when bullying is at a discount, and the Notions reflect a community in which minds scintillated and tongues toyed with words in a manner only possible when fear is in abeyance. One also suspects that stories of bullying have been exaggerated by the type of author who sets out to show that he was badly treated, but is none the worse for it. My own experience in this field is that a boy's first two years at boarding school were hard to the point of austerity, but there was a magic formula for surviving them: to do your best at everything. Once it was realised you were doing this, the tyrant stood back a pace and respected you. In any case, the two years were soon over, and then, in a trice, you had achieved seniority, and size, and the world lay at your feet: and one of the first things you asked yourself was whether to bring up your juniors more leniently than you had been brought up yourself. Over-permissiveness, you knew, might produce chaos. Great severity, on the other hand, went against the grain of most of us. Inevitably you settled for a compromise policy; and so the school went on, each generation of boys trying to do things a little better than the last: not always wisely, perhaps, for the judgement of the adolescent lacks the maturity which only experience can confer. But they did what they then thought was right. And it is because so many young men have gone on doing what they thought right, for so many centuries, in the same place, that the attitude of Winchester boys became a part of Englishry, and their school is still an exemplar to the educationist.

These are not just the after-thoughts of a veteran, gazing myopically at his remote schooldays. They are something we realised while we were still at school. This is a most remarkable fact, and one of which latter-day iconoclasts are seldom aware. It is another way of explaining the great power of continuous tradition. It is a shining example of how a good and godly manner of life can persist in a stable institution, almost untouched by the national vicissitudes which have gone on around it. Nobody told us this when we went to Winchester, but we soon learned it, not only, as Cicero says, from our pastors and masters, but also from the inarticulate place itself. As you walked round Chamber Court or Cloisters in the evening, the stones could preach their sermons: and on a summer afternoon the running brooks of the Itchen were books, for those who had the wit to read them. It was a great privilege to be admitted to the freemasonry of this ancient place, and one for which I have never ceased to be thankful.

Charles Stevens.

La Grange,
St Mary,
Jersey

25 January 1969

Author's Preface

Every community has its own special phrases, its slang, and its 'in-jokes', and retains them as a lubricant to the community machine. In certain circumstances they have proved to be a valuable coagulant against external menace. This was never more clearly shown than during the German Occupation of Jersey, when the resurrection of Norman patois enabled the Islanders to express themselves freely about their invaders, under their very noses. In a less dramatic way, English counties preserve a dialect in which nuances of various kinds can be shared by the indigenous, to the exclusion of strangers in their midst. But that has not been the intention. Dialects survive because they enshrine words passed by mother to child, and by that child to the succeeding generation. Dialect is, in fact, mother-tongue, however small the area to which it applies: and the same is true of community-slang, composed as it is of a vocabulary passed by one generation to the next, to express subtleties of meaning known only to members of that community. It is the way that people of that place speak, because it is the way they have always spoken. It has the dignity of unbroken tradition, and offers to the scholar an almost irresistible challenge to trace that speech to its original source.

If you turn to the Concise Oxford Dictionary you will find that the fifth and last meaning of the word 'notion' is 'traditional special vocabulary of Winchester College': an accurate definition, within the severe limits imposed by the conciseness of this excellent book. But the word 'special' strikes an unjust note, implying as it does that the boys of Winchester were too proud to speak Englishman's English, and invented a language of their own to show their superiority. That, of course, is not how Notions were created. The reason why Winchester has more in-words than most English institutions is that it has gone on so much longer than they. It is much older, for example, than the Church of England, and its scholars maintain, in twentieth-century England, the costume and behaviour of a pre-Reformation monastery, and language drawn straight from the Latin or medieval Catholic liturgies, or from the crude vernacular English of Chaucer. It is a pity that the word 'notion' was applied to this venerable vocabulary, as it apparently was in about 1856, because 'notion' implies a freakish personal idea. The College Under-Porter, Joel, used the word in this way when he showed visitors over College in the 1920s. Timidly opening the door of VIIth Chamber, and pitching his voice low lest he disturb us at books-chambers, he would say: 'This is Seventh Chamber, the old School-room. The cubicles are called toys. Preparation-time is called Toy-time. Curious notion, isn't it?' From him and similar disciples sprang the fallacy that the words he used were infantile, perverse and rather silly, and the preservation of them was boring. But by the boys themselves, with their keenly trained minds, notions were recognised as a fascinating heritage, and they insisted, with all the discipline and sanctions they wielded, that Notions should pass unscathed from one generation to another.

But in spite of this conservatism, Notions, like any other language, have always been on the move. Old words were dropped when their *raison d'être* vanished, and new words were coined to match some innovation. But behind the successive accretions, one can discern a solid nucleus of Notions dating from the foundation itself, including the names of certain buildings, customs and functionaries. There are a few ancient nouns, verbs and adjectives that Chaucer might have used, but which have long since vanished from ordinary English: such as baker (a cushion), thoke (to rest), cud (beautiful). There is also some pure Latin, which formed the basis of medieval education, both at lessons and in casual talk, in accordance with the ancient Wiccamical precept that at all times and places boys must eschew their mother tongue and speak Latin. That is why you find words like licet (permissible), sum (I am present) and socius (companion) in the Notion Books.

The Reformation, with its effervescence and ebullience of spirits, expanded and stimulated the Notions vocabulary. Free at last from monastic inhibitions, scholars discovered the fascinating pastime of making play with words and their equivalents: and the young and enthusiastic headmaster, Christopher Johnson (1561–71), broadened the boys' minds still further by letting them loose on Hills and in Water Meads, where they came in contact with the farmers, millers and bargemen of the Itchen Valley and picked up from them, as boys will do, inflections and phrases of the Hampshire dialect. The vernaculars of other counties also began to make their contribution to the store of Notions, for the scholars were no longer drawn merely from Hampshire and adjacent country, but from homes all over England, and now and then a neat phrase from a Northumbrian boy, for example, appealed to his fellow-scholars and stuck in the Notions vocabulary. For once a word had been adopted in College, it was not lightly discarded. Thus it comes about that word after word in this lexicon is found to survive in county dialect, and at Winchester, but not in English.

One gets the feeling that the post-Reformation masters were beginning to treat the boys less as a dumb herd of monastic novices, and more as individuals with brilliant academic careers ahead of them. They were encouraged to take interest in their surroundings, in the great institution to which they belonged, and the part they were playing in its continuation. Indeed Johnson used to discuss their activities with the boys up to books, a startling innovation, but traditionalised by him by conducting the discussions in Latin: and his 'Themes', or exercises on subjects such as Books and Hills, survive in the British Library. He also composed couplets on past Wardens and Headmasters, wrote a life of the Founder, and revised (in Latin of course) the Founder's school rules on the notice board known as Tabula Legum. A little later, an able young scholar named John Hoskyns, as a tribute to the College men-servants, painted a picture of the

'Trusty Servant' outside the kitchen, and wrote competent verses beneath it in Latin and English, extolling the virtues of these worthy men. A century after the Reformation another talented scholar, Robert Mathew, wrote a competent poem of 267 Latin hexameters describing in detail what life in College was like [*De Collegio seu potius Collegiata Schola Wicchamica Wintoniensi*, by R. Mathew (Scholar 1643–7)]. Talents such as these, combined with the new-found intellectual freedom, added pages of new words to the store of our particular dialect.

The Notions vocabulary was handed from generation to generation of boys through the seventeenth and eighteenth centuries, with a few words added here or discarded there. In the early nineteenth century a certain number of words were adopted from Regency slang, and survive at Winchester, but are lost to standard English. But later in the century all sorts of changes took place, buildings vanished, customs were discontinued, and large areas of the Notions vocabulary vanished with them. Among these events were the abolition of Old Commoner buildings in 1842 and then, in a rush, about 1869, New Commoner buildings were converted to class-rooms, going on Hills ceased, the great festival of Election Week was shorn to the bone, and School with its wealth of tradition ceased to be a school-room. You might have thought that these upheavals would deal a death-blow to Notions, but the Wiccamical community, preoccupied as always with the manipulation of words, continued to preserve all it could of its traditional speech, and to match each innovation with a page of new Notions. To take but one example, the 1914 war revived the ancient Notion of beavers, and produced malt buns, meatlessers, starva and War Scholars.

Nor must one forget those citizens who innocently contributed new Notions: those Dons, new men, pitch-up and townspeople who strove from time to time to offer the correct idiom and got it wrong. Their mistakes were gratefully pounced upon by the boys, and added to the existing hotch-pot of fascinating or entertaining words.

Before adopting a word from outside as their own, the boys tended to put their mark upon it by altering it slightly, in one of several ways. One does not know how many, if any, of these word-changes followed an example set by county dialects, or arise merely from an adolescent urge to be different. But the changes are there, they follow certain patterns, and are well worth scrutiny. They are: (1) *the addition of -ster to familiar words to denote an agent*: e.g. brockster (a bully); mugster (a worker); thokester (an idler). A genuine Old English suffix, -ster originally indicated the feminine: thus, sangere (singer), sangestre (woman singer), seamer (sewer), seamestre (needlewoman). In the fourteenth century this suffix was dropped in favour of the Norman-French suffix -ess, and words ending in -ster lost their feminine meaning. Thus Wyclif uses dwellster (m) and dwelleresse (f). In the change-over period one gets double-feminines which still survive, like songstress and sempstress. By the time College was founded, words ending -ster were no longer exclusively feminine, and this type of word-change looks rather early. (2) *the addition or -er or -ers to a name or word*: e.g. the Jacker (Mr Jackson); chozzers (a chouse or nuisance); uppers (up-game). This is not confined to Winchester, and probably has no deeper significance than the -ie or -y suffixed to familiar names: e.g. Willie for Will. (3) *the alteration of the vowel in the middle or a word*: e.g. chince (chance); crocketer (cricketer); houstle (hustle); roush (rush). This word-change is deliberate, and fairly consistent. In some cases it represents Hampshire or other dialect; in others, a policy of changing a word before accepting it. (4) *pluralisation of words*: e.g. crockets (cricket): Hills (St Catharine's Hill); Meads (the College meadow). There is no obvious explanation of this. (5) *omission of the definite article before the names of familiar places and people*: e.g. Chamber Court; Chapel; School; Meads; Hills; Praefect of Hall. For some reason, the Nipperkin was always awarded a definite article. This may be due in part to the fact that such words were originally spoken in Latin, which has no definite article. (6) *the abbreviation of -ation into -ā (pronounced like star)*: e.g. examinā (examination); Illuminā (Illumination). This trick appears to be no earlier than c. 1850, though it is recorded outside Winchester of a Wicklow innkeeper named Judy in Sir Walter Scott's *Journal* (c. 1820), who used to say consolā and botherā. But it is not part of standard English slang. It may derive from the fact that penmen of all periods, from classical manuscripts to the present day, have found the Latin -atio (English -ation) consumed too much time and paper to write in full, and put a broad stroke over the -a to indicate the omitted letters. What was in origin a legitimate time-saver has been injected in a rather juvenile way into words not qualified for it: e.g. gymnā (gymnasium); steeplechā (steeplechase). It has even been carried further, *per ludibrium*, into Debā Sā (Debating Society), and in 1960 Museum was called Musā. This kind of prank brings Notions into disrepute. On the other hand, competî (competition) is sound medieval practice.

NOTIONS EXAMINATIONS

One of many things which became quite apparent to me during my five and a half years in College was that the boys were determined to perpetuate Notions, and to this end they devoted a good deal of time and trouble. One manifestation of this was the Notions examination. You might suppose that this insistence on Notions was just a subtle form of bullying the younger boys. I, who was there, know it was not so. Senior boys regarded Notions as a heritage, and in their minds it was part of their duty to the place to pass that heritage on intact. There was nothing irksome in this. On the contrary, many of the Notions held great interest for boys of scholarly mind.

Professor C. H. Turner (Coll. 1872–9) told me that up to 1872 Notions Examination was conducted in VIIth Chamber, the whole of College sitting round three sides of it, and taking places on the result of answers given. Similar examinations were held in Commoners. It was an ordeal for all except Senior Praefects, and for those found wanting there was severe punishment. This of course was carrying tradition too far, and in Short Half 1872 the whole thing boiled up into the famous Tunding Row, after which the mass Notions exams were abolished. What happened was that a Praefect of a new house who was not in full power was ordered to attend a Notions exam, and refused. The Senior Commoner Praefect lost his temper and thrashed him savagely. The facts became public, and an inquisition was held by the authorities into the extent of tundings (beatings) of juniors by seniors. Up to this moment, said Turner, life in College was a hell. In the twenty-two days between 18 September and 9 October he had himself had fifteen tundings. But after the Row, life in College became very comfortable.

By the time I got to College in 1917, some forty-five years later, discipline, though strict, was milder. But Notions were taken seriously. On the second Sunday of term the Praefect of School sent for all new boys and heard from them the words of 'Domum' and 'Jam Lucis' in his upstairs Chamber. Some translation was also required, and the catches here were that in 'Jam Lucis' 'mundi' means 'clean' (not 'of the world'), and that the Holy Spirit in 'Jam Lucis' was 'paraclitus', not 'sanctissimus' as in 'Te de profundis' [see Dictionary: 'Domum', 'Jam Lucis' and 'Grace']. The real test came on the last day of the first fortnight of term, when the Senior Praefect of each upstairs Chamber examined the Chamber in general, and new men in particular, in Notions. Often two Chambers combined for the session. The Chamber assembled after Preces, tollies were lit, a beneficent Praefect sported refreshments, and all sat in slack chairs round the fire, though in some Chambers the examinees sat up in bed. The two Praefects stood on the fender with their backs to the fire and asked questions in turn, beginning with the junior man. Few of the questions asked reached the In Loco. Corporal punishment for Paters and Sons was strictly forbidden by the Headmaster, who indeed had outlawed the holding of any Notions exams, and it seldom took place unless a Pater had obviously done nothing to help his Son. The more usual procedure was to hold the examination again.

By this time a conscientious Pater, such as the excellent Arthur Foot, whose Son I was privileged to be, should have taught his Son, orally or by book, most of the current Notions, and also some of the obsolete ones, which it was strongly felt should be preserved on account of their interest. He should have taught him how to call, how to light fires, and his other miscellaneous duties: and also have:

sweated him to get a Pempe;
taken him to Amphitheatre and Third Pot;
pointed out to him the most important Dons and Commoners;
taken him round the Houses and shown him the entrances.

The Child had also to know:

everyone in College;
School Caps in College;
any members of the Go.Bo. who had recently been on view;
what members of the staff were Blues; in 1923 there were:

cricket: Rockley Wilson (Camb.), Harry Altham (Ox.);
soccer: the Headmaster (Camb.).

He had also to give his opinion (amid universal merriment) who was the cuddest and who the ugliest man in College (excluding his own Chamber).

It was hoped he would know what were *bad notions*: (1) under 4 years: to sport a speckled straw hat. (2) under 3 years: to sport a satin ribbon on a straw hat; to walk across Flint Court when men are (or a quarter of an hour before men are) up to books, unless you are in VIth Book or have a school cap. (3) under 1 year: to sport a line, unless the other two have been in the school over a year. (4) to say 'I think' unless you have twenty men junior to you in College: in Commoners this was a bad notion under 2 years. (5) for all: to toll Meads without a socius between hours. (6) for College: to talk to a Don without buttoning the gown (originally the Aul.Prae. was included also). (7) for College Inferiors: to take the gown off the waistcoat, except for two purposes (see College waistcoat); to go a solus walk. (8) for all College men: to wear brown shoes on Sundays; to eat food, fruit or ices in Chamber Court. For other bad notions, see: angle, barricade, fringe, halo, hiatus, hot roll, tail, three at a toys.

The following words were extremely bad notions: Deba. Sa. (for Debating Society); Hills (for Junior Game); Long Table (for Middle End); Skiers (for Porter's Lodge).

Some Commoner notions were bad notions in College:

Aunty Norton (for Mammy Norton)
brew cad (a junior who makes tea)
brewing (for having tea)
british (for an English)
Cathers (for Cathedral)
in sweat (for still liable to be sweated)
meader (for a tug cap)
Micla (for St Michael's Passage)
Preffy (for Praefect)
Sick House (for Sanatorium)
Southers (for Southampton)
teejay (for Pater)
tozzie (for sixpence)
uppers, up game (for game in yard)
up to House (q.v.)

If any of the following notions were asked, the answer had to be given verbatim from the Beetleites' Notion book:

Adam and Eve: 'A stream . . . First Pot'.
Birley's Corner: 'The corner . . . in 1897'.
Hell: 'A gloomy copse . . . embankment'.
Jupiter: 'A notorious rascal . . . time immemorial'.

Everybody had to know how to

raise leave continent.
get a book out of Mob.Lib.

Sometimes the names of the last five Headmasters and Second Masters were asked.

Examinees had to know what Long Stinkers and Short Stinkers tolls were.

Ties, colours and hat-ribbons offered a wide field for the questioners, who usually put the question thus:

'If you saw a man going down College Street wearing . . .'

The house hat-ribbons had to be given word for word, e.g. 'plum, straw, plum, light-blue, plum, straw, plum'.

Favourite questions were:

Lords hat-ribbon: plain blue, silk.
Soccer XI ditto: white, half: dark-blue, half.
Sixes ditto: in three stripes, the centre white, the other two blue, red, or brown.
narrow full-house-tie ribbons, especially College East and West, and F.
the form and names of College XV and VI ties: tramp, brightest and best.

The answer to 'who may wear a house-tie ribbon on a zephyr' was 'Thorntons only.'

Examinees could be asked to distinguish between

Buttress and Colson's Buttress.
a snack, a squish, a whiteball.
Log Pond Champions; Meads Champions; Og, Gog and Magog.
the many corners: Amen, Angelus, Birley's, Darius, Misery, Pen and Ink, Salve Diva Potens.
the obsolete types of blow: boner, clo, con, greaser, muttoner, muzzler, rabbiter.
the Courts: Chamber, Flint, Job's, Moberly, Outer, School, Tout.

[They could be asked:]

the difference between: Bullfinches, Goldfinches, Greenfinches.
the five meanings of dean; and of bishop.
about the foricas:
about the Tents: Meads, Old, Webbe.
about the Gates: Blue (2), Commoner, Garden, Meads, Middle, Moberly, Non-Licet, Outer.
about the Paradises: Lost and Regained.
about the passages: Du Boulay, Good Friday, Hewett's, Non-Licet, North-West, Pseudo-Good Friday, St Michael's, Seventh Chamber, Young Augustus.
the difference between Audit Room and Cheese Room.
about the various utensils, all obsolete but intriguing: biggin, bob, jack, joram, nipperkin and Waterloo.

There were many *catch* questions: 'A' is the correct and only answer:

'Which way does College clock face?'
A. 'It hasn't got a face.'

'What is College Walk?' (When the answer had been given correctly, there followed:) 'What is Boat Club walk?'
A. 'The way men in Boat Club walk.'

'Where is Blackberry Lane?' (When the answer had been given correctly, there followed:) 'Where is Tubby Lane?'
A. 'In Armoury.'

'Why is Hat Place so called?'
A. 'Because there are never any hats there.'

'What is Moses and Aaron?'
A. 'The double arms on Old Tent.'

'Which is Moses?'
A. 'The one that isn't Aaron.'

'What is "Let us now praise famous men"?' (q.v.)

'What is a top-hat called?'
A. 'A cathedral.'

'What is a hat-box called?'
A. 'A hat-box.'
(*Not*, as an ingenious junior suggested, a 'cathedral close'.)

'What is on the top of Hills?'
A. 'Clump.'
'What is on the top of Clump?'
A. 'Feathers.'

'How many Pinnacles are there?'
A. 'Thirteen.'

'Why is Forder's Piece so called?'
A. 'Because the Headmaster said it was not to be called Forder's Piece.'

'Can you sing?'
A. 'All people that on earth do dwell.'

(The origin of this answer is seen under Candlestick, and is recorded from 1820.)

'Who is Senior Commoner?'
'What is Senior Commoner?' (q.v.)

'Who is Senior Wreck?'
'What is Senior Wreck?' (q.v.)

'Who was in Do.Co.Ro.Fo?'
A. 'Mr Munro.'

'What is the hexameter on Aut Disce board?'
A. 'Aūt dĭscĕ, aūt dĭscĕdē, mănĕt sōrs tērtĭă căēdī.'
(This had to be pronounced in accordance with the above false scansion, thus:
'Ought dissy, ought dissydee, manet sors terteia kay-edi'.)

'Who said, and when: 'Hymn number 200?'
A. 'Quirk.'
'Is this College East Melhuish Cup?'
A. 'The Headman.'
'Lies, devilish lies'?
A. 'Bertie Lucas.'
(And there were many others.)

Some of the more striking inscriptions were sometimes asked: e.g.

(in the Aul.Prae.'s place in VIth): 'ἀρχὴ ἀνδρὰ δείξει.'
(Sick House Continent Room): 'ψυχῆς νοσούσης εἰσὶν ἰατροὶ λόγοι.'
(Mob.Lib., north face): 'Si haec scitis beati eritis, et si feceritis ea.'
(Commoner Gate): 'Leaving to those who pass where they passed an undying memorial of faithful and willing service.'

A knowledge of Dons' nicknames was desirable: see **nicknames**.
Of course, no junior could possibly learn all this in his first fortnight, and no Praefect expected him to. It is a compendium of questions asked at many Notions examinas. There was much good humour on these occasions, and no punishment for those found wanting. But the new boy perceived immediately, as the examination proceeded, that those who had trod the path before him valued, and intended to preserve, the corpus of College lore, which they had inherited from their predecessors.

Preface

The histories of schooling and of special languages are enticing and fruitful fields in their own right; even more so when they meet, as they do in the study of school slang. The archives of the English public schools contain a mine of information on the subject, but by far the richest deposit is that held in the Wiccamica archive at Winchester College. Here are to be found a long series of manuscript lists of Notions (Winchester College slang) made by pupils at the school, from the 1840s to the present day. I am glad to be able to record my thanks to the headmaster of Winchester and current guardian of Wiccamica, James Sabben-Clare, who has patiently endured visits and queries over several years, and has allowed me to borrow and copy material in his care. My thanks also to his secretary, Suzan Rae, for her cheerful welcome and unobtrusive help, and to the College archivist, Dr Roger Custance, for access to non-Wiccamical material.

As well as the manuscript word-books, Wiccamica also contains a set of heavily illustrated typescript volumes on life at Winchester assembled by Charles Stevens, who was a pupil there from 1917 to 1922 – a labour of love which occupied much of his spare time during a long life. Among them is his dictionary of Notions, the most comprehensive ever assembled, which forms the basis of the present book. I am very grateful for the generous and unstinting help of Richard Stevens, who has discussed his father's life with me, lent me material, and with his wife Jo made me welcome on several occasions. His brother Philip Stevens kindly allowed me to quote from his helpful comments on a draft text. My thanks too to Chris Collard, Mrs Carolyn Dalton and James Lawson, for information on Charles Stevens' career at New College, Oxford and at Shrewsbury School.

Introduction

In the introduction to his *Public School Slang*, Morris Marples wrote that
'Westminster, Christ's Hospital, and most of all Winchester, have a speech
rich in relics of the past . . . No other school can even approach Winchester in
this respect, and its slang . . . is worth a detailed study in itself.'[1] Marples was
not very explicit about his sources for 'Notions' (the term used at Winchester
to refer to its slang) though he declared that the best glossaries were provided
by R. G. K. Wrench's *Winchester Word-Book* (1891) and the 1930 issue of the
official school booklet, *Notions and Rules*.[2] Nor did he make any mention of the
manuscript word-books compiled by boys, of which a large collection is held
in the College archives. One such book was assembled by Charles Stevens,
who entered the school in 1917. He later transcribed earlier word-books, and
intermittently added new material, producing a finished typescript only in 1969.
This was presented to Winchester College by his family after his death in 1979,
and forms the basis of the present volume.

My aim in this introduction has been to give an account of the history of
Notions and of their lexicography, in relation to the history of Winchester
College. In dealing with the various glossaries that have been compiled, my
concern has been less to discuss the linguistic details of their content than to
explain why they appeared when they did. In the case of Stevens' own glossary,
I have tried to provide a biographical context. Dictionary-makers are, after all,
human, though their readers may be forgiven for forgetting this on occasion. We
are reminded of it by a story told of H. G. Liddell, the co-author of what remains
the standard Greek-English dictionary, 'Liddell and Scott', first published in
1843. Liddell was from 1846 to 1855 headmaster of Westminster School, and
used the dictionary in his classical teaching. When pupils queried the accuracy
of entries, he is alleged to have replied, 'Scott wrote that part'. This prompted a
Westminster boy to recite the following when a prize was offered for epigrams:

> Two men wrote a Lexicon, Liddell and Scott;
> Some parts were clever, but some parts were not.
> Hear, all ye learned, and read me this riddle,
> How the wrong part wrote Scott, and the right part wrote Liddell.[3]

Marples' personal views are occasionally made explicit. In his entry on
Winchester College, he claims that in his listing of Notions will be found
'all except place-names, technicalities, and certain trivial and unimportant

Winchester idioms' (186). The last two exclusions make one wonder just
what Marples' criteria were. In his entry on 'Forms, nomenclature of', he tells
us that 'Eton has a unique and elaborate, but not particularly interesting, system
of classification of its own', and mentions only the Remove (82). Yet as with
other schools, these names encapsulate the history of teaching and learning. Two
of the lower forms at Eton, for example, were called 'Nonsense' and 'Sense',
referring to the teaching of Latin verse, which in the first year was required
to be no more than metrical, and in the next year also to make some sense.
Such naming systems are outcrops of semantic geology, preserving valuable
evidence of practices long since abandoned. One of the most striking features
of Notions is the sedimentation of layers of vocabulary over a long period to
make a palimpsestic record. Anglo-Saxon forms include mug = study, thoke
= leisure, brock = misfortune, cud = smart or nice. Latin gives us licet =
permissible, preces = prayers, remedy = holiday, continent = confined to bed.
In the nineteenth century common Victorian slang entered the stock: quill =
narrow hollow stem, but in Devonian dialect = a faucet for a cask used to tap
liquor, hence to ply electors with drink, hence to curry favour. Thus to 'raise a
quill' is to win favour, and a schoolboy homosexual liaison is referred to as 'being
in quill with X'. The complexities of this dialect are given an added dimension by
the differences of vocabulary between boarding houses, so that particular routes
and places are given unique descriptive phrases. One account mentions that if a
boy asks you to 'nip on' if you are going 'round by' you will know both where
he proposes to go, and that he belongs to a particular boarding house which alone
uses these terms.[4]

Stevens' dictionary of Notions, the fullest ever compiled, is rich in the
names of people and places: headmasters, staff and their families, servants
and tradesmen, buildings, passages, walls and ponds. And this is because
any person or thing that acquired an importance in the life of the school,
or possessed some interesting individuality, was likely to 'become a Notion'.
Thus a listing of Notions as comprehensive as Stevens' provides an encyclopedic
pupil's-eye guide to Winchester College. And here we return to the humanity of
the dictionary-maker; for as I shall suggest below, Charles Stevens' collection
and listing of Notions, begun in boyhood and pursued in retirement, were driven
by a powerful emotional commitment to his old school.

RE-CREATING PARADISE:
CHARLES STEVENS AND WINCHESTER

Charles Guy Stevens was born in Edgbaston in 1903, and died in Jersey in 1979.
As a boy he spent several years in South Africa, where his father was engaged
in trade. When the family returned to England in 1909, he entered Bromsgrove
School, and when they moved to Pevensey in 1913, went to Dunchurch
Hall preparatory school near Rugby. From there, he gained a scholarship to

Winchester College in 1917. At Winchester he had a successful academic career, winning the Greek verse prize and being *proxime accessit* for others. He narrowly missed appointment as Aul.Prae. (Prefect of Hall, the Wintonian equivalent of Head Boy), and served as 'Cap.Prae.' (Prefect of Chapel: for both terms, see the Dictionary). He also played cricket and fives with some distinction. Plate 1 shows him in school dress in about 1920. In 1922 he gained a scholarship to Winchester's sister institution, New College, Oxford. Here he continued to develop his cricketing skills, acting as secretary and then captain of the college XI. The classical course at Oxford consisted of a linguistic and literary section (Honour Moderations: 'Mods') followed by a section devoted largely to ancient history and ancient and modern philosophy (Literae Humaniores: 'Greats'). Stevens gained a First in Mods, but could manage only a Third in Greats. The reasons are unclear, but it may be that his linguistic skills and interests, so finely honed at Winchester, were not enough to carry him through a course that may have been less to his liking.[5] His disappointing final degree must have been a shattering blow to a young man whose academic success had previously been so consistent. It seems also to have followed (and was perhaps associated with) the erosion of a firm, if conventional religious faith by the scepticism inculcated by the philosophy course in Greats. This was certainly the opinion of J. N. L. Myres, a close friend of Stevens' at Winchester and later his brother-in-law. In a letter to Stevens' son, Myres wrote:

> He began . . . by taking basic Xtianity . . . for granted as the foundation for the good life – but I think this was one of the losses he suffered from Oxford philosophy when reading Greats, where nothing was supposed to be taken for granted . . . he lost something solid and comforting at the back of his thought at that time and had to make do thereafter with an idealism which had no basis in anything beyond this world, and too often led to failure and frustration in the day-to-day business of life . . . one has always to remember that he never wholly recovered from the disastrous disappointment of his Oxford years, when his failure (by no means wholly his fault) to fulfil the golden promise of his time at school had such a devastating and traumatic effect on his idealism and self-confidence. He could not come to terms with this as a schoolmaster, and though for a while Africa went a long way to satisfy his frustrated passion for worthwhile service, the eventual collapse of the whole colonial mise-en-scène drove his idealism back once more to feeding unhappily on itself with a deepening sense of failure and futility.[6]

On leaving Oxford in 1926, he joined the teaching staff at Shrewsbury, a school famous for its classical teaching since the great days of Samuel Butler, headmaster from 1798 to 1836, and his pupil and successor Benjamin Kennedy, author of a celebrated Latin primer, who reigned from 1836 to 1866. Here he continued to play cricket and fives. His performance in a masters vs pupils match was commented on in the school magazine: 'it is obvious to the most casual and ignorant observer that before very long he will be a player of the highest class'.[7]

Between 1925 and 1928, Stevens served on the committee supervising the excavation of St Catharine's Hill, a steep and imposing landmark outside Winchester with a long history of College associations. He also drew diagrams and maps for the published report, which appeared in 1930, his co-authors being his Winchester contemporaries Christopher Hawkes and Nowell Myres.[8]

In 1929 Stevens left Shrewsbury. A common career pattern would have been to remain until a boarding house became available – the normal route to increased influence and income within the school. At that point, however, there were several long-established staff members ahead of him in the queue, and prospects for a house must have seemed poor. Stevens entered the Colonial Administrative Service, serving first in Northern Rhodesia, with a short-term attachment to the Colonial Office. He was promoted to District Commissioner in 1945 and retired in 1949. He was then 46, well below the normal retirement age; but he seems to have been increasingly at odds with his superiors in the Colonial Office. He felt that the desk-bound functionaries in London and Lusaka were unable to make the imaginative leap to life in the boma and the bush, and that they were unappreciative of the dedicated work he carried out in difficult and demanding conditions.[9]

Stevens was in fact always happier in the field than in the office. During his period in the colonial service he travelled constantly, learning native dialects and assembling maps of the districts of which he was in charge. On one occasion, travelling in Northern Rhodesia by barge in February 1930, he played his native paddlers a record of Paul Robeson singing 'Old Man River'. Finding that they liked the tune, he translated the words into Sikololo for them.[10] The result was recorded in a poem, one of his 'Rhymes at Random'. Several of his 'rhymes' reflect the irritation of the man on the spot at the demands made by his masters back in London. This feeling comes across in 'An African Survey' (1947), prompted by Lord Hailey's book of that name.[11]

An African Survey

(a lament, sung by District Commissioners, on the eve of publication of yet another book about Africa; this time, by a Lord Hailey, whom we never met)

Air: 'A bicycle made for two'

Hailey! Hailey!
    Here are your answers. Whew!
We toil daily
    Writing your book for you.

And when the pundits quote it,
Please don't pretend you wrote it.
    It was written, you see,

By each tired D.C.
On those stations you never knew.

On his retirement, Stevens went to live in Jersey; his wife Joan, born Joan Collas, was the daughter of a Senator of Jersey. He went in for farming, at first in potatoes, then after a coronary in 1958 concentrating on a small milking herd. He spent much of his spare time collaborating with his wife, who became a distinguished historian of the island. Together they assembled a definitive study of Jersey place-names, illustrated with detailed maps drawn by Stevens.[12] He contributed a long series of articles to the *Bulletin* of the Société Jersiaise, which elected him a *Membre d'Honneur* in 1976. One of these described a game of fives played in Jersey in the summer of 1463, and went on to suggest that fives became tennis, as the glove was developed into the racket.[13] His last article, published after his death, was entitled 'Caesar and Jersey'.[14] Here he argued that Caesar may have sent Legions VII and X to Jersey in 55 BC. Reminding his readers of the long tradition which allotted to Jersey the name 'Caesarea', and drawing on his knowledge of etymology and local place-names, he suggested that two strange names, Sedeman and Diélament, may come from Septimana and Decumana castra (i.e. the camps of the Seventh and Tenth Legions). Recognising that 'the learned' might dismiss his argument, he concluded, 'For my part, I shall cling quietly to my fancy, for (if true) it would have so many attractive side-effects. It would solve the riddle of two of our most obstinate place names; it would put beyond reasonable doubt our right to the name Caesarea; it would underline our connection with the great Julius.' Plate 2 shows Stevens in his study in retirement. He relied heavily on a small collection of reference books, using the ninth edition of the *Encyclopedia Britannica* for general information and the *Century Dictionary* for etymologies.[15] In a sense, Stevens' life on Jersey was a continuation of the semi-exile of his period in Africa: the hermit had come to prefer life in his cell, on the margin of the larger world. To his eldest son, he remained an enigma: 'he was very accomplished and very good-looking, and yet a man of the greatest integrity, and shy, lonely and ill at ease in the world.'[16]

Wherever he lived, Stevens not only collected information and organised it, but illustrated it with finely detailed maps and drawings. His contribution to the archaeological report on St Catharine's Hill has already been mentioned; he also provided illustrations for his own dictionary, 'Notions'. His fascination with language and the byways of its local usage was paralleled by a visual curiosity about the unique details of particular places. As well as producing his 'Notions', finally finished in 1969, he gathered together a large collection of material on every aspect of Winchester life in six volumes entitled 'Winton'. At the beginning of the first volume, Stevens quotes from Cicero: 'Which of us who has had a liberal education does not remember those who taught him, and even that silent place itself where he was educated, with a grateful memory?'[17] The 'silent place itself' (*locus ipse mutus*) is extensively recorded in 'Winton'. Its several hundred pages constitute a miniature archive in themselves. Photographs, some taken by Stevens himself, offer a snapshot of life in the school just after the First World War. Ephemera of all kinds letters, sermons, circulars, invitations, notices are inserted and commented on. Headmasters and their staff are described, and their speech mannerisms recorded; they are caught for eternity in photographs and caricatures by pupils. All in all, 'Winton' is a unique resource for the history of Winchester College: at once an exploration of its development over several hundred years, and a detailed insider's account of its life in the early twentieth century.

Linking 'Winton' with the dictionary is a further volume containing transcripts, made in 1923, of three word-books. The first is by Robert Gordon (1842), the earliest which survives; the second (extracts only) is by James Foord, who was at Winchester from 1868 to 1872; the third is Stevens' own word-book. At this point, just after leaving Winchester, he was already concerned, as he writes in his preface, to 'bring together all the existing knowledge on notions'. At the time, this was contained in seventy pages of typescript. By 1969, when 'Notions' was finally completed, the total had risen to 267 pages.

In a letter from which I have already quoted, his brother-in-law J. N. L. Myres concluded that Stevens 'developed a kind of personal pantheism in which his sense of the sacred focussed more and more on the beauties of nature and the innocence of the beasts of the field and the birds of the air . . . He had very strongly the Greek feeling for the personification of natural forces'. Stevens himself, in his Author's Preamble, recalled that 'As you walked round Chamber Court or Cloisters in the evening, the stones could preach their sermons: and on a summer afternoon the running brooks of the Itchen were books, for those who had the wit to read them'. Wherever Stevens lived – Winchester, Africa, Jersey – he sought to capture this sense of place. But the greatest of these was Winchester. To a boy whose home life seems to have been unhappy, it offered an encompassing alternative world. It could never be re-entered – the only true paradises are those we have lost – but it could at least, through minutely detailed description, be re-created in imagination. Just before his death, Stevens wrote a poem called 'Illumina':

> If I die tonight
> (and I might,
>   you know),
> stay in my sight
>   until I go.
> Be close at hand
> (you understand)
> in the kindly glow
> of candle-light.
>   I loved it so.

At the end of his natural term, he looked back to the custom of his schooldays, when lighted candle-ends were placed in a wall niche to mark the end of a school term.[18] The simple eloquence of the final line encapsulates his commitment to

Winchester. The quizzical parenthesis 'and I might, you know', on the other hand, suggests a gentle sense of humour which can be seen in others of Stevens' poems, and also in some of his Dictionary entries. It is heartening to think that it survived the experience of disappointment and frustrated idealism which might have been expected to destroy it.

THE LEXICOGRAPHY OF NOTIONS

The earliest known listings of Notions are manuscript glossaries compiled by boys at the school. The first of these was assembled in 1842 by Robert Gordon, who was in the school as a Commoner from 1838 to 1843. The Commoners – originally *commensales*, boys who shared meals with the scholars on the foundation – were pupils who had not gained scholarships.[19] The scholars lived in College, a building containing a series of 'chambers'. Many of the Notions recorded by Gordon had to do with 'Old Commoners', a building which was converted into classrooms during his time at the school. All the later word books assembled in the nineteenth century seem also to have been written by (or for) Commoners. Each of these two segments of the pupil community had its own Notions; but many were held in common, and individual boarding houses, when these were erected, also developed their own vocabulary. Charles Stevens stands outside this tradition, since he was a scholar; but he was certainly aware of this history of difference and overlap.[20]

The several dozen manuscript word books which survive from the nineteenth century seem all to have been compiled by Commoners. Of the two parallel streams of Notions, one was repeatedly recorded in writing, while the other (College Notions) was passed on orally. How are we to explain this disjunction? A clue may be found in the timing of Gordon's word-book, written in the final days of 'Old Commoners'. It was replaced by 'New Commoners' in the early 1840s, but after his installation as Headmaster in 1867, George Ridding turned this into a classroom block, and separate boarding houses were set up. Meanwhile the scholars continued to occupy their traditional rooms in College. It may be conjectured, therefore, that the long line of Commoner word books has something to do with the successive moves and divisions which the Commoners experienced. The need for fixity in writing was greater for them than it was for the scholar, whose existence was more stable. This conjecture can be supplemented from Stevens' entry on 'Commoner examina', in which he states that when Commoners were tested on Notions in their new building, from 1842, the six who scored lowest were made to write out a list of Notions: 'hence', he suggests, 'the number of excellent Commoner word-books which have survived'. Here we catch a glimpse of the mechanism underlying the transmission of Notions.[21]

New Commoners was converted into a classroom block in 1869–70, and the Commoners were housed in several newly built boarding houses. It seems to have been at this time that the testing of knowledge of Notions became known as

'Notions examina'. The role played in the preservation of the vocabulary by both examina and the Commoner word books was suggested by a *Spectator* reviewer in 1891:

> 'Winchester Notions' are differentiated from ''Tother School Notions'
> in two important particulars, in their character and their unique method
> of perpetuation. Indeed, it is this method that is at the bottom of it all.
> Other schools, had they adopted a similar plan, might be able to furnish
> an equally interesting vocabulary . . . The institution of 'notions' is a
> very serious business at Winchester. All 'new men' are given a fortnight
> to master the dialect, at the end of which time they are summoned before
> the assembled prefects for 'notion exam.', ranged in seniority, and plied
> with questions . . . whereas the slang of other schools has only an oral
> currency, that in vogue at Winchester is kept alive by examinations and
> 'notion-books', in which all the words are carefully recorded.[22]

Winchester and Eton had much in common, since they were both collegiate schools, founded to supply students to Oxford and Cambridge respectively.[23] The two schools, however, were very different in style. Eton was near London and the Court, and a worldly place; Winchester, on the other hand, rested in provincial seclusion, and in consequence was markedly more introverted. In the second half of the nineteenth century, the outside world began to obtrude on Winchester. Its traditional ties with New College were disrupted by the reforms which followed the Royal Commissions on Oxford and Cambridge of 1850 and 1872, as well as by the 1871 Winchester statutes which flowed from the legislation passed in the wake of the Clarendon Commission's report of 1864.[24] The Commission's investigations in the early 1860s revealed a range of financial abuses and led to a long list of proposed reforms. A willingness to accept these, and to move in new directions, underpinned the policies of George Ridding, installed in 1867, in effect, to carry out the recommendations of the Royal Commissioners.[25] The memoirs of Old Wykehamists make it clear that the ethos of the school changed markedly in his reign. William Fearon declared that when he entered the school in 1852, he had been 'plunged straight into the Middle Ages'.[26] Sir John Furley (1867–73), by contrast, remembered that 'I came to the school at a very interesting time . . . I was in time to know something of the old Winchester, and the Winchester of 1873 when I was left was completely different from the Winchester of 1867 in organisation, in spirit, in buildings and local conditions.'[27] The number of boys in the school increased rapidly (from 275 in 1867 to 385 in 1873), and as a result more boarding houses were founded. (This development in itself is likely to have encouraged the creation of Notions specific to particular houses.)

It was probably during Ridding's early years as headmaster, in the later 1860s, that 'Notions examina' was instituted. New boys were given printed word-lists and tested on them after their first two weeks at the school. 'Examina', pronounced 'Examinā', stands for 'examination', and belongs to a group of Notions in which endings are removed and vowels lengthened – hence also Illuminā for illuminations, Athlā for athletics.[28] This ritual is best seen as a control mechanism set up in response to the increasing numbers of boys in the late 1860s and early 1870s. Locating it in this context also enables us to explain why the 'Great Tunding Row' occurred when it did. (Tunding = beating: see the Dictionary.) In 1872 a boy was given a lengthy beating by a prefect and complained to his father. The resulting scandal led to a thorough investigation by Ridding, which revealed that unknown to the staff, wholesale and arbitrary beatings were taking place.[29] Stevens himself mentions that C. H. Turner, a pupil at the time, received fifteen beatings in twenty-two days.[30] Both examinations and beatings date from just this period of rapid change and increased numbers. One of the official accounts of the Tunding Row describes how 'the senior commoner prefect had thought it well to examine the boys in his house, which was a new one, in what the boys call "notions", as one small way of assisting to bring the house into unity with the school'.[31]

The Etonian comment quoted above comes from a review of the first published dictionary of Notions. This appeared in 1891, and was the work of R. G. K. ('Piggy') Wrench, a modern languages master at Winchester. Wrench printed almost 300 entries, of perhaps a thousand words then current. In his introduction, he makes plain the motivation of his work:

> The Glossaries hitherto published have done these words scant justice;
> and in assuming that an imbecile Wykehamical ancestry composed them
> by spelling words backwards, or by choosing a word at random out of the
> Classics, have relegated them to the position of nonsense. If *thoke* came
> from θῶκος, *ferk* from *furca*, and *scob* from *bocs*, they would be unworthy
> of any consideration; but the slightest investigation proves them to be
> full of interest to the philologist, and worthy of the tenderest respect from
> Wykehamists.[32]

Wrench's scathing remarks were directed against the two glossaries published before his book appeared, both of them included in books about Winchester College. R. B. Mansfield's *School Life at Winchester College* had been brought out by J. C. Hotten in 1866. It belonged to a sub-genre inspired by the publicity given to the nine leading public schools by their investigation by the Royal Commission of 1861 (the Clarendon Commission). In a note to his glossary, Mansfield explained that it reflected the usages of his own schooldays at Winchester (1834–40), and that since he had never seen the words written down, he had spelled them 'as phonetically as the nature of our alphabet will allow'.[33] Mansfield was followed in 1878 by H. C. Adams' *Wykehamica*. Adams had been a Commoner in the 1830s, and retained vivid memories of life in Old Commoners.[34] Let us take Wrench's final example, *scob*. Mansfield defines it as 'An oaken box with a double lid', and adds, 'So called from the Box spelt phonetically backwards'. Adams is more cautious: 'said to be derived from box (bocs) spelt backwards. Against this is to be set the fact, that "scob" in early documents is sometimes spelt "scobb".' If we turn to their treatment of *thoke*, used in Notions to mean 'idle[ness]', Mansfield defines it simply; Adams adds '(θῶκος a resting place)'. The Greek origin is unlikely, especially as this form of

the word is found only in Ionian and Epic Greek (it can mean 'seat', and is once
used to refer to a privy). Although its origin is unclear, it is found as an adjective
in early middle English to refer to unsound fish. The sense 'limp, relaxed, inert'
seems to underline both these early uses and the Notional usage.

Wrench's reference to 'spelling words backwards' surely refers to the
disparaging remarks of J. C. Hotten on 'Ziph'. This was a mechanical slang
which involved repetition of vowels and the insertion of medial 'g'. 'Shall we
go?', for example, would become 'Shagall wege gogo?'.[35] In the third edition
of his *Dictionary of Modern Slang* (1864) Hotten had written, 'The "Language
of Ziph", it may be noted, is another rude mode of disguising English, in use
among students at Winchester College. Some notice of this method of conveying
secret information, with an extensive Glossary of Words, Phrases, Customs, &c.,
peculiar to the College, may be found in Mr Mansfield's recently-published
"School Life at Winchester College". It is certainly too puerile a specimen
of work to find place here' (p. 26).[36] In his entry sv *Ziph*, Hotten refers
to De Quincey's account of it in his autobiography, published in 1853. De
Quincey remembered being taught it by the sons of a Dr Mapleton, who had
acquired it at Winchester.[37] Ziph remains something of a mystery, especially
as De Quincey's mention of it seems to be unique.[38] Almost more mysterious
is how Hotten came to confuse it with Notions. The passage quoted above from
his dictionary suggests that he thought Ziph and Notions were identical. Certainly
the latter appear not to be listed in his dictionary. The explanation may be that
when he wrote, he had not yet seen Mansfield's text (which makes no mention
at all of Ziph). Surprisingly, Eric Partridge followed Hotten, classifying it as
'ziph gibberish' as opposed to 'slang proper', and thought it hardly worthy of
mention.[39]

In Wrench's campaign to defend Wintonian dignity against Hotten's dis-
missive remarks, his most powerful weapon was the philology imported from
the continent in the 1820s and 1830s and currently being applied to English
lexicography by Skeat and Murray. This linkage of institutional uniqueness with
linguistic dignity is illustrated by an editorial in *The Wykehamist* in February
1880 (doubtless also directed against Hotten) which declared that 'notions are
not slang but the Wykehamist dialect'.[40] The link between lexicography and the
assertion of uniqueness had been made by Dean Trench in his paper 'On Some
Deficiencies in our English Dictionaries', given to the Philological Society of
London in 1857, which led eventually to the publication of *OED*.

There are many who conceive of a Dictionary as though it had this
function, to be a standard of the language; and the pretensions to be this
which the French *Dictionary of the Academy* sets up, may have helped
on this confusion. Those who desire, are welcome to such a book: but
for myself I will only say that I cannot understand how any writer with
the smallest confidence in himself, the least measure of that vigour and
vitality which would justify him in addressing his countrymen in written
or spoken discourse at all, should consent in this manner to let one

self-made dictator, or forty, determine for him what words he should use, and what he should forbear from using.[41]

This privileging of individual judgement over generalised prescription can be found, allied to a celebration of assimilative change, 'muddling through' and irrationality, in a vast array of statements on politics, cultural life, schooling – and language.[42] Trench's paper draws on a powerful contemporary ideology of 'Englishness' which celebrated the national freedom from rule(s). In contrast to a stereotyped continental practice of regimentation and centralised control, England was depicted as a land whose own freedom was mirrored in the autonomy of its citizens.

James Murray's *New English Dictionary*, which later became the *OED*, was intended to focus on the common stock of English; but other projects of the same period concentrated on dialect. The most notable of these was Joseph Wright's *English Dialect Dictionary* (8 vols, 1896–1905). Wright included a few words from Notions (e.g. 'books-chambers'), and acknowledges the help of two Winchester informants, A. D. Hill and L. L. Shadwell. The latter had assembled a word-book in 1864.[43] Hill had compiled a list of Notions, and had helped Wrench with his glossary, as had James Murray. Slang dictionaries (notably J. S. Farmer's *Public School Word Book* [1900], Eric Partridge's *Dictionary of Slang and Unconventional English* [1937], and Morris Marples' *Public School Slang* [1940]) included Notional terms, drawing on Wrench, the Beetleites and on personal communications from Wykehamists. In 1901 Wrench brought out a revised edition of his *Word-Book*, which included illustrative quotations supplied by A. F. Leach, the author of a recent history of the school.[44] In the same year, Wrench's only rival appeared: *Winchester College Notions*, by 'Three Beetleites'.[45] The editors' preface drew attention to their inclusion of place-names, which Wrench had excluded. They also explained that they had omitted derivations, which Wrench had given in his book. In 1910, however, a second edition appeared in two volumes; the second volume contained examples and etymologies, and was to be 'read concurrently with the first'.[46] In their Preface to this volume, the editors adopted an elegiac tone:

> Elsewhere old and simple methods of life and speech are being gradually overwhelmed and swept into the torrent of modern progress . . . It is only in a few scattered and remote country districts that men and women may be found who, untroubled by the stridencies of latter-day reformers . . . still speak the tongue and live the lives of their forefathers. They too will pass away . . . there is something of melancholy in the thought that the ancient customs . . . manners, and . . . forms of speech sacred to so many generations of Wykehamists may share a similar fate.[47]

Contempt and confusion from without, as might have been expected, prompted a loyal defence, both here and in Wrench's preface; it is also reflected in Stevens' subtitle: 'an English dialect maintained in a Hampshire community since the 14th century'.

The publication of these dictionaries aroused attention and comment at Eton. The first edition of Wrench's *Winchester Word-Book* received a generous review in the *Eton College Chronicle*:

> The tongue of our Wykehamist friends is indeed as strange to us as ever was ancient Pistol's, but now it seems that many of their words claim to be relics of our mother tongue as it was spoken in the days when Winchester was an experiment, when New College deserved its name, and when Eton did not yet exist. These, by the pious tradition of Winchester 'Notions', for which many a tunded junior has ere this righteously smarted, are still preserved, not like dry specimens in a museum, but as the natural use of daily talk; so that words, for which the barbarian consults his Skeat or waits for his Murray, are there familiar in the gossip of an 'inferior' . . . as Etonians, we are . . . concerned to find how barren is our own tongue, and how little we have kept from the past. [Readers] will find at all events a school slang formed on a higher principle than that of substituting 'er' for every termination.[48]

This final remark is a sideswipe at Harrow School, which seems to have been the origin of the habit of adding final -er to words; the fashion spread quickly, especially at Oxford. (The most extreme example was perhaps 'wagger-pagger-bagger' for wastepaper-basket.)[49] The philosopher A. J. Ayer wrote in his memoirs that when he reached Eton 'there was . . . a certain amount of slang to be learned, though little in comparison with the pedantic profusion of Winchester notions'.[50] An *Eton Glossary* was produced by C. R. Stone in 1903, and went into several editions, but his list was relatively meagre in comparison with the Winchester dictionaries. Marples claimed that the appearance of Stone's glossary demonstrated how numerous were the 'peculiar technical terms' used at Eton. It is surely more likely that the publication of Wrench's second edition, and 'Three Beetleites'' first, spurred him into action.[51] This is perhaps also the case with a Westminster memoir of the same year, which includes a 'Westminster Glossary' of words in use in the early 1840s.[52]

With the 'Beetleites'' second edition of 1910 we come to the end of the golden age of Notions dictionaries.[53] By the 1920s, the heyday of the public schools was over; it would not be long before the empire they supplied with proconsuls and administrators also faded away. Stevens' dictionary is thus located in a kind of historical limbo. It is clear that its assembly was driven by a powerful personal motivation, but it is tempting to see it in Hegelian terms as symbolising the end of an era: the lexicographical owl of Minerva taking wing at dusk. The idea would surely have appealed to Stevens' Notional animism. In his book on Winchester College, Firth pinpoints the turn of the century as a crucial moment in the history of Notions:

> [Notions] crystallised at the beginning of this century. Their use, or at any rate the insistence upon it, came in much more recently than is commonly supposed. The Notion, for example, which everybody knows – the use

of 'man' for 'boy' – did not exist in Fearon's schooldays and made
Moberly laugh when he first heard it used in the sixties . . . No mystical
virtue was held to inhere in . . . such words and forms . . . But by the
turn of the century they had acquired, almost suddenly, a rigid fixity and
veneration . . . To the same period belongs the *Mushri Dictionary* . . .
Such works, and the extreme enthusiasm for special and local customs
as they presuppose, require a society stable and proud, with immense
margins for 'extras' . . . All contemporary influences . . . tell against
Notions. The outside world impinges powerfully and disturbingly upon
them. It is best to consider them, therefore, as they were in their zenith.[54]

The weak point in this perceptive summary is Firth's assumption that stability
and pride were givens: in fact, they were at issue in a dialectic of challenge and
response. Stevens' first epigraph, taken from Bunyan, is 'They are for holding
their notions, though all other men be against them': we might replace 'though'
with 'because'. The dictionary-making of the 1890s, as we have seen, responded
to the denigration of Notions by outsiders. It was also, in part, a response
to the perceived challenges of state intervention in the public schools.[55] The
'zenith' which Firth refers to was the product of that 'rigid fixity' – a phrase
which itself indicates that we are dealing with reactive assertion, not just with
a 'society stable and proud'. The sudden 'veneration' of Notions stems from the
challenges described above to the independence and uniqueness of Wintonian
life. 'All contemporary influences . . . tell against Notions', writes Firth. It would
be more accurate to say that the 'fixity and veneration' he ascribes to the turn of
the century reflected a resistance to a threatening outside world.[56]
One of the most attractive aspects of Notions is their beatification of the
particular. They celebrate the uniqueness of Winchester; in detail, that of objects,
places, customs and people. Many of the school staff, not just masters but also
porters, cooks and others, themselves became Notions. Their idiosyncrasies of
speech and behaviour led to their being given nicknames, which in turn often
gave rise to Notional phrases. Thus C. E. Robinson, known as 'The Bin' to
distinguish him from Major Robertson, was also called 'The Beast'; his habit
of allowing bare leg to show between trousers and socks then became 'sporting
a hairy beast'. (See the Dictionary: 'Beast', 'sport a Bin'.) Any individual could
become a Notion by becoming part of the school's life or by impinging on it
notably from outside. The redoubtable Margot Asquith, who came to visit her
son Anthony at Winchester, 'became a sort of notion' according to Stevens: 'she
over-idolised Puffin [her son's nickname] and over-dramatised herself; but we
enjoyed that'.[57] The most remarkable and richly developed example of staff
individuality – indeed, idiosyncrasy – is that of Edmund Morshead ('Mush'),
who spent most of his life at Winchester, first as a pupil, later as a classics
master. Morshead's speech mannerisms were observed and recorded by several
generations of his pupils, who wrote out, and later had printed, a pronouncing
dictionary of 'Mushri'. The succession of editions, three of them printed, over a
period of more than twenty years, reflects not just the persistence of an elaborate

joke, but the recognition of changes in this idiolect. The name probably derives from his pronunciation of his own surname with a heavy aspirated medial s. It has recently been pointed out, however, that the name Muṣri occurs in the Old Testament, apparently denoting a region in south-eastern Asia Minor.[58] Winchester pupils were commonly taught, and tested in, knowledge of the Bible, and it is likely that one of those involved in preparing the *Mushri Dictionary* looked in a Bible dictionary for words beginning with Mus.[59] Mushri will have seemed a fitting addition to a family of human languages which already included Hindi, Maori and Pali. Notions begat Mushri: in both cases, words are deployed to assert uniqueness, at the institutional and personal levels respectively. Mushri was perhaps the most exotic plant to grow in the rich seedbed provided by Notions.[60]

COMMONER WORD-BOOKS AND THE APPEARANCE OF 'NOTION'

I have referred above to 'word-books'; but by the end of the century, the preferred title for the boys' manuscript glossaries was 'Notion books'. Nevertheless, the earliest glossaries do not include the word 'notion'. The earliest word-book to gloss the word 'notion' dates from 1866; the earliest entitled 'Notions book', from 1872.[61] Thereafter 'word-book' and 'Notion book' coexisted for some time, but by 1914 the latter seems to have become the accepted title.[62] *OED* refers to Notions (*Notion*, I.3, 'a phrase or term') but, remarkably, offers no citations, even though the relevant fascicle of *OED* did not appear until September 1907, and though James Murray's help had been acknowledged by Wrench in the preface to his *Winchester Word-Book* (which is cited sixteen times in *OED*). The *OED* entry offers two citations from the 1650s, and suggests that the Wintonian use of 'notion' may be a survival of this. This is a rather unconvincing notion, and we will do better to look at usages current in the mid-nineteenth century. The philosophical uses of the term were accessible to students through such sources as Fleming's *Vocabulary*.[63] They also filtered down into textbooks through the writings of the philosopher and HMI J. D. Morell, who popularised the work of the German grammarian K. F. Becker. In his influential book on sentence analysis (1852), Morell explained that words could be divided into classes, notional and relational, containing the matter of thought and its relations respectively.[64] Morell's views were in turn popularised by his follower C. P. Mason, as, for example, in *First Notions of Grammar for Young Learners*.[65]

Exactly how the term was imported into Winchester is another matter, but we should remember that the writings of Max Müller and others were making an interest in comparative philology fashionable. In the case of one Winchester master, we have precise evidence of this interest. George Ridding, himself a Wykehamist, was appointed Second Master in 1863, becoming Headmaster in January 1867. Ridding had New Testament texts printed in fourteen languages and dialects; he studied Romansch and compiled a grammar-sheet of Gothic accidence. His return to the school, a few years before the first written use of 'Notion', makes him a good candidate for the importation of the term.[66]

A NOTE ON THE TEXT

Stevens' original text has been reproduced with a minimum of alterations of substance. Minor errors have been corrected, and formatting altered for the sake of consistency and clarity. A very few minor entries have been omitted, a few additional entries and cross-references inserted. Some articles contain references to so many other Notional terms that consistent marking of cross-references would have overburdened the text. The reader is therefore encouraged to pursue any terms which raise a doubt or an eyebrow through the Dictionary as a whole. Stevens often refers to a few standard sources for the history of the school; these are listed below.

BOOKS ON THE HISTORY OF THE SCHOOL

Adams H. C. Adams *Wykehamica*, Oxford: Parker 1878.
Leach A. F. Leach *A History of Winchester College*, London: Duckworth 1899
Mansfield R. B. Mansfield *School Life at Winchester College*, London: J. C. Hotten 1866.
Trollope T. A. Trollope *What I Remember*, London: Bentley 1887–9.
Tuckwell W. Tuckwell *The Ancient Ways: Winchester Fifty Years Ago*, London: Macmillan 1893.

OTHER WORKS BY C. G. STEVENS HELD IN THE WICCAMICA ARCHIVE AT WINCHESTER COLLEGE

'Winton', 6 vols, typescript, n.d., c. 1,200 pp.
'Notions', typescript, n.d. Transcripts of word books by R. Gordon (1838–43), J. Foord (1868–72: extracts), C. G. Stevens (1917–22).

ILLUSTRATIONS

Some of the illustrations have been reproduced from Stevens' own line drawings, some of which are in turn copied from published accounts of Winchester. Other illustrations have been taken direct from such sources. The decorative initial capitals in the Dictionary are taken from the 1866 word-book of J. M. Callender; the first such book which glosses the word 'Notion'. The most elegant of all the word-books in the Wiccamica collection is that assembled by Edward Deas

Thomson in 1855. Its atypical title, *Winchester, Illustrated. A Dictionary of the Traditional School Vocabulary*, accurately reflects its contents, since it is profusely illustrated. Several of Thomson's pen-and-ink drawings are reproduced in the present volume. Thomson entered Winchester as a Commoner in 1854. He went on to New College, Oxford, and in the 1880s and later served as a senior civil servant in Australia. His word-book eventually passed to his distant relative Richard Jebb, Regius Professor of Greek at Cambridge, on whose death in 1906 it was given to Jebb's successor Henry Jackson. Jackson, who was a fellow of Winchester College, donated it to the college archives, suggesting that it might be reproduced in facsimile.

NOTES

1 M. Marples *Public School Slang*, London: Constable 1940, p. xii. His entries on these schools list 28 words for Westminster, 125 for Christ's Hospital, and 153 for Winchester.

2 Marples used the second edition (1901) of Wrench's book. He acknowledges the help of 'several hundred . . . correspondents' (p. v) but gives no further details; of those singled out for thanks (p. vi) none had to do with Winchester.

3 H. L. Thompson *Henry George Liddell DD . . . A Memoir*, London: Murray 1899, p. 109. Liddell approved of the poem, and gave it a prize.

4 For this and other examples, see J. d'E. Firth *Winchester College*, London: Winchester Publications 1949, pp. 215–16.

5 Stevens recorded in 'Winton' (vol. 5, p. 1193) that he was taught philosophy at New College by the then Senior Tutor, H. W. B. Joseph ('Jobags': see Dictionary). Joseph was thus almost certainly Stevens' Greats tutor. He aroused strong feelings in his pupils: some loved, others loathed him. His obsession with linguistic accuracy led to tutorials in which nothing he said could be comprehended by an average person. In a whole hour, some pupils never got beyond having the opening sentences of their essays demolished. (Stevens reports that Joseph described one of his essays as 'solemn nonsense').

6 Myres to Richard Stevens, 10 January 1983. I am grateful to Richard Stevens for allowing me to quote from this letter.

7 *The Salopian* 46.8, no. 475, 12 March 1927, p. 159.

8 C. F. C. Hawkes, J. N. L. Myres and C. G. Stevens *Saint Catharine's Hill Winchester*, Winchester: Warren 1930. The excavations uncovered Iron Age earthworks, a medieval chapel and an eighteenth-century labyrinth.

9 Stevens would have sympathised with the Duke of Wellington, who in August 1812 responded to a demand from Whitehall for a complete inventory as follows: 'Each item and every farthing has been accounted for, with two regrettable exceptions for which I beg your indulgence. Unfortunately the sum of one shilling and ninepence remains unaccounted for in one infantry battalion's petty cash and there has been a hideous confusion as to the number of jars of raspberry jam issued to one cavalry regiment during a sandstorm in Western Spain. This reprehensible carelessness may be related to the pressure of circumstances, since we are at war with France, a fact which may come as a bit of a surprise to you gentlemen in Whitehall.' (I owe this quotation to Philip Stevens.)

10 Sikololo is a Bantu dialect, one of several in which Stevens was fluent.

11 C. G. Stevens 'Rhymes at Random, 1916–1977', p. 47. The first edition of W. M. Hailey's *An African Survey* had appeared in 1938, the second in 1945, the year in

which Stevens was promoted to D.C. On Hailey's *Survey*, see J. W. Cell *Hailey. A Study in British Imperialism, 1872–1969,* Cambridge: Cambridge University Press 1992, pp. 215–40.

12 *Jersey Place Names. A Corpus of Jersey Toponymy,* La Société Jersiaise, 1986. Stevens also provided maps and drawings for his wife's *Old Jersey Houses* (vol. 1, 1965; vol. 2, 1977) and for her biography of Sir John Le Couteur, *Victorian Visions* (1969).

13 'A Game of Fives in Jersey Five Hundred Years Ago', *Bulletin de la Société Jersiaise,* 1977, pp. 96–7.

14 *Bulletin de la Société Jersiaise,* 1979, pp. 281–5; the article is preceded by an obituary notice.

15 The *Century Dictionary* was edited by the noted American linguist W. D. Whitney, and had originally appeared as part of a larger, encyclopedic work in the 1880s. See J. Green *Chasing the Sun. Dictionary Makers and the Dictionaries They Made,* London: Cape 1996, pp. 276, 362–3. In its presswork it 'outranked any other dictionary of its time' (Carl Rollins, printer to Yale University, quoted in J. Blumenthal *The Printed Book in America,* Boston: Godine 1977, p. 31).

16 Philip Stevens to the author, 1 January 1998.

17 'Quis est nostrum, liberaliter educatus, cui non educatores, cui non magistri sui atque doctores, cui non locus ipse mutus ille, ubi alitus aut doctus est, cum grata recordatione in mente versetur?', *Pro Plancio* 33.81.

18 See the Dictionary: 'Illumina'. One is reminded of Colonel Newcome's deathbed cry of 'Adsum' as he remembers his schooldays at Charterhouse, in Thackeray's *The Newcomes.*

19 Their Eton equivalents were the Oppidans: *oppidani,* town boys.

20 Stevens' copy of Wrench's *Word-Book* is annotated to distinguish College and Commoner words; those used in Old Commoners; those used in Notions examina; and those used throughout the school.

21 It also prompts the somewhat alarming thought that the word-books we possess are largely the work of those whose tested knowledge was poorest. But several of the books were written by amanuenses, and consultation probably took place.

22 'Winchester Notions', *The Spectator,* 11 July 1891, p. 55; reviewing R. G. K. Wrench's *Winchester Word-Book,* on which, see below.

23 Winchester College was founded in 1382 by William of Wykeham to supply students for his 'New College' at Oxford, and is thus the oldest of the great public schools.

24 Winchester and New: see H. B. George *New College 1856–1906,* London: Frowde 1906 for the impact of the Commissions. An undergraduate's impressions of the changes at New College are recalled in C. W. C. Oman *Memories of Victorian Oxford,* London: Methuen 1941, pp. 89–91. The Clarendon Commission: C. Shrosbree *Public Schools and Private Education,* Manchester: Manchester University Press 1988.

25 Ridding was a Wykehamist through and through – a former head boy, the great-great-nephew (and godson) of a former Warden, son of a former Second Master, son-in-law of the previous Headmaster – and was seen in conservative quarters as something of a traitor to Old Winchester. See the memoir by his widow: L. E. Ridding *George Ridding, Schoolmaster and Bishop,* London: Edward Arnold 1908.

26 W. A. Fearon *The Passing of Old Winchester,* privately printed, 1924, foreword. Fearon succeeded Ridding as Headmaster in 1884.

27 J. S. Furley *Winchester in 1867,* Winchester: Warren 1936, p. 5. Furley was the third Housemaster of 'Beetleites', and in the early twentieth century the House had become known as 'Furley's'.

28 The copy of Wrench's *Winchester Word-Book* (1891) in the British Library has an MS examination paper in Notions inserted. This contains two 'papers', of 3 hours each, for translation from ordinary English into Notions and vice versa.

29 The boy was given thirty strokes, during which five sticks were broken by the force

of the blows. See the vivid account of the whole incident in Oman *Memories of Victorian Oxford*, pp. 35–8, and the detailed analysis in Peter Gwyn 'The "Tunding Row". George Ridding and the Belief in "Boy-Government"', in R. Custance (ed.) *Winchester College. Sixth-Centenary Essays*, Oxford: Oxford University Press 1982, pp. 431–77.

30 See the section on 'Notions Examinations' in his introduction to the Dictionary.

31 Winchester School Archives, 40280 (1872). Cf. N. G. Annan *Our Age*, London: Weidenfeld & Nicolson 1990, p. 57: 'The house was . . . responsible for teaching the new boy the tabus and rituals of the tribe. He had to learn the tribe's language – school slang – within a few weeks or he (or his initiator) was beaten.' Annan seems to claim that this was true of public schools in general; on what basis is unclear, since his book is without references.

32 R. G. K. Wrench *Winchester Word-Book*, Winchester: P. & G. Wells 1891, pp. vi–vii. A second, revised edition appeared in 1901.

33 R. B. Mansfield *School Life at Winchester College*, London: J. C. Hotten 1866, p. 197. The glossary is on pp. 197–243. Mansfield had been a scholar; which helps to explain why he had never seen a written list of Notions.

34 H. C. Adams *Wykehamica,* Oxford: Parker 1878, pp. 213–15; his glossary is printed at pp. 415–39.

35 Wrench's reference is thus inaccurate, since Ziph is not a back slang.

36 *Dictionary of Modern Slang*, 3rd edition, 1864, p. 26. Later editions were renamed *The Slang Dictionary*. Hotten was, to say the least, optimistic: he did not bring out Mansfield's book until 1866.

37 T. De Quincey *Collected Works*, ed. D. Masson, A. & C. Black, vol. 1, 1896, pp. 201–3. Two Mapletons appear in the school lists in 1789.

38 The passage from his autobiography provides the earliest of the three citations in *OED*; the others, from Partridge and from Otto Jespersen, refer back to De Quincey.

39 E. Partridge *Slang Today and Yesterday*, 2nd edition, London: Routledge 1935, p. 203. 'Ziph' is Partridge's word for children's language produced by deliberate distortion. Note that Hotten also lists *Ziff* = young thief. This suggests that Ziph was a thieves' cant.

40 *The Wykehamist* 141, 1880, pp. 325–6. It may be relevant that the first (manuscript and jellygraphed) editions of the *Mushri-English Pronouncing Dictionary* were circulating at Winchester at this time.

41 R. Trench 'On Some Deficiencies in our English Dictionaries', *Transactions of the Philological Society of London*, 1857, p. 5. The 'forty' of course refers to the forty Immortals of the Académie Française. France and Prussia functioned at different times as England's contrastive (centralised, regimented) Other.

42 For the background, see D. Simpson ·*Romanticism, Nationalism, and the Revolt against Theory*, Chicago: University of Chicago Press 1993; R. Colls and P. Dodd (eds) *Englishness: Politics and Culture 1880–1920*, London: Croom Helm 1986. The depiction of 'normal change' as evolutionary rather than revolutionary can be seen in James Murray's Romanes lecture *The Evolution of English Lexicography*, Oxford: Clarendon Press 1900: 'The English Dictionary, like the English Constitution . . . is a growth that has slowly developed itself adown the ages.' For a discussion of this which emphasises the importance of Liddell and Scott's Greek lexicon, not mentioned by Murray, see H. Aarsleff 'The Early History of the *Oxford English Dictionary*', *Bulletin of the New York Public Library* 66, 1962, pp. 417–39.

43 See Wright's list of correspondents and unprinted sources, *English Dialect Dictionary*, vol. 6, pp. 60–2. Wright also drew on the lists in Mansfield's and Adams' books.

44 *A History of Winchester College*, London: Duckworth 1899. Leach's son was at the school in the 1890s, and may well have supplied his father with information on Notions, as he did on the sixth-form timetable. See C. A. Stray 'Schoolboys and Gentlemen: Classical Pedagogy and Authority in the English Public School', in N.

Livingstone and Y. L. Too (eds) *Pedagogy and Power: Rhetorics of Ancient Learning*, Cambridge: Cambridge University Press 1998, pp. 29–46.

45 W. H. Lawson, J. F. R. Hope, and A. H. S. Cripps. For 'Beetleites', see the Dictionary.

46 Vol. 1 was edited by Lawson, Hope and R. S. Cripps; vol. 2 by W. G. I. Hope and R. F. Hope.

47 *Winchester College Notions*, vol. 2, pp. v–vi.

48 *Eton College Chronicle*, 7 May 1891, p. 636. 'Skeat' refers to W. W. Skeat's *Etymological Dictionary of the English Language*, which had appeared in 1882; 'Murray', to the *New English Dictionary* (later *OED*), whose most recent fascicle, *Cast–Clivy*, had been issued in November 1889.

49 Similarly the Prince of Wales was known as 'Pragger-Wagger'. For the Harrovian origin, see M. Marples *University Slang*, London: Williams & Norgate 1950, p. 73, and his entry on '-er suffix' in *Public School Slang*, pp. 67–9.

50 A. J. Ayer *Part of My Life*, London: Collins 1977, p. 36.

51 Marples, *Public School Slang*, p. 70. Once again Marples is distinguishing 'actual slang' from other categories (here, 'place-names, words descriptive of various garments, terms connected with games and rowing [etc.]'), without explaining what criterion he is using to distinguish them.

52 F. Markham *Recollections of a Town Boy at Westminster*, London: Edward Arnold 1903. The Glossary (pp. 226–32) was provided by the author's cousin Sir Clements Markham (Westminster 1842–6).

53 In 1914 the College authorities issued an 'official' list of current Notions, together with a summary of school rules, under the title *Notions and Rules*. Several subsequent editions have appeared: the 1949 edition, for example, contained about 120 Notions.

54 Firth *Winchester College*, p. 213.

55 This is discussed in the introduction to *The Mushri Dictionary*.

56 Resistance later gave way to accommodation. A turning point came with the appointment of a non-Wykehamist, H. M. Burge, as Headmaster in 1901.

57 Stevens met her later at dinner in Oxford: 'friendly, kind, brilliant . . . she dominated the table'. 'Winton', 327. Her impact on the pupils was, of course, heightened by being that of a glamorous and sophisticated woman in a semi-monastic and almost womanless environment.

58 I and II Kings. See W. O. E. Oesterley *A History of Israel*, Oxford: Oxford University Press 1932, vol. I p. 341. I owe this reference to Ian Michael.

59 Biblical knowledge is reflected in several Notions: see *Moab*; *Gaspar, Melchior and Balthasar*.

60 The text of the final edition of the Mushri dictionary is reproduced, with an introduction, in C. A. Stray *The Mushri-English Pronouncing Dictionary. A Chapter in 19th-Century Public School Lexicography*, privately printed, 1996. (ISBN 07049 0774 7.). The introduction relates the Mushri phenomenon to a variety of factors, including Morshead's adherence to political liberalism, something which underlined his commitment to individualism.

61 The 1866 book was written by J. M. Callender; its spine title is *Commoner Word Book*, the title page has *Winton Notions*. The 1872 volume was the work of C. L. Cripps. (Both are held in the Wiccamica collection, Winchester College.) Stevens (see Dictionary: 'Notion book') believed that the transition occurred c. 1870.

62 Thus in 1915 the Greek scholar Henry Jackson (who had been elected a Fellow of Winchester College) referred to 'an ms notion book': R. St J. Parry *Henry Jackson OM*, Cambridge: Cambridge University Press 1926, p. 151. Jackson's second son was 'The Jacker' (see Dictionary).

63 W. Fleming *A Vocabulary of Philosophy, Mental, Moral, and Metaphysical, with Quotations and References; for the Use of Students*, London and Glasgow: R. Griffin 1857. As the Glaswegian connection suggests, this volume is a product of the Scottish

educational system, in which 14- and 15-year-old boys began their university course with a general grounding in philosophy.

64 J. D. Morell *The Analysis of Sentences Explained and Systematised, after the Plan of Becker's German Grammar*, London: Longman 1852, p. 52.

65 London: Bell & Daldy 1872.

66 See further C. A. Stray 'Notions', *Henry Sweet Society Newsletter* 26, May 1996, pp. 24–6.

Ablers   J. B. Poynton (Coll. 1913–19): Don 1928–60: a brilliant classic. The notion probably arose when a Don called one of his compositions 'able'.

Abner   Mr Abner Dean, manager of School Shop c. 1917–22: an ex-naval man with pointed beard, and maker of wonderful ice-creams and iced coffee.

abroad   up and about again after being ill: especially in the phrase 'to come abroad' e.g. 'He came abroad this morning'. Thus used by Sir Thomas More c. 1520, Shakespeare c. 1600 and Defoe c. 1720, and still so used in provincial dialects: recorded as a Notion from 1831, and still in use. It is a specialised use of 'abroad', used by Udall (1522), Burton (1621) and Swift (1710) as the normal English equivalent for Latin *foris* (out-of-doors): boys at Winchester, with the precept of Tabula Legum 'Patrium sermonem fugito: Latinum exerceto' before them, would have described a sick school-mate as 'continens cameram' and, when recovered, as 'foris'; and today we still say a man is 'continent' and 'abroad'.

abs   (adj.) away: short for Latin *absens*, *absentes*: written on rolls against the names of absentees to show they had not attended Chapel, Hills, Commoners, or any other place where names had been called; or were away from College from health or other reasons (1831 on); or that they had neglected some duty (1868).
(adv.) away: e.g. 'get abs' (get or go away; 1831–92); 'toll abs' (run away; 1914 on).
(vb) take or go away: e.g. 'He absed my wind and then absed' (1856–92; obsolete by 1917).

Ada   the maid-of-all-work and retainer of Miss Wellsman at College Sick House: she left in 1921.

Adam and Eve   a stream flowing from Birley's Corner through Dalmatia, and running parallel to Old Barge till it rejoins River immediately below First Pot. In 1831 part of the stream was tolerably deep and free from weeds, and hence a favourite bathing-place for seniors at Evening Hills. In 1838 the stretch near Tunbridge is mentioned as deep, narrow and weedy but with good fishing. The

Adam and Eve

derivation is either from the fact that bathing costumes were not worn; or from the riddle:

> Adam and Eve and Pinch-me went down to the river to bathe.
> Adam and Eve were drowned. Who do you think was saved?

Adam, Eve and Pinch-me   three goldfish in the miniature pond in Monty Fiasco: also called Gaspar, Melchior and Balthasar (1920). For derivation, see **Adam and Eve**.

ad Coll and **ad Stag**   (for 'ad Collegium' and 'ad Stagnum Log', Log Pond): the alternative directions of play in College canvas: the skipper winning the toss called out to his side 'ad Coll' or 'ad Stag'. It is possibly a survival, or revival, of medieval terminology.

Ad Portas   the ceremony of receiving distinguished visitors under Middle Gate with a Latin Speech, delivered by the Praefect of Hall: if the visitor is up to it, the reply is in Latin also. Originally the only persons thus received were the two Posers, on the Tuesday of Election Week, and two other 'declamatores' gave the 'Fundator' and 'Elizabeth and Jacob' speeches; and they and the Praefect of Hall each received 13s 4d left by the will of Miss Lettice Williams, whose portrait is preserved in College. Recorded since 1831.

ad rem   to the point. In 1868 a task was declared to be ad rem, or nihil ad rem, when it was, or was not, appropriate to the words of the theme. From the Latin: not confined to Winchester, but recorded as a Notion from 1856.

ad Stag   see **ad Coll**.

advertisement, to sport an   to turn down the collar of a College gown to show the velvet. This was licet for Officers only (1892): by 1917 Officers had the velvet sewn on the outside of the collar as well as inside.

aetna   a boiler used with spirits of wine, chiefly by Commoners, who 'cannot get boilers such as are used in College on their fires' (1838); also in use in New

Aetna

Commoners 1868; by 1917 it had come to mean an oil or spirit stove used for College Chamber teas in Cloister Time when there was no fire. Named after the volcano in Sicily.

afternoon school   the school hours from 3 p.m. to 6 p.m. on whole-school days (1868–84).

'All down!'   called by the names-docker (1917–22) as soon as all the players had arrived for canvas: the game then began.

all-nighters   a College Notion (1917–22) for work done late at night by tolly-light, in Ist, IVth, or some other quiet place, in preparation for Goddard, New College, or other important examina. Leave to work late had to be raised by Inferiors from the Second Master, who sanctioned it till 10.45 or 11 p.m.: but men often went on much later, especially for New College.

Alps   the plank bridge at the end of Bull's Drove (1917).

amahagger   a game played by two persons with dressing-gown cords slung between two windows: the cords were threaded through the handles of two china vessels which slid down the cords, met and exploded in mid-air: though it was no longer played in 1917, the tradition continued and it was then reputed to be fifteen years old. The Amahagger were a cannibal African tribe in Rider Haggard's novel *She* (c. 1885), who slew their victims by placing red-hot basins on their heads.

Amen chapel   a long service originally performed in Chapel on the four days set apart for commemorating the Founder, and on the anniversary of his death (Founder's Com. and Ob.). Recorded 1831–1892. In 1868 it is noted that responses were chanted to the organ, and that instead of the regular psalms

Amen Corner

and first lesson, Psalm 145 and Ecclesiasticus 44 were used. A commemoration service including this lesson was still held once a year in 1922, but the notion Amen chapel was obsolete. Derived from the harmonising of the 'amens' at the end of prayers in that service.

Amen Corner   a curious point or angle in the middle of the south side of Meads Wall, behind the pavilion called Tent (1868), Meads Tent (1922). Originally two streams which formed the boundary of College land joined here, and Meads Wall, enclosing every inch it could, followed them to the exact point of their confluence. The Notion, quoted since 1831 and still in use, has been given various derivations: (1) Chapel was originally here 'but now there is only a small portion of the wall of it left: my father's name is cut there, R. Gordon' (1838): the writer was misled by fragments of medieval tracery from St Elizabeth's College used in the building of this part of Meads Wall in 1548. (2) in the earliest days of College the whole collegiate body made a daily round of its property singing prayers and hymns, and it was at this point that the final Amen was sung. It is more likely that they ended up nearer their dispersal point in Chapel or Chamber Court. (3) this was the ultimate (i.e. most southerly) point of College property, cf. Amen Corner at the end of Paternoster Row in the City [of London]. This theory, produced by Adams [*Wykehamica*, p.416], is probably right but the inscription, which he quotes inaccurately, is not evidence in his support: it is contained on three stones, which are obviously not *in situ* and which probably refer to a strip of land owned by St Elizabeth's College; it reads: 'in occidentali parte huius muri ab hoc angulo solum Eccl(es)i(a)e (extendit) 78 pedes in longitudine, 10 in latitudine'.

ammuni (pronounced ammunī)   blank ammunition issued on field-days or march-outs (1920).

Amphitheatre   a natural hollow in the form of an amphitheatre on the north of the Petersfield Road, about 3 miles [4.8 km] out of Winton below Telegraph; also called Devil's Punch-bowl.

Angelus Corner and **Angelus Gate**   the corner which lies between Cloisters and Non-Licet Gate, and the gate leading from it to the Warden's Garden. Derived from Latin *angulus* (corner): so spelt, 1880.

angle, to sport an   to wear your straw hat crooked: a bad notion (1920).

Ante-Chapel

annals   records of important events and matters, kept in 1892 by each of the five Officers, the Sen.Co.Paes, captains of games and Rifle Corps, and the Senior Praefect of each House. By 1920, Officers kept no annals, but some Chambers had them and the Aul.Prae. had a book. The annals of Old and New Commoners were for many years kept on the fly-leaves of books in Commoner Praefects' Library: these were copied into books, which were later destroyed. By 1868 the annals had been rewritten with the aid of contributions from various quarters and were still kept up by Senior Praefects. Between 1770 and 1790 memoranda of a ribald nature were scribbled by College Praefects in Chamber copies of the Statutes, now in the Warden's Library.

annexe   the Headmaster's Notion (1920) for the six or seven desks on his left as he sat up to books in Senior Div class-room.

anoint oneself, to   to put on ointment. This had to be done in bidet room (1920).

Ante-Chapel   Chapel was formerly divided into two unequal portions by the rood loft and screen, a gallery surmounted by a crucifix with images of the Virgin and St John on either side. The western portion was called Ante-Chapel. The rood loft was reached by an outer stair on the south side of Chapel, and its position is still shown by a blocked-up door in the third light of the fourth window: it was taken down in 1572 and a pulpit and choir screen erected, which were removed at the restoration of 1874–5. Evening Chapel or Preces at 9 p.m. were always held in Ante-Chapel (1838).

appeal, to   a man who thought he was being beaten unjustly in College (1920) could appeal to the Second Master; if a Co.Prae. was beating him, the appeal lay to the Headmaster.

apple-pie bed   a common trick in College and Commoners 1838–68; thus described: 'one sheet of a boy's bed is taken away and the remaining one is doubled up inside the bed so as to turn over the counterpane: which seems as if the bed was all right: the effect of this is that when a boy gets into bed he cannot get his legs down more than half way'. Not confined to Winchester.

Apple-pie Day   the Thursday in Sealing Week, variously dated as the last Thursday in Short Half or the first Thursday in December, when there were apple pies for dinner in College, one to three boys, and the Fellows of the College got their money. It was a Hatch Thoke, and Six and Six (College vs Commoners) was usually played on it. See **Warden's Om**. Recorded 1831–92; obsolete by 1917.

Arcadia   (1) the Warden's stables, forming the west side of Outer Court, where College pack-horses were kept in the early days. By 1917 the stables had become a cycle-shed and out-houses. (2) the passage from Outer Court along the west of College buildings and through Blue Gate into School Court. (3) generally for all the western part of Outer Court and the passage down to School Court. Recorded from 1868. Derived from Arcadia in Greece, a land of rural bliss: this effect being created by the trees in Paradise.

Arethusa   a spring on Twyford Downs, south-east of Hills, above Second Chalk Pit; also called Shepherd's Well, 1880. Recorded from 1868. By 1914 it was described as a clump of bushes. Derived from the name of a fountain near Syracuse.

arma scholastica   pens, ink and paper. If, c. 1918, anyone in C. W. Little's div failed to bring these necessaries up to books, he had to write out the 'In Scola' section of Tabula Legum (1566–71), in which occurs the phrase 'arma scolastica in promptu semper habeto'.

Armoury   the room near South African Memorial Gate where Corps rifles were stored (1900–20).

article   the regulation wooden stool in a toys. cf. stump. Recorded from 1892.

assassinate, to   to play for a Chamber VI when you did not belong to that Chamber (1920): an assassin in English is one who undertakes to kill for a reward.

Athla (pronounced Athlā)   sports; which took place at the end of Common Time. Recorded from 1892. Derived from Greek ἀθλος (contest).

Audit   College audit, held by the Warden and Fellows between 28 October and 1 November, when rents were paid by tenants of College property: also called Pay Day and Apple-pie Day. Recorded 1838–92.

Aut Disce board

Audit Room   the first room in the turret west of Hall, entered through hall, where College Audit was held. The Founder's original lockers, in which College moneys received at Audit were deposited, were still there in 1892, though the wood had needed renewing. The floor is paved with patterned Flemish tiles, which were much used in the Founder's day. On the walls hung three tapestries, which were placed in the bedchamber of the Warden of New College when he came down for Elections; by 1917 these had been framed and hung at the west end of hall, being later removed to School. At the north-east corner is the table where the Bursar used to dine with the principal tenants on Audit days, the remaining tenants being seated in the body of the room. The original proportions of the room were impaired by the erection of a wooden partition in later times, reaching to the ceiling, and used as a hatch at audit time.

Aulae (pronounced Auly)   the Praefect of Hall (1920).

Aul.Prae. (for Aulae Praefectus)   the official title of the Praefect of Hall, added beneath his name on marbles, notices and official documents. cf. Bib.Prae., Cap.Prae. and Officers.

auly-auly   a compulsory game (for all-y, all-y, i.e. compulsory for all) played on Grass Court by Commoners on Saturday afternnons after chapel. Boys stood in a ring and threw an india-rubber ball at one another: it was originally a game of catch. First recorded 1868; obsolete by 1892.

Aunty Norton   the Commoner Notion (1920) for Mammy Norton, proprietress of the Kingsgate Street Post Office, much used by men in the School: she had high entertainment value.

Aut Disce board (pronounced Ought Dissy)   the tablet on the west wall of School, displaying the hexameter 'aut disce, aut discede, manet sors tertia caedi' ['either learn, or leave, or be beaten'], interspersed with illustrative emblems which have probably been altered at successive repaintings, and surmounted by a coat of arms. Such a tablet was on the west wall of the old school-room (VIIth) in Mathew's day (1647), and according to one story was noticed by Queen Elizabeth (1570).

[**B**   see **bidet roll**.]

baby   the bundle of unwashed linen which is given to each man to take home at the end of the half. Recorded from 1892.

babylonightish   College Notion (1920) for a dressing-gown: a composite word, from Babylonish and nightshirt. From Joshua 7.21: 'and Achan answered . . . "when I saw among the spoils a goodly Babylonish garment".'

back staircase   the achievement of getting into VIth Book by moving from Senior Part l.b. to VIth Book.b. The more tortuous manoeuvre from Senior Part l.a. to VIth Book.b. was called 'climbing over the banister' (1920).

back up, to   in 1831, it meant to vent any opinion or retort energetically, usually in support of one's friend or party; by 1856 it had come to mean to call or shout out loud, especially in support of a team in the field; in 1920 it meant to shout out something as loud as one could. In English, to back up means to support in cricket or football, by standing or following behind a player: our word seems to be an extension of this to include shouting from the boundary or touch-line.

backings-up   odd ends of faggots put on to a low fire to bring it to life. Recorded from 1856; obsolete by 1914. In dialect, backing is small coal, slack, cinders or even turf, put at the back of a fire to damp it down or keep it in all night: faggot-ends would have the opposite effect, so our use is an adaptation of the normal one, but is in line with the sense, the fuel being added at the back of the fire.

bad notion   a word or phrase not used, or a thing not done, at Winchester: see introduction.

bag, to   to steal. Recorded in 1838, but not confined to Winchester; 'jockey' would have been used in 1920.

Baker

bagster   a thief. Recorded in 1838; long since obsolete. From bag (steal): not found in ordinary English.

bait, to   to tease, annoy. Recorded in 1868, but not confined to Winchester.

baize   a College Notion (1920) for a shelf protected by a flap of red baize or cloth, above each man's bed, for hats, clothes, etc.. On top of the baize stood each man's hatbox. In his baize the First Junior kept newspaper, brown paper and matches.

bake, to   to sit, lounge or lie at ease. Probably a Notion since the foundation, but obsolete by 1917. Bake is a medieval word variously spelt, the commonest form being beake, meaning to bask (a word of different origin) in the warmth of the sun or a fire: e.g. bekand (fourteenth century), beikand (1460), baking (1470), beake (1577) and beaking (1640).

baker   a medieval word for a cushion to put on a bench or hard seat, used at Winchester since the foundation and continuing there after it had vanished from normal English. For some reason such cushions ceased to be used in College after 1840, but the Notion, and the bakers themselves, survived in Commoners. The bakers (c. 1838–72) were large green baize cushions stuffed with hay or horse-hair, used chiefly by Commoner Praefects, and by Inferiors who had studies. Described in 1880 as stuffed with wool: green bakers for Praefects, red for Inferiors. The word was also used (1830–50) for anything else comfortable to sit on, e.g. a blotting book or portfolio, and (1868) for something to kneel on, e.g. the small red cushion about 1 foot [30 cm] square used in Chapel and Cathedral.

Originally banker: this word appears in College account rolls as bankarii made to fit the benches in hall; in 1410 there are bankers and cuschyne; in 1417, three bankers and six quyssons; in fifteenth-century Bursars' rolls of New College, bankars and cussons; and in the will of a Winchester scholar in 1550, six quissions and a banker. Ever since Aristophanes joked about sore buttocks at Salamis, the need for a pad between flesh and wood has been recognised by galley slaves, scholars in Hall and School, men sitting at toys or chests, and even at the Oberammergau passion play, where cushions can be hired at the door. Our

Saxon, English and French ancestors called a hard seat a *banc, benc* or *baunck*. Toy-time at Charterhouse is called banco, the Italian word for a money-changer's bench or bank. The requisite bench-pad was naturally called a banker, and the word has descended to us in this atmosphere, not from bake (above).

The original baker was not small or suitable for kneeling on; it is always distinguished from the smaller and more numerous cushions, and was evidently something long and wide, tailored to fit a bench in hall, the top of a chest, or the broad seat of a toys: the fitted cushions in railway carriages, and on the picnic-seats in farm wagons, are true bakers.

baker-layer a junior who took a Praefect's green baker in and out of hall in New Commoners. Obsolete by 1869.

bakester one who bakes, i.e. lounges. In use 1856; obsolete by 1914.

baking leave leave given by the owner to bake in his study, pigeon-hole, or toys in New Commoners. Obsolete by 1869.

baking place a sort of sofa in Commoner studies, or any comfortable place where a man might bake, generally a toys. Obsolete by 1869.

balk, baulk a false alarm, signal, report or rumour. A good example of an old English word surviving as a Notion: in medieval English balca or balk, and in dialect baulk, was a ploughman's term for a strip of ground which had been accidentally missed in ploughing. Hence it came to mean a wrong turning and, as a verb, to miss the way: thus Spenser (1579) says 'balke the right way', Sir Henry Wotton, a Wykehamist (c. 1600) 'baulk the beaten road' and Feltham (1659) 'baulk your road', all in the sense of going astray. From this it came to mean causing others to go astray: thus Ben Jonson (1598) 'to balk me'; and later on the word appears in baseball as a feint by the pitcher when pretending to pitch without doing so: this is exactly the baulk sported by the Tolly-keeper (see below). The idea of misleading by false information easily follows from this, and there is no need to look to the Norse word *balk* (a beam of timber), which conveys hindrance rather than deceit or practical joking. 'Sporting a baulk' meant starting a false rumour. In College (1920) it denoted a special kind of false alarm: when Hall was nearly over the Senior Tolly-keeper, by way of a joke, imitated with his own stool the scraping made by the Praefect of Hall's stool when the latter got up to say grace: the result was that half the men in Hall stood up, and had to sit down again in confusion. This was an ancient privilege, and might be indulged in three times a half, but no more.

Ball Court (1) a large court at the back of School where College men played bat-fives, small crockets and soccer-on-Ball-Court. It was divided into three fives

Ball Court

courts and separated from Meads by a low back wall, built c. 1890. In 1838 the games played on it were bat-fives, hand-fives and rackets: the floor is now cement, but at that time was chalk, as the following passage shows: 'in the beginning of the season the court is generally good, but sometimes towards the end of the half year the chalk gets worn away, and holes are made which prevent the balls from bounding properly.' (2) a ball court in Old Commoners (1742–1842) by Wickham's, near Commoner Gate.

ball-keeper   an Inferior appointed to look after football and cricket balls in New Commoners: he got off going down to football and watching-out at cricket. Obsolete but still in use 1884.

bangay   see **bangy**

bangies   trousers of brown, light brown, or drab cloth; recorded 1831–8, and then 'reckoned very low' (vulgar); later used for brown clothes generally, also considered vulgar. Long since obsolete but still in use 1884. From bangy (brown sugar).

Bangor chapel   a landing and door between Upper Cloisters and North Gallery (later the upper part of Moberly Library) in New Commoners (1842–69).

Benjamin Hoadley, Bishop of Winchester 1734, preached a sermon as Bishop of Bangor in 1717 before George I, which started the Bangorian controversy; Bangor (Maine) is the seat of a Congregational theological college: but the origin of the Notion is obscure.

bangy, or **bangay**   brown sugar; also used as an adjective, for brown. Recorded 1831, and still in use 1920. Said to be from Bangalore, capital of Mysore, which had a trade in many things including coarse sugar: if so, the notion may date from its capture by Cornwallis from Tippu Sahib in 1791: or it may have been introduced, like poon, by a boy with relatives in the East India Company, and be an echo of some Indian word: e.g. (1) bhang (Indian hemp), used principally for smoking but also made up into a sweetmeat with flour and sugar. (2) banghy, a pole for carrying a package; hence a parcel received by post.

bangy boots   boots of brown cloth. Recorded 1838 only, and then considered very vulgar.

Bangy Gate   a brown gate formerly leading from Grass Court into Sick House Meads (recorded 1831). Applied later to the gate leading into Kingsgate Street, opposite St Michael's Passage, subsequently called Commoner Gate: in 1907 a new gate was erected here in memory of casualties in the Boer War, and was known as South African Memorial Gate, or Memorial Gate.

banns (for bands)   the white linen neck-band with the two ends hanging down in front, prescribed by Queen Elizabeth as part of the uniform of churchmen, and worn by masters and College boys on formal occasions. Mansfield says that white neck-cloths and bands were worn by all, except when on leave-out. Recorded 1838 only, when it is noted that if the bands were long and fastened over the tie of the neck-cloth, they were called 'pious banns'; another name for them was 'bands of innocence'. The white bow-tie worn by College men on Sundays (1920) may be a relic of them.

Baptistery   the vestry at the south-east corner of Chamber Court, where Choir assembled before coming into Chapel. In medieval times it was called the vestibulum, but got the name baptistery when Chapel font was moved there from 1862 to 1875 during rebuilding of Chapel tower.

Barge (Old Barge and New Barge)   in Water Meads the main stream of the Itchen is called Old Barge, and the canal is called New Barge, or River. There is a story behind these names: as long ago as the eleventh century the main stream was called 'old', to distinguish it from later diversions and channels: barges plied upon it, and some of the building stone for Cathedral may have come that way: there are still (1960) two large squared blocks of stone to be seen in the water on the western bank of the stream about 80 yards [73 m] north of Double Hedges, and these may have been spilled from a barge which was bearing them upstream.

New Barge was cut in about 1195, probably by Bishop Godfrey de Lucy, to carry merchandise to the city in barges, and flows from the Alresford Pond, which serves as its reservoir, to Northam (the old Southampton). It was equipped with a series of locks, of which First, Second and Third Pot are survivors: towards the end of the middle ages traffic subsided, but was revived by Act of Parliament in Charles II's reign, and again in 1767; and there is still an Itchen Navigation Company, but it does not operate, and all navigation ceased in about 1870. At some time the School appears to have obtained an exclusive right to row on River between Black Bridge and First Pot. The mentions of bargee in old word-books, and the title Master by which it was prudent to address them, must date from c. 1670–1770, when barges were often encountered by boys in the school on their way to and from Hills, and at Underhills; and the names Old and New Barge for these waterways are no doubt the old watermen's abbreviations for the old and new bargeway or bargewater.

bargee   a bargeman. Recorded 1838–82; but not peculiar to Winchester.

barn   a thatched pavilion in the south-east corner of Kingsgate Park, and the cricket pitch near it (1920).

barricade, to sport a   to place a light bookshelf on the outside edge of one's slab, thus partly shutting one off from the rest of the Chamber (1920). The same as an 'erection': this has successively been a VIth Book Notion, and a bad notion, but varied with times and Chambers.

barter   (1) a half-volley at cricket: described in 1838 as 'a hit made when the ball pitches on guard and bounds from thence to the bat, when a moderately hard hit will send the ball a long way'; also to hit a man with a bat for fielding badly (1880; this use obsolete by 1900). Named after R. S. Barter (Coll. 1803–7), Warden 1832–61, a fine all-round cricketer who was famous for hard hitting, especially when dealing with this class of ball: he is said to have hit a ball from Turf into Kingsgate Street, about 130 yards [120 m]. (2) barters and bartering still used (1920) for fielding and catching practice at cricket, when the ball had to be thrown in to the hitter half-volley.

barter, to   (1) to hit a half-volley; obsolete since c. 1900. (2) to hit hard at cricket (1868); obsolete since c. 1900. (3) to hit balls for fielding and catching practice: recorded from 1856, still in use 1920.

bather   a basin pudding in College, especially in the phrase ginger bather (1920). Named from a supposed resemblance to Rev. A. G. Bather, Don 1894–1928.

bathing-leave   leave sent down by the Headmaster, usually at the beginning or middle of May, before which it was non-licet to bathe. The official day for asking

Batmugger

for bathing-leave was 12 May, but in 1838 'boys never wait for that leave to begin bathing: but if nailed by a Master or Tutor bathing before that leave is down, the boy is liable to punishment'.

bathing-place   a section of Old Barge surrounded by palings, where only boys in the school were supposed to bathe (1880).

bath room   a room in Lower Cloisters in New Commoners 1842–69, fitted with a cold water tap.

batmugger   a wooden instrument like a rolling-pin, formerly used for oiling bats. Recorded from 1868; obsolete by 1914, but surviving in the nickname 'the Batmugger', borne by C. W. Crawley (Coll. 1911–17), presumably because he used to oil bats.

batlings, battlings   a weekly allowance of one shilling to each boy. In New Commoners (1868) they were given out at Saturday teatime by Commoner Steward, James Williams; in 1920 Commoners received them from the House Don, and College men from the Senior Praefect of their upstairs chamber. Now merely pocket money, these were originally intended to enable boys to supplement their meagre diet on Fridays, Saturdays and other fast days, and in Lent, and they thus appear in the Hutton accounts (1620), while in his Manual of Prayers (1674) Bishop Ken enjoined devout boys to content themselves with College commons and divert part of their battlings to charity. At Eton the extra food was received in kind by Collegers from their Dames under the name battel: carried on to Oxford, the word there slightly changed in form and meaning, becoming the battel (Lat. *batella*), a College account for food and drink supplied outside the normal College commons, and since 1706, if not earlier, battels have meant College bills in general: the verb 'to battle' appears in the 1670s for running an account with a College kitchen and buttery for extras; while in 1744 a Batteler or Battler was a grade of student one step up from a Servitor (the latter received no commons and had to buy his meals from College kitchen). Literally a battling is something to grow fat on, from the verb battle, battill, or batten (to grow fat, or fatten), derived from an Anglo-Saxon root: early examples, both from 1590, are Spenser, to battill in this sense, and Green, who uses battling as fattening.

batters bat-fives, played (1920) with a short or a long bat on Ball Court by College men, and in Old Fives Courts by Commoners.

beak! an exclamation by an Inferior, when anything unlawful (e.g. smoking) was going on, to warn that a Praefect was approaching. Recorded 1838 only; not confined to Winchester. A beak, or beck, sort for beck-harman, is old slang for a magistrate, constable, or schoolmaster: harman is an old word for the stocks, and beck-harman was the man who beckoned you to them.

Bear, the Dr W. A. Fearon (Coll. 1852–9), Headmaster 1884–1901, who wore a luxuriant beard and moustache.

Bear Cages, or Bird Cages the three semi-open fives courts adjoining Old Fives Courts on the south, so called from the wire netting which took the place of the back wall. They were very ugly, dirty and slow, and let in the wet; in 1922 they were demolished to make room for the War Cloister. Bear Cages is a misnomer, as the courts were built [not by the Bear (Dr Fearon) but] by Dr Ridding, Headmaster 1867–84.

Bear's Corner the corner formed by the junction of Southgate Road and Culver Close. Named after the Bear, who was House Don of D House 1868–82.

Bear's Delight a foricas in the Headmaster's house; it was said to be the small compartment over Moberly Gate.

Bear's Names see **Names-calling**.

Beast, the C. E. Robinson, Don 1909–45; also called the Bin. 'Beauty' was originally M. Robertson, Don 1905–46, but this Notion soon fell into disuse.

Beast's div, the the 1920 notion for Senior Part l.a.

beating the modern notion for tunding. The rules current in 1920 were: (1) any Praefect may beat any Inferior in his House. (2) any Co.Prae. may beat any Inferior in the school, and in theory anyone who is not a Co.Prae. (3) the Aul.Prae. may beat even Co.Praes, if the Headmaster requires him to do so, but he never does. For these purposes Tolly-keepers counted as Inferiors. Beating was more often on the bottom than on the back (a three-year man could demand the latter privilege). No beating was of more than ten strokes. In College, ground-ashes had to be raised by a Praefect from the Aul.Prae., who satisfied himself that the punishment was necessary; the culprit was sent back with them afterwards. Beatings took place at the beginning of breakfast and tea, and after Preces: it was a Notion in College for the Praefect to toast for his victim at the next meal, to show there was no ill will. A beating from the Headmaster, only for thoking or grave offences, was called a bottoming; beating was the only form of corporal punishment he sanctioned. Spanking, however, was used in College for trivial offences or carelessness, and was performed with any handy weapon such as a short bat or swaggerstick. Very Old Wykehamists remembered the historic Tunding Row, and one version of it which reached us was that a visitor had met a junior on his way to Hell to procure ground-ashes for use upon himself: letters were written to *The Times*, an enquiry revealed a disproportionate amount of beating, and it was restricted.

Beauty of Holiness, the   a pre-1820 nickname for Dr David Williams (Headmaster 1824–36), known as the Gaffer from 1820 to 1828.

beaver's weam, a   the pin fastening up a bundle of laundry. From weaver's beam: I Samuel 17.7: 'the staff of his [Goliath's] spear was like a weaver's beam'.

'Been through!'   at Winchester football, when the ball has passed through the legs of any up in the front row of the hot on either side, the hot-watcher calls 'Been through', and the hot breaks up.

beeswaxers   (pronounced bëswaxers) thick, heavy, laced football boots with square toes. Recorded 1831–72; long since obsolete. Came from treating them with beeswax; dubbin was used c. 1920.

Beetle, the   The Rev. H. J. Wickham (Coll. 1839–47), House Don of A, 1859–88. From his presumed resemblance to one.

Beetleites   men in the Beetle's house. Recorded from 1868; obsolete by 1917, when they were called Furleyites.

beavers, beevers, or **bevers**   a light intermediate meal of bread and beer laid out in College Hall during an interval in afternoon school called bever time, which in 1831 was 4.30–4.45; in 1836–8, a quarter of an hour in hot weather in Cloister Time only; in 1856, 4–4.30. Obsolete by 1868. In 1831, beer only is mentioned: in 1838, the beaver is only a piece of bread placed in Hall for each boy, 'but the boy who gets up into Hall first gets as many as he wants, and the next boy the same: so that unless a boy gets up into Hall in time he gets none, which is generally the case with juniors'. This interval was observed long after bevers ceased, and towards the end of the First World War, when School Shop was closed and extra nourishment was needed, bevers of tea and biscuits were introduced under the old name at 4–4.15 p.m. Until 1890, Eton also had a bever or beever of bread, salt and beer laid in Hall at 4 p.m.; at Charterhouse a beaver was an extra piece of bread taken with drink. The word and the practice still survive in rural areas, and farmers recognise an obligation to give labourers, especially at harvest or haymaking, a bever or bayver at 10 a.m. and 4 p.m., consisting of beer with or without bread and cheese; in Jersey it is at 10 and 3, and called lunch; in Bedfordshire it is called 11 o'clock and 4 o'clock; all the world over, mid-morning coffee is called elevenses.

Bever descends from the Latin *bibere* (to drink), through French *bevre*, *boivre*, and Italian *bevere*, to bever and beverage; it appears as bever or biberium (drinking time) in 1440; as bevarages or nuntions in 1577; as beaver in 1585; as bever in 1590 (in Marlowe's *Faustus*, where Gluttony has ten bevers a day); as nunchions and beavers in 1599; as beaver in 1730, 1733; bever time occurs in 1725. In Commoners in 1868 the pedigree of this venerable word was forgotten, and bevers were a time of leave-out in the afternoon, when none but Praefects might wear (beaver) hats.

behind (1) a kick or back at Winchester football. In XVs there are three behinds, called Second, Middle and Last Behind; in VIs there are two, called Second and Last Behind: their duties are to kick every ball which comes back through their ups and hot-watchers, to stop all rushes and to hold the ball in ropes until the ups come round. They are allowed to stop the ball with their hands. Last behind kicks off after a goal, and after a behind. (2) when a ball passed over worms, having last been touched by a player on the defending side, it is called a behind, or said to go behind.

behind your side at Winchester football, when a player fails to go back to where the ball was last kicked by one of this own side, he is said to be behind his side: the penalty is a hot one post back from where he broke the rule.

Belfry the room where bells are rung, between gallery and the head of gallery stairs.

Bell Gate a gate in the east side of Cloisters, made in 1921, with a stone stair and balustrade, and an almost illegible inscription in florid characters. The gate led into the Warden's Garden and replaced a very shabby door, which had existed at that point; given in memory of G. M. Bell, Don 1900–17 and House Don of H from 1908, killed in action at Ypres 1917.

bells go Chapel bells were rung to summon the congregation for fifteen minutes on Sundays, for five on saints' days and weekdays, and for about three minutes for College preces. They rang in three different ways, and one had to know these to calculate the time left to get in: they were called 'bells go rotten', 'bells go double' and 'bells go single':

- 'bells go rotten' meant three successive bells in descending scale, each rung three times, with an interval of nine or ten seconds between.
- 'bells go double' meant the full peal of six bells; or, on weekdays, two bells only.
- 'bells go single' meant a rapid monotonous toll on one bell only.

'bells go down' meant they stopped (a Notion at least as old as 1838, when 'bells down' meant they had stopped).

In 1920, on Sundays bells went rotten for five minutes, double for five minutes, single for five minutes; on saints' days, double for two minutes, single for three minutes; on weekdays, double (two bells) for two minutes, single for three minutes; for College preces bells went rotten with about a one-second interval between each group of three; and then single for seventy strokes, which represented the fixed number of scholars.

Beloe's K House: Kingsgate House. Original House Don, Rev. R. D. Beloe, later Headmaster of Bradfield.

bend over to put yourself in a position to receive a spanking, by touching your toes, etc. Quoted 1868 as a Notion in New Commoners; not confined to Winchester.

Bendle College carpenter and odd-job man (1920). He mended lights, div room chairs and College Praefects' slack-chairs; his workshop was in Arcadia, at the top of a wooden ladder and he was summoned thence by a shout of 'Bendle!' A favourite commendation of an efficient job of work was 'Bendle done it'. His alias was Bush, on the analogy of Rendall, Push.

Bendle's Hole the workshop of the above; called Downer's shop in 1838.

benjamin (1) a ruler; from Psalm 68:27: 'there is little Benjamin [with] their ruler'. (2) a small table in College Hall, between Dais and Simon and Jude, which in 1918–19, when College was overfull, accommodated four men; from Genesis 43.34: 'but Benjamin's mess was five times so much as any of theirs. And they drank and were merry with him.'

ben in halo see **Funkey**.

Ben Stephens, or Ben Stuggins Capt. E. E. Byng Stephens, on the staff 1909–32, as Headmaster's secretary, and in charge of gymna.

Bertie Lucas, or **Bertie** Rev. E. de G. Lucas (G 1891–7), priest in charge of the Winchester College mission at Rudmore, Portsmouth (1920).

between hours the interval between hours (1900).

bible, to to inflict a **bibling.**

Bible Clerk in medieval times, he was the boy who read the Bible [aloud] during Hall dinner; later used for the Praefect responsible for law and order in School, and finally for the Praefect who read the lessons in Chapel; long since obsolete. In monastic institutions a member of the community was chosen each week to read the Bible during dinner in hall, and at Winchester one of the boys performed this function: during his week of office he was called Bible Clerk or Biblioclericus (1647). The readings, which in the seventeenth century were from the Old Testament only, were known from sixteenth century as ἀναγνώσεις and the reader as ἀναγνώστης, and on his scob at the east end of School was inscribed 'τῷ ἀεὶ ἀναγνώστῃ' (for the Bible-reader for the time being). The name and function of Bible Clerk are as old as College: in 1220 boys were holding similar office at Wells Cathedral, except on special days when choir and organ performed, and similarly our Bible Clerk did not perform on days set apart for celebrating the Founder. Under a benefaction of 1574 the Bible Clerk at Christ's Hospital received a white loaf on three days in his week of office.

At some stage readings in Hall ceased and the Bible Clerk became, with the Ostiarius (doorkeeper), the representative of law and order in School, and the inscription on his scob was changed to 'τῷ ἀεὶ θυρωρῷ'. In 1836–8 he is described as a College Praefect in full power, in course for a week at a time, with the duties of collecting the verse and prose tasks; keeping School quiet; giving in names which had been 'ordered' to him and presenting their owners to the master for bibling; taking the place of Praefect of Hall when that man was absent. While holding office the Bible Clerk did not have to go up to books. In 1868 he had also to open the door for masters and keep up the fire.

When School ceased to be used as a school-room, the title of Bible Clerk reverted to its original meaning of bible-reader, and the College Praefect who was in course for a week at a time to read the lesson at morning chapel was called Bible Clerk. But by 1914 the title had lapsed.

bibler (later **bibling**: wrongly spelt bibla 1838) a flogging of six cuts administered with the bibling rod. The victim was 'taken up' (i.e. his shirt was held up to expose a hand's breadth of the small of his back) by the Bible Clerk and Ostiarius. The tradition in 1820 was a space equal to the diameter of a crown-piece. A bibling was usually given by the Headmaster but sometimes by the Second Master. A Warden's bibling was of nine cuts, and one in VIth Chamber (1838) was of an indefinite number of cuts. Recorded from 1831; obsolete by 1870. Bibler is from Bible Clerk, i.e. a flogging administered with the official approval of the Bible Clerk, with a possible echo of 'booking' and other euphemisms in dialect for punishment or beating.

bibling-rod a rod made of four apple twigs tied to a handle; there was still one in Porter's Lodge in 1920.

biblos a Bible. Recorded from 1892; obsolete by 1917. Derived from Greek βιβλος (a book).

Bib.Prae. Bibliothecae Praefectus, the official title of the Praefect of Mob.Lib.

bicolour a cropple of lines set by A. E. Broomfield, Don 1903–24, to be written out with alternate letters in red and blue ink. There was also tricolour, in three inks.

bidet (pronounced biddy) a round flat hip-bath of zinc or galvanised iron, used in College, with handles for emptying it. Recorded from 1856; still in use 1922. From French *bidet* (bath).

bidet, to to immerse forcibly in a bidet. Obsolete by 1917.

bidet motto a quotation or original epigram in verse or prose connected with baths and bathing, to be produced by Inferiors in each shop in College (1920) on the first Saturday or Sunday of the half. Entries were judged by the Praefects of the shop, and the first choice of bidet-nights was given to the winner.

bidet roll the roll made out in each chamber at the beginning of the half to show when each man was to have his weekly hot bath. Pinned up above half-faggot in each upstairs shop, it took the following form (1920):

VIIIth Chamber Bidet Roll
Common Time, 1920
τὸ πᾶν
J. Smith, K.C.B.
S. Jones, C.B.
F. Brown, B.
A. White, Tuesday
B. Green, Friday

At the foot the winning motto was quoted, with the owner's name: the whole was initialled by the Junior Praefect, who wrote it out. For τὸ πᾶν , see Toe-pan Roll. In the Praefect of Hall's chamber only were G.C.B., C.B., and B. [an apt allusion to the grades of the Order of the Bath].

bidet room bath-room. There were five in College (1920): *upstairs*, 6th bidet room (for 6th and 7th upstairs), 8th bidet room (for 8th and 9th upstairs) and 12th bidet room (for 10th, 11th, 12th, Ken and New chambers); these were used by all for cold bidets in the morning and hot bidets at night; during the day, they were used only by Praefects, Tolly-keepers, and senior men and men on XV roll whom Praefects invited to change upstairs; *downstairs*, Ist Chamber (for Inferiors in IInd, Vth and VIth during the day) and IVth Chamber (for Inferiors in VIIth and Thule during the day).

biggin, bigging a coffee-pot in two parts. The upper part was a strainer and held the grounds, on to which boiling water was poured, passing through the perforations to the lower compartment. In an illustration from 1868, the spout

Biggin

has a cap secured by a chain, and there is a handle at right-angles to the spout. Recorded from 1856; long since obsolete. Came not from the Elizabethan biggin (a child's cap or nightcap) or from piggin (a small wooden vessel) but from one Biggin who invented this type of coffee-pot c. 1800. [See *OED*, biggin[2].]

bikkers   biscuits (1920).

Bill Brighters   miniature faggots, originally used for lighting College kitchen fire. Neat bundles of dried twigs, about 9 in. [22.5 cm] long, in 1917 they were still in use in upstairs chambers for lighting the fire in the evening, and in the morning the Second Junior had to light one for the Senior Praefect to dress by; they were also used for lighting the faggot in Ist and IVth during changing after football. Named after Bill Bright, a College cook c. 1834, who had charge of them.

Bin, the   C. E. Robinson, Don 1909–45; so called to distinguish him from Ro*bert*son.

Bingo   an unattractive dog, part-collie and part-bobtailed sheepdog, belonging to W. D. Munro, Don 1911–33: always about (1920), and always de trop.

Birley's Corner

Black Bridge

Bird Cages   see **Bear Cages**.

Birley's Corner   the corner between Hatch and Tunbridge at the northern end of Reach, where Adam and Eve leaves River. Recorded from 1868. Named after Robert Birley (Comm. 1839–43), who was the first to bathe there: in legend he was also drowned there, but in fact died in 1892 at the age of 72.

Bishop   (1) the Lord Bishop of Winchester. (2) Johnny Bishop, College Porter c. 1920. (3) the second senior chaplain, who officiated in Chantry, was called Bishop of Chantry (1920). (4) a querister who left in 1919. (5) the hazel withy which bound a faggot together (1920); possibly from the name of the plant, e.g. bishop's-weed, bishop's elder: or from the name of the man who supplied, or prepared, faggots.

black asses, or **three black asses**, or **two black and one brown**   a College dean, introduced in the First World War, consisting of squares of Yorkshire pudding with hard outsides, covered with dark jam: most unpopular. The third name was adopted on the suggestion of Walker, a College sweater, who was the first person to give them a name.

Blackberry Lane, or **Stanmore Lane**   led up from St Cross Road over Level Crossing, and across open country beyond (1920). There was a tradition that [William] Rufus' body was brought along this lane from the New Forest.

black book   a book kept by the Warden (1838) in which were entered names of College boys who had 'committed any[thing] out of the common way': if a boy's name was entered three times, he was expelled. Long since obsolete.

Black Bridge   the bridge at the foot of Wharf Hill, near what was Mant's Wharf. Originally black (probably wood), by 1892 it was of conspicuously white stone. In 1838 it was the largest bridge over the river, and boys crossed it on their way to Hills.

black jack, or **jack**   black leather beer jug used in College. Made of stitched, waxed leather, they had wide mouths and bases, narrowing slightly at the waist,

black jack

with tough leather handles sewn in; there were two examples in Porter's Lodge (1920), and replicas in china could be bought up Town. The jack or black jack was in general use in England in the seventeenth century, and the word occurs in Beaumont and Fletcher (1609), in other examples (1630–52), and in W. H. Bellamy's song 'Simon the Cellarer'. Ben Jonson uses the term jack (1622), and Tom Warton in 'the happy junior of VIth Chamber' (c. 1750) mentions jacks among the items contibuting to his happiness. The jack is shown as the cause of the slothful porter's undoing in the mural in Porter's Lodge, executed in the reign of the nineteenth-century porter Locke: it shows a porter asleep over his jack, and the keys being stolen from him, with the verse:

> The slothful porter loves too well his jack,
> and College keys are stole behind his back.

To the right is a more reliable porter, with:

> The trusty porter's figure here you see,
> and kept is College under Locke and key.

Like billy and jemmy, jack is a personal name used as a noun for something which does the work of a servant and is subjected to rough handling.

Jacks are now obsolete and the word has disappeared from current English, but survives at Winchester, where 'jack' rather than 'black jack' was the word for these jugs.

black-sheeping   in Cloister Time, when two divs sometimes went up together, a man in Junior Part might jockey (go up above) one in Middle Part: this was called to 'jockey a black sheep', or black-sheeping; and was applied later to a man in Junior Div Middle Part jockeying one in Senior Div Middle Part. Recorded 1868; obsolete soon after, when School ceased to be used for teaching and taking places up to book was discontinued. Came from the idea that the men thus jockeyed were the ne'er-do-wells or black sheep of the div above.

Bleeder, the   William Bleaden Croft, Don 1874–1915.

blood line, to sport a   to walk in a line with three or more people (1920): only done by very senior men. From blood, in the sense of a man of fashion.

Bloody Hand, the   a dark patch about 2 in. [5 cm] in diameter on the marble of William Williamson in the bottom row on the west wall of VIIth: a natural discoloration of the stone. The following legend was told of it. In the dark ages of College, before Functures were used in chambers, a junior in VIIth was unmercifully brocked by the Senior Praefect and, suffering beyond endurance, resolved to slay him; late one night he took a knife, crept across the chamber to the Praefect's bed, and stabbed him. When a light was struck it was discovered that he had murdered his brother by mistake. To eliminate any danger of error in future, Functures were instituted. It is not recorded how bloodstains could have found their way to a marble 10 feet (300 cm) above the floor.

Bloody Lane   a lane on the way home in Senior Steeplecha course (1920), leading from Parker's Gallop to Portsmouth Road: it was generally very muddy, and full of mosquitoes. The name reflects the attitude of runners to the conditions it offered at this critical stage of a gruelling run.

blow, to   to blush. A survival of the Shakespearian verb to blow (bloom), used (1595) of wild thyme, roses and other flowers, it came from Old English *blowan* (to bloom) and was in use to 1914.

bluchers   From blucher (the half-boot). (1) the blucher, or half-Wellington boot. Recorded 1868 as non-licet; not peculiar to Winchester, and long since obsolete. Named after Marshal Blücher of Waterloo fame. (2) College Praefects in half-power, now called Junior Praefects, who formerly had authority only 'on Chamber side of Gate', i.e. in Hall and Chambers. Recorded 1836; obsolete by 1914.

blue bills   tradesmen's bills, sent in at the end of the half to the House Don, who, on what was called Blue Bills night in Commoners, gave them to their owners to check; the owners either took them home, or gave them to the House Don who sent them home. So named from being formerly wrapped in blue paper; in 1922 in College they were still enclosed in a long blue envelope. Recorded in 1880.

Blue Gate   (1) the gate which stood between School Court and Arcadia. Through the grating in this gate La Croix's cad sold ices; Commoners similarly bought food at Hatch. Masters came from School into Commoners through this gate up to c. 1870, when it disappeared. The name was then transferred to (2) the medieval arch leading south from the Warden's stables. Finally it passed to (3) the little modern gateway leading down a step from Moberly Court into Arcadia.

blue patrol   see **patrol jacket**.

Blue Roll   the School calendar: a small book in blue paper cover which was sent to one's pitch-up in the summer holidays. The Blue Roll showed each man's place in his various divisions, and in Senior Part Order, the names of all winners of medals and prizes since their inception, and a list of all work done by each div during the year. Recorded 1880, it survived to 1922, but has since vanished.

Boat Club   the school Boat Club. In 1880 it had a president, a committee of four, and numerous rules.

Boat-house   School boat-house on River, just below Plank Bridge and opposite what was called Domum Wharf: a little below Red Bridge (1880).

bob   (1) a large white beer jug, holding about a gallon [4.5 l], used in College. Bobs are recorded in 1820, when they were filled by juniors at midday hall and brought down for afternoon consumption. Obsolete since c. 1860. The name is perhaps from their price: bob has been slang for a shilling since 1812, if not before. (2) a shilling. Recorded 1838–80 as a Commoner Notion. Bob, or bobstick, is English slang for a shilling: derivation unknown.

Bobber, the   Major M. Robertson, OBE, MC, Don 1905–46.

bog-owlers   brown buttoned boots, which might on no account be worn (1917). A complex Notion, based on the word bob-owler (a large moth), built up from bog (brown) and Latin *bubo* (horned owl).

bogwheel   a bicycle. A Notion, and common slang (1920), which has given place (1960) to bogle.

boiler   any vessel used for boiling water. In 1838 it meant a kind of tin saucepan with a cover, in which coffee was made and water boiled. Other patterns, all long since vanished, were the funnel-shaped Waterloo boiler; the mess boiler, similar to a teapot; and the biggin boiler, a two-tiered coffee percolator. By 1917 a boiler was an ordinary kettle used on chamber fires.

boner   a smart rap or thump with the fist on the lower vertebrae. Recorded 1831–80; obsolete by 1900.

booby trap   a can of water balanced over a door: recorded as a Notion in New Commoners 1868, but not confined to Winchester.

books   a word with a long history and some interesting meanings.
  (1) Naturally it meant written and printed books (mentioned 1820).
  (2) Up to 1563 'books' also meant the oppressive practice of making scholars repeat orally at bedtime the passages they had heard read from books at supper

'up to books'

in Hall: this spoiled both supper and bedtime, and appears to have been abolished in 1563. In 1673 the fifteenth-century Warden who introduced it was still remembered as *durus* (harsh); and it is possible that the phrase 'go *up* to books' echoes the days when scholars climbing hall stairs for supper realised that they were ascending to a Latin lesson which they would later have to recite.

(3) From the first the school was divided into six classes, after the standard text-books taught in each, the VIth being top and Ist bottom. William Horman. Headmaster 1494–1502, calls a class a 'boke' or 'classis'. For some reason the lower classes have gradually faded out. In 1529, Class I is not mentioned; in 1645 III, II and I have given place to a composite class called IV–II (Quarta-Secunda); IV was still there in 1843, but has since gone and by 1917 the only survivors were VI, V and II (Queristers).

(4) The benches on which the classes sat were named books after them. In the original school-room (VIIth Chamber) there were three tiers of stone benches in each of the three window embrasures: they are still there, in the two surviving windows, and still called books. When School was built in imitation of VIIth these books were reproduced in three tiers of wooden benches, called books (but by 1836 the name had changed to rows), at each end of the room: those at the east have vanished, but those at the west are still there, and still called books. Here the classes were ranged to recite or construe their lessons, and change places on the result of question and answer, and to be at lessons was called being 'up at books': to go to lessons was to go 'up to books'. Chichester Cathedral had benches of this nature and also called them books. The procedure in School c. 1868 is thus described: 'when a Part or division are up to a Master saying a lesson, they sit at one of the ends of School on three "rows": the Master sits on his chair with his side to them, and the fellow who is "set on" gets up from his place and goes to the end of the front or Senior Row, stands about 6 feet [1.8 m] from it facing the Master, and construes'.

Nowadays 'up to books' means in school, and going up to books means going from College or one's house to a div room.

(5) When form prizes were provided in the shape of books, by the Duke of Buckingham, and later by Lord Saye and Sele, these were called books: to win them was to 'get books' (from 1838), and to 'raise books' (later). Originally the two boys at the top of each part at the end of each half, or at the top of the Classicus paper in the lower forms, and two chosen by the Doctor were awarded books. In 1868 there were fourteen such prizes, and when the year was divided into three terms, each div was awarded one prize at Easter and midsummer and two at Christmas. Other prize books available c. 1920 were:

French books: school prize for French, given in Cloister Time
German books: school prize for German
Senior Part Order books: at the end of Cloister Time the marks of all men in senior part for classics, French, mathma and science were scaled and added together: the two or three senior men, and others down the list who were much higher than expected, got books
Task books: given in VIth Book Junior Div twice a year for the half's classical compositions, independently of div books
Tutor's books: given by a Tutor to his Pupil at the end of the half if he raised a remove, and often if he did not
Valet's books: given by a Praefect to his valet
Writer's books: given by an Officer to his Writer.

(7) The tall bookcases on either side of the fireplace in School were called books. By 1917 they had only one shelf each, the height of a bench, and on them the New Roll sat at concerts and lectures.

(8) By analogy with (5), top score at cricket or first place in anything could be called books, and to achieve this could be called to 'make books' or to 'get books'. Recorded from 1836.

books-chambers a school hour spent in chambers (College) or up to house (Commoners) preparing for an hour up to books: in the evening called Toy-time. A curiously built phrase, it appears in 1838 as books chamber time, signifying either chamber time spent preparing to translate a classical text up to books, or up-to-books work done in chambers. It is comparable with the phrase 'in chambers', when a judge disposes of a matter in his private study instead of in court. The term must date back before 1687, when School was built and boys were locked out of chambers in the daytime, but continued to mean daytime preparation hours. In 1831–43 it meant the hours from 10 to 12 and from 4 to 6 on whole remedies (4–6 only on half-remedies), when College boys sat in School in charge of their Praefects, no master being present, and Commoners in Commoner hall under one of their Tutors: during these hours School was liable to be entered by any master. By 1868, books-chambers in Commoners were from 9 to 11 on remedies and half-remedies, and 3.45–4.45 in Easter and Cloister Time, but by then the afternoon books-chambers were obsolescent. Tutor did not sit in Hall, but sometimes came in and had names called by one of the two Praefects in course. By 1892 the hours were 5–6 on half-remedies in Short Half and Common

Boots and Leathers

Time, and 9–11 on Thursday mornings in Cloister Time, the Praefect in course keeping toys. By 1917 a man was unlucky if he did not have one, if not two, books-chambers a day. Recorded from 1831, and still in use.

books lesson translation of a classical author up to books. Recorded from 1892, but dating back to the time when the standard text-book in forms was classical.

bootlace a narrow black necktie of even width throughout its length: a type worn by small untidy men in College c. 1920.

Boots and Leathers a Commoner peal; see **peal**.

bottoming see **beating**.

bowled croppled in standing-up. Recorded as a Notion in 1868 but is ordinary slang.

box over toys a moveable box like a cupboard placed above a toys in New Commoners (1868) and Houses (1880).

'Boy!' when Election Chamber became College Library in 1922 it was decided that there would be accidents if men ran down the spiral staircase to answer the call 'Junior'; so a law was made that if on such occasions no junior appeared from any other part of College, a Praefect might back up 'Boy!', on hearing which the junior man in Election Chamber should descend.

Bradley a man who swept out div rooms and did other odd jobs in that region, c. 1920.

bread-pickers each of the four Senior Praefects in Commoners used to choose a junior as his bread-picker, an office which exempted him from all sweats except that of putting tollies in foricas: this sweat was considered an honourable one. Trant Bramston (Comm. 1856 and Comm. Tutor 1868–9) used to say that the correct definition of a bread-picker in a Notions examina was: 'one who picks bread: also one who puts tollies in foricas; a piece of patronage once of great value'. Recorded from 1831; obsolete by 1868. Whether they ever had to choose slices of bread for the Praefects, or the title is an euphemism, we shall probably never know.

Bread Room   a room in Hatch in New Commoners, where cargoes were kept (1868). Still recorded in House (1880).

brew   From Anglo-Saxon *briw* (pottage, broth, porridge, which appears in Old English and dialect as *brew*, *brue*, *bree*, *brewis*: in Old French as *broez*, and French as *brouet*. a Commoner notion for tea, coffee, or drink in general, by 1920 usually meaning afternoon tea. Recorded from 1856.

brew, to   to partake of a brew, or to prepare brew for a Praefect. From Anglo-Saxon **briwan** (to prepare food); it is thus used by Shakespeare and Swift.

brewed beer   made in two ways: in hot weather, by mixing sugar and rice with the beer to make it up; in cold, by adding spice, lemon and sugar, and heating it. Obsolete by 1892.

brewers   a notion in New Commoners for Juniors who had to make a brew of coffee, cocoa, or spiced beer for Praefects and spree men. Brewing beer was non-licet by 1868.

Brewery   adjoining Porter's Lodge on the west, and separating Outer Court from College Street. Originally there were five or six brewing days in the year, but by c. 1900 College was no longer brewing its own beer. The full equipment of wooden shovels, etc., survived in Brewery until 1922, but unfortunately disappeared when the building was converted into Mob.Lib. Beer was served in College Hall until 1915, when it was stopped as a wartime economy.

brewing   in Old and New Commoners, when a boy first came, he was put on the brewing roll of some Praefect, and had to abstract a certain number of soda-water bottles full from the public jorums at dinner time; it was considered infra dig. at supper time.

brightest and best   a knitted College VI tie, of even width, which could be worn (1920) by anyone who had been on VI Roll the previous year. Came from the hymn 'Brightest and best of the sons of the morning' (tune by H. J. Gauntlett; words by Bishop Heber), no. 56 in Hymnarium (1910), no. 58 (1928 edition).

bring down, to   to read out a Lords, Sixes or other roll; usually done by a Don at the request of the captain. Probably from being brought down to School Court, from College or Commoners.

British   a Commoner notion (1920) for an English, i.e. a translation or crib of a classical book. The word was also used as an adjective (1920) for over-enthusiastic or hearty, whether of a man or house: a reaction to wartime jingoism.

brock   a shame, bad luck, nuisance, unfair treatment, injustice, bullying; e.g. 'What a brock' (what a nuisance, what a pity). From Anglo-Saxon *broc* (affliction), thus used by Aelfred (871–901): our word has acquired the special sense of misfortune when better luck was deserved.

brock, to   (1) to tease, chaff or badger. (2) to treat unfairly, inconvenience, handle roughly, hurt or bully. Either the meaning has oscillated between these two in successive generations, or two distinct words are preserved in this term. It is usually derived from brock (a badger), used by Ben Jonson (1636) and surviving in dialect, and taken to convey the general idea of tormenting, getting a rise out of, or maltreating, and in support of this it is noted that badger-baiting was a recognised school sport until 1870. However, a marginal note of 1775 in the Statutes shows that the boys at that time used badger, not brock, for the creature baited. It is more likely that we are here dealing with two words: (a) brok, which in a document of 1315 apparently means to speak plaintively or provocatively. It appears as 'brokkynge' in Chaucer's 'Miller's Tale', as an epithet for the nightingale's song, meaning something akin to teasing. This obscure word may be the source of our brock, when used for verbal teasing, which was its sole meaning up to 1850, and its more usual meaning in 1920. (b) the Anglo-Saxon brocian, a violent word meaning to afflict or oppress: in the *Anglo-Saxon Chronicle* 'gebrocod' means overwhelmed by conquest or affliction: the bullying sense of our brock might easily derive from this.

brockster   a tease or bully.

Brodgers   a farm near the Portsmouth Road belonging c. 1868 to a man named Stratton; also called Bridgers (1880).

brodrick   the peaked service cap used in the Officers Training Corps c. 1920: an army word, probably from its inventor's name.

brolly   an umbrella; National slang, but recorded as a Notion from 1836. cf. tolly, yolly.

Brolly Tree   a tree in Salve Diva Potens Corner, so called from its shape.

brown   a penny; national slang for a halfpenny or other copper coin. Recorded as a Notion in 1838 only.

brum   (1) out of funds, penniless, stony-broke; usually in the phrase 'dead brum'. Recorded from 1831; still in use 1922. (2) stingy; so used 1856, but this meaning soon lapsed. From the Kentish dialect word brumpt (bankrupt).

brum penny   one's last penny. 'To raise a brum penny' was a College Notion c. 1920 for levying a penny from each man in the Chamber to alleviate one's own distress. It was a privilege of the Senior Praefect of the Chamber but he seldom if ever exercised it. From brum (above), or possibly an echo of the adjective brummagem, for Birmingham (i.e. counterfeit), in allusion to the counterfeit groats made there in the seventeenth century.

Bryant's   a small white wooden house situated at the end of College Street, under the walls of Wolvesey Palace. Recorded from 1838 to 1884: near Foster's Corner. In 1838 it was 'a favourite resort of Commoners, where they buy dispars and porter. Praefects never go there, so that Inferiors smoke and drink there as they like.'

buck   handsome, well turned-out. Recorded 1856–92; obsolete by 1917. From Regency slang, buck for a man of fashion, dandy, fop, first appearing in print in Dickens. [*OED* cites the word in this sense from Fielding and Gray.]

buck down, to   to grieve, to be unhappy. In use c. 1880; obsolete by 1914. Means the opposite of buck up.

buck up   (1) hurrah! In use c. 1850–1900: obsolete by 1914. (2) cheer up, hurry up. (3) to be happy (1880). National slang: this group of Notions was a temporary frolic with the word buck, and has not survived, except in so far as buck up (cheer up) is still current.

bucked up   smartly dressed. In use c. 1900: obsolete by 1914. It may simply mean dressed up like a buck or dandy, or may descend from the dialect phrase busk up (from Icelandic *buask*, to prepare oneself), meaning to smarten up one's appearance prior to departure. This occurs from 1377 onwards; the Scotch version is buskit up. As the word grew older, its element of departure came to the fore, and busk up came to mean to repair or hasten to some place: in this sense it survives in slang as buck up (hurry up).

bucksome, or **buxom**   cheerful. In use c. 1880; obsolete by 1914.

bulky   rich, generous, liberal (the opposite of brum). In use 1831–1900; obsolete by 1917. Not used thus in English, as being comparable with big-hearted, but *amplitudo* is thus used sometimes in Latin.

bull   a crown (five-shilling) piece; half a crown (two shillings and sixpence) was half a bull. In use 1856; half a bull survived till 1914; both since obsolete. The old five-shilling piece had various nicknames: in polite society called a cartwheel, in thieves' slang it was bulls-eyes, and bull is from this. Dickens' characters use half a bull but not bull, which may be slightly older. [cf. *OED*, bull[2], a seal.]

Bullfinches and **Greenfinches**   Notions in College c. 1920, possibly for two farms: the exact meaning is forgotten. A bullfinch can mean a strong fence, being a corruption of bull-fence.

Bull's Drove   strictly the south-western portion of New Field, next to Double Hedges, but used generally for the whole of the southern section, on which School Game (soccer) was played. Like Dogger's Close, the name is a relic of old lands that were merged into College grounds.

bundle   clean clothes returned each week from the wash and put out on each man's bed.

Bungy, or **Bungay**   a nickname for Bryant, the owner of Bryant's, (q.v.). In use 1838–68.

Bungy's Corner   see **Foster's Corner**.

Bunny   Dr Roberts, doctor to some Commoner houses c. 1920; the College doctor was Dr Child.

Bunny's Own   College Junior Junior (cricket): it was formerly College junior XI. In use c. 1900; obsolete by 1914. Either called after the nickname of its founder, or because the players were 'rabbits'.

Burgess   (father) a College under-porter c. 1920, usually seen with a broom, bucket and keys: hence called St Peter with the Keys, which became the hereditary title of the third porter. (son) a College chamberman and keeper of bicycle shed, c. 1920.

Burgess' Hole   the small sweater's room off 12th bidet room, used by Burgess junior and Crute c. 1920.

Bursar's gown   each year, c. 1917, the Bursar supplied material for one gown and waistcoast, thus named, for every man in College, who paid for the cloth being made up; his second gown was paid for by himself.

Bursary   the Bursar's offices above Outer Gate, formerly the Steward's rooms.

Bush (pronounced Büsh)   see **Bendle**.

butter-washer

bust a punt, formerly called a kick-off, at Our Game. When a man caught the ball before it had touched the ground, he had the right, subject to certain restrictions, to take a bust. Also used as a verb, dating from c. 1890: probably from burst.

buttered roll when a boy forgot to retrieve, on returning to his chamber, the roll he had put up on leaving it, the roll was well rubbed in tallow, toasted over the candle and given him to eat: this was a buttered roll. Recorded only 1838: long since obsolete. cf. hot roll.

butter-washer an instrument for washing butter, recorded as obsolete in 1868. In origin, it probably meant a boy employed to wash butter: see **wash butter**.

Buttery (1) the lobby outside College Kitchen, approached from Chamber Court: it had a buttery hatch, long since disused. Men in A and B Houses used to leave their hats in Buttery before going into Chapel. By 1917 it was called Trusty Sweater's Hole. (2) the three hatches at the west end of College Hall. Shakespeare uses buttery for pantry in 1603, and Ben Jonson uses it in 1633; Webster uses buttery-hatch in 1612. The word is from Old English *botelerye*, Old French *bouteillerie* (a place for bottles and liquors), from Latin *buticularia* (a wine-taster's office).

In Mansfield's day the three buttery hatches at the west end of Hall were:

Whiteman's hatch: for trenchers, knives and forks.
Dear's hatch: for bread and cheese.
Colson's hatch: for beer, butter and salt.

Colson was evidently a Hall butler, and his hatch was the buttery hatch, *par excellence*, because it yielded butter. There may be a pun here between buttery and buttress.

Buttress the westernmost buttress of Chapel in Chamber Court, flanking Chapel gate. In use since 1868.

buy a Chamber, to   to behave in someone else's Chamber as though it were one's own (1920).

buxom   see **bucksome**.

B.W.   for belly-worship or greed. This Notion was introduced by A. E. Broomfield, Don 1904–24, for eating suction up to books.

bysshe   a boil or pimple on the face or neck. From Percival Bradbury Tudor (Coll. 1911–16), afflicted with these, whose initials P. B. earned him the name Bysshe, from Shelley.

cad From late Latin *cadetus*, French *cadet* (younger brother), English cad (errand-boy, inn-yard loafer), Scotch caddie (errand-boy, golf-club carrier). (1) a blackguard (1838), in conformity with normal slang. (2) an errand boy (1856), e.g. La Croix's cad: and (in Commoners only) a fag or junior who had a regular sweat, e.g. brew cad, library cad: it was still so used in 1920. (3) in College (1920) a special sort of tie (see **tramp**), worn only by cads.

calendar some boys in College used to make a calendar of the term and ink each day in as it passed. Recorded 1838 only, with directions as to how it was done, ending nostalgically with: 'and so [till] the number of days we have to stay here for the half year are finished'.

calling see **peal**.

Candle-keepers, known by 1892 as **Tolly-keepers** the Inferiors who had been longest in College. In 1831–6 there were seven; in 1838–42, six: by 1917, three. They were excused from all fagging, though if absolutely no juniors were available, Praefects in full power had the right to fag them, but rarely exercised it. They were allowed a breakfast fag in hall, and a valet in Chambers, and the senior Candle-keeper had the power of fagging the twenty juniors on the School side of Seventh Chamber Passage Gate. Each Candle-keeper chose his chamber at the beginning of the half. These privileges were of the boys' own devising and not recognised by the authorities, and much of their power was taken away in 1838.

Their original function is obscure. They sat at the ends in Hall, as seniors of the messes, and may have been in charge of the candles supplied to each end in the dark months of the year. But they did not keep candles in 1838. They may have kept stocks of tollies for retailing to the juniors who had to supply them in chambers, or have stocked functures. Or the title may be jocular, as in the case of Bread-pickers. It could be a play on the Shakespearian term candle-holder, which meant a non-participant in some undertaking (here fagging): or the opposite of a candle-waster, which occurs in Shakespeare and Ben Jonson as one who burns the candle at both ends, i.e. either a dissolute person, or a book-worm.

candlestick a candidate for admission into College. In the past the Warden of New College, the Posers, the Warden, Sub-warden and Headmaster of Winchester each had the privilege of nominating a boy for admission: his election followed as a matter of course. The boy was given some Latin to construe, and was then asked if he could sing; whatever his answer, he had to say after the examiner: 'All people that on earth do dwell.' In continuous use since 1820; a facetious version of candidate.

Canon Street street leading from Kingsgate Street to Southgate Street. In 1920 it was rather a slum, and out of bounds.

canvas the ground, measuring 80 by 27 yards [73 by 24.5 m] on which Winchester football is played. Its shape may derive from the days when football was played in a confined space such as a road or (as at Old Charterhouse) in a cloister. When it was first played, the walls were supplied by two long rows of juniors, who had to kick in the ball; in 1843 their place was taken by canvas stretched on wooden poles, but this hid the game from spectators, and about 1862 the present method of wide-mesh netting was substituted, stretched first on wooden poles, later on iron ones: this is still called canvas. In 1920 the canvases were situated as follows: College, between Cloisters and Log Pond; Commoners, in Doggers Close, running parallel with Kingsgate Street; O.T.H., adjoining Commoner canvas but further from the street. Junior game canvases were: College, in the south-west corner of Meads; Commoners, in New Field, parallel with Logie; O.T.H., in Lavender Meads, parallel with Logie. In 1910 there were middle game canvases for Commoners and O.T.H. in Kingsgate Park, and in New Field, between Commoner junior game and Doggers Close.

canvas book a book kept by the skipper of College VI, c. 1920. It contained the names of the sides, goals scored and criticisms of all XV and VI canvases, games and players.

canvas roll see **roll**.

canvas slip a slip of paper bearing the names of those playing in Commoner and O.T.H. canvas, given out to a junior in each House by the names-docker at morning lines.

Cap.Prae. Capellae Praefectus, the official title of the two Praefects of Chapel. A book of plans, information and duties of Cap.Prae. and a box containing all chapel rolls and papers were bequeathed to succeeding Cap.Praes in 1922.

cargo a parcel or hamper of food sent by friends or relations; a hamper of game or eatables (1836). In use since 1820.

carry your gown, to   to hold up the skirts of your gown in the gap between the elbow, when bent with hand in pocket, and the body; a Praefects' and Tolly-keepers' Notion, 1920.

Carthage   a Notion c. 1920 for: (1) Debating Society room, off the east end of Mob.Lib. (2) the smaller half of the upper room above School Shop, which in College could be used only by three-year-men and their socii. (3) the house of Dr E. T. Sweeting, Music Don 1901–24, opposite Culver's Close. There is no record of why this name was chosen for any of the three places.

carving table   a table in a shallow recess at the near end of Grubbing Hall in New Commoners, where the Steward and other men carved at dinner, and where jam, etc. was put out for its owner to take at breakfast or tea. Obsolete since 1869.

Caryatid   a bracket carved in dark wood in the shape of a lady supporting a shelf for a cup, fixed to the screen in hall above Middle End; put up by Herbert Chitty, the Bursar, c. 1919. Named from the caryatids in the Erechtheum, which were named after Carya in Laconia.

cat   see **cat's head**.

Cathedral   (1) Winchester Cathedral, about five minutes walk from College through the Close gate. From about 1890, the school had its own service there on the second Sunday of each month, from 5.30 to 6.30; by 1917, the time had changed and was from 4.45 to 5.45, and the school occupied the whole choir area east of the screen, the Senior Cap.Prae occupying the Dean's stall. Formerly the school had attended Cathedral every Sunday, mingling with the congregation, but this was discontinued owing to complaints from the townspeople. The school no longer attends Cathedral. (2) a top-hat: because one had to be worn in the past for Cathedral.

Cathedral Sunday   the second Sunday in the month: see above.

cat's gallows   the poles set up for practising high-jump in Meads. Recorded in 1892; obsolete by 1917.

cat's head   the end of a shoulder of mutton (see **dispar**). Recorded in 1831; obsolete by 1860.

cause money   money formerly paid by College to maintain the raised footpath from Blackbridge along River to Hills. From causey (causeway), a dialect word meaning a raised and paved sidewalk or footpath across a farmyard, mud, or marshy ground, it appears as cawcy (1440), cawchie (1450), causay in Scotland (1520), causeye (c.1620), cause in Devon (1670–80), causey in Milton (1667) and in Oxfordshire (1710). Derived from Latin *calceata*, meaning a road (*via*) paved with broken limestone or gravel: hence Old French *cauchie*, French *chausée*.

caves calves of the legs. Recorded 1856 only. cf. haves for halves.

C.B. see **bidet roll**.

Cecil Range the miniature rifle range erected in memory of G. E. Cecil (B 1909–12), killed in the First World War. Until 1921 it lay just inside the old wall between Commoner Gate and David's Kennel. It was then pulled down, with the old wall, and rebuilt in Forder's Piece with the new fives courts; the memorial tablet was transferred thither.

Ceiling Room the space between the ceiling and roof of Chapel. Recorded 1892; obsolete by 1917.

Cellar College cellar. It lies beneath hatches in Hall and west of VIIth Chamber: access to it is by a stone staircase at the south-west corner of Buttery. It has a fine groined roof, resting on a single central pillar.

C.F. *consanguineus Fundatoris*: the official suffix for Founder's Kin (q.v.).

Chalk Pit (1) on the north side of Hills, facing Tunbridge: called simply Chalk Pit. (2) on the side of Twyford Down, between First and Second Pots: called Second or Twyford Chalk Pit. Recorded from 1868.

chalks much (with a comparative), e.g. 'chalks better than . . . '. Recorded 1892; obsolete by 1917. From common slang 'better by a long chalk'.

Chamber see **Chambers**.

Chamber, the the six Electors to New College. In use 1820; long since obsolete. From the fact that they sat in Election Chamber.

Chamber annals a record of the inmates and doings of a Chamber, written in light-hearted vein. In 1922 there were still in existence comparatively

60

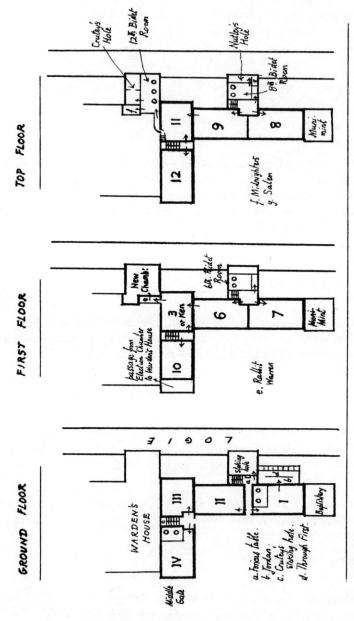

Plan of floors, north-east side of Chamber Court.

Chamber Court Conduit

old annals of IVth and VIth, and annals of IInd and New Chamber had been started.

chamber can   a large tin can for washing water in each upstairs shop in College c. 1920, which had to be filled night and morning by the First Junior.

Chamber Court   the inner court in College, surrounded on three sides by chambers and on the fourth by Chapel. Between 1838 and 1868 it was variously called Quadrangle, the Quadrangle, or Quadrangle Court.

Chamber Court Conduit   a long recess in west wall of Chamber Court, containing a drinking-water tap and a heavy silver cup on a chain. Originally it had a pent-house over it, which was rebuilt in 1651 as a timber shelter or portico supported on five Ionic columns. The pediment was an elm board carved with the Founder's arms, and it and the whole structure were richly painted and gilded. It was destroyed in 1837. Inscribed on the base of the cup is 'pote, repone'. This was formerly College washing place. The inscription on the cup could be read as 'potere, pone' (Take hold of [the cup], then put it down), but this is an awkward phrase. At first sight it appears to read 'repone post te', but there is no 'st'; 'drink, and put it back' would be *pota, repone*; *pote* in Latin can only mean rather.

chamber day   a day when College boys were allowed access to chambers all day, e.g. on the Sunday, Tuesday and Thursday in Standing-up week, all Election week and the last day of Short Half. At other times, chambers were locked directly after morning chapel and opened at 6 each evening. In use 1831–4: latterly it had come to mean the last day of each half, when School was cleaned and College boys retired to Chambers.

chamber deity a mascot fixed to chamber post or some other prominent place in the chamber (1920). It did not attract many devotees.

chamber library shelves set apart in each chamber for books in general use, such as *Corpus Poetarum Latinorum* and *Indices in Tragicos Graecos* (1920).

chamber post the solid oak pillar holding up the ceiling in IIIrd proper, Vth, VIth and VIIth.

Chamber Roll a list of the occupants of a chamber pasted up by men inside the door of their toys cupboards. The list followed a standard form. For a downstairs chamber, it was as follows (the number in brackets signifies the upstairs chamber):

IInd Chamber Roll
Short Half 1914

(8)	G. R. S. Snow, Cap.Prae.	
(9)	J. F. Duff,	
(9)	G. C. Glossop,	Praefecti
(8)	D. W. Pye,	
(8)	P. J. Campbell,	
(9)	F. J. W. Roughton,	Custodes candelarum
(9)	P. B. Tudor,	
(8)	H. H. Price,	Ganymedes
(9)	J. d'E. E. Firth,	
(8)	J. T. Christie,	
(9)	M. Beevor,	
(9)	J. Single,*	
(8)	V. H. Boileau,	Iuniores
(8)	K. B. Constable,	
(9)	G. E. R. Sandars,	
(9)	R. H. D. Campbell,	

* qui has nuces habuit (habebat).

For an upstairs chamber, it was as follows (the full details were not always given):

VIIIth Chamber Roll
Common Time 1920

A. Black, Cap.Prae.	(Senior Praefect)	
B. White,	(Junior Praefect)	
S. Holmes, (Candle-keeper)	(In loco)	
D. Watson,	(Shebe)	Sixth Book
D. Johnson,	(Hebe)	Inferiors
M. Boswell,	(Ganymede)	
A. Freeman,	(3rd Junior)	

B. Hardy, (2nd Junior) Juniors
C. Willis, (1st Junior)

Chamber VI after Sixes were over, some chambers produced a VI, and matches were arranged with other chambers or individual houses (1920).

chamber tick each chamber's deposit account at School Shop for Praefects' teas (1920).

Chamber Srogus a reading of a play in a chamber (1920); see **Srogus**.

Chambers the rooms in which College men have lived and slept since the foundation. There were originally six, corresponding with the six books or classes; the Praefect of Hall was always therefore in VIth Chamber. Organisation into six units also appears in the six 'chambers' into which all boys were grouped for Easter Speaking.

The first four chambers (I–IV) were on the east of Middle Gate, and the other two (V–VI) on the west, and were originally used both for sleep and study. When School was built in 1687 the school-room, whose windows looked out on to School Court, was converted into VIIth Chamber.

In 1838 the occupants and furnishings of the seven chambers were:

Ist 7 Inferiors: 2 Praefects: bedsteads, iron: clothes kept in drawers.
IInd 7 Inferiors: 3 Praefects: bedsteads, iron: clothes kept in drawers.
IIIrd 8 Inferiors: 3 Praefects: bedsteads, wooden, with sacking at the bottom: clothes kept in chests: post in centre.
IVth 7 Inferiors: 2 Praefects: bedsteads, wooden, with wood at the bottom: clothes kept in chests and large boxes or cupboards on top of the bed: post in centre.
Vth 6 Inferiors: 2 Praefects: bedsteads, iron: clothes kept in drawers: post in centre.
VIth 7 Inferiors: 3 Praefects: bedsteads, wooden, with wood at the bottom: clothes kept in chests: post in centre.
VIIth 10 Inferiors: 3 Praefects: bedsteads, iron: clothes kept in drawers.
$\overline{52}$ $\overline{18}$

Chroniclers of this period all testify to the cosiness and comfort of chambers in the evening, and Gordon's word-book of 1842 contains a note of items for further attention, including 'Chambers, bread, beer allowed'.

Between 1869 and 1871 the Fellows' Chambers on the first and second floors were converted into dormitories for the boys and some downstairs chambers were fitted with toys as work-rooms. By 1892 there were four such mugging-rooms, II, V, VI and VII; at this date, dormitories were IV downstairs, and 6, 7, 8, 9, 10, 11 and 12 upstairs: I had become a changing-room, and III a linen room.

In 1903 a room above III was taken from the Warden's Lodging as a dormitory, and called 'Ken'. In 1906 a downstairs chamber named Thule was added west

VIIth Chamber

of VI: it was first used as a changing-room and then fitted as a work-room: IV had also become a changing-room. In about 1914 a further dormitory was added beyond Ken and called New or War Chamber.

By 1917 the living- and mugging-rooms, fitted with toys, were I, V, VI, VII and Thule: sleeping-rooms, all upstairs, were:

6th: slept in by the men in VIth
7th: slept in by the men in Vth
8th & 9th: slept in by the men in IInd
10th & Ken (or 3rd) slept in by the men in Thule (so called as it was above IIIrd
11th & 12th: slept in by the men in VIIth
New (or War) Chamber: slept in by overflow from VIIth and one Praefect from Vth
Changing-rooms were Ist and IVth; linen room was IIIrd.

Chamber was the normal word for the lodgings of the secular clergy, and appears thus in Edward VI's Injunctions to cathedrals (1547): from the Latin *camera* (vaulted room). In 1647 six *camerae* were allotted to the scholars and one to the choristers. The room in which Election was held was called Election Chamber.

chancel chairs   chairs placed in Chapel between choir stalls and the altar steps, for extra accommodation in emergency. Recorded c. 1890; obsolete by 1917, but the chairs were still being brought in to relieve congestion at Confirma, and other times.

Chandler's finger   a macabre notion c. 1920 for a long roly-poly pudding. At this time Chandler was head butler in College Hall, and had the misfortune to cut off a finger in the bread-machine.

Chandler's Hatch   see **hatch**.

Chantry   Fromond's chantry, the two-storeyed chapel in Cloisters built by John Fromond, steward for the Hampshire and Wiltshire estates of College until 1420. Suppressed under Henry VIII, it was in 1629 converted into a library for the Fellows by Robert Pinke, Warden of New College, and so remained until 1875, when it was converted into a chapel for juniors: it holds about 100 men, who must spend at least a year there before passing into Chapel. On Advent Sunday 1899 Communion was celebrated there for the first time since the Reformation.

Chantry is unique, being the only perfect specimen of a chantry chapel left in England. The glass in the east window is original. The upper room was designed as a scriptorium. When the lower room became a chapel, the Fellows' and Dons' library was moved upstairs. In 1917 all that remained of this library were a few shelves of folios, since removed to the Warden's Lodging. In about 1923 Mr R. M. Y. Gleadowe fitted the upper room as an art-school, but by 1948 it had become a Wiccamica room presided over by Budge Firth. The reredos in the chapel below was presented by Dr Freshfield in 1896, and shortly afterwards he also gave a silver cross. The coats of arms of the ceiling were repainted c. 1900 at Dr Fearon's expense. The chapel is 36 feet [nearly 11 m] long, 18 feet [nearly 5.5 m] broad and proportionately lofty.

A chantry (Old English *chaunterie*, low Latin *cantaria*) was a chapel endowed with lands or revenue to provide the fees of a priest to sing daily mass for the donor's soul.

Fromond's chantry was always called Chantry. There was another chantry in the College buildings but it was never known as such; this was Thurbern's chantry, known (1920) as Tower Chairs, built about 1470 under the bequests of Warden Thurbern (1413–50). Soon after it was built, the tower of Chapel was erected above it, but it became insecure, and in 1862 had to be taken down and rebuilt. Each stone was numbered as it was removed, and the outward appearance of the tower was thus preserved.

In Cathedral there was Wykeham's chantry, built by the Founder in the nave before his death in 1404. It fills the space between two piers in the south aisle and contains his tomb, with his effigy, clad in pontifical robes, above. The chantry was repainted in 1664 after the Civil War, and in 1893 for the Quingentenary celebrations.

Chantry Roll   a plan showing the seat allotted to each man in Chantry. It used to be prepared (1920) by Mr Bather, printed and posted up on a notice board in Cloisters.

Chapel   forming the south side of Chamber Court, externally has changed little since the Founder's day. It was the first part of the College to be built by him, and was probably completed in time for divine service on the opening day, though the altar was not consecrated till 1395. Chapel is in the perpendicular style.

Between the third and fourth buttresses there is a blocked-up doorway, and in about 1780 Mr Purnell inserted above it a stone bearing the Uvedale coat-of-arms

Chapel (from the Quadrangle)

with the legend 'Uvedallus patronus Wiccami': this coat-of-arms was repaired c. 1900 at the expense of G. W. Leveson-Gower but had vanished by 1917. Though rather low, the doorway was the original entrance to Chapel. It was blocked up in 1680. The heraldic stone was given by the Rashleigh family c. 1780 when they demolished the old Uvedale manor at Wickham, and the legend was added in the mistaken belief that the Uvedales had been patrons of the Founder.

The main entrance to Chapel is through the vestibule known as Crimea, the choir entering through the vestibulum or sacristy, known as Baptistery.

Internally, Chapel is 93 feet [28.3 m] long, 30 feet [9.1 m] wide and 53 feet [16.1 m] high. The reredos, given by an unknown donor in 1470, was restored by Sir William Earle: it was cased in wainscoting in 1567, and so remained until the restoration of Chapel in 1874–5. At this time the original miserere seats were replaced in the choir, and the nave was fitted with new oak pews facing east. Between 1822 and 1829 most of the original stained glass was removed from the windows by Messrs Betton & Evans of Shrewsbury and replaced with exact copies, but the copies are greatly inferior to the originals in richness of colour. In 1908 Gallery was erected on the west wall, to house the organ, and provide seating for about 50 juniors. Six pieces of tapestry found in College were hung on the walls of Chapel c. 1910 but have since been moved elsewhere. There is seating in the nave for about 300, with 20 to 30 more in the chancel and Tower Chairs, and 50 in Gallery. Each row seats six or seven men, and a Praefect at the end to dock the names of absentees. A Don sits in every third or fourth row.

Chapel times have varied down the ages. In 1838 they were:

morning chapel: Sundays and saints' days, 8–9; weekdays, 6–6.30
middle chapel: Fridays and saints' days, 11–12; Saturdays 5–6; Sundays, 5–6 (Cathedral)
evening chapel: every day, 9–9.15

In 1892 there were ten services for the School each week:

Sunday: 9–9.45; 11–12; 5–6.10
weekdays: after Morning Lines, 7.30–8.5
Saturday afternoon: 5.35–6.5.

By 1917 there were only nine services:

Sunday: 10.30–11.30; 5–6.10
weekdays: as before
Saturday afternoon: 5.45–6.15 (6.45–7.15 in summer)

Attendance is compulsory for all.
College Preces are held in Chapel each evening for College men, at 8.45 in 1892, 9.0 in 1917. Commoners have Preces up to house.

Chapel Roll   [two usages]
   (1) the plan of Chapel, showing the seat allotted to each man, was written out by the Prefects of Chapel and pinned on the door of VIIth Chamber Passage, with another copy on School Notice Board (1920).
   (2) *Chapel Tardy Roll*: in 1838 names were called by the Praefect of Chapel when boys were in, and those not answering were reported to the master next morning by Ostiarius on a roll reading:

Jones	precibus matutinis (meridianis, vespertinis)
Brown	abfuit (abfuere) [day of the month]
Smith	A.Johnson, Cap.Prae.

The imposition for being tardè was 30 lines, and 60 for shirking altogether. 'Boys often say they missed their names, i.e. they did not hear their name called and could not answer it: again others say that they did answer their names.' Later these rolls were written on blue paper, the day of the week (*Solis*, Lunae, *Martis* [etc.] *die*) being added before the day of the month, which was given in the Latin manner. In 1892 they were brought round during Middle School with continent rolls. Saturday evening and Sunday rolls came round on Monday morning. By 1917 they were pinned up by Chapel Writer in Dons Common Room.

Chapel Rolls   a slip of cardboard put at the end of each row by Chapel Writer, on which Praefects and Dons dock the names of absentees.

[**Chapel Tardy Roll**   see **Chapel Roll**.]

Chapel Writer   duties set out in full in the Cap.Prae.'s book of 1922. They included: (1) writing out a roll of men absent from Chapel after each service. (2) putting round the cardboard rolls before each service. (3) wheeling out the Pandemonium (q.v.) for Preces, and giving out the number of the hymn at the door.

charades   acted at College Chamber Sports (1917–20) and similar occasions by two sides in turn. There was one scene for each letter in the word chosen and one for the full word. The scenes were drawn from classical mythology, the Old Testament, and episodes involving Dons and men in the school. Witty, and performed with zest, these charades were not considered as a children's game.

charge, to   to run fast, or run at. Recorded as a Notion in 1868, but normal slang.

Chawker Pot   Hawkins Cup, presented by the Chawker (below) for inter-house first XI soccer. In 1920 it was played on the Bull's Drove, Webbe Tent and Dogger's Close grounds. See **Pots**.

Chawker's   F House or Southgate House, named after its first House Don, the Chawker (Rev. C. H. Hawkins, 1869–1900).

Cheese Room   above Audit Room. Originally a library, in 1628 it became a store-room for cheeses. Later on, it became a mere lumber room.

chest   'a large long box which boys who have no drawers under their toys keep their clothes in'. Recorded 1838 only.

child   Latin *puer*. A Notion long obsolete, in both its meanings.
   (1) It meant a scholar on the foundation, as distinct from the other two sections of the school, Commoners and Choristers; thus children (1547), puer (1563), pueri (1645), pueri (1653 Long Roll), child (Bishop Ken, 1674), children (late eighteenth century). Children are now called Scholars or College men, but in the seventeenth century scholars included children, commoners and choristers.
   (2) It also meant a scholar on the foundation chosen by each of the Electors to wait upon him at Election time. Latterly their duties were nominal, and consisted chiefly in pocketing a guinea or a sovereign (1836). We hear of the Warden of New College's Child, the Warden's Child, who (1836) used to receive a sovereign and had the privilege of dining with the Candlesticks (q.v.) in Election Week. The Headmaster's Child was always the head scholar in Cloisters, and the Warden's Child the second.
   On Domum Day the Children got off all fagging, and at Election Dinner they sat at the same table with Writers and Election grace singers, where the fare was

better than that served to the other scholars; and afterwards they had wine and dessert in the Child's room in the Warden's House.

During the year following the appointment of a Warden, the Warden's Child had the duty of applying to the Headmaster for every remedy and half-remedy, in the set phrase: 'the Praepostors' duty, and they would be obliged for a remedy' (or 'for a half-remedy'). If the application was something more than mere form (e.g. when a leave-out day disturbed the ordinary arrangements of the week), it was made by the Praefect of Hall.

By 1860 the festivities of Election Week had been much curtailed, and the 'Children' had disappeared.

chince, or **chintz** a chance. In use 1836–68, but long obsolete; an example of the Wiccamical alteration of a vowel.

chinner a grin. In use 1831–92; obsolete by 1914. From Latin *cachinnare* (to grin), or Greek γένειον (chin): i.e. that done with the chin.

chisel, to to cheat or injure. Also used as a noun: a chisel, meaning a cheat. Thus chizzel (1821), chisel (1870). [cf. *OED* chisel v¹ where Winchester evidence is mentioned, but not cited.] From chisel, meaning to pare with a chisel and thus to cut close in a bargain. Associated in 1831 with a carpenter named Crutch, known as Chiseller Crutch, who used to overcharge for mending cricket bats.

chiseller a cheat. In use 1831–92, but long since obsolete. See Chiseller Crutch, above.

choir half-rem a half-rem given once a term to all members of Chapel and Chantry Choirs (1920), to make up for spare time occupied in choir practice.

chossers a shame; the Wiccamical form of chouse. Long since obsolete.

chouse a shame, especially in the phrase 'What a chouse'. In use 1831–92, but obsolete by 1914. It is universal slang for a swindle, a trick: derived from *chaush, chiaus*, a Turkish interpreter or official messenger, one of whom in 1609 swindled a group of London merchants: hence a swindler, a rascal, and so used by Ben Jonson (1610) and John Ford (1639). From this it came to be used as a verb, in the forms chiauzed (Gayton, 1608–66), chews'd (1664), choused (Pepys, 1659–69). Derivative meanings of chouse are: somebody easily tricked (1662) and the trick itself (Johnson's *Dictionary*, 1755).

circum (pronounced sircum), **going** a phrase often found in the early College records. For some time after the foundation the entire Wiccamical body used to walk in procession round the College precincts each evening, singing hymns and chanting prayers. The custom seems to have survived the Reformation, for in the seventeenth and eighteenth centuries boys still 'went circum', which meant repairing at about 5 p.m. to a bench in the ambulatory (now the Crimea Memorial) to kneel there for private prayer.

In 1887 the original form of going circum was revived. After a short chapel service, at which 'Te Deum' was sung, the school assembled in Chamber Court and marched in procession round Cloisters, singing 'Jam Lucis'. This ceremony took place at morning lines on or about 25 March, in memory of the Founder. But by 1897 it was abandoned, and the phrase is long forgotten.

Clark's   a house standing between New Barge and Commoner Field, with a garden in which Domum Tree stands (see Domum Cottage). Recorded 1868: obsolete by 1914.

classicus   the junior boy of each part or class, whose duty it was to get the lessons set, and the themes for composition made known. But it is emphasised (1838) that he need not tell boys what lessons were set unless they asked him. Other duties of his were (1831) to give in the list of names of those absent from the lesson, and to keep the classicus paper: and (1838) to put up pen and ink to the master he was under when either was wanted. In 1836 the Classicus was the boy who had the lowest score in Classicus Paper at the end of the week. By 1868 the word meant the junior College man and Commoner in each division, whose duty it was to get lessons and tasks set and tell the others. College Classicus went up to the master for particulars and passed them on to Commoner Classicus. At that time no one was obliged to be Classicus during his first three months in the school. In 1900 Classicus was the junior Coll-man, if any, in each div, otherwise the junior man; and the duties were the same. By 1914, in Commoners, it included the junior representative of each div up to house. In 1922 it still meant the junior College man in any div, but was used primarily to mean the junior College man in Senior Div, who got work set and collected tasks. The title is at least as old as 1645. From Latin *classicus*, the (junior) boy of the class.

classicus paper   in the period 1820–43 this meant the large mark book with which each division was provided, said to have been introduced by Dr Gabell (Headmaster 1809–23). Every day after morning school the position of each boy was marked, the lowest receiving 1, the next lowest 2 and so on. These marks were added up, and the boys were arranged anew in their form order each week. At the end of every half-year the marks were totalled, and the result determined the prizes and the school order for the next half-year. At first the classicus paper was not used above Middle Part, and there was no place-changing in Senior Part except at Senior Part examination. This was introduced by Dr Moberly (1836–66) and took place at the beginning of each half-year, and considerable changes in the order were sometimes made. Later the classicus paper was introduced into Senior Part. Place-changing eventually ceased, and the Notion classicus paper passed on to the mark-book kept by each div don: and finally to the form list on which the week's marks were posted up by the Div Don, but the word was shortened to 'cus or cuse (to rhyme with use). In 1892 no div above Senior Part 3 had a cuse, marks

Cloister roush

being made out only at the end of the half. In 1922 there were cuses in Senior Part 1 and 2, but none in VIth Book. From Latin, *(liber) classicus*, the form book.

class-rooms   usually called div rooms. The buildings comprising New Commoners were altered and adapted in 1869 to their present function of class-rooms for the whole school.

clean straw   clean sheets. See **straw**.

[**climbing over the banisters**   see **back staircase**:]

clo, or **clow**   From the Anglo-Saxon *clawian*, surviving in claw, clutch, clout. a box on the ears, to box a person's ears. It seems to have been the sort of blow in which fingers are used in a clawing or scratching motion: examples are clowe (Langland, c. 1377), clawed (Ben Jonson, 1622). It was in use at Winchester between 1830 and 1900 but obsolete by 1914. In dialect it came to mean any blow on the head, as in 'clew o thee yead' (Wiltshire, Gloucestershire), or 'clow' (Cumberland), for to beat about the head. Regardless of spelling, it was always pronounced clo: cf. sew/sow, shew/show.

cloister a ball, to   to kick a football over into Cloisters while kicking in Ball Court: a big kick, but a bad one from the point of view of practice for canvas, as it is unnecessarily high. In use in 1920.

Cloister pealing   in Cloister Time, Cloisters (see below) used to stand up to books and express their approval or otherwise of praefects in rhymes and songs, composed in College by Tolly-keepers and in Commoners by Course-keepers. (See **Peal**). Long since obsolete.

Cloister roush   an annual engagement in School at the beginning of Cloister Time, between Cloisters and Senior part, who charged each other from opposite ends of School. Recorded from 1836. In 1892 the occasion for this contest was that a Maltby prize had been won by a man in Middle Part, and the roush took the place of pealing.

Cloister Time   originally the last ten weeks of Long Half, i.e. mid-May to July, because formerly lessons were said in Cloister in the summer months. When

College Cloisters, 1395

Long Half was divided into two terms the name Cloister Time was applied to the summer term.

Cloisters (1) the medieval cloister, completed 1395, enclosing Fromond's Chantry, completed 1437. (2) a covered side-walk running round three sides of Flint Court in New Commoners, 1842–69. It had a flat roof supported on iron pillars, the holes for which are still visible in the paving stones. In 1880 it was called Commoner Cloister. (3) the name given to Middle and Junior Part, when amalgamated during the last ten or twelve weeks of Long Half, beginning at Whitsun and ending at Standing-up week, these weeks being known as Cloister Time. Recorded from 1831. In 1838 it is remarked that formerly Middle Part were allowed to learn their Standing-up in Cloisters. Obsolete by 1860.

Cloister, Lower first-floor galleries in New Commoners (1842–1869) on the west side of Commoner (Flint) Court: corresponding roughly to class-rooms 12, 13 and 14.

cloisters, to run see **run**.

cloister, to toll a College notion (1920) for walking round Cloisters with a socius before Preces.

Cloisters, Upper second-floor galleries in New Commoners (1842–69), above Lower Cloisters: corresponding roughly to class-rooms 15, 16 and 17.

clothes-brushers juniors in New Commoners (1842–69) who had to brush Praefects' clothes every morning before Chapel.

clothes inspeccer, or a **First and Fourth raid** made by the Aul.Prae. once or twice during the term in Ist and IVth (1920). Owners of clothes that were untidy or lying on the floor were beaten or otherwise punished.

clothes-keeper in New Commoners every Praefect and Six-and-Six man had an Inferior to look after his football clothes, get him hot water to swill with after football, etc. Clothes-keepers of Senior Praefects and Six-and-Six men got off all football; those of other Praefects, only when their Praefects played. Recorded from 1868 to 1884: long since obsolete.

Clubs from about 1880 to 1910 the best cricketers in the school, who could wear white flannels, were organised in three clubs:

- Senior Club: men in Second XI, or near it.
- Middle Club A and B: the pick of Toye Cup men, and some seniors.
- Junior Club: Toye Cup men, when not playing in a match.

By 1917, only Senior Club survived.

Clump a clump of Scotch firs and beeches on Hills. There is a suggestion of a clump there in Warden Chandler's drawing (c. 1460). If so, it had doubtless been planted as a windbreak round St Catharine's Chapel: but had disappeared by 1647 as Mathew does not mention trees in his poem, and the hill is bare in the painting (c. 1692) in the Warden's Lodging. A clump was planted over the Chapel ruins in 1762 by Lord Botetourt, and replanted in 1897, but was so seriously depleted by 1924 that a fresh clump was planted round it.

cobb, to to hit hard at cricket (recorded 1880 only). Either from cobb, to strike or beat; or from Arthur Cobb (E. 1877–83), Lords player and a free hitter. He died in 1886, and has a brass in Cloisters.

Co.boat a boat reserved for the use of Boat Club Committee; a 1920 Notion.

Co.Boat Corner some point or other on River, known only to rowing men.

coffin a Commoner notion (1892) for a wooden box in which clothes were kept round galleries. Obsolete by 1914.

Co.Fo. Commoner foricas, immediately south of the western wing of div rooms.

College Collegium Beatae Virginis Mariae Winton prope Winton, or the College of St Mary Winton.

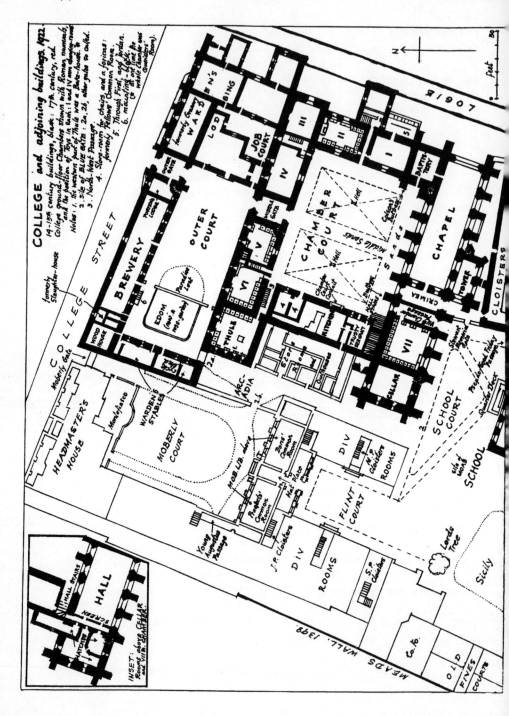

Entrance to College Hall and Kitchen

In 1382 William of Wykeham bought from the monks of St Swithun's Priory their 'viridarium and deambulatorium' as the site of his college, and laid the foundation stone of Chapel on 26 March 1387. To the original Dummer's Mede and Otterbourne Mede he added two strips of land on the north and west in 1392. On 28 March 1394 the Warden and Scholars entered into possession, having been temporarily housed on St Giles' Hill for the past twelve years.

On 11 September 1400 the Founder issued revised Statutes, providing for a community of 115 persons: a Warden, Headmaster, 10 Fellows, 3 Chaplains, an Usher, 70 Scholars, 10 extranei commensales, 3 Chapel Clerks and 16 Choristers. All members over the age of 15 had to take an Oath of Allegiance to the Statutes, a custom maintained till the nineteenth century.

Owing to its fortress-like construction, College has suffered little change from outsiders in the last six centuries, and the layout is substantially the same as it was in 1394. The gate on the street, Outer Gate, leads into Outer Court: beneath the gate is Porter's Lodge, with Bursary above, with Brewery (now Moberly Library), workshops, Arcadia and Paradise Lost to the west: and to the east the Warden's Lodging, built by Warden Harman in 1597, and enlarged by Wardens Nicholas and Lee: it occupies the site of the Slaughter-house, Bakehouse and Granaries, and the space that originally existed between them and the north façade of Chamber Court.

On the south of Outer Court is Middle Gate, leading into Chamber Court. Above Middle Gate is Election Chamber, which became College War Memorial Library in summer 1922. At the south-east corner of Chamber Court is Muniment Tower and the sacristy, known as Baptistery: at the south-west, the stairs leading up to College Hall. North of the stairs was the Buttery, known as Trusty Sweater's Hole, and the entrance to Kitchen.

At the west end of Hall are the original Buttery and Hatches, and in the south-west corner a stairway down to Cellar, and up to Audit Room and Cheese Room.

Adjoining Cellar is VIIth Chamber, the original School-room, entered from Seventh Chamber Passage, which leads into School Court. On the east of School Court was Stewart Memorial, since moved elsewhere. West of School Court is Flint Court, and to the south of it Fives Courts, which gave place in 1922 to War Memorial Cloister. The north side of Flint Court is called Hat Place, and leads into Moberly Court, on the north of which, on College Street, stands the Headmaster's House.

'College!'   a yell emitted by College men to encourage College XV or VI, when they were playing Commoners or Houses. Pronounced 'Cau-au-au-ledge'. (See **epideixis**.)

[**College boy**   a Winchester scholar, as opposed to a Commoner. Usage in the later nineteenth century shifted to 'College man'. 'Colleger' is used at Eton, but not at Winchester. An example is quoted by A. K. Cook in *About Winchester College* (p. 500), from an unnamed Commoner of the early nineteenth century, who seems to have used it from ignorance.]

College cat   in 1920, a black tom named Peter, owned by College Cook.

College competis (pronounced competīs)   College bat-fives and fives competitions in Common Time. In 1922 they were:

- *with the long bat*:
     Long Bat: for Praefects and Tolly-keepers
- *with the short bat*:
     Short Bat: open
     Double Bat: doubles, senior and junior men partnered
     Officers' Bat: for men under Toye Pot age: prize given by Officers
- *hand-fives*:
     Single Hand: open
     Double Hand: cf. Double Bat
     Officers' Hand: [not known]
     Tout Bat: hand-fives for men under Toye Pot age: prize given by College Tutor. It should have been called Goddard, Parr, etc. Bat after successive Tutors, but Tout (nickname of C. V. Durell, 1909–20) seems to have stuck.

Handicaps were given in all except Double Bat and Double Hand. The prize for singles was 10 shillings, for doubles 10 shillings each.

College Cook   in the period 1917–22, Miss Easton, owner of William of Wykeham, Roger and Peter. She lived in the Warden's Lodging, and cooked

College Mill

all College meals (and the Warden's when he was down) in the antiquated Kitchen.

College dog   See **William of Wykeham**

College East and **College West**   the seventy College men were divided, principally for games purposes, into two halves of thirty-five men each, called College East and West, according to whether their chamber lay to the east or west of Middle Gate. By 1917 the distinction was no longer based on this factor, every chamber containing men from both halves.

College Gate   a Commoner notion (1868–84) for Outer Gate.

College ghost   several phenomena answering to this name in 1920: (1) an unseen presence, said to be that of Bishop Ken, which was felt to pass through Ken Chamber into New Chamber. (2) footsteps descending Hall Stairs late at night, first on the wooden treads, then on stone, followed by a tinkle of the handle of Chapel Gate. (3) a mischievous force which played noisily in the small hours with shoes put out for cleaning on the landings outside 10th and 12th. This was the best attested. Nothing was ever seen.

College goal   a goal-post for College men to practise at, which stood (1920) just south of Ball Court wall, facing Bear Cages.

College horse   a contemptuous name (1920) for a man who boasted of his strength or endurance.

College Library   originally Election Chamber, this room was equipped as a library, and a common room for Inferiors, in 1922. It is College War Memorial, and has a carved overmantel with an inscription and the names of College men killed in the First World War. The books are kept in the passage-way between Election Chamber and 10th (see plan). The Second Master gave the leather couches. The senior praefect not an Officer became Praefect of College Library, and had a writer. The next junior to him was jocularly called Praefect of Foricas.

College Mill   immediately south of Non-Licet Gate. By 1917 its milling equipment had gone, the upper floor being used as a workshop and a store for chairs. The lower part was Meads Foricas.

College Oath   an oath of allegiance to the College, taken by all scholars over the age of 15. It has long since lapsed, but was still being administered in 1842, when Robert Gordon preserved the text of it in his word-book. Gordon concludes: 'On the last day of Standing-up week all the College boys who are going to take the oath have to go to chapel, and service is performed: and afterwards they all stand by the Warden's pew, and then each boy reads a small part of the oath: then when all have read a piece the Warden holds a Testament in his hand and each boy kisses it: then he says something to them about the importance of it and that sort of thing: and then they all go out of chapel. Their names are all entered in a book kept by the Warden for that purpose: a boy is expelled if he refuses to take the oath, and from that the boys argue that as it is a forced oath it need not be observed.'

[The Oath ran] 'I, Robert Gordon, having been heretofore admitted as a scholar of St Mary's College of Winchester near Winchester, do swear that at this time I have no certain revenue of my own whereof I may spend above forty pounds by the year.

'Also I swear that if I shall happen to know any of the secrets of the same College, I will not reveal them to any stranger to the loss and prejudice of the same College.

'Also that I will be helpful to the same College in any business that may concern the bettering of rights of the same College, or privileges of the same: and that I will do my best endeavours to promote their affairs by my faithful advice and furtherance as long as I live in this world, to what state soever after I may come.

'Also that I will not procure the diminution or change or abolishing of the number of persons appointed by the Founder's statutes to live in this same College nor, as much as in me lies, suffer the same to be made, or anywhere consent to the same.

'Also that I will keep the statutes of the same College which the Right Reverend Father in God, William of Wykeham, founder thereof, made, so far as they concern me in the plain literal and grammatical sense and meaning: and, as much as in me lies, cause the same to be kept and observed by others: and that I will not admit of any statutes and deviances, interpretations or injunctions deviatory or repugnant to the same statutes or the meaning thereof, by whomsoever they shall be made, unless by the same William of Wykeham during his lifetime: neither will I consent unto the same or be governed by them, or make any use thereof.

'Also that I will not be a detractor or talebearer that shall stir up any strife, quarrels or dissensions between the scholars of the same College, by making odious comparisons between person and person, kindred and kindred, country and country: by upbraiding anyone with the lowness of his birth, poverty or meanness of his friends, or any other thing in any way tending to the disparaging or disgrace of another.

'Also that I will not make any unlawful conspiracies or conferences at home or abroad against the statutes of the same College, or the state or honour or profit thereof, against the Warden, Sub Warden, Schoolmasters, or against any usher or fellow therof: nor will I procure nor permit the same to be made by others, as much as in me lies: nor will I give my counsel or assistance or willingly consent thereto. And if I know anything that shall procure or make any such conspiracies aforesaid, I will reveal the same to the Warden, Sub Warden, or Bursars of the same College, either by word or writing: and that, as much as in me lies, I will preserve the tranquillity, peace and honour of the said College, and the amity by all good means I can: and also cause the same to be observed by others.

'Also that if it should happen (which God forbid) that for my demerits I should be expelled or removed by the said College, by virtue of the statutes of the same I will not trouble or molest the Warden, Sub Warden or any of the Fellows, or the usher thereof for my said expulsion, or cause the same to be troubled or molested on my behalf: but do renounce all actions, complaints or appeals to be made in any court whatsoever, Civil or Ecclesiastical, and all letters of great persons whereby I might recover my former state interest or possession of the same College: and the same I will renounce in writing if I be put to it in my expulsion or removal aforesaid.

'Also that I will observe and keep all the statutes and ordinances of the same College, as far as they concern me, or else I will personally submit to the penalties appointed and limited in the same, without opposition and contradiction thereto.

'Also that I will not procure any dispensations against this oath of mine, or against the statutes and ordinances of the same College, or any of them, nor willingly suffer that any such dispensations of this kind should be obtained or gratuitously offered or granted by whomsoever it might be, whether it be granted in general or special terms or in what terms or words it may be, I will not make use of it in any mannner or consent unto it.

'SO HELP ME GOD.'

College photo   taken once a year at the end of Cloister Time, when Praefects' and Officers' photos were also taken (1920). It took place immediately after Hall, on Hall Staircase. The new Roll sat on the bottom step, with any pots College had won in front of them. Senior men stood on higher steps. Hall Writer perched in the window of Trusty Sweater's Hole.

College Plate   a rich collection of silver and silver-gilt table plate, kept (1920) by the head butler, Chandler, in his safe; of many different dates. The Headmaster sometimes borrowed pieces for dinners.

College Play　play performed by College men, originally only in years when the school was up for Easter: latterly (1920) this condition was not observed and there were plays at the end of each Common Time. Usually serious in character.

College Roll　a printed list of men in College, used chiefly for namers (1920).

College Singing　an informal concert held in VIIth Chamber after tea on a day when College had won a Fifteen or a Six. Corresponding with Commoner Singing in Commoners and Houses. In 1900 every man called upon to sing had to give a song, whether he could sing or not, but this custom had lapsed by 1917.

College song-book　a small red book stamped with the school arms in gilt, used at College Singing. Identical with the book used in Commoner Singing.

College subscrippers　a subscription of from 10 to 15 shillings collected (1920) by Hall Writer from each man at the beginning of each half: to meet some of the expenses not covered by College fees of £7 per half.

College Tutor　a junior Don chosen to assist the Second Master and take his place when absent. He lived in College, above Thule. Unlike House Tutors, he had nothing to do with mugging in College (1920).

College waistcoat　a black long-sleeved waistcoat worn under the gown by all College men. These two garments had always to be taken off together, as it was a bad notion to wear the waistcoast alone, except when standing round for a beating or (in the case of the First Junior) for sweeping. Made (1920) only by Cliftons of High Street. In Mansfield's day, some College Praefects wore green or brown waistcoats.

College Walk　the road from Non-Licet Gate to Black Bridge.

College ware　crockery which fell without breaking. In use 1836–92; obsolete by 1917.

College wash　the Winchester Steam laundry. The term was also applied to the women who worked in IIIrd Chamber sorting and mending laundry. There was no charge for laundry in Blue Bills.

Colson's Buttress　the buttress between Ist Chamber and Baptistery door, in Chamber Court. ('Buttress' is between VIIth Chamber Passage and Chapel door.) In use 1917. There is no record of who Colson was. A William Colson of St Thomas, Winchester was admitted as a scholar in 1645; and a Nicholas Colson of St Lawrence, Winchester, admitted 1709.

come about, to 'when a master comes round Chambers in Toy time or after Chapel to see if all is right, he is said to come about.' Thus recorded, in 1836 only. A survival of Old English about, meaning round.

come down, to the passive of to bring down: (1) to be read out in public: thus, Lords Roll comes down just before Eton Match. (2) (of a roll) to be posted on School Notice Board. (3) to come to Winchester, usually from London or Oxford.

'Comfort ye' an anthem sung about once a half in Chapel which, owing to the stirring imitas of the lay-clerk Mr Brown doing the solo part, became a Notion (1920).

committee book the skippers of College East and West games each kept (1920) a book recording the games played by their houses. Originally the skippers of crockets, Our Game and soccer formed a committee, but as they were so often the same man the committee lapsed and the Senior House Tie filled in the book.

Commoner a member of the school not in College (*commensalis et oppidanus*).

Commoner annals records of the School's Athletics kept by Senor Commoner Praefects. Obsolete by 1917.

Commoner bell rung by a sweater in new Commoners (1842–69) five minutes before school time.

Commoner Court the court round which the buildings of Old Commoners stood (1742–1842), later called Moberly Court.

Commoner examina (pronounced examinā) a Notions examination for new men in Commoners at the end of their first fortnight. From 1842 to 1869 it was held in New Commoners Mugging Hall by the senior Praefect. Later, all who had not been in the school two years were included. The men took places, new men starting top. Those in the six bottom places had to write the Notions out: hence the number of excellent Commoner word-books which have survived.

Commoner Field a three-cornered field between River and the Newbury line, on the way to Hills from Boat-house. Cricket and football were played there by Commoners, and Middle Game canvas was in the field. Later called Delta Field, from its shape, and finally Palmer Field, after G. E. H. Palmer (c. 1918–23) whose family gave it to the School as an extra games field. In 1836 Commoner Field was used from 12 to 1 on whole-school days, and in the afternoon on holidays.

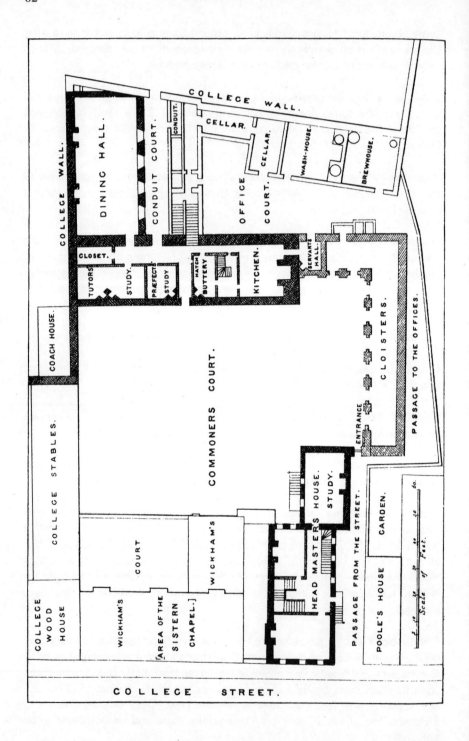

Commoner Gate (1) (up to 1869) a name for Moberly Gate, by which Commoners entered College Street. (2) (1920) name for South African Memorial Gate, which, owing to its brown colour, inherited for a time the name of the disused Bangy Gate.

Commoner grub a feed given by Commoner Praefects to College after cricket matches. Recorded 1836; obsolete by 1868.

Commoner Passage a Notion (1900) for St Michael's Passage. By 1917 Commoners called it 'Micla'.

Commoners [used of men and their houses.]
(1) It is used to mean all members of the school not in College. In 1960 there were about 450, an average of 45 per house.

As at Oxford, this word meant a student who does not rely on the foundation for support, but eats his commons with the scholars. He was a *commensalis* (sharer of the common table). The first Winchester Commoner mentioned (1395) was a *commensalis extraneus*. From the outset there were two types of Commoner. Type (a) were 'filii nobilium et valentium personarum', or 'gentlemen commoners', ten of whom were provided for in the Statutes. They lodged with the Warden, Fellows or Masters and ate in Hall. In 1653 there were seven: in 1690, two. Type (b) were 'oppidani', 'commensales extra Collegium' or 'town Commoners' (cf. oppidans at Eton). They were in effect day-boys lodging in St Elizabeth's College, the Sustern Spital, and rooms in the town. They attended Chapel and School, but provided their own meals. Many of them later entered College. There were 80–100 in 1412; 68 in 1690; 49 in 1702; 20 in 1717. Oppidani were abolished in 1809.

In 1742 Dr Burton converted the Sustern Spital (Sisters' hospital, lying to the west of College) and added to it various buildings to form a boarding house for all Commoners, and it was known as Old Commoners. The oppidani now dwindled and the number of Commoner boarders rose, to 50–60 in the years 1766–93 and, after the Sustern Chapel (Wickham's) was added, to 136 in 1810. In 1838 there were about 200.

Old Commoners was a 'rambling rabbit-warren of a place'. Its buildings were of many dates and styles, in indifferent repair, and windows and doors fitted so badly that it was draughty: though this was recognised later as an advantage. Dr Moberly had it demolished between 1838 and 1842, replacing it with the buildings called New Commoners. But here the doors and windows fitted so well that there was no real ventilation. At the same time, the foundations blocked a City sewer called the Lorte Burn, forming a malarial marsh which soon caused an outbreak of fever. The buildings were cheap and ugly, and preserved none of the medieval features of the Sisters' Chapel, Conduit Gallery and other buildings which they replaced.

Two resident Commoner Tutors were appointed, but could not supervise New

Commoners adequately because the galleries were designed to hold only four men each, and only one gallery in four had a Praefect. From 1859 to 1869 new Commoners dispersed into boarding-houses, the first (A) being opened in 1859 by Rev. H. J. Wickham, who had been a Tutor in New Commoners. For this reason a group of the resultant boarding houses were named Tutors' or Old Tutors' Houses. After A came B (1860) and C (1862). In 1869 the residue of New Commoners moved into a block of four houses in Culver's Close (D, E, G and H), with a fifth (F), opposite D. The buildings of New Commoners were now vacant, and after extensive rebuilding were converted into classrooms. Two houses were finally added: I (1871), and K (1905).

(2) It also means the buildings occupied by Commoners; i.e. Old Commoners (1742–1842); New Commoners (1842–69).

(3) To achieve parity in Winchester College football, men in D, E, G, H and K are called Commoners: as distinct from Houses (or O.T.H., for Old Tutors' Houses), who are A, B, C, F and I.

(4) It was a post-1869 Commoner Notion for the Kingsgate Street and College Street area, where Commoner buildings used to be.

(5) It was also a post-1869 Notion for the buildings forming Moberly and Flint Courts, which were a modification of the buildings of New Commoners.

'Commoners!'   a yell emitted by supporters of Commoner XV or VI. cf. *College!*

Commoner Singing   (1) (in New Commoners, 1868) 'the first week after stove comes into Mugging Hall, after tea, Praefects sit round stove, swig brew and have singing. The songs are given out at Senior Praefect's bidding by a new man. Some fellows also sport solos.' (2) (since 1880) an informal concert, similar to College Singing, held up to house after a Commoner or Houses victory in Fifteens or Sixes, and at the end of the half. Solos and choruses are sung, and the concert ends with 'Domum'.

Commoner song-book   identical with College song-book (q.v.).

Commoner Speaking   (1) (1831–80) a day of public recitation early in May, when Praefects who had composed the best Easter-tasks, and Inferiors who had done best at the six recitations during Easter Time, were chosen to deliver speeches and tasks in the presence of visitors. (2) later the notion was transferred to speeches made at the end of the half in Mugging Hall by men who were leaving. The speeches followed a set pattern, expressing regret at leaving, and hope for the success of the School. 'God save the Queen' and 'Domum' were sung. Later again, these speeches were delivered at House Grub (House Supper).

Commoner tables   two tables for Commoners on the stove side of School. Praefects, VIth Book, and Senior Div Senior Part sat at Senior table on the right:

Commoners (from Commoners Court)

Junior Div Senior Part, and anyone in Middle Part who had been in the school a year, sat at Junior table on the left. Obsolete by 1869.

Commoner temples   the temples in the ancient wall which ran behind Old Fives Courts and alongside Cecil Range. These were saved in the 1923 demolition and built into the east wall of War Cloister.

commonplace book   a notebook in which every boy wrote difficult words encountered in translation. The Rev. C. Wordsworth, Second Master 1835–45, was 'very particular about the words being written neatly in them'. In 1868 it is described as small (7 by 4 in. [17.5 by 10 cm]) and black, and used by Middle and Junior Part for notes. By 1917 it was known as a Middle Part note-book.

Common Rooms   two rooms on either side of Hat Place: that on the east being for Dons (first recorded 1880); that on the west for Co.Praes.

Common Time   when first recorded (1836), this meant the whole of Short Half plus the first six weeks of Long Half, up to Easter time: 'common' meaning the time common to both terms. In 1866 three terms were recognised, Long Half being divided into Common Time and Cloister Time.

compos paper   paper for compositions, described (1892) as large, smooth sheets of white paper ruled with alternate lines of blue and brown. Obsolete by 1917.

con   a rap on the head, administered with the knuckles, the edge of a roll of paper, the cover of a book, or any other firm substance. The Praefect of Hall

Con

(1831) used to go round examining men's white ties, and if any was not neat, its owner was conned with a cricket ball. In 1620 and 1670, to con or conne was a normal English verb, signifying to give such a rap; the noun survives in north country dialect for a flick or fillip with the finger. Sometimes derived from Greek κόνδυλος (a knuckle), but probably from the French *cogner* (to knock). Mansfield says the con was given with a cricket-ball to anyone attending 1 p.m. Hall (and therefore singing Grace) who had no bands attached to his neck-tie.

condensers   a College Notion (1920) for condensed milk.

conduit   (1) a water tap. Recorded with this meaning from 1836. The tap in Upper Cloisters in New Commoners was called Conduit. Mansfield describes 'Conduit' as six brass cocks in the west wall of Chamber Court, and gives a picture of it (p. 62), showing the wooden lean-to erected over it. The tap in Chamber Court, used originally for washing and latterly for drinking water, was called Conduit, or (1917) Chamber Court Conduit. The original use led to the two derivative meanings that follow. (2) (in College) a wash-basin or wash-stand. In 1917 a Conduit was an enamelled tin basin in upstairs chambers. Conduits was the long wooden washstand frame down the middle of each upstairs chamber, on either side of which conduits were fixed in holes. 'Head under conduits!' was an order to get oneself into a convenient position for spanking up in chambers. (3) (in Commoners) a lavatory. In new Commoners (1842–69) senior Conduit was beside Fives Courts, entered from Flint Court. It was in two parts, one for Praefects, the other for Senior and Middle Part. Junior Conduit, used by all other Commoners, was near Brewery. After 1869, Conduit, or Commoner Foricas, was beside Old Fives Courts.

Conduit, as a water-pipe, is used by Ben Jonson (1611) and John Ford (1633), and conduit-pipe by Donne (1620–30). Johnson's *Dictionary* (1755) defines it as a pipe or cock at which water may be drawn. There was a Great Conduit in London's Cheapside.

If used nowadays, as it sometimes is by builders, it is pronounced con-du-wit. At Winchester it was always cun-dit, as in pundit: cf. constable.

From Latin *conductum* (something brought: a canal), thus a pipe or tube. The word, and its pronunciation, may well date back to the foundation, occurring, as it does, as *condyte* and *Condite*, both about 1420.

Confirma (pronounced Confirmā)   confirmation by the Bishop of Winchester, generally on the Saturday afternoon before Advent.

continent   confined to Sick House or Sanatorium. In commoners, confined to continent room or Sick House (i.e. Sanatorium). To go continent is to go sick, the opposite of to go (or come) abroad. In the phrase 'continent forbearance' in *King Lear* (1608), which is followed by 'stir abroad', the word implies restraining indoors, but not on account of sickness. At first sight our word looks like a mistake for 'contained', an active for passive; it is in fact the anglicisation of the classical Latin phrase 'se continens ob valetudinem' (keeping himself indoors because of illness), and this may well have been the formula used in medieval continent rolls.

continent cad   a Commoner Notion (1900) for a junior detailed to take on the sweat of anyone continent.

continent roll   a list of men continent. In 1868 such rolls were compiled by the Ostiarius and taken round to each of the Masters. By 1900 each house had its own continent roll, showing under three headings those absent: viz. *aeger* (ill); *absens* (away); and '*leave off lines*' (i.e. Morning Lines). it was signed by the Praefect in Course and the Housemaster. In 1880 it used to be placed on Bible Clerk's scob, to be copied by him and taken round to the dons concerned. By 1917 rolls of College men continent and absent were made out daily after breakfast by School Writer and left in Praefects' Common Room for the Corps Sergeant-Major, who compiled a roll of all men in the school continent or absent, and put it up before first hour in Do.Co.Ro.

continent room   in New Commoners, continent rooms, in which men slept when they were very ill, were in Linen Gallery, and Old Continent Room was in the passage at the end of Linen Gallery. Upper Continent Room was the second room in Lower Cloisters. Men were said to be 'upper' or 'lower' continent. Subsequently each house had a room or rooms for men continent. In College Sick House, the south-west ground-floor room, a sitting room for men continent, was called Continent Room.

Cook's   C House, Southgate Hill, named after A. K. Cook, Esq.; its first House Don was Rev. J. H. T. du Boulay.

Co.Prae. (short for Commoner Praefect)   a School Praefect, i.e. one (whether in College or Commoners) with full powers, as distinct from a House Praefect. He could sweat or beat any Inferior in the school.

copy-book   an exercise-book for fair copies, versions or notes: not in the usual meaning of a book for handwriting. A VIth Book copy-book was a large copy-book with stiff covers. In 1917 these were still being beautifully half-bound in vellum. A Tug copy-book was a smaller book with limp covers.

Corinth   probably upper School Shop.

Corporal 'Arris   an old soldier named Harris, who was Tubby Lane's right-hand man in Armoury (1920).

Corps tailor   a Mr Smith (1920), who lived nearly opposite Commoner Gate in Kingsgate Street. He supplied, altered and mended all Officers Training Corps uniform.

Corpse   nickname of F. P. Burch (Coll. 1912–17), a man of cadaverous appearance.

corpses   see **headless corpses**.

Course   Short and Long Course (rowing) on River, both finishing at Birley's Corner. The start of Long was nearly at First Pot; of Short, above Half-way house (1920).

course, in   on duty in rotation. Thus the two Praefects of Chapel were in course in alternate weeks, calling the names at the end of Preces. Praefects in each chamber were in course for a week in rotation, and during that time were responsible for all that went on in the chamber. [cf. the account by W. A. Fearon in the *Report of the Clarendon Commission* (1864), I. 571, Q. 1153.] In houses, the Praefect 'keeping toys' each week was said to be in course. Up to 1869 the offices of Bible Clerk and Ostiarius were taken in succession by the ten senior Praefects in College. In Old Commoners (to 1842) three Commoner Praefects held office in each week. In New Commoners (to 1869) there were two Praefects in course from Saturday to Saturday, the senior of whom was Ostiarius till Wednesday, when the junior took his place. Commoner Tutors and Chaplains also took turns in course. A junior, after his first fortnight's exemption from sweating and punishment, came into course like the rest.

Praefect in course

From Latin *cursus* (running, course), which is used in 1470 of choir duty at Southwell. In II Chronicles 8.14 Solomon appointed the 'courses' of Temple priests, i.e. times when they were on duty: and in Luke 1.5 Zacharias was 'of the course of Abia' (*de vice Abia*: ἐξ ἐφημερίας Ἀβιά).

Course-keeper an Inferior in Commoners, not higher than Middle Part V, appointed by the Praefects as their deputy to superintend fagging. He had to be of reasonable bodily strength, to have been three years in the school and to know the customs of fagging. 'A sort of popular, muscular thick, generally in Lords or Sixes.' In 1831 in Old Commoners he arranged the breakfast, kicking-in and cricket fagging, and made out the football lists. In 1868 in New Commoners he made out sweat rolls, i.e. assigned gallery sweaters to each Praefect. In return for this he had many privileges (not recognised by the authorities) of which the chief was fagging juniors. He was reckoned in 1838 to correspond with Deputy in College. On rising to Senior Part he became Ex-Course-keeper, and retained his privileges but not his duties. Recorded from 1831; obsolete by 1870.

Court in New Commoners (1842–69) this meant Grass Court: and 'to go down to Court' meant to keep in balls there.

court leave given by the Headmaster (1920) to Praefects to hear cases in the Assizes, as part of their general education.

cowshooter a bowler hat; called a wide-awake hat (1868) and a billycock (1892): in those days worn only by Praefects. By 1917 a bowler was worn by nobody in term, but was still called a cowshooter: a parody of 'deer-stalker'.

Coxe's Wallow a small depression in front of Meads Tent where a College junior named H. R. H. Coxe (1876–82) and his friends, with their gowns tucked up, used to play informal kick-about football in their spare time. The area was soon churned into mud, hence the name. Coxe was to serve in India, becoming Puisne Judge in Calcutta. In the Register he is noted as 'eponymous hero of Coxe's Wallow'. The Notion was kept up at his own request.

Crab Wood on the right of the Old Sarum Road, just beyond Teg Down, about 2 miles [3.2 km] out of Winton: a favourite place for naturalists and botanists in the school. It is so named in the Ordnance Survey map; perhaps from crab-apple trees, or some past owner.

Crimea the memorial on the west wall of Ante-Chapel to the Wykehamists killed in the Crimean War, 1854–6. Commoner Praefects put their hats there and waited before entering Chapel.

Crimia a College mason of 1868: probably a nickname arising from the way he pronounced Crimea.

crockets, crocketts   simply cricket, with the Hampshire change of 'i' to 'o', and the Winchester plural. Defined (1836) as miniature cricket, played with a stump and fives ball: but subsequently meant ordinary cricket, as it still does. To get crockets meant (1836) to fail in a lesson of Standing-up: and later, to score 0 at cricket. See also **small crockets**.

crocketer   a cricketer.

crocks' game   an Our Game football match (1920) against a side of Old Wykehamists or grown-up men. So named from the false assumption that they would be 'old crocks'.

Crofts   a grocer's shop next to Mammy Norton's (1920), with a branch at St Cross. At neither shop might food be bought by men in the school.

cropple   an imposition given for not preparing the lesson properly. The verb to cropple means to find that a boy does not know the lesson, to plough him in an examination, or to punish him with an imposition; the passive of this is to be croppled. In 1820 the form 'crippled' was used, and the offender had to go to the bottom of the class. 'Cropple' and 'croppled' are still in use. Cropple is Hampshire dialect for cripple, which means in standard English to limp like a cripple; or to disable a person, depriving him of the free use of his limbs. Our usage could derive from any of these: to find a man limping through his lesson; to inflict severe punishment on him; or to deprive him of the use of his limbs by keeping him in.

Crutch   Commoner carpenter in 1868. His real name was Lee, but he inherited his name from a predecessor named Crutch, who used to mend bats c. 1831. See **chiseller**.

Crutey, or **Crutie**   (1) a labourer who worked in Meads, c. 1838: short for 'recruit', which he was called on first arrival. (2) bed-maker and chamberman on 12th staircase (1920), whose surname was indeed Crute.

Crutey's Hole   (1) the sweaters' room off 12th bidet room (1920). cf. Burgess hole. (2) the stoking-hole at the bottom of 12th staircase (1920) where Crute stoked the fires heating the boilers for the staircase.

crux   a problem, or a difficult situation. Standard English, borrowed from classical criticism. From the Latin *crux* (cross).

cud   pretty: hence, decorated, coloured. Still in use in these two senses. Originally it could also mean nice, cosy, comfortable, pleasant. Recorded from 1831. There is an example of couthe, meaning cosy, c. 1350, and cud, which is the same word, persisted at Winchester with this meaning till 1830, as is shown by the example 'a cud thoke', and the fact that 'cud' was used in Commoners for comfortable. The other example of this date, 'a cud girl', has been erased in the word-book, showing that the new meaning of 'pretty' was coming in but not yet approved of. Cud then broadened a little, to mean also coloured or decorated as distinct from plain, coloured socks being 'cud socks'. The word 'kiddy' is similarly used at Eton.

Cud is pure Anglo-Saxon, being a form of the adjective cuth or couth (from *cunnan*, to know; *cuthian*, to be known). It meant known, familiar, intimate, cosy, kind, affectionate, cuddlesome. It was obsolete in English by the time of Spenser, though its opposite, uncouth, meaning unknown, unseemly, unlovely, survives. But cud endures in dialect and at Winchester. It may also be perceived in the verb to cuddle in standard English: and up to 1850 at Winchester, to cud as a verb could mean to hug, cuddle, fondle, or beautify.

cud handkerchiefs and **cud socks**   handkerchiefs other than white, socks other than black, which (1920) it was a one-year Notion to sport. At that time a **cud tie** was a Praefects' and Tolly-keepers' Notion.

Cups   See **Pots**.

'cus   Mr R. L. A. Du Pontet (Don, 1892–1926) always spelt cuse (q.v.) in this way. He was of course correct.

cuse   classicus paper (q.v.), or weekly division order. In use 1831; spelt kuse (1838); still in use. It is the last syllable of classicus.

Custos   the Warden's official title, dating from the foundation. From Latin *custos* (guardian).

cut   a stroke with a ground-ash. The maximum in 1892 was twelve. By 1917 more than ten was unheard of.

cut, to   to refuse further acquaintance with anybody (1868); standard English.

cut for grub, to   to draw lots for food. It was done thus: two men agreed on a line, say line 5 on the right-hand pages of a book (usually Vergil), and opened the book at random to see what the first letter of line 5 was. Whichever had the later letter in alphabetical order, paid for the food, and the winner went to Gate to fetch it. This was a Notion in Old Commoners, c. 1831; long since obsolete.

cut in a book, to   a method of drawing lots (identical with that described under 'cut for grub'). Recorded in a College word-book, 1836.

cut into, to   to beat with one stroke of a ground-ash across the shoulders (1856). By 1892 it meant a beating, given by a Praefect with a ground-ash, of any number of cuts up to twelve. The phrase is long since obsolete. In College this was called to 'lick' in 1914, and by 1917 had changed to 'beat'.

cut-shorts   shorts, i.e. trousers cut short above the knees. An example of the original idiom surviving at Winchester.

Cyclops   an ageing labourer to be seen (1920) working in and around the purlieux of College. He had one sightless eye. Named from the one-eyed Cyclops in the Odyssey.

Dais   standard English for a platform or high-table for dignitaries in a hall. From the Latin *discus* (table or platter). But the word is seldom used today. The dais in College Hall was probably always called that. In or about 1393 Chaucer wrote 'deys' for such a platform, and Langland wrote 'deyse'. [Two platforms were so named]: (1) the platform at the east end of College Hall. On the panelling above it a portrait of William of Wykeham, now fixed there, used to be hung during Election week. Other Wiccamical portraits hanging there were moved to the Warden's Lodging in 1920. (2) the platform at the end of Grubbing Hall in New Commoners, at which Tutors dined up to 1869.

Dalma   (pronounced Dalmā) (short for Dalmatia)   a bathing-place in Water Meads between Waterman's Hut and Tunbridge, on the north of the road known to townsmen as Garnier Road, but to the school as Double Hedges. Dalma is traversed by Adam and Eve but is shallower than that stream for which reason juniors (1831) favoured it. By 1880 Dalma belonged to the Town, whose property it still is. It is likely that in the early 1800s, as also happened with Hills, the right to use this place was in dispute between Town and College, each claiming ownership of it. At that time the country of Dalmatia on the Adriatic was much in the news, changing hands every few years (between 1797 and 1814 it passed from Venice to Austria, to France and back to Austria), and its name would have been appropriate to this controversial bathing-pool.

Damme Hopkins   College manciple or provisioner, c. 1820–8: well-to-do, pompous and bonhomous. His brother was one of the Chaplains. He was so called from his habit of relating conversations with the Warden and others who, according to him, always prefaced their remarks with 'Damme, Hopkins'.

Dan   see **Dog Dan**.

Darius Corner (pronouned dairy-us)   the corner made by the walls of Grass Court and Sick House Meads. Both walls, and consequently the corner, having long since vanished, the name was used up to 1923 for the south-east corner of Cecil Range. But that has also gone, and the Notion is dead. One can only guess why this name was chosen. The pronounciation shows that it is not Darius the

Persian King, but a corruption of some similar word, e.g. (1) Darien, the old name of the Isthmus of Panama. Grass Court ended at this corner in a narrow strip which might have been likened to an isthmus connecting Grass Court and Meads, and called Darien's Corner. (2) derries, a word of Indian origin, for white cotton cloth with blue or brown stripes, perhaps in reference to football jerseys which were hung there to dry on wash-day.

Dark Wood a copse on the southern edge of Twyford Downs. Junior Steeplecha started at its north-west corner.

David block see **paper**.

David's Kennel an ammunition hut on a concrete base, which stood on the small triangle of grass between Bear Cages and Cecil Range; destroyed in 1922. It was named after Rev. F. P. David, Commander of the Officers Training Corps, 1900–8.

dead (1) as an adjective, badly hurt (1838). cf. kill, and modern slang 'dead beat'. (2) as an adverb, meaning utterly, especially in the phrase 'dead brum' (absolutely penniless). It thus survives in dialect and slang, in phrases such as 'dead right'. It does service for 'deathly', in phrases like 'dead tired' and 'dead pale'.

Dead Man's Hole a cavity in the river bed of New Barge near Birley's Corner, where Birley was supposed to have been drowned. Recorded 1868–1914; then obsolete.

Dean in College (1920) this had five meanings. (1) any tart, pudding, pie or sweet: see **bathers**, **black asses**, **Chandler's finger**, **Dog Dan**, **Ellenberger and Antrobus**, **frog-spawn**, **ginger bather**, **gobbets**, **King's daughter**, **open cesspool**, **rokeby**. In this sense, perhaps named after a man called Dean. (2) the five or six men who eat the pudding, and the part of the table they sit at: formerly called a mess or pitch-up. (3) the withy binding a Bill Brighter (by analogy with bishop, q.v.). (4) the Dean of Winchester. (5) the proprietor of School Shop (see **Abner**).

Deanesly, to do a to insinuate oneself between two people to a warm place on Half-Faggot: from R. M. Deanesly (Coll. 1916–22), who used to do this.

dean plate a pudding plate: for some reason very hard to get on Junior End in College Hall (1920).

Death Pits (called Plague Pits by the townspeople) mounds and cavities in the valley south of Hills. These were said to be the common graves of victims of the Great Plague (1666), and this would have been a suitably remote place for the corpses. Some of them may be natural undulations in the chalk, others old excavations for lime and flint. It was also the name of the College toll which passed that way (see **tolls**).

Deba.Sa. a Commoner Notion for Debating Society: a bad notion in College.

Debating Society Library (or **Room**) contained (1920) an old Commoner table, books ousted from Mob.Lib., and periodicals taken by the Society. See **Carthage**.

Delta Field named from its triangular shape, resembling the Greek capital D. Its sides (1920) were formed by Domum Cottage garden, Reach and the Great Western Railway. Before the building of this branch line the field was larger, and called Commoner Field. In 1868 it was Delta Fields in the plural, and they lay between New Barge and the path leading to Hills, stretching from Clark's garden to Tunbridge.

Depot the Rifle Depot, or units of the Rifle Brigade and 60th Rifles quartered at Winchester Barracks. The officers were on good terms with our staff: they judged Drill Pot, and played against the school at cricket in Greenjackets match, and also at football.

Deputy the next senior boy below the Candle-keepers in College (1831–8), or the junior Candle-keeper (1836). He acted as the Praefect of Hall's deputy, helped the Senior Candle-keeper to keep Hall quiet, organising the fags, and thrashing the juniors in Hall (1836), and also saw that all but Praefects and Candle-keepers, 'with whom it is optional whether they choose to go up into Hall', were in Hall in time, morning and evening (1838). The name survived to 1892 for the senior man in College who was neither a Praefect nor Tolly-keeper, but was obsolete by 1914.

Detective, the a nickname (1868) for the Rev. H. E. Moberly, Housemaster of B (1860–80).

Devil's Punch-bowl the Ordnance Survey map name for Amphitheatre (q.v.).

διαπρωτίζω from δια and πρῶτος to 'go through First'. Not to be found in the lexicon; also used Anglicè as diaprotize. [See **Through First**.]

dibs money, coin. Recorded from 1838, but by 1917 obsolete except in 'journey dibs' (journey money). Dibs were the knuckle-bones of sheep, and [the name was applied to] the games and dicing for which they were used. Dibs or dubs has been national slang for money generally from the early nineteenth century, if not earlier.

Wiccamical slang for standard coinage, at various times, was:

6*d* [sixpence] a tozzie (for tizzie)
1*s* [one shilling] a shig, or bob
2*s* 6*d* [two shillings and sixpence] half a bull
5*s* [five shillings] a bull
10*s* [ten shillings] a half-sog, or half-skiv
£1 [one pound] a sog, or skiv

By 1917 only tozzie survived, in Commoners.

Dick Shield   Richardson Shield for gymna: house teams of three, under 16 years
of age. Given by Rev. G. Richardson (Dick), Second Master 1873–99.

dicky from Dutch *dek* (a cover, or horse-cloth),   a flannel waistcoat worn next
the skin. Recorded with this meaning in 1838 only. In modern English it has
meant a leather apron, bib or false shirt front.

Dimond's Hole   a large depression or bog, which existed (1838) between
River and Tunbridge. 'So called because a boy named Dimond often used to
sit there.' One wonders why. If Dimond was a Wykehamist and not a local
farmer or waterman, he was possibly an ancestor of C. B. Dimond, admitted to
Commoners 1860.

disper, or **dispar**   a helping of mcat, usually mutton, at dinner; hence a
commons, or any share of food. Tom Warton (c. 1760) mentions dispars as
one of the amenities of life in College. In 1776 there was a dispute between the
Praepostors and Oll.Prae., who had refused to sell any more dispers: his trading
in surplus food brought him in about £80 per annum, of which the Praepostors
no doubt received their share, and when he decided to stop selling, they saw their
interests threatened. The word disper remained in use till 1860. The dispers or
cuts from a joint of mutton were:

cat's head
cut
fat flab (part of the breast)
fleshy (a thick slice out of the middle of a shoulder)
long disper
middle cut (a thick slice out of the centre of a leg)
rack (a cut from the neck or scrag of mutton).

'Cut' and 'rack' were still in use in 1907. Mansfield says there were six dispers
to a shoulder of mutton, and eight to a leg: middle cut and fleshy were as stated,
racks were the ribs, long disper was the loin. Inferior dispers were cat's head (the
end of the shoulder), and fat flab (the breast). Juniors ironically derived disper
from Latin *dispar* (unqual), implying unfair division of the joint between them
and seniors. Actually it is from Latin *dispertio* (divide, serve out), which probably

passed straight into the monastic butler's vocabulary as verb and noun. Spenser (c. 1590) and Milton (1641) use dispart, and we use disperse.

dittos from Latin *dictum* (that which has been said before),   a suit of coat and trousers made of the same material. Considered 'very low' (1838); non-licet by 1868. 'Ditto blues' (1831) was a suit of clothes all of blue cloth. The term dittos is used in this sense by Southey (1834) and was national slang.

div for division (a word in use by 1838), a form or class. In 1836–43 the divisions were:

Sexta Classis
Quintae Classis,   Senior pars
                            Media pars: Senior and Junior division
                            Junior pars
Quartae Classis,   Senior pars
                            Media pars
Secunda Classis, (the Choristers, with a school and a schoolmaster of their
                            own)

In 1892 the divisions were:

VIth Book
Vth Book, Senior Part, Senior Parallel (2 divisions)
                                    Middle Parallel (2 divisions)
                                    Junior Parallel (2 divisions)
                  Middle Part, Senior Parallel
                                    Second Parallel
                                    Third Parallel
                                    Junior Division
                  Junior Part
(From Third Parallel upwards, promotion was from parallel to parallel, not divison to division.)

In 1920 the divisions were:

VIth Book: (a) Senior Div
                  (b) modern parallel to (a) and (c), which were classical
                  (c) Junior Div (known as Frank's Div, from Frank Carter, who
                  then took it)
                  a Science div, recently added
Vth Book: Senior Part 1 (2 parallels)
                  Senior Part 2 (2 parallels)
                  Senior Part 3 (2 or 3 parallels)
                  Middle Part 1 (2 or 3 parallels)
                  Middle Part 2 (2 parallels)
                  Middle Part 3 (2 parallels)

                            Junior Part 1 (2 parallels)
                            Junior Part 2 (no parallels)

div books   form prize given at the end of each half.

Div Don   form master.

Diver, the   a Notion of 1820–8 for one of the Chaplains who, in order to read the prayers at maximum speed, used to submerge, i.e. omit a line or two while drawing breath.

Divina, or **Divinner**   Divinity. Generally at Morning Lines on Monday and Tuesday (1920).

dock   (1) to tear out (1831–60), especially in 'dock a book', i.e. tear the pages out. It had five other meanings, all in use since 1856. (2) to curtail: e.g. to 'dock one's gown' (to tuck it up behind), to 'dock the light' (to turn it out). (3) deprive of, prevent from, withdraw a privilege from: e.g. 'he was docked leave-out'. It could also mean (1920) merely to reprimand. (4) to stop doing something, leave off: e.g. 'time to dock' in a game. (5) to defeat in a team game: e.g. 'we docked them 4–3'. (6) to dock, or dock out was to rub out, scratch out, mark off a name on a list: thus the names-docker in canvas struck out each man's name as he came down.
   The first five uses derive from the old Icelandic word *dokr* (a short stumpy tail), yielding Old English *dock* (to cut or clip short a tail or hair): thus, dokked in Chaucer (c. 1380) and dockyd (1440). In standard English to dock means to curtail, reduce (of wages), abridge, cut off (of an entail), eliminate ('docking every 6*d*'). The sixth use may come from the North Country incantation 'in dock, out nettle', used when dock-leaves are rubbed on a nettle-sting to draw out the poison: this became a proverb, to express sudden change or inconstancy, and occurs thus in seventeenth-century poets. The plant-name dock is derived from Anglo-Saxon *docce* (dock).

Do.Co.Ro.Fo.   the foricas attached to Dons' Common Room.

Doctor, the   in the first half of the nineteenth century, and probably earlier, the Headmaster was always known as 'The Doctor', and with good reason: of the eighteen Headmasters from Bilson (1572) to Moberly (1866), fourteen were Doctors of Divinity, four were DCLs.

doctor's room   the north-east room on the ground floor of Sick House (1920), where medicines were dispensed, and the bundle put when one went abroad.

Dog Dan   (1) an old spotted spaniel belong to Mr Bather (Don 1894–1928): a great finder of cricket balls. (2) a suet roly-poly, with currants in, in College: from its resemblance to the above.

Dogger's Close   the southernmost but one of the four component parts of New Field, added in 1894. Richard Dogger was part-owner of a tenement in Kingsgate Street in 1457–66. His wife was paid 8*d* in College accounts 1454–5 for sewing six towels or napkins for the high table and Fellows' table in Hall. He or his descendants probably owned the field, which was already known as 'Doggersclose' in 1543.

dogs   the iron cross-bars on which the faggots rested when they were burning in chambers (1838). Fire-dogs is standard English.

dole   from Greek δόλος, Latin *dolus* (a trick), a trick, dodge, clever invention, stratagem (sometimes to get one out of bed). In use 1830–1900; obsolete by 1914. It survives in dialect as tole, toll, toil, all meaning to entice or draw away: a toll-bird is a decoy. It also survives in Scots law with the meaning of guilty intent (*mens rea*), without which a crime cannot occur.

dolifier   from dole, as above: a trickster. In use 1831–92; long since obsolete.

domes   rubber soles and heels fitted to boots and shoes. Introduced in England as an economy in the First World War. Frowned on when first used at Winchester, as they enabled the wearer to creep silently about, but accepted later as cheaper than boot leather. Their trade name was 'Phillips' Military Soles & Heels'. Probably derived from 'domes of silence', a type of metal boss fixed to the bottom of chair-legs, to enable them to slide smoothly over the carpet.

Dom Fox et Burton   one of the headings on Long Roll. Under this heading were the names of men who had left, and who received during their university career about £15 to £25 per annum, from a fund left to College in 1729, for deserving boys who were superannuated, by Bohun Fox, CF (in College 1688–92; died 1750), and John Burton, CF (in College 1705–9; DD; Fellow; Informator 1724–66). This bequest formed the nucleus of a fund which later provided four exhibitions annually of £50 each, tenable for four years at the university. It was awarded (1920) to applicants whose parents were in monetary distress, and was in no sense a scholarship.

'Domum' (pronounced Dōmum)   from Latin *domum* meaning 'homewards'. This meaning underlies its use on Hills, at breaking-up ceremonies at the end of term, and in the school song. The 'o' is short in Latin. The invariable pronunciation of Domum with a long 'o' is due to a fluke, that the song 'Domum' was set to a tune that demanded this. The contexts in which Wykehamists have felt impelled to exclaim or sing 'homewards' have been three in number, but they have been hopelessly intertwined, and the legends invented to disentangle them have merely tightened the knots. One has to unravel them, like unloading hay, to establish the order in which they were fastened upon each other. For greater clarity we shall take them in chronological order.

(1) In 1561 an energetic young Headmaster named Christopher Johnson decided that the boys needed regular fresh air and exercise, and sent them up Hills as part of their curriculum: and there they diverted themselves in various ways until it was time to go home again. The Praefect of Hall originally gave the call of 'Domum', ten minutes before it was time to descend from Hills and return to College. By 1820 we find this duty of 'calling Domum' delegated to the three juniors in College, two of whom walked round Trench, and the third across the crest of Hills, shouting 'Domum' as loud as they could from stated distances, calculated to ensure that the warning was heard from every part of the hilltop. As soon as they heard it, the boys assembled at 'On Place', and awaited the order 'On' from the Praefect of Hall. By 1868 they no longer cried 'Domum' on Hills, but below it, at Pot, Double Hedge and Portsmouth Road, but by that time, as a Commoner lexicographer remarks, Dr Ridding had largely abolished Hills 'as our fellows never came back in time'.

(2) At Whitsun 1666 the Plague descended on Winchester, and the boys were sent home or dispersed to uninfected areas, leaving in College only Roger Oades, who had charge of College pack-horses and used to ride provisions out to a group of scholars sequestered at Talmage's farm at Crawley. I have suggested (in my 'Winton', vol. 3, pp. 503 *et seq.*) that the school song 'Dulce Domum' was written at this time by a party of boys kept back from the Whitsun recess in mid-May: and that they composed it either by a Chamber fireside, with 'Sumer is icumen in' as model, and an exhortation to Roger to bring the homeward coach next morning, or at Talmage's farm, with a tune such as 'Lillibullero' in their minds, and urging Roger to press forward the pack-horses with their next meal, and after it their return to their homes. They were not expert Latinists, but their poem was memorable enough to be kept by one of them, and set to music later by John Reading, College organist 1681–92. Unfortunately his harmonisation ignored the original lilt and scansion.

This song 'Domum', with its alien music, is recorded as being sung from 1768 onwards on the eve of the Whitsun recess, at Domum Wharf, Blackbridge and College gates. By 1804 it was being sung also round Domum Tree, and in 1835 in Meads. By 1852 it was sung not only round Domum Tree, but in Hall on the last six Saturdays of Long Half. In 1868 it was sung in New Commoners Grubbing Hall, after leave out of hall, on the last six Mondays of Long Half.

By this time a blanket of legend had smothered its origin, and the accepted tale was that 'Domum' was composed by a boy who was kept back for the holidays, spent his time moping on Hills, cut Domum Cross, carved the words on Domum Tree, and committed suicide. The legend's connection between the song and Hills is, of course, false, arising from the homing call of 'Domum' in (1) above.

(3) The breaking-up festival of Domum was at the end of the school year. In 1836 this was on the last Friday evening in Long Half after Election; since 1892 it has been from 6.30 to 10 p.m. on the last day of Cloister Time. There was a large assembly of neighbouring gentry and others, and 'Domum' was sung over and over again. Latterly a band attended and interspersed other music. The singing of

'Domum' continued in School, and finally in Chamber Court, followed by cheers for popular characters.

'Dulce Domum'

Concinamus, O sodales:
   Eja! quid silemus?
Nobile canticum,
dulce melos, Domum,
   dulce Domum resonemus.
   Domum, Domum, dulce Domum,
   dulce Domum resonemus.

Let us sing together, companions:
   (Ha! why are we silent?)
the noble song,
the sweet tune, Domum,
   let us re-echo sweet Domum.
   [*Domum, Domum, sweet Domum,*
   let us re-echo sweet Domum.]

Appropinquat, ecce, felix
   hora gaudiorum:
post grave tedium
advenit omnium
   meta petita laborum.

See, the happy hour
   of rejoicing draws near:
after heavy strain,
the longed-for goal of all
   our toil is getting closer.

Musa, libros mitte fessa,
   mitte pensa dura,
mitte negotium:
jam datur otium.
   Me mea mittito cura.

Tired Muse, leave the books,
   leave the hard tasks,
leave duty:
leisure is now granted.
   May my care leave me.

Ridet annus, prata rident,
   nosque rideamus.
Jam repetit domum
Daulias advena,
   nosque domum repetamus.

The season smiles, the meadows smile,
   and let us smile also.
Already the nightingale
is returning home,
   so let us return home as well.

Heus! Rogere, fer caballos,
   Eja! nunc eamus.
Limen amabile,
matris et oscula
   suaviter et repetamus.

Ho! Roger, bring the horses,
   Ha! let us now be going:
and blithely let us seek again
our beloved threshold,
   and Mother's kisses.

Concinamus ad penates,
   vox et audiatur.
Phosphore! quid jubar,
segnius emicans,
   gaudia nostra moratur?

Let us sing together at our hearth,
   and may our voice be heard.
Morning star! why does your beam,
shinging out so lazily,
   delay our joy?

Domum Ball   a ball given by superannuated College Praefects on the first night of the summer holidays (1858–92).

Domum Cottage   a cottage between New Barge and Commoner Field, or at the north end of Delta Field, formerly called Clark's, in the garden of which Domum Tree stood. So called from the singing there of 'Domum'.

Domum Cross   a cross cut in the turf of Trench on the south side of Hills. Every new man had to put into it a stone taken from Chalk Pit, and then kneel down and kiss the cross. The cross is mentioned in 1868, and this custom (still in force in 1922) in 1892. The cross is said to have been cut by the author of 'Domum', but this is a fallacy arising from confusion between *Domum* (1) and (2) above. It was called Domum Cross because from it the College juniors used to start their tour of Hills calling 'Domum'.

Domum Day   see **Domum** (3) above. 'The last day of Long Half when a platform was put up in Meads and the school walked round singing Domum at intervals' (1880).

Domum Dinner   a dinner held in College Hall on Domum Day, the last day of Cloister Time, at which the Governing Body, Dons, all College men and distinguished Commoners were present. In 1922 the senior half of College attended. Recorded from 1874–5.

Domum Tree   a great elm round which 'Domum' used to be sung after Evening Hills and on the last day of term; mentioned by Warton (1768–71) and Huddesford (1804). It stood in the garden of Clark's, or Domum Cottage. It was blown down in the gales of 1904. There was another tree (1880) called Domum Tree, between Red Bridge and Boat House, on the further side of River. The name derives from the singing of the song there, not, as stated in legend, from the carving of the words of the song on the tree.

Domum Wharf   a wharf on new Barge, described as between Scards and New Bridge (1868); opposite Boat-house (1880); extending from Black Bridge nearly up to Clark's (1892). Named from the singing of 'Domum' there.

Don   from Latin *dominus* (master), a master. A Div Don is a form master; a House Don, a housemaster. Recorded from 1880. It is a university word.

Dongas   a series of ridges on the south of Portsmouth Road and east of Death Pits: a natural conformation of the chalk, accentuated by medieval pack-trails. Junior Steeplecha course passed through Dongas. From the South African word *donga* (gully, ravine): a word brought home from the Boer War.

Dons' Common Room   the room on the east of Hat Place, to which only Dons are admitted.

Dons' Library   an 1880 Notion for the room above Chantry.

Domum Tree and Wharf

'Door!' shouted when someone entering a chamber had not closed the door (1920).

Double Hedges a lane, called Garnier Road by the townspeople, leading from Waterman's Hut, over Tunbridge, to Portsmouth Road. It had a hedge on either side. In use since 1838, when it was called Double Hedge.

Dowlings chocolates from Dowlings in High Street: generally bought by one's pitch-up or sported by an Old Wykehamist. The boys could not buy them themselves (1920). Also used for any chocolates not bought at School Shop.

'Down!' (1) 'in the morning Hall about 9 clock Whitesman calls "Down" in the middle of Hall, when hatches are shut: in the evening when he calls "Down", Deputy sends every one out of Hall who is not fagging, but candle-keepers and Praefects' (1838). (2) shouted by any man in the hot at Our Game who had touched the ground with his knee or body (1920).

down, to be (1) a College man was said to be down when watching out at nets (1856). Obsolete by 1917. (2) the opposite to being up (to books) for any hour (1920). (3) of one's pitch-up, to be staying in Winchester (1920).

Downer's shop a carpenter's workshop near Paradise and Shoe Hole (1838): known as Bendle's Hole (q.v.) (1917).

down hot (for **knuckle-down hot**, q.v.). a kind of mons in VIIth Chamber: the stoutest man stood at the door, holding on to a bar fixed there, and the rest of the chamber tried to hot him out (1920).

down river, to be or **to go** to exercise oneself on River, of members of Boat Club (1920).

down ropes   inside ropes, of a hot, or the ball (1920).

down shops   at or to School Shop.

dress   a reserve, of about seven men in XVs and three in VIs, who stood on a board at the end of canvas just behind their side's worms, ready dressed so as to be able to take the place of anyone injured. These men, who were expected to shout loudest of all the supporters, were said originally to be 'in dress' (i.e. dressed for the fray), later changed to 'on dress', thus obscuring the meaning. Recorded from 1880.

Dress Match   an annual match between dress men of the three XVs, played after XVs. Rrecorded 1900; obsolete by 1917.

Drill Pot parade   parade of a house section by the house commander to practise for Drill Pot (1920).

Duboulay Ho!   a facetious word for Hurrah (1922), fabricated from Du Boulay (below) and the American Bully-Ho!

Du Boulayites   obsolete name for men in Cooks: from Rev. J. T. H. Du Boulay, first Housemaster (1862–93).

Du Boulay note-book   a small note-book with red paper cover, introduced by Mr Du Boulay; still in use 1920.

Du Boulay Passage   leading from Southgate Road to Southgate Hill; used chiefly by men in C and I houses.

dubs   double (1868 only). Borrowed from the game of marbles, in which 'doublets' is when a player knocks two marbles out of the ring: he cries, 'Dubs', and claims both.

duck   face, facial expression (1831); 'ducks' used for grimaces (1880). Obsolete by 1917. Derived from a dying duck turning up its eyes in a thunderstorm, not from Hans Andersen's ugly duckling story, which was published long after the Notion was in use.

duct   from Latin *ductus* (conduit pipe), the copper pipe in each chamber, used for taking water from a conduit (i.e. pipe) to a bidet. The 'ductus' of Chamber Court Conduit is mentioned in the poem of 1647. The remains of a duct were visible below the west window of Ist Chamber (1920) but it had not carried water for years. Obsolete by 1890.

Duke of Wellington   an old man about College (c. 1838): so called from his resemblance to the Iron Duke.

dump, to   to put out a tolly. In use 1856: obsolete by 1900. Derived from an extinct English word, which is related to the following. (1) to damp (moisten, exinguish), from Old German *dampen* (extinguish). So used by Donne (c. 1630), and still current in the phrase 'to damp down the fire'. (2) to dump (throw down a load): from Old English *dumpen* (to cast down suddenly), derived from Dutch *dompen* (to immerse). It appears in dialect as domp (to sink). (3) dump, usually in plural form as dumps (dejection): from German *dumpf* (moist, dull), which also gives the English adjective damp (humid). Thus used by Sir Thomas More (1573), Shakespeare, and Swift (as damp, 1730); still in use in the phrase 'down in the dumps', and in 'dumps' (twilight).

Duncan   two prizes for mathematics given in 1841 by P. B. Duncan, senior Fellow of New College, and competed for the week before Heathcote, i.e. three weeks before the end of Short Half. In 1868 the senior prize was awarded to VIth Book, the junior to the remainder. In 1880 Dungy (as it was called) included two prizes for maths, one for reading and one for an historical essay: Senior Dungy was open to VIth and Senior Part, being awarded at Easter; Junior Dungy was for the rest of the school, and awarded at the end of Short Half. Duncan was still competed for in 1922, but the Heathcote had lapsed.

Dungy   (1) College blacksmith and bell-ringer (1838). This nickname became a title, which in 1868 was borne by Commoner locksmith, whose real name was Stripp. (2) Notion for Duncan (q.v.) in 1880.

eagle   the lectern in Chapel (1868), from which Bible Clerk read the lessons, was the gift of two Praefects of Chapel, and was made of oak. The eagle of 1880 was presented by Rev. James Baker.

Earliers   early Communion service, at 7.45 on Sundays (1920).

Easter Speaking   on Saturday mornings in Easter Time, all the boys had to speak before the Warden and masters in School. They were divided into six Chambers, corresponding with those in College, and were rehearsed for a week beforehand by the Praefects assigned to them. A speech of fourteen to eighteen lines of Shakespeare was chosen, and if this was well said, the speakers got off three tasks. Praefects also recited their Easter Tasks at Easter Speaking. The best performers in each week had to speak again at Commoner Speaking. Obsolete by 1868.

Easter Task   a poem in Latin or English composed voluntarily by any Praefect who chose to do so, and recited at Easter Speaking. Recorded from 1831; obsolete by 1868.

Easter Time   the six weeks after Common Time, beginning just after mid-March and lasting till the end of April, so that Holy Week was sure to fall within it (1831).

East Hall   on the east side of Flint Court in New Commoners (1842–69), over Mugging Hall: converted into div rooms for physical science.

Ebenezer   when a ball hits the wooden bar in racquets, fives or bat-fives, and flies straight up; in use from 1900. The word is Hebrew, meaning 'stone of help'. It was the name of a stone erected as an altar by Samuel after defeating the Philistines (I Samuel 7.12). In giving it this name he said: 'Hitherto hath the Lord helped us', as a fives-player might say on suffering this disappointment.

Edom   the space round College boot-holes, opposite Arcadia. Recorded from 1892; obsolete by 1917. Taken from Psalm 60.8: 'Moab is my wash-pot; over Edom will I cast out my shoe.'

Edward Wickham's, or **Old German Room** a room in New Commoners (1842–69) to the west of Hat Place, and between it and Praefects' Library. In it German was taught, and 'sometimes whippings were administered by the headmaster'. Named after Rev. E. C. Wickham, Don 1857–9. Not to be confused with 'Wickham's', formerly the Sustern Chapel in Old Commoners, named after a doctor who lived there 1794–1801.

egg-flip hot spiced beer, with egg and lemon added. It was made on Apple-pie Day and drunk in School round Stove (1856–68). In 1880 it was served at a party given at 4 p.m. in School, on the last Hatch Thoke in Short Half, after VIs, by College Praefects; to which they invited Commoner Praefects, to share this drink and join in a sing-song, together with all members of VIs. By 1892, Dons, Old Wykehamists and all men in College attended, and there was singing and cheering. By 1914 Egg-flip had come to mean the entertainment itself, which was a recognised fixture on the evening of the Hatch Thoke in Short Half. By 1917 the guests included all important Commoners, and Dons' ladies, and glasses of lime-juice, spiced with lemon and a dash of spirit, were handed round to the company by the New Roll in College.

Egg-flip is standard English for a cocktail, with a recipe approximating to the above, known also as a 'yard of flannel' from its fleecy appearance. Mansfield (1836) describes these convivial evenings as a regular occurrence in Short Half, and gives a picture of one of them [Mansfield, p.41].

Egg-flip Night the night of Apple-pie Day, when egg-flip was provided (1831). Obsolete by 1914.

ekker exercise.

ekker rolls from 1892 onwards, if not before, it was laid down by Praefects in most Commoner houses that from four to six hours' compulsory exercise (per week) must be taken by everyone who had not been in the school three years, and rolls showing the number of hours taken were put up once a week. At first, this was confined to the first six or seven weeks of Common Time, but it was later extended. In 1920 ekker rolls were adopted for the first time in College.

Eleckers election, of Scholars to Winton (1920).

Election (1) the examination of Praefects and Senior Part for New College (1836). By 1892 this had become the choice of men for New College after the examination at the end of Short Half. By 1917 the examination was just called 'New College'. (2) the election of candidates for admission as scholars of Winton (1836). In 1916 the examination was held in June, and the list of Scholars and Exhibitioners was published a few days after it was over.

Election Chamber the panelled room over Middle Gate where election for New College and Winchester scholarships was held by the Electors. Scrutiny was also held there. At one time it was the Warden's apartment. In 1892 it was used by College Tutor. By 1917 it was being used for occasional meetings of the Governing Body. In Cloister Time 1922 it became College War Memorial Library.

Election Dinner　see **Domum Dinner**.

Election Roll　the list of men elected to scholarships and exhibitions at Winchester. In 1892 it was brought down at noon on Hatch Thoke in Cloister Time, and put up for public inspection in Wells' shop. By 1916 a short list was posted at Wells' of candidates required on the third day of the exam, and a few days later the final roll was posted at Porter's Lodge.

Election Week　the last week of Long Half and, in the early Victorian era, by far the most important and glittering moment in the Wiccamical year. It is now of little or no significance. [Its decline followed the breaking of the Winchester/New College connection by the 1850 Royal Commission on Oxford and Cambridge.]

　It was set apart for elections to Winchester and New College by the Electors, that is, both Wardens, two Fellows of New College (called Senior and Junior Posers), the Sub-Warden and the Headmaster of Winchester. They used to arrive on the Tuesday after the feast of St Thomas of Canterbury, 7 July, and were received Ad Portas with two orations, the 'Fundator' (in honour of the Founder), and the 'Elizabeth and Jacob' (in honour of Queen Elizabeth and James I). The Candlesticks, and the three Fardels for New College, were then examined. A cricket match was also played 'between the Collegians and the Town gentlemen, i.e. those gentlemen who live in or near Winchester and are good cricketers' (1838). On the Wednesday, Thursday and Friday grand dinners were given, and 'Domum' was sung: and the festivities ended with the Superannuates' Ball at St John's House.

　By 1892 Election Week had been stripped of its glamour, and was merely a week towards the end of Cloister Time during which, one understood, next year's Winchester Scholars were chosen.

Electors　see **Election Week**.

eli　an *e*lectric *li*ght bulb (1920).

Elizabeth and Jacob　a speech in honour of Queen Elizabeth and King James I, formerly delivered by the Praefect of School on 24 March, the date of Elizabeth's death and James' accession in 1603. Later it was delivered in School on the Tuesday in Election Week, after Ad Portas. Long since obsolete.

Elkins　(senior) a Cathedral verger (1920), who would take one up the Tower if tactfully approached. (junior) his son, an assistant at Wells', and member of Chapel Choir and Glee Club (1920).

Ellenberger and Antrobus prunes and custard. From G. F. Ellenberger (Coll. 1909–14) and either M. E. Antrobus (Coll. 1908–14) or P. R. Antrobus (Coll. 1911–16).

end at morning and evening Hall in College (1831–42) a Candle-keeper sat at each end of the three long tables for Inferiors; and below him, sitting three a side, were six Inferiors who fagged for him, the junior of them putting up his bob, salt and pepper and making his mustard. These six groups or messes of seven boys each, and the ends of the tables at which they sat, were called 'ends'. The word survived to 1922 in the names of the three tables, Senior, Middle and Junior End. But the three Tolly-keepers all then sat at the head of Senior End, and there were no messes or fagging.

English a crib: a printed English translation of a Latin or Greek book or books-lesson. In 1920 they could be used in Senior Div or in mugging up for an examina, but were otherwise illegal. Standard English, but recorded as a Notion from 1838.

entry a piece of unseen translation written out in Senior Div and Frank's Div; an **entry version** was the hour in which the entry was given back and gone through (1920). A special use of a standard word, in the sense of an item entered in writing: or entered in a competition. [Described in the 1890s as an importation from Harrow: A. F. Leach *A history of Winchester College*, 1899, p. 534.]

epideixis from Greek ἐπίδειξις (a demonstration). On the night before the first XV, the skipper and second skipper of VI went round to each upstairs chamber, and called on all new men to give an epideixis, i.e. to stand on top of conduits and back up 'Cau . . . llege', in preparation for XVs, as loud as he could. The best performer was complimented. The skippers often called on some old stager in the chamber to do so as well (1920).

erection, to sport an see **barricade**.

Etheridge's a public house on the river above Winchester where boats were kept (1868).

etna a spirit stove; see **aetna**.

Eton match the annual cricket match between Eton and Winchester, usually played on the last Friday and Saturday in June, at each school alternately. The visiting team arrives the day before the match and is entertained at the expense of the rival school. Each school used to invite seventy men for the second day, providing them with their meals. When the match is at Eton, men can stay away over Friday night if they have pitch-up to go to.

The first match was played in 1826. From 1832 to 1854 the triangular contest

Etheridge's

of Eton, Harrow and Winchester was played at Lords. In 1855 our match with Harrow was discontinued, and the Eton match played at Winchester. The first Eton match to be played in New Field was in 1870.

Evening Hills   see **Hills**.

Ex-Course-keeper   see **Course-keeper**.

exhibi (pronounced exhibī)   an exhibition. (1) men on Eleckers Roll who went into Commoners were called Exhibitioners. (2) an exhibition at the university, won by a man in the school. (3) a school exhibition (q.v.).

expedi (pronounced expedī)   any excursion on a leave-out day or whole rem (1920).

ex trumps   unprepared (up to books). To 'go on ex trumps' is to be put on to construe when you have not prepared the lesson; to 'go up ex trumps' is to go up to books without having looked at your work. This notion may have arisen from a new boy's attempt to say 'ex tempore', which is used in the sense of unprepared by Ben Jonson (1598); or may mean 'out of trumps', i.e. winning cards (trump deriving from Latin *triumphus*); or may reflect the use of trump (French *tromper*) in 'trump up a story', meaning to devise or fabricate, a use as old as Fletcher and Massinger (1621); or may echo the phrase 'to put one to one's trumps' (to call for one's utmost efforts), thus used by Peele (1593).

eyesight, to sport   to deliver all the blows on the same spot in beating (1920).

fag   a junior performing household chores and other duties for a Praefect. Fag and fagging were used in this sense at many schools, including Winchester, from 1820 if not earlier: but by 1880 the words 'junior' and 'sweat' had begun to take their place and they have long been obsolete. In standard English the noun fag can mean a drudge, or a wearisome task: Jane Austen wrote: 'It is such a fag' in 1818. The verb means to be weary or make weary, and is probably a form of flag (to hang limp).

fagging   Thackeray uses 'fagging out' for fielding at cricket. Fagging done by College juniors at Winchester (in 1838) included: 'In a chamber, the junior takes care of the mop, broom, candlesticks, snuffers and extinguishers, which together with a candlestick and candle he puts up to each boy. He has to provide a towel to wipe up mess things and dirt with; to provide foricus and fire paper, clean and put the boilers on the fire, and put on faggots when wanted. In School side of Gate, as many juniors as are wanted watch out at cricket, and every junior kicks in [i.e. except candle-keepers and seniors at candle-keeper's end]. Any boy with 20 juniors [i.e. 20 men junior to him] may, if told to do anything by a Praefect, tell one of his juniors: and may also keep his juniors in School to fag when wanted. There are also other kinds of fagging:

> . . . quae spatiis exclusus iniquis
> praetereo, atque aliis post me memoranda relinquo.'

Compare the duties of First and Second Juniors in 1920 (see under Junior). In 1836 fags did everything except make beds and clean shoes.

faggot   a large faggot which was burned in College chambers from the earliest times until grates were put in. In 1820–8 a faggot was 4 feet [1.2 m] long, and it was the duty of bed-makers to put the nightly ration of four faggots in each chamber. They were burned over the fire-dogs. In 1917 they were still in use in Ist and IVth chambers, which had open grates, and had to be lighted after soccer or canvas by the junior man changing at the time, and men warmed by them after their bidet. They were then stopped as a war economy and never started again. See also **half-faggot**.

family ticket   a man who took a family ticket in Athla could go in for all events except handicaps and obstacle races, thus saving the expense of a separate entrance fee for each. It usually cost 5 shillings. Used in 1892; obsolete by 1917. A metaphor from railway travel.

Fang, or **Little Fang**   Mr R. L. G. Irving (Coll. 1890–6: College Tutor 1901–9: Housemaster of E 1909–37): also called Twitch or Little Twitch in Commoners. The name Fang derived from his rather long teeth, displayed when smiling, which he often did; Twitch, from his habit of twitching, said to be the result of a fall while mountaineering. As College Tutor he had rooms in and above Election Chamber, and from this, Middle Gate was called Fang Tower.

fardel   from Anglo-Saxon *feortha dael* (fourth deal or part), appearing as *feorrthe dale* (1200), *ferthe del* (1283), and finally as fardel: a division of VIth Book into four parts for New College Election, at the end of Long Half. From 1831 to 1860 (when they disappeared), there were only three fardels, and in 1836 Senior Part seem to have been included also. It survives only in the South Country, in the old law term 'fardel of land' (the fourth part of a yard-land), and in this Notion. It has no connection with Shakespeare's fardel (a burden), which is from Old French *fardeau* (a pack).

Farley Mount   about a mile on from Crab Wood, south of the line of the Old Sarum road. The monument on it is a well-known landmark. Men often went to or past it on expedis.

fast   unusually well dressed: particularly fastidious over one's clothes (1838). In use at the university (1852) for a man who dressed flashily. In standard English the word refers to conduct rather than clothing.

fat flab   a cut off the fat part of a breast of mutton; see **disper**.

Fearonites   the Notion (1868–82) for members of Rev. W. A. Fearon's House (D): now called Kennyites.

feathers   the tops of the trees in Clump, and the cry given when they first come into sight over the sky-line; in use since 1900 or earlier. The question is still (1960) asked in some House Notions examinas: 'How many leaves are there on top of the trees in Clump?' Correct answer: 'None. They are feathers.' Trollope (1820–8) remarks that the trees were tall and spindly 'with not a branch until the tuft at the top is reached'. But there seems no special reason for the word feather, except in the sense it can have as a verb, to become thin: thus Tennyson: 'the edge of the wood began to feather towards the hollow.' See **Hills**.

Fellows   the Fellows (Socii) of Winton were unobtrusive, and we hear little of them. They occupied the first- and second-floor rooms round Chamber Court,

Field (Commoner Field)

which were later converted to dormitories. In Mansfield's plan of College (1835–40) there was a Fellows' Common Room between Kitchen and VIth Chamber.

ferk   see **firk**.

Fever Time   during Cloister Time every superannuated College Praefect was allowed a week to prepare his 'Election business', i.e. work for Election Week; during which time he did not appear in School at all but mugged in his room at Sick House (1838). By 1868 the week had extended to a fortnight, and later they went down two at a time to Sick House to work in quiet. Long since obsolete. The notion implies that they were working at fever pitch, or that it was generously assumed they were suffering from fever.

fib, to   to get a boy's head under your arm and then punch his face (1838). To fib was English slang for striking with a succession of rapid blows and was thus used by Southey (1811).

Field   the field near Domum Wharf where Commoners played cricket and football (1838); usually called Commoner Field.

field, to   to help a man when bathing, to look after, to protect. When a new man went in for the first time, another man went in beforehand to help him if necessary. If a man got out of his depth, to field him was to rescue him. In use 1856–1900; obsolete by 1917. Not used thus in standard English: it might be a metaphor from cricket, but there our word was 'watch-out' or 'fag-out'.

Fifteens   the annual matches at Winchester football between College, Commoners and Houses, played on Tuesday, Thursday and Saturday early in November, usually in College canvas. There were fifteen a side, and several men in dress. Play began when College clock struck 12.15, and lasted an hour (1892). Fifteens superseded the old matches of twenty-two a side between College and Commoners in 1867.

Fifteens Roll   lists giving the names of men in each XV and dress, brought down in Hat Place by some Don at the request of the Captain of VI, two days before the event, after last hour at night, amid applause (1920).

fifteens sport   given in a Chamber by any men in it on Fifteens Roll, consisting of a meal varying in quantity and quality, and followed by charades or some game (1920). See **sport**.

fifteens spot   after the first fortnight in Short Half, new men in College had to compose a conjectural roll of XVs and dress. The two skippers came round to each shop, as in epideixis, and called on somebody to bring down these rolls from the top of conduits. The authors' mistakes in names, order and initials could be amusing. The custom was designed to show whether new men were taking an interest in the prospects of College XV, and whether paters were instructing them sensibly (1920).

Fillet, the   see **Fillies**.

Fillies, the or **the Filly**, **the Folly** and **the Fillet**   the three daughters of Mr R. L. A. Du Pontet (Don 1892–1926). Their mother was called the Mare (1920).

fill-up   a bottle or stone jar of ink to fill inkpots or fountain pens. It was the duty of the First Junior to have one ready (1920).

Filly, the   see **Fillies**.

finge (also spelt **fingy**, **finjy**)   an exclamation, pronounced 'finjy' to 1843, as 'finge' by 1917, used in College; it excused one from a chore, if one uttered it quickly – the last man to say 'finge' had to do the chore. Commoners used 'jockey not'. Recorded from 1831. Examples given (1838) are: 'Fingy greasing the ball', or 'Fingy taking up the stumps', after cricket: a later example (1920) is 'Finge table!'; the last man to say this amongst the juniors sweated to wash up in a Chamber, had to clean the table as well as do his share of the washing-up.

This is the 'fains I' of prep. schools: the books say it is from Latin *fingo* (I feign), in which case finge would mean 'pretend thou', not 'I refuse': while 'fains I' would appear to mean 'I would fain [like to] do it'. The real origin is 'fen', a corruption of 'I fend', an exclamation used at marbles meaning 'I forbid a manoeuvre by my opponent': and when Dickens says: 'Fen larks, you know', he means 'No nonsense, mind you'. This fen was misspelt as fain or feign, feign was Latinised to *fingere*, with the termination -y or -e, overlooking the fact that *fingere* cannot mean to refuse to do something. cf. knuckle down.

firk (also spelt **ferk**, **furk**)   (1) to send: e.g. 'ferked up to house', 'firk abroad'. So used 1856–92. (2) to send away. (3) to expel from Winchester, a specialised use of (2): firked means expelled. This was wrongly derived from Latin *furca* (pitchfork), and the phrase 'naturam expelles furca, tamen usque recurret' (Horace, Ep. 1.10.24) inspired the picturesque but groundless legend that an expelled boy's clothes were pitched to him over Non-Licet Gate on a long-fork. The story that expelled boys left by this gate is as old as 1831. (4) to pay up. This is a variation of fork out: a temporary use of firk, c. 1870.

In the first three meanings, firk is from Anglo-Saxon *fercian* (to bring: hence to lead, or to send away). It appears as *ferke* (1400), *fferke* (1469), and at this time also had the intransitive meaning of to set out, proceed, ride. Ben Jonson uses firk (1610). In sixteenth- and seventeenth-century slang firk and fyrk meant ferret out, worry like a dog, flurry, hustle. Firk (send) was still being used by the older townsmen of Winchester in 1860. It also survives in dialects in the sense of rapid movements such as jerking, fidgeting, scratching and worrying.

First and Fourth raid   see **clothes inspeccer**.

first hour   the first hour up to books in morning or afternoon (1920).

First Junior   see **Junior, First**.

First Peal   a bell in Chapel Tower was rung by Joel three-quarters of an hour before Morning Lines, and could just be heard in the nearer Commoner houses. After it had rung, Crute and Nutley aroused the First Juniors in the Chambers on their staircases (1920).

First Pot   a lock on River. See **Pot**, and **Hills, to do**.

Fishcroft   a house in Southgate Road, which borders on the south-west corner of Kingsgate Park and has given its name to that part of it. Ellis Pot and Jun-Jun (crockets) were played on Fishcroft (1920).

Fives Courts   up to 1921 there were three groups of them. (1) four in Old Fives Courts, a red-brick building just south of Co.Fo., presented in 1862 by Rev. C. H.

Ridding, father of Dr Ridding. It was divided in half by a passage leading to a stair, which rose to a spectators' gallery above. To the left of the entrance were the two courts named 'Senior and Junior College'; to the right, 'Junior and Senior Commoner'. The courts named 'Senior' had a buttress. These four courts were so slow (1920) that they were only used for squa ra, and by Commoner juniors for batters. Rain got in by the roof. They were used one summer during the First World War for storage by a regiment. (2) three in Bear Cages, or Outside Fives Courts, next to the above on the south, numbered 1, 2, 3 from Museum side: presented in Short Half 1882 by Dr Ridding. Open to the weather on the back wall side. Very old and ugly (1920), and used only by juniors. (3) five in New Fives Courts, provided by subscriptions from Old Wykehamists, with entrance next to Racquets Courts. Nos. 1, 2, 3 and 4 lie together, with 5 to the south. Used for fives only, they were good, fast and clean, and far the best we had (1920). In 1921–2 Old Fives Courts and Bear Cages were demolished to make room for War Memorial Cloister. New Fives Courts still stand, but are now called Old, others, called New Fives Courts, having been built in Forder's Piece.

Flannel Roll   a list which originally came down twice in Cloister Time, giving the names of those who might wear white flannel trousers for distinguishing themselves at cricket. By 1917 it came down once, after Eton Match. It was compiled by the Captain of Lords and posted by him on School Notice Board. It usually contained about eighteen names.

flannels   flannel trousers used for football and crickct, and also on very hot days as being cooler than any other kind. Boys were not allowed to wear them on school days (1838). By 1917 flannels meant only white flannels; see **Flannel Roll**. Grey ones were 'greyers'.

fleshy   the name of a disper: a thick cut out of the middle of a shoulder of mutton. Long since obsolete.

Fletcher's Dust Hole   a hole in the panelling of the Second Master's chair at the lower end of School (1868). cf. Pulver's Dust Hole. Perhaps it was from J. R. Fletcher (Comm. 1838–41).

flier, flyer   a long high kick at Winchester football, when the ball is caught on the instep and goes well over the opponents' heads. Thus used since 1831. In 1838 if such a kick was made with the toe (called a toe-bang in 1917) and not the instep it was considered unfair. In 1856 flyer was used for a half-volley kick, but by 1917 it meant a kick with the instep when there was no restriction as to the height one might kick it.

   A **made flyer** is described in terms difficult to follow. In 1856, it is when the bound of the ball is gained from a previous kick against canvas or any other obstacle, or is dropped in as a drop-kick: this is now confused with a kick-up. In 1892, a player having last kicked the ball himself, may not kick up, nor may it be taken as a flyer by any other member of his side, if it should rebound from a post or be an own-side kick. A violation of this rule is termed a made flyer. In 1900, when a player has passed all the opposing side in a rush towards their worms, he is entitled to take a flyer, even though he himself last kicked the ball. Such a flyer is termed a made flyer.

A good flyer literally flew through the air, hence the name: but is is not used in this sense outside Winchester, and Clough's lines in the 'Bridge of Peschiers':

> Your comrades chase e'en now the fliers
> And, but for you, possess the field

do not, as some have suggested, refer to football.

flimsy   a £5 note. Recorded 1880 only. It is standard slang for a bank note, from the fineness of the paper used.

Flint Court   the flint-paved court surrounded by classrooms. As part of New Commoners (1842–69) it led from Hat Place to Grass Court, and its sides were formed by Mugging and Grubbing Halls, above which were East and West Hall Galleries. Down the sides were Cloisters. Good Friday Passage led from it into School Court. It was swagger (non-licet) for juniors to walk across it (1880), and in 1917 they still kept to the pavement round the edges.

flogging   see **bibling**, **beating**. The term was noted for attention by Gordon (1842) but he never completed the entry. It was not used in the 1820–8 period.

floored   found wanting in a lesson up to books (1820–8). Standard slang for being unable to answer a question, or being silenced by a decisive retort. cf. settler.

Flower de Luce, the   an ancient inn near College named the Fleur de Lys, where T. A. Trollope put up in 1820, as his father had known it in his College days.

Folly, the   see **Fillies**.

Fol.Sil.   *Foliorum Silvula* by H. A. Holden: a book of pieces to be done into Latin prose or verse. Used in Frank's Div (1920). There was a companion Greek volume.

football   Winchester football, or Our Game. For its origins, see **Canvas**. It has this notice in 1838: 'When a game is played between the ropes it is called a "game". Then there is "kicking in" when played between SS and Trees. A "long game" when there is no kicking in, but every boy may play that likes.

At the beginning of the Short Half every Inferior subscribes a shilling which buys two footballs, and pays the man for blowing them and providing bladders. A football costs nine shillings and a man is paid two shillings and sixpence a week for blowing and finding bladders. Inferiors have 2 footballs and Praefects have 2 also. They pay for theirs out of "Subscriptions".'

The notice given c. 1900 reads: 'It is played in Short Half, and begins on the first Monday in October. The fundamental rules of the game are: (1) always kick the ball as hard as possible: dribbling not being permitted. (2) no player may pass to another on his own side. (3) never to touch the ball with the hands, except for saving a goal, for busting, or kicking off after a goal, and (in the case of behinds only) for placing the ball in a convenient position for kicking. (4) a goal, to be counted, must always be a clean shot, i.e. it must not have been kicked . . . from under ropes, not touched either ropes or canvas, or any of the defending side, before passing over worms. (5) the side which loses a goal must have touched the ball at least once beforehand. The position of the twelve players in a fifteen-a-side game is as follows. Firstly, the ups are spread irregularly in two lines across Canvas, or combined for the hot into three lines of three each: supported by the three hot-watchers. Secondly, the three behinds, Second Behind taking one side, Middle Behind the other, some yards to the rear, and Last Behind about the same distance behind him, standing . . . in the middle of the ground. The arrangement is essentially the same for six-a-side games: three men in the hot, one hot-watcher and two behinds.

Owing to the confined dimensions of the ground the game is always interesting, and often highly exciting. Scoring is reasonably frequent. In a good game the number of goals (adding the scores of both sides together) varies from ten to twenty. If lower than that, the game has been slow: if higher, one side has been too strong for the other.'

Since 1922 the method of scoring has been changed.

Football Place   the forerunner of College canvas. In his frontispiece plan of College (1835–40), Mansfield shows it as lying between Turf on the north, and Log Pond and Amen Corner on the south.

Football Rolls   recorded thus in 1868: 'each day during the Winchester football season the Captain of football in Commoners and the next best player made out lists of those whom they would have to play with them in Canvas, and what coloured jerseys they were to wear. The rolls were taken round to the players by a junior, who got off playing football for the morning.'

Ford   (1) where Adam and Eve runs through Double Hedge (1868). (2) a plank over Adam and Eve near Birley's Corner (1892). Both obsolete by 1917.

Forder's Piece   a piece of land south of Kingsgate Park, next to Barn, containing allotment gardens (1917). In 1924 a hard tennis court, Stinks Hut, Cecil Range and all the new Fives Courts were built on it. If asked why it was called Forder's Piece, the correct answer (1920) was: 'because the Headmaster said: "Ah will NOT have it called Forder's Piece".' There was a Henry Forder in College 1702–9 who came from St Cross. His family may have owned it. cf. Dogger's Close.

foreign non-Wykehamist. Used for non-Wiccamical personnel visiting the school. Thus: foreign preacher (not one of our Chaplains or staff); a foreign match (against any outside team); foreign four (the racing boat used by visitors rowing against the school); foreign oars (oars used in that boat).

foricas WC, privy: 'quod omnibus necessarium est'. Also wrongly spelt foricus, cf. vulgus for vulgars. The word is peculiar to Winchester, and in use there since at least 1647; see Mathew's poem: 'pars abit ad foricas, et pars ascendit in aulam'. It may be the accusative case of medieval Latin *foricae*, from Latin *foris* (outside). The following foricas existed in 1920:

Bear's Delight	(in the Headmaster's House)
Co.Fo.	(south of div rooms)
Do.Co.Ro.Fo.	(through Dons' Common Room)
Meads Foricas	(College Mill)
midnighters	(through 12th bidet room)
Old Tent foricas	(at Old Tent)
Olympus	(at Boat Club)
Pawson's Place	(behind Webbe Tent)
Praefects' foricas	(same as Through First)
Through First	(between Ist Chamber and Warden's Garden)

foricas table a table at the bottom of the staircase leading to 6th, 7th, 8th and 9th Chambers. Above it was College Notice Board and an electric light. On it, School Shop boy put all food for Praefects' teas (1920).

form of work a printed form supplied by Wells on which one entered one's weekly timetable of hours up to books, and books-chambers. In use since 1900.

For.Prae. Praefect of Foricas; a facetious title for the senior praefect below the Officers in College. He had no duties. When College Library was made, the 6th senior man became Praefect of College Library, and the 7th was awarded this title as a consolation.

Forster's Corner, or **Foster's Corner** the corner at the end of College Street near Wolvesey Palace: also called Bungy's Corner, from Bryant's house, which used to stand there, Bryant's nickname being Bungy. Recorded from 1880.

Founders see **Founder's Kin**.

Founder's Com and Ob four days in the year, set apart (1831) for commemorating the Founder, and the anniversary of his death. On these days, which were Hatch Thokes, there was Amen chapel, the Fellows and Masters gave a

120

Founder's Kin

dinner in Common Room, and Founders received a sovereign each (1836). By 1892 there were only two commemorations: of the Founder's birth, on the Thursday after the first Tuesday of December, in Sealing Week; of his death, in Cloister Time. (See **Amen chapel**, **Apple-pie Day** and **Hatch Thoke**.) By 1917 the Hatch Thokes still occurred, but their original title and purpose were forgotten.

Founder's Kin, or **Founders**   boys who could prove descent from William of Wykeham['s family] were elected as such, by vote among the Electors. Only two were admitted to College each year, and only two to New College, but they always headed the Roll, whatever their previous position in VIth Book might have been. They lived at the expense of the two Colleges, to which they could be admitted without any other qualification. They added the letters C.F. (*Consanguineus Fundatoris*) after their names on rolls and on marbles. Commonly supposed to have thick skulls: their claim to be Founder's Kin was tested, on their entering College, by banging a trencher on their heads (1836). If the trencher broke, no further proof was needed. Unlike other boys, they were not obliged to leave at the age of 18, but could stay till they were 25: and the tale is told that a smart stroke in a Lord's match was once applauded from the crowd by a child's voice crying: 'Well hit, Daddy.'

It is not known when this nepotism began, but it was abandoned long ago. Descendants of the Founder's family, such as the Twistleton-Wykeham-Fiennes, continue to gain entry to the school in open competition.

four-holed middlings   ordinary walking-shoes (1836).

IVth Book   the form below Vth Book (see books). By 1836 it included all boys below Vth Book except Quiristers (IInd Book). A room called IVth Book was provided for it in 1833 between Walford's and College Praefect's Library, but was later used for mathematics: and in 1868 IVth Book worked under their own master in the room (also called IVth Book, and later 7th Chamber) above Ist Chamber in College.

fragment   a private dinner ordered by the Warden, a Fellow, or a Master (the host not attending) for a boy he knew, who could invite five others to join him. It was cooked in College kitchen and eaten in hall after Middle Hall time, or at

Frampton's Hatch

Evening Hall time. It was supposed to consist of three dishes, the limit imposed by the Founder on the dinner served to the Warden and senior Fellows. Recorded 1831–60; long since (alas) abandoned. The Notion reflects the deprecatory way in which hosts refer to the fare they offer: 'pot-luck' in standard English usually means a robust meal: and Monty Rendall's 'buns and pea-soup' was famous in 1920 [M. J. Rendall, headmaster 1911–24].

Frampton's Hatch   a red-brick hatch on the right bank of New Barge about 200 yards [about 185 m] below Tunbridge, between Tunbridge and Pot, just above the gate of Half-way House. Through it water was drawn off into Water Meads. In 1868 nobody could bathe in Pot until they had swum from Tunbridge to Frampton's Hatch. Recorded from 1831 to 1872; obsolete by 1917. John Frampton of St Michael's, Winchester, was admitted as a scholar in 1652.

Frank's Div. see **div**.

Frank's Div Room, or **the Mushroom**   the southernmost ground-floor div room in the east wing of div rooms, used by Frank's Div (1920). Its outstanding feature was its great height, due to the fact that it and the div room opposite used together to form Commoner Mugging Hall. At one time it was fitted as a science theatre; at another was used by the Mush (q.v.). Its chief ornaments were the back wall (padded, for acoustic reasons), a large cupboard, a table, and roller maps, which vanished into a case on the east wall. The Mush (E. D. A. Morshead, or Doidge) was Don 1872–1903; Frank Carter was Don 1903–22.

frater   from Latin *frater*, brother. A Wykehamist's pitch-up (family) consisted of: pater (father), mater (mother), frater (brother), soror (sister). Nunky (uncle) and nevy (nephew) were obsolete after 1856.

Freddy, the   Frederick Morshead, Don 1868–1905. He and E. D. A. Morshead were probably seventh cousins.

Freddyites   members of E House.

Freddy's   E House, Southgate Road. Original House Don, the Freddy.

Functure

fringe, to sport a   to allow the bottom of one's gown to become tattered: a bad notion (1920).

frog-spawn   a tapioca pudding in College (1920).

frout   vexed, angry, fierce. In use 1831–90; long since obsolete. Hampshire dialect still uses frit, fright, or frout for terrified, and the word may be a lost past participle of fright, originally spelt frought, meaning startled, hence annoyed: or it might be from Anglo-Saxon *froht*, **froht** (terrible, frightened): or again a contraction of froward, an Old English word derived from 'from' and 'ward' (petulant, peevish, perverse).

frow   From Latin *frons* (forehead), hair. Mentioned only in 1838. Probably from Old English *frounce* (to curl or frizzle the hear); so used by Spenser (1589).

frowsy   hairy. Mentioned only in 1838. Derived from frow, above. In standard English, frowzy means unkempt or dirty, especially of dress or hair: and frousty means musty, stuffy. Both may stem from our frow.

frowt   see **frout**.

Functure   (wrongly spelt **Functior**; known since c. 1914 as **Funkey**) an iron bracket candlestick or sconce, fixed in a ring in the wall over the fireplace (half-faggot) in each College Chamber, with a tallow rush-light or dip fixed in a socket in the bracket. Since 1838 it has been the duty of the junior in the Chamber to light Funkey after Evening Chapel (Preces). Originally it was kept burning all night, as a night-light (see **Bloody Hand**) but by 1917, probably as a war economy, it was blown out by the Tolly-keeper, In Loco, or the last man to bed. In 1776 the functure in IIIrd Chamber is called a sconce, but functure was universal by 1831. In 1820–8 it was the responsibility of the Praefect in course to keep it alight.

Funkey, which is a proper name and never has an article, has in the past meant the ring, the bracket, or the rush-light, but in 1917 it meant, as it had in 1820–8, the candle itself. It was long, narrow and tapering, of dark yellow tallow, with a rush as a wick, and burned with a small but steady flame. The term is probably from *fulctura*, an early form of fulture (a prop or stay), from Latin *fulcire* (to prop); or from Old French *fonture*, a casting or article of cast-iron.

Funkey had two eccentricities (1920): (1) a **ben in halo**, or the pungent smell of Funkey burning: or when it had burned right down and the oil burned on in the socket, giving out a glow. The spelling is uncertain: perhaps Benin halo, or ben-and-hale-o, from the shop of Ben & Hale, said to have stood in Kingsgate Street where Bicycle Shop now is, which had a similar smell. (2) a **thief**: when a bit of burning wick fell down the side of Funkey and carved away a scar, so that Funkey burned away quickly. So used in standard English in 1642, and still used in dialect. The French *suif* (tallow) was sometimes used for a drip down the side of a candle.

Fundator   a speech 'in honorem Fundatoris' delivered formerly on 21 December, and afterwards in School on the Tuesday in Election Week. In 1615 Dame Lettice Williams gave £200 to ensure the continuation of this. It was spoken by the senior Founder's Kin till 1864, when H. L. Cripps was the first non-C.F. to deliver it. Long since obsolete.

Fungy Brown   the nickname in 1820–8 of Mr Brown, writing master, who sat at a low desk in School. He never taught writing, but used to mend pens and add up the marks in the classicus paper. Probably from Latin *fungi* (to perform).

funk   fear (noun and verb). Standard slang, but recorded as a Notion 1838–84.

Funkey   see **Functure**.

Funkey bracket   the round iron bracket in which Funkey was fixed (1920).

Funkey grease   the tallow of which Funkey was made: an obnoxious substance. (See **hot roll**.)

funkster   one who is afraid. In use 1868; the slang 'funk' with the Wiccamical termination.

furk   see **firk**.

Furley's   A House, Chernocke House: the first house to be opened (1859). It was originally in St Thomas Street, later becoming Ludford's boarding house, and its fives court was still standing in the back yard in 1920. The present house is in the north-west corner of Kingsgate Park. Its first Housemaster was Rev. H. J. Wickham (1859–88), known as the Beetle, and men in the house were called Beetles or Beetleites. For some reason its present name is that of its third House Don, J. S. Furley (1894–1909).

G, the in Chamber Court, a mysterious G carved back to front in the middle of one of the flagstones in Middle Sands. Some theories advanced to explain it were: (1) that it is where Warden Golding (1757–63), who died suddenly in Chamber Court on 25 November 1763, fell. (2) that it is where King George V stood Ad Portas in 1910. (3) that it stands for gas. (4) that it is one of a batch of gravestones which, as Herbert Chitty the Bursar used to say (1920), had been bought wholesale by College from Cathedral churchyard at intervals as paving stone (there is a fragment of a seventeenth-century tombstone below the window of IInd Chamber). None of these theories explains why the G is so deeply incised, why there is no sign of letters before or after it, and why it is back to front. Was it, for example, a mould used in a brick-works?

Gaffer, the the nickname of Dr David Williams, Headmaster 1824–36. Gaffer is a rustic contraction for grandfather, used in the countryside as a term of respect for a man of advanced age or rural habits. The boys probably called Williams the Gaffer because he used to ride out on a white or grey horse towards Hills, intercept the school column returning therefrom, and have names called. [More straightforwardly, gaffer = boss.]

gags an exercise introduced by Dr Gabell (Headmaster 1810–23) of criticisms of some celebrated poem, written in Latin in a book by VIth Book and Senior Part (1831); of comments on some Greek or Latin author (1836); or of notes taken from Greek plays. Below Senior Part, gags were an analysis of some historical episode, written in English (1831–43). Sent in about once a month (1831), eight times a year (1836), or weekly in the case of history gags (1838), or read out to the master by the united divisions, by 1850 they had been abandoned.

Said to be an abbreviation of gatherings, a term used by bookbinders for the collection in proper order of the sections or leaves of a book for binding. At New College in 1922 a similar word, 'Collections', was used for periodical exams held by College Tutors. Gag is also standard stage slang for interpolation of one's own words into a set part, being derived from some old onomatopoeia like gaggle or cackle, meaning to choke, stutter, or falter.

gain a year, to a boy who was not Founder's Kin had to leave the school at the Election following his eighteenth birthday; if his birthday fell shortly after

Election, he could stay till he was almost 19, thus 'gaining a year'. Used thus 1836; long since obsolete.

gallery   a Commoner dormitory. Taken from the tradition of galleries in Old Commoners. In New Commoners (1842–69) the galleries were six long passages, each leading to three, four, or five bedrooms. They were named: Upper and Lower Cloisters; North Gallery; East and West Halls; and Linen Gallery. Senior Tutor's rooms were in North Gallery. Junior Tutor's bedroom was by East Hall and Hag's rooms, Lower Continent Room, etc., were in Linen Gallery. When houses were built, dormitories were automatically called galleries. In some houses they were divided into cubicles. 'Round galleries' meant 'in the dormitories'.

gallery nymph   a housemaid in Commoners (1892).

gallery sweat   (1) in New Commoners (1842–69), each Praefect had: (a) a valet, who brought him warm water in cold weather and took down any books he happened to have upstairs. He generally came about Half-Hour every morning, and again at Gates. (b) a clothes-brusher, who brushed his Praefect's clothes every morning; he also came about Half-Hour. (c) a water-carrier, who brought his Praefect a jug of cold water every Sunday morning, the Praefect having used his in his toe-pan the night before; he also came about Half-Hour. When a fellow was continent, the junior in the gallery without sweat had to do his sweat for him. (2) in Commoner houses (1892), gallery sweat consisted of peals-calling and clothes-keeping, duties performed by the First or Second Junior of the gallery. Each Praefect also had a valet, to take books up and down stairs and to get hot water.

gallery sweat roll   in New Commoners (1842–69), a roll of each fellow's gallery sweat made at the beginning of each term.

galvanise, to   used metaphorically in English to mean 'imparting a semblance of life to', galvanising (the surfacing of metals by galvanic electricity) had two special meanings: (1) to stick a knife or pin into somebody (1838). This was organised into a practical joke in Commoners. A hole was bored in the seat of A's toys, and a needle fixed therein in such a manner that when B pulled a string, the needle passed upwards through the seat and baker into A. Long since obsolete. (2) (of the skipper of College VI) to make a point of rebuking a certain player throughout one canvas for idleness, oiling or other faults.

Games   anyone not playing in College, Commoner or Houses canvas was organised into Games for Winchester Football. In Commoners and Houses there were Middle Games A and B, and Junior Game. In College, on account of smaller numbers, there was only Junior Game. Games went on till the end of XVs week.

Ganymede   the junior VI Book Inferior in an upstairs College Chamber (1920). His functions were: (1) to brew cocoa, mix lime-juice, etc., for Praefects up in Chambers at night. (2) to refill Chamber Can for Praefects if it was empty by the time they wanted to wash. (3) to switch off all electric lights in the Chamber after Joel had turned off the main at 9.30 p.m. (as he turned it on again early in the morning). (4) to superintend distribution of cake or food sported by any member of the Chamber up in chambers. In Greek mythology Ganymedes became cup-bearer to the Gods in place of Hebe.

Garden Gate   the gate of the garden of Half-way House, down River, just below Willow.

Gards   the shop of Albert Gard, successor to R. H. Northall as 'Tailor to the Commoners of Winchester College' (cf. Stanley). It was next to Toye's in Kingsgate Street and had two large bow windows.

Gaspar, Melchior and Balthasar   three goldfish in the pond in Monty Fiasco (q.v.); see **Adam, Eve and Pinch-me**. These were the Kings of Orient in the nativity legend.

Gate   The following gates are listed: (1) in College (1838): (a) Commoner College Gate, between Moab and New School: leading from School Court into Commoners. (b) Commoner Gate, leading from Commoners into College. (c) Middle Gate, between Quadrangle and Outer Court. (d) Non-Licet Gate, near Mill and Cloisters. (e) Outer Gate: the first gate as one enters College. (f) Seventh Chamber Passage Gate, leading from Quadrangle Court into School Court. (2) in Old Commoners (1742–1842): (a) Blue Gate, at the back of Commoners, through which Commoners came into School. (b) Gate, Commoner Gate and other gates. (3) in New Commoners (1842–69): (a) an iron gate on the stairs at the end of Lower Cloisters. (b) a smaller gate opposite (a), leading into Linen Gallery. (c) New Gate, by the foot of Cloister stairs before Hatch.

'Gate!'   (1) in New Commoners, if a boy wanted to see someone who was continent, he backed up 'Gate!', and the other boy's name; if he wanted to get anything out of Linen Gallery, he backed up 'Gallery nymph'. (2) on the arrival of the evening post in College, c. 8.15, College Porter used to stand with it under Middle Gate and call 'Gate!' Originally this was done every night, but Johnny Bishop, Head Porter c. 1920, seldom did it. On hearing 'Gate!' the Second Junior in course in each Chamber went out to receive letters and parcels addressed to men in his Chamber and delivered them.

gated   confined within College gates. An Oxford term, this was recorded in 1831 and 1892; long since obsolete.

gate-locking   at the end of leave-out day the Steward, or some sweater in New Commoners (1842–69), used to back up 'Gate-locking!', which was passed on from mouth to mouth till it reached Commoner Field. Anyone who came from leave-out after Gate was locked had to come through College or the Headmaster's house.

gater   (1) a leap head-foremost over one of the projecting handles of Pot Gate (the canal lock-gate) into Pot (1831–6). (2) a jump head-first over a gate or hurdle placed by the side of any deep part of the river, so that a boy comes head-first into the river (1838).

gates   VIIth Chamber Passage gate. When the boys were assembled in Seventh Chamber Passage, preparatory to going on Hills or to Cathedral, they were said to be 'at gates'. Shortly before time to assemble a junior went round Chambers calling 'Gates!' (1836–8). In 1892, when men assembled at this gate before entering Chapel, it was still called Gates. Obsolete by 1917.

'Gates!'   (1) see **gates**, above. (2) the call in New Commoners when Chapel bells went single (see **Peal**).

gatherings   see **gags**.

Gattrell's, also called **Hollis's** (q.v.)   a house in Watermeads near College Mill, outside Non-Licet Gate. In use 1868–92; obsolete by 1914.

G.B.   the ginger-beer served in jugs in College Hall as a substitute for beer, the original drink of College, until 1916, when it was stopped as a wartime economy.

G.C.B.   see **bidet roll**.

genealogies   genealogical tables of Paters and Sons in College. Many men made a copy of the family tree to which they belonged. In 1922 all extant genealogies were collected, but it is not known what became of them.

General Books   the first or last twelve books of the Iliad or Odyssey, and the Georgics or Horace's Odes, prepared during Cloister Time for one of the papers in Goddard. Translation only was required (1920).

genuine   praise; an abbreviation for 'genuine praise', or perhaps '*laus genuina*'. In use 1831, usually with 'immense', and in reference to a comment by a master; e.g. 'He got immense genuine from the Doctor.' From 1850 it was also used as a verb (cf. to blackguard, to lord). Quoted 1892; obsolete by 1914. See also **tight genuine**.

German Room   between Junior Tutor's Room and New Gate in New Commoners: used for mathematics (1868).

Goal

getting off, getting off to New   a boy is said to get off when he succeeds in passing off to New College, Oxford (1838).

ginger bather   a ginger basin-pudding in College (1920); see **Bather** and **dean**.

gips   the focus. Recorded 1838 only, with an aetiological derivation from a boy named Gips, who was so short-sighted that he took a long time to focus on the paper before he started writing. There is no such name in the school lists, and the notion is really an elaborate play on words. The Latin for hearth is *focus*, hence the focus in optics. The stone used for whitening hearths, or hearth-stone, was *gypsum*, a Latin word from Greek γύψος. Hence gips.

glope, or **globe, to**   to spit. In use 1836–84: then disused. From Old English **glub** (swallow greedily, gulp): thus 'gloppyng of drynk' in Piers Plowman's 'Crede' (c. 1394). It also survives in dialect as gloup (gulp, swallow), from Norwegian *glupa* (swallow).

Glory Hole   a small room in Sick House at the top of the second flight of stairs, with a sloping ceiling as it is up in the rafters. Usually it was a maid's bedroom, but was used for one patient if Sick House was very full (1920).

goal   (1) a boy standing at the centre of either end between two gowns rolled up at his feet, in a line with the end of ropes, and in the middle of 'football place' (i.e. between the ropes), was called 'the goal'. The object was to get the ball past him without his touching it; and he was umpire or referee of whether this had occurred, and if so in what manner. If the ball crossed the line on either side of him and he had not touched it, it counted as a 'pass'. If it passed over either gown, also untouched, it was a 'gowner', equal to two passes. If it went over his head or between his legs, also untouched, it was a 'goal', equal to three passes (1836–8). (2) a goal scored, and assessed as above (1836–8). The manner of play and scoring has changed several times since.

Go.Bo.   the Governing Body, comprising the Warden, Fellows, Head and Second Masters, Bursar and other distinguished men. They dined on High Table in Hall about twice a half, the Warden presiding. On the same morning the Aul.Prae. was wont to put up a notice in these time-honoured words: 'The

Warden and Fellows will be lunching in Hall today. Men will therefore be dressed accordingly' (i.e. clean collar, face and hands) (1920).

go down   (1) about ten minutes after 'Down' in Morning Hall, Praefect of Hall called 'Go down!', whereupon Deputy sent out of Hall all Inferiors who were not fagging (1838). (2) the school goes down (breaks up) at the end of the half.

gobbets   a roly-poly pudding cut in slices and covered with treacle: a favourite dean in College (1920). The name was inspired by a ballad rendering of the Cyclops' indigestion in the Odyssey, after eating too many hunks of meat.

Goddard   the Goddard Scholarship examination, founded in 1846 in memory of Dr W. S. Goddard (Headmaster 1793–1809) who died in 1845. it was Senior Div's examinations at the end of each Cloister Time. The papers were on all books-lessons done during the half: General Books; Divina; History; and a General Paper. Senior man on Goddard Roll received a sum of money, (£25 p.a. for four years in 1868), and every fourth year £5 was added to Goddard from the Pitt Scholarship Fund. No man might raise Goddard more than once.
   Goddard was of vital importance to most men in Senior Div (1920): to men leaving, because the first four men on Goddard roll were usually awarded the four School Exhibitions; to men staying on, because it decided Officers and Praefects for the ensuing year. Consequently a very great deal of work was done for Goddard.

Godfrey block, or **Godder block**   a writing block of plain unruled paper. Named after Mr C. Godfrey, senior Mathematical master 1899–1905 [co-author of well-known mathematical textbooks ('Godfrey and Siddons')].

God's bench   the two desks, occupied by the two senior members of the div (one generally the Aul.Prae.), on the Headmaster's right as he sat up to books in Senior Div Classroom (1920). Formed by analogy from Monty Rendall's 'front bench', 'back bench', etc., for the rows of desks in Senior Div.

Goldfinch, or **Goldfinch's**, or **Goldfinches**   The identity and derivation are uncertain, but on no account to be confused with Greenfinches and Bullfinches. Two possible sites are: (1) a house of flint and red brick in Water Meads (1880) (perhaps as early as 1868?). (2) a mill in Water Meads beyond St Cross near Second Pot (1917).

golf links   the school Golf Club had a private course (1900) on the hills beyond Half-Mile Road, along the Southampton Road. By 1920 the Club was extinct, but golfers used the Hockley Course (q.v.).

Golf Links Hill   the hill on Southampton Road which led up to the school golf links.

gomer a word with an intriguing pedigree. (1) a large pewter dish used in College for meat and potatoes. In a 1778 inventory of utensils in Hall and Kitchen we find, among the dishes and brass pots, 24 gomers. In 1820–8 the Oll.Prae. used to march into Hall followed by four Queristers each carrying a gomer of dispers, and take them round to the various tables. It probably comes from the hebrew measure *khomer* (also spelt *homer*, *chomer* and *gomer*: and meaning a mound). As a measure of wine the homer was 75 gallons 5 pints [about 344 l]; or as a dry measure, 10 ephahs or 11.1 bushels [about 23,900 cubic inches or 391,650 cubic cm]. It appears in the Vulgate (AD 400) as *gomor*. John Bradford (1510–55) wrote: 'fill up our gomers daily'; and Donne (1610–31) uses *gomer* for a measure of solids. The size of the original Hebrew measure must have been lost sight of, and the word used to mean a container of reasonable calibre. (2) when it first appeared, a beaver hat was called a gomer hat, probably because its brim resembled a gomer dish: cf. the porringer hat of Shakespeare, and the later chimney-pot hat. In Old Commoners it came to mean the type of hat worn when going home, and one of the end-of-term peals was 'Gomer hats' or 'Gomers and hats'. This led to the idea that Gomer meant Go-home-er. (3) in consequence, the suits which College boys wore instead of gowns to go home in were called gomers by 1868, and still so called in 1920.

Goodchild a chamberman on 8th Chamber staircase in College c. 1917; succeeded by Nutley. He was famous for having raised a leaving subscription for himself and then not left.

Good Friday Passage the passage which formerly led from Flint Court to School Court, between Moab and College Praefects' Library. It vanished in 1871, and the name was transferred to the passage leading from School Court to Ball Court, between School and Cloisters, though this should really be called Pseudo-Good Friday Passage (q.v.). For derivation, see **Good Friday Prose**.

Good Friday Prose a discourse formerly delivered by the Headmaster in School on Good Friday, reviewing the school's progress during past months. Later, it was given on the last day of the half. Men used to assemble in Good Friday Passage and wait there until the Headmaster had passed through into School. The passage is named after this custom.

goodgodster a brown bowler hat. From the exclamation necessarily uttered by anyone seeing so strange a thing (1920).

Good Resolutions, or **Paths of Good Intent**, or **Paths to Destruction** the narrow lines of stone sets which lead diagonally from the corners of the cobbled areas in Chamber Court, to Hell (q.v.) in the middle. In use 1916. As is known, the path to hell is paved with good intentions.

go on, to (up to books) to be put on to translate.

go over, to   to prepare a books-lesson or other mugging with another man in his toys, in books-chambers or Toy-time, in College (1920). If the other man was in the same Chamber, one asked the Praefect in course: 'May I go over with Smith?' If he was in another Chamber, one did not mention his name, but asked: 'May I go over in Fifth?'

gosh, to   to spit. In use 1856; obsolete by 1892. From the onomatopoeic words goush, gowshe, dialect forms of gush, which is from Old Dutch *guysen* (to flow out with a gurgling noise).

gown   (1) the gown worn by all College men. (2) thick, coarse brown paper. In use 1831–92; obsolete by 1917. Perhaps so named because its texture resembled the broadcloth of which a gown is made.

gown-cupboard   there was one in each upstairs Chamber in College, near the door. One partition was reserved for Praefects' gowns; beneath it was a partition for dirty clothes (1920).

gowner   in a primitive form of football played in College (1831–42), Goal (the goal-keeper) stood on worms, with legs outstretched, between two gowns rolled up at his feet. When the opponents kicked the ball over one of the gowns without Goal touching it, it was called a gowner and scored two points. When the ball was kicked over worms outside the gowns it was called a schitt and scored one point. When it passed between Goal's legs it was called a goal and scored three points.

Grace, gratiarum actio   the following graces were used at Middle Hall or dinner in the period 1820–40.
   (1) *In ordinary time* there was grace before and after the meal. (a) Before dinner the Praefect of Hall said the 'ante cibum' grace, viz:

> Benedic nobis, Domine Deus, atque iis donis tuis quae de tua largitate
> sumus sumpturi. Per Iesum Christum Dominum nostrum. [Response:]
> Amen.

(b) After dinner the 'post cibum' was sung by seven boys chosen each half by the Praefect of Hall, viz:

> Agimus tibi gratias, Omnipotens Deus, pro his et universis donis tuis
> quae de tua largitate accepimus. Qui vivis et regnas, et es Deus, in
> saecula saeculorum. [Response:] Amen.

This was followed by the hymn 'Te de profundis, summe Rex', which was a metrical version of Psalm 130 ('Out of the deep'), probably written for College, and set to the tune 'Bishop' by J. Bishop (1665–1737). The words were the same as in the 1910 Hymnarium no. 77, except for minor variations.
   (2) *In Easter Time* the hymn 'Iam lucis orto sidere', dating from the fifth

century, set to another tune 'Bishop' by the same J. Bishop, was sung, taking the place of 'Te de profundis'.

(3) *In Election Week* the two best singers in College, a treble and a bass, sang graces harmonised by John Reading (1686–92): (a) the 'ante cibum', as above, was sung on one note up to 'Christum', and the 'Dominum nostrum. Amen' in harmony. (b) the 'post cibum' grace was a set of canticles for one voice, and responses in harmony for four voices:

Benedictus sit Deus in donis suis,
   R. et sanctus in omnibus operibus eius.
Adiutorium nostrum est in nomine Domini,
   R. qui fecit caelum et terram.
Sit nomen Domini benedictum,
   R. et hoc nunc usque in saecula saeculorum. Amen.

This was followed by the canticle of thanks for the Founder:

Agimus tibi gratias, Omnipotens Deus, pro Fundatore nostro Gulielmo
de Wykeham, reliquisque, quorum beneficiis his ad pietatem et studia
literarum alimur: rogantes ut nos, his donis tuis and nominis tui honorem
recte utentes, ad resurrectionis tuae gloriam perducamur immortalem. Per
Iesum Christum . . . [breaking into harmony] Dominum nostrum. Amen.

This canticle was followed by an anthem for four voices:

fac Reginam salvam, Domine:
da pacem in diebus nostris,
et exaudi nos in die quocunque,
   invocamus te. Amen.

In 1920 the 'ante cibum' and 'post cibum' graces were said at lunch every day in College Hall by the Aul.Prae. or the next senior man present, standing on Dais beside the Second Master. Before the next 'ante cibum' the Aul.Prae. called all men to their feet with 'Surgite!' (pronounced with a soft g). Similar graces were said at lunch in each house by a Praefect.

'Sung Grace' was the 'post cibum' above, sung on one note and breaking into harmony at the end: followed by 'Te de profundis'. In 1892 this was sung every Sunday after lunch, but by 1917 on one or two Sundays only each half, by a chosen choir of College men, and only the first and last verses of 'te de profundis' were sung. When the meal was over, Aul.Prae. rose and called 'Grace!', whereupon the choir took position in the middle of Dais facing Simon and Jude, with all the occupants of Senior and Middle Ends grouped on their left, and Junior End on their right. The Second Master stood in front of the carving table, with Aul.Prae. beside him, and Praefects between them and Screen. Grace was then sung.

At Domum Dinner (c. 1920), the Election Week Grace was sung by a chosen choir standing in the body of Hall. It was introduced by the Warden rising, banging on the table with a knife-handle, and calling 'Grace!'.

Grace   Margaret Grace Stewart, wife of Rev. A. T. P. Williams, Second Master. He once delighted the congregation (1920) in a sermon by saying: 'We can none of us get on without grace.'

Grace Place   another name for Dais in College Hall (1892), where graces and 'Domum' were sung; obsolete by 1917.

Grass Court   a court in New Commoners where football was played. It led into Meads, from which it was divided by a wall. On one side of it were Fives Courts, and on the other Walford's.

Gravel Court   see **Moberly Court**.

greaser   rubbing a boy's head with the knuckles, a mode of torture practised in College (1836); long since obsolete.

Greenfinches   probably a farm in the St Cross area (1920). cf. Goldfinches.

'Green Grow the Rushes'   a song sung at Officers Training Corps camp or on march-outs, with a good marching tune (1920). It is a folksong, of the cumulative type, like 'The house that Jack built', and seems to refer to some astronomical system. It is known in several versions outside Winchester. The words we used were:

> I'll sing you one, O; green grow the rushes, O.
>   What is your one O?
> One is one and all alone, and ever more shall be so.
>
> I'll sing you two, O [etc.]
> Two, two for the lilywhite boys, clothed all in green, O;
> One is one [etc.]
>
> Three, three, the rivals (or rifles):
> Four for the gospel-makers:
> Five for the cymbals at your door:
> Six for the six proud walkers:
> Seven for the seven stars in the sky:
> Eight for the eight bold rainers [or rangers: April rainers]
> Nine for the nine bright shiners:
> Ten for the ten commandments:
> Eleven for the eleven went up to heaven:
> Twelve for the twelve apostles.

greyers   grey flannel trousers, worn for fives, crockets, expedis, etc.; but might not be worn up to books (1920).

Gripe's Hole   a hole about 6 feet [1.8 m] deep in Water Meads behind Boat-house where the water was very cold, and well known as a thirst-quencher. Used from 1880; obsolete by 1914. Probably from the Old English *gripe* (trench, drain), used in the form gripple (1440), from Anglo-Saxon *greop* (ditch, channel); or from gripes (intestinal cramp), used by Purchas (1613), which is from Anglo-Saxon *gripe* (grasp), and also gives the dialect gripe (pitchfork) and gripe (small boat) used by Hakluyt (1589).

Grotius Time   the period 7–7.45 on Sunday evenings in Cloister Time when VIth Book and Senior Part (1836) (in 1838, Praefects), were up to books in School to translate 'De veritate religionis Christianae' by Hugo Grotius (1627). By 1838 they did Greek Testament instead. Long since obsolete.

ground-ash   a young ash sapling. Used by College Praefects for beating since 1836. Originally obtained from Hell (q.v.), but by 1917 from Simons' shop. A Praefect who had to give a beating raised ground-ashes from the Aul.Prae., who kept them standing in a pot in his place, whither they were returned by the culprit (1920). Ground-ash is provincial English for an ash sapling of a few years' growth.

groyse   grease of any kind, especially brilliantine (1920). Of a person, **groysy** meant mean or insinuating, like the slang 'oily'.

grub   food. So used in *Tom Brown's School Days* (c. 1835). Standard slang for food, as the product of grubbing or hard work.

Grubbing Hall   (1) the dining hall in new Commoners (1842–69), on the ground floor on the west of Flint Court; converted to classrooms 5 and 6. (2) the dining hall in each house.

grubster   one who eats, or who eats too much: a glutton.

Gundry's Hole   a cupboard in School above the scob of the Praefect of Hall (or School), from which the gas used to be turned on (1892). By 1920 the name had been transferred to a small door in the east wall of School, giving access to a stairway to the concert platform. Possibly from F. W. Gundry (Comm. 1839–?43): or J. P. F. Gundry (Comm. 1850–6).

Gunner's Hole   the school bathing-place, first used in 1872. It was a section of Old Barge, fenced off, between Non-Licet Gate and Boat House: greatly improved at Dr. Fearon's expense in 1900. Donated by Rev. W. H. Gunner (Coll. 1824–30), Chaplain to the school 1839–59, who lived at Blackbridge House.

Gurdler   an old bricklayer who had (1838) been in the service of College for a very long time. He and Long John (q.v.) were working on Ball Court one day,

136

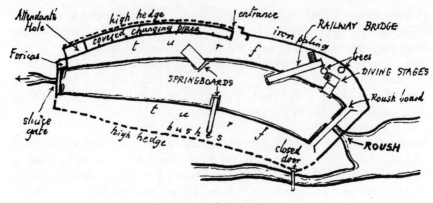

Gunner's Hole (1917)

when a boy asked Long John what he was doing. 'Nothing, Sir,' was the answer. the boy then asked Gurdler what he was doing. 'Helping Long John,' he replied. It was also related that when there was no work to be done about College, Gurdler used to break the tiles on Cloisters so that Long John could go up and mend them. The writer concludes: 'Men like working in College because the boys give them beer, bread, cheese, beef, potatoes, meat &c'.

gutter   a dive in which the performer falls flat on the water instead of going in head-first. In use 1836–92; now obsolete. In standard English a gutter is a man who guts fish; our use of the word implies that such a dive hurts the stomach: standard slang is 'belly-flopper'.

Gymna (pronounced Gymnā)   Gymnasium. It adjoins racquets courts. When the foundations were being dug a stone coffin was discovered, and put in Cloisters.

Hag an unkind Commoner notion for the house Matron. The original hag, in New Commoners (1842–69), was Mrs Thompson.

half a school term, of which there were originally only two in each year, Short Half (September to December), and Long Half (February to July). The six weeks of Long Half between 15 March and 30 April were known as Easter Time, the remainder of Long Half being called Cloister Time, and in the third week of it there was the Whitsun recess. After 1867 Long Half ceased, having for some time been divided into two terms by the lengthening of the Easter holidays to three weeks.

The result was that the school year was composed of three terms, or 'halves'. Short Half, the autumn term, which begins the school year; the January to March term, or Easter term, which took on the name Common Time (which originally meant Short Half and the first six weeks of Long Half); and Cloister Time (the summer term). The Christmas holidays and Easter holidays are four weeks each, and the summer holidays eight weeks, with twelve-week terms between each.

half-baker a small cushion. Commoner Notion c. 1900.

half-faggot the stone slab in front of the fireplace in a College Chamber, upstairs or down. Formerly it meant the fireplace itself, faggot signifying the hearth where long faggots were burned. Half-faggot suggests the small fire-baskets (for coal fires), which gradually superseded the fire-dogs (for long faggots) and which could take only a short faggot. In 1892 the only coal fire was in VIIth Chamber. By 1917 faggots survived only in Ist and IVth Chambers, and were discontinued soon after.

'Half-Hour!' see **Peal**.

Half-Mile Road, or **Half-Milers** a road leading from the Southampton Road across the Itchen valley to the Portsmouth Road: and the name of the unending toll that followed it.

half-vessel half of a vessel (q.v.), i.e. one-sixteenth of a piece of Long Paper. A stock of half-vessels had to be kept by the First Junior in a College Chamber,

College Dining Hall

as it was the only size and type of paper which might be used by Inferiors for 'veniam exeundi petit' rolls during Books Chambers or Toy-time (1920).

Half-way House   (1) 'a low house near Second Pot' (1892). (2) a house supposed to be half-way between Pot (i.e. First Pot) and Tunbridge (1868), or between Pot and Birley's Corner (1880) on River. Here lived 'Pot Cad' (1868). It was out of bounds (1900). The notion was still used by oarsmen (1920) for some building or other.

Hall   (1) College Dining Hall was a large, high room, 'and beautiful' (1838), measuring 63 by 30 feet [19.2 by 9.1 m] in length and breadth, over VIIth Chamber. Approached by a wide flight of stairs south of Trusty Sweater's Hole, it is of noble dimensions, with an open oak roof, and is lighted by five tall, double-light windows. Archbishop Warham's tapestry has gone, but the Elizabethan panelling remains. In the centre stands the stove named Simon and Jude, which superseded the original brazier. At the east end is Dais, with a portrait of the Founder above it. Various other Wiccamical portraits, which hung above Dais and on the north and south walls, have been moved to the Warden's gallery. Three large tapestries that hung high on the west wall (1920) were later moved to School. At the west end is a screen with three servery hatches behind. In front of Screen is Tub, originally used for the reception of broken meats for the poor. In 1836 the three tables on the north side of Hall were allotted to Praefects, and called Tub, Middle and Junior Mess. Those on the south had a Candle-keeper at each end, and were called Senior, Second, Middle and Junior End.

  In 1838 three meals were served in Hall: (a) Morning Hall (breakfast): obtainable at any time between 8.30 and 9.15, when VIIth Chamber Passage gate was locked. College servants stood at the hatches and gave out to each boy a small loaf and a pennyworth of butter. La Croix provided 1 pint [568 ml] of tea per head, paid for by College. Previously boys had had to buy it at Sick House at fourpence a pint. (b) Middle Hall (dinner): at 1.15 to 1.35, broiled or roast mutton being served every day except Wednesday, when there was beef. There were potatoes, and occasionally greens and carrots. Each boy also had cheese and a quarter of a small loaf. On Friday and Saturday there were baked plum puddings, 'but they are not eatable. We can have as much beer as we like, but it is not very good or strong, as unfortunately for us the brewer keeps pigs.' A Tutor walked about Hall throughout the meal. (c) Evening Hall (supper): from 6 to 7. On Sunday, Tuesday, Thursday and Saturday there was cold roast beef, and bread and cheese on the other days. Unlimited beer was again available. When 'Down' was called, all except Praefects and Candle-keepers had to leave hall. 'Some of the boys smoke &c up there.'

(2) The name was also used for the midday meal in Hall.

(3) It was also a Commoner notion for Mugging Hall.

Hall Writer   the Praefect of Hall's writer: like all writers, a man in his second year. His main duties (1920) were: (1) taking namers-board to the Aul.Prae. or next senior man present and standing behind him as he read it, and taking back the board when namers was over. Copies of College Roll could be obtained from him. (2) collecting subscrippers; and getting particulars of journey dibs required, and destinations, at the end of the half. (3) batters courts on Ball Court were raised from him in Common Time.

halo, to sport a   to have one's hat tilted like a halo so that hair was showing in front: a bad notion for everybody (1920).

Hammond's Mill   near Waterman's Hut; formerly owned by J. Hammond. Long since vanished.

hand up   (1) to give up a thing (1838). Obsolete by 1917. (2) to throw back a ball to anyone who has hit it near you (1838). Obsolete by 1917. (3) to give information against, to report an offender to a Praefect or master (1856); from the idea of propelling an offender by the hand to authority. Still in use 1920.

hard up   in standard slang, means only short of money, but for us had two special uses: (1) exhausted in swimming. In use 1856–92; obsolete by 1917. It probably meant at the end of one's physical resources; at a loss what to do. (2) embarrassed, shy. In use 1856–1920. This probably meant short of small talk, at a loss for what to say.

Hardy Tower   Middle gate: also called Fang Tower. From H. J. Hardy (Coll. 1874–9: Don 1883–1921: College Tutor 1884–1900), who had rooms there.

harlequin   (1) the wooden nucleus of a red india-rubber ball (1856–1914). Obsolete by 1917. (2) a ball used for cricket in yard: a Commoner Notion 1914.

The derivation is not obvious, unless used because harlequin in pantomime is invisible to Clown and Pantaloon.

hatch, hatches   basically, a half-door or wicket-gate, from the Anglo-Saxon *haec*. (1) a sluice or flood-gates in Water Meads (1838–1900). Hatches (1838) meant Water Meadows in general. Hatch (1868) was a particular hatch between Birley's Corner and New Bridge, used as a bathing place. In standard English hatch means a sluice-gate, and heck or hext appears for a grating in front of a sluice-gate; in dialect it can also mean a garden gate. (2) buttery hatches opening off the west end of College Hall, where trenchers, bread, cheese and butter were given out (1838). The term was used by Ben Jonson (c. 1610). In 1916–22 they were named after the College butlers of the time: they all had half-doors. The southernmost one (Underwood's Hatch) contained a sink and the salt-cellars from all the tables; from it a stair led down to Cellar, and there was also a door that led through to the middle hatch, called Hatch (*par excellence*) or Chandler's Hatch. It contained a bread-bin and bread-cutting machine and, near the entrance, the shelves on which jams and other food belonging to individual boys were 'set up' (q.v.). Cargoes were kept there. A tiny room leading off to the west contained the safe where College Plate was kept, and Chandler's writing-desk and account books. The northernmost (Meacher's Hatch) contained two large sinks, and the urns in which tea and cocoa were made. In Mansfield's day (1836) the three hatches were: Whiteman's Hatch, for trenchers, knives and forks; Dear's Hatch, for bread and cheese; Colson's Hatch, for beer, butter and salt. (3) a similar hatch opening into New Commoners Grubbing Hall (1868). (4) from (3), Hatch was applied to the whole suite of Steward's rooms in New Commoners.

Hatch Thoke   a day of Commemoration of the Founder. So called from the custom of staying in bed till breakfast, which was provided at Hatch. There used to be five Hatch Thokes, one Founder's Com every quarter, and the Founder's Ob. By 1868 there were two in Short Half and three in Long Half. By 1892 there were two only, the Saturday following the July meeting of the Go.Bo., and the Thursday after the first Tuesday in December.

In New Commoners boys did not have to be down in Hall till 9, and Amen chapel was at 11. In 1880 Hatch Thoke was a whole rem with no leave-out: Chapel was not till 11, and one could stay in bed till then. In 1892 Chapel on a Hatch Thoke was at 9 in summer and 10 in winter. By 1917 the reason for Hatch Thokes was forgotten and they had become leave-out days. See also **thoke**.

Hat Place   the passage leading from Moberly Court into Flint Court. So called from the depositing there of hats at some stage in the past; this was no longer done in 1917.

Haunted Room   the room in North Gallery nearest East Hall in New Commoners (1842–69), corresponding roughly to the room opening off Mr W. B. Croft's classroom (1892). So called from the curious shadows cast by an old tree outside whenever there was moonlight. A man is also said to have died there.

have the Chamber, to   before giving a beating, a Praefect requested the men in the Chamber to go out, with the words: 'May I have the Chamber, please?' (1920).

haves (pronounced hāves) (for halves)   half-Wellington boots. These were strictly non-licet. Recorded 1831–92; obsolete by 1914. In medieval English, we find haef, hafe (half), and haeves (halves); and in Cheshire dialect, hafers (half of any treasure-trove).

headless corpses, or **headlessers**   a breakfast dish of fresh herrings, served once a week in College Hall (1920): poorly cooked and seldom eaten.

Headmaster, Head Man, or **H.M.**   Headmasters from 1724 to 1954 were:

Dr J. Burton	1724–66
Dr J. Warton	1766–93
Dr W. S. Goddard	1793–1809
Dr H. D. Gabell	1809–23
Dr D. Williams	1824–35
Dr G. Moberly	1836–66
Dr G. Ridding	1867–84
Dr W. A. Fearon	1884–1901
Dr H. M. Burge	1901–11
Dr M. J. Rendall	1911–24
Dr A. T. P. Williams	1924–34
Dr S. S. G. Leeson	1935–46
Dr W. F. Oakeshott	1946–54.

Dr Rendall (old Harrovian, Second Master 1899–1911; awarded doctorate by Toronto University 1921), Headmaster 1911–24, was also known as Monty, and as Push, an exclamation he used (a form of pish, used by Middleton in 1608), meaning 'bother'.

heads down   at the start of every hot in XVs and VIs, the three front-row men in the hot on each side were standing upright: when the whistle blew for the hot to begin, they put their heads down – a painful business. In 1921 this was changed, and hots started with heads down.

heart-to-hearters   a confidential talk (1920).

Heathcote   a prize of 30 guineas [£31 10*s*] established in 1832 by Sir William Heathcote, Bart, of Hursley House near Winchester: to be competed for annually at the end of the Short half-year by boys in the upper part of the school.

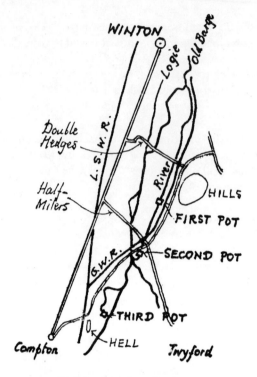

Hell (and the three Pots)

Hebe   the VIth-Book Inferior in a College chamber next senior to the Ganymede: above Hebe came Shebe, and then In Loco: but in smaller chambers there was often only an In Loco and a Ganymede (see **Chamber Roll**). Hebe was cup-bearer to the gods, until dismissed by Jupiter in favour of Ganymede.

heeler   a jump into the river feet-foremost. So used 1838–92; obsolete by 1914.

Hell   From the Anglo-Saxon name for the abode of the dead. (1) a place, corner or copse (1838–84) famed for violets, below Third Pot on the west bank of the river about 3 miles (4.8 km] out of Winton. It was rather dark, and through it flowed a stream. By this date it was not a place of ill omen. But before long the marsh near it was the place to which juniors were sent to get ground-ashes. It then became a 'gloomy copse', and the stream was named Styx. In 1892 we are told that juniors could no longer find ground-ashes here, but there were plenty on the neighbouring railway embankment. The notion was still in use in 1920, but ground-ashes were obtained elsewhere. (2) in 1868 Hell was also a name for old IVth Book, but whether the class or the classroom is not clear. (3) the drains in the centre of the cobbled areas in Chamber Court, to which descend the paths named

Good Resolutions (q.v.). In use from 1914. The Anglo-Saxon name originally meant a hidden place, and in Hampshire dialect still means a dark place in the woods. It appears in other dialects as hele, hill, hull and heal, all meaning to cover up; to heel in a plant may come from this root, if not simply from pressing in with the heel.

hen-coop, or **hen-roost**   the gallery above stalls in Cathedral, where pitch-up and Dons' wives sat on Cathedral Sunday (1920).

Herbert   Mr Herbert Elliott, groundsman, who, with the aid of his daughter, Hochstapler the horse, and occasional male help, kept all the cricket pitches, canvases and soccer grounds in order during the First War. In summer he also umpired.

Herbert Chitty   D 1876–82; Captain of Commoner VI for two years; Bursar 1907–27. He had a profound knowledge of the antiquities and documents of College, and from time to time wrote about them in the *Wykehamist*.

Herbert Chitty Memorial   a low wall erected by Chitty between Logie and Through First, to screen the latter from the Warden's garden, which it failed to do. A stone let into the wall was carved with 'H.C.1921': hence the name. Other monuments to his Bursarship were the Caryatid (q.v.), and a fine oak door put in place of the old one in Angelus Gate.

'Here!'   the call used by a Commoner Praefect when he required the attendance of a junior (1836). The junior in Hall who was not fagging had to run to him (1838). All juniors up at house had to come without delay, the last to arrive usually being employed (1892). The call corresponds to 'Junior!' in College.

Hewett's Passage   a passage between Lower Kingsgate Street and Southgate Road. Named after Rev. G. M. A. Hewett (Don from 1882; House Don of G 1896–1916).

hiatus   from Latin *hiatus* (gap), a gap between the top of one's trousers and the bottom of one's waistcoat: it was a bad notion to sport one (1920).

highlows   very thick, strong shoes. Described as high (1838); as low, but not half-boots (1836); as with no nails in them, and used for football (1831–60). Long since obsolete. In standard English of the past, high-low meant a high shoe or ankle boot fastened with a leather thong in front. They are mentioned by Bishop Fox (c. 1515).

High Table   the long table put out on Dais, at which the Go.Bo. ate Go.Bo. lunch and Domum Dinner (1920).

Hills St Catharine's Hill, a steep-sided oval chalk hill 328 feet [100 m] high, standing on the east bank of the Itchen a mile [1.6 km] south of the town. The summit is encircled by an earthwork enclosing an area of about 23 acres [9.3 hectares]. Excavations carried out in 1925–8 by past and present members of the school Archaeological Society showed the site to have been an early Iron Age settlement occupied from the sixth to the second century BC, containing many pit dwellings. There was a fortified entrance on the north-east which had been violently destroyed by fire. Relics of this occupation included pottery, a saddle quern, picks of red-deer antler and a remarkable bronze duck of the sixth century BC from northern Italy, slotted for fastening to a brooch.

The only traces of human contact on the hill during the next four centuries were scraps of Belgic pottery, a Roman bronze fibula of the first century AD, some Roman pottery of the first to third centuries AD, and a coin of Carausius (286–93). From this time till the Norman period the hill was deserted.

Between 1110 and 1125 a cruciform church with a central tower was built on the apex of the hill, abutting on the west end of a small oratory, which had been built some years earlier. Adjoining the oratory on the north-east were rooms occupied by a priest or caretaker. To the north-east of the church a ditch was dug to enclose a rectangular burial-ground. The church was called St Catharine's Chapel, being dedicated like many hilltop chapels to St Catharine of Alexandria, owing to the legend that after martyrdom her body was buried on top of Mount Sinai. Her cult, which reached England c. 1100, was very popular for a time, but waned after the Black Death in 1348.

The church was built in flint and Quarr stone decorated with billet and other mouldings. The drums and bases of three of the piers in the crossing are still *in situ*, one of them standing to a height of 7 feet [2.1 m]. The roof was of red and glazed tiles, and also of blue slate from north Devon, a great rarity in medieval times. Finds included a fragment of a statue, some scraps of stained glass and glass-leading, and a silver penny of Henry I (1120–5), which may have been dropped by one of the builders.

The chapel was part of the great estate of Chilcombe, which was the main endowment of the Christian Church in Wessex, and the hill is still church property. The first mention of the chapel is in 1284, in a grant by Edward I to John Pontissara, Bishop of Winton. Belonging to this period was a late thirteenth-century finger-ring, probably part of an undertaker's equipment. In 1331 there is mention of oblations in the chapel on the feast of St Catharine, 25 November. Finds of this period included a large number of broken pitchers and other pottery of the fourteenth century, lying near the priest's room, a door-key of c. 1300–50, knives and other implements, and a silver Edward II halfpenny (1369–77).

By 1460 the chapel seems to have been surrounded by a clump of trees, if Warden Chandler's drawing has been interpreted aright, but the chapel itself is not shown because at that time the boys had not begun to visit the hilltop, and any buildings on it would not have been of significance to them.

In 1528–9 the chapel was suppressed by Wolsey, and the oblations in 1536–7 were nil. In 1538 the chapel and the 'cymytorie dycched abowte the same' were leased to Thomas Wriothesley, later Earl of Southampton, and between 1538 and 1540 he demolished it and sold the materials: but did not complete the work, as the excavators found roof slates stacked at the west end ready for removal, three piers of the crossing left standing, and the south transept walled off and used as a hut or fold for some years after.

Hills has never been the property of College,* but in about 1561 the young and popular Headmaster Christopher Johnson (1561–70) introduced games for the boys, chose Hills as their playground, and established a right of access to it that is still respected. Until then the boys had never gone there, and Hills is not mentioned in the Statutes. Among the Latin themes which Johnson dictated in School is one of c. 1565 which refers to shirking games on Hills and idling on Hills, the word used being '*montibus*' in each case: showing that games on Hills were already part of the curriculum, and that the hill had been awarded its Wiccamical plural. It has been called 'Hills' in print from 1820 to the present day. Tabula Legum, the school rules compiled c. 1570, probably also by Johnson, includes rules for orderly behaviour in the two-and-two processions up Town and to Hills ('in Oppido. Ad Montem'). The clump of 1460 had by now dwindled, and Speed's map of 1611 indicates that few trees were left.

By 1647 the boys went up Hills twice every remedy (Tuesdays and Thursdays), and Mathew's poem of that year describes how the procession, starting soon after 6, marched to the summit (he evidently called the hill Hills: 'mont*e*sque revisant cum sociis pueri'), where they dispersed for quoits, hand-ball, bat-ball (a sort of tennis played with a long bat), and football (a primitive form of the Winchester game, but without the enormous hots that appeared in the eighteenth century). This was called Morning Hills. At 9 the Praefect called 'Domum', and they returned to breakfast. After school and dinner they went up again (later called Middle Hills) till 3 p.m. Mathew hints at certain illegal pastimes, among which Gordon (1842) mentions smoking; some of the seventeenth-, eighteenth- and nineteenth-century clay pipes found by the excavators may be a relic of this. Mathew does not mention trees, so they had probably died and vanished. A find of this period was a 1657 trade token of Anthony Wiseman, draper of Winton. Hills appears in a painting of c. 1692 in the Warden's lodging, but it is treeless.

At about this time Labyrinth, known as Mizmaze in the Town and in an 1838 Notion book, was cut in the turf east of the chapel site, one side of the cemetery ditch being used as a base line, by someone unconnected with the school, to supply a diversion for townsfolk visiting the hilltop. By 1838 the story in the school was that it had been cut by a boy who was 'kept'. A plan of it was drawn by J. Nowell, probably a townsman, in 1710. There is no earlier evidence for its existence, and it is unconnected with the medieval idea of treading mazes for penance.

In about 1742 Commoners were added to the Hills processions, and some time later Evening Hills, or Underhills, started: it was between tea and 8 p.m.

---

* Hills was bought by the Old Wykehamist Lodge for the School in 1930.

in summer, for bathing in selected spots at the foot of Hills. Tom Warton (c. 1755–60) describes the view from the 'tumulus' on the summit, but did not realise that the mound he stood on was the rubble of the chapel tower. He does not mention trees, so the clump had not yet been replanted. He records that boys had to remain within the bounds of Trench, and that there was football and bathing. His reference to some of the boys treading the maze implies that it was not a school institution. In 1762 Colonel Norborne Berkeley (later Lord Botetourt), commanding the Gloucestershire Militia then stationed in Winton, set his men to plant a new clump of fir and beech over the mound, a task they performed in one day, no doubt for a wager. Two brass aiguilette-ferrules, and a Brown Bess musket-ball of lead, found in the excavations, may be souvenirs of this event. A Wykehamist reminiscing of the years 1767–75 remarks that boys ran the maze as a race, and that it had been cut by a College boy. From these memoirs, and from the cry of 'Domum' when it was time to leave Hills, arose a mass of false legend connecting Hills with the Domum ceremony. In 1799 the school's use of Hills was challenged, and Warden Huntingford claimed the right 'from time immemorial'.

During a Napoleonic scare in 1811 the government put a beacon on Hills, but due respect was paid to the rights of the boys there; and between 1812 and 1817 the school vigorously repelled intruders. In 1820–5 Meads came into use for games and the popularity of Hills declined, though badger-hunting continued there, and there was rifle-shooting in Chalk Pit between 1830 and 1840.

By 1832 Labyrinth was obliterated and Long Game was being played over it. Warden Barter had it re-cut, using the 1710 plan but making the area 16 feet [4.8 m] larger either way. But the boys had always regarded it as a town game, and a tame one at that, and ignored it: and Fearon (1852–9) never trod it if there was anything better to do. In 1842 Gordon had said: 'It is fast going to ruin.'

Writing of the period 1838–42, Gordon says: 'in summer we play cricket on Hills, and in winter football: and at all times boys smoke &c on there.' He thus describes the Hills procedure:

'On remedies, Morning Hills was from 7.30 to 9.15. Leave from "going on" could be got from a Master, with some excuse: and the Praefect of Hall could give three leaves, which were "jockeyed for", to College boys with 30 juniors to them. Middle Hills: boys 'went on' at 2, until 3.30. Similar leave could be obtained. Evening Hills: at the end of May, when bathing leave was down, until the end of Long Half, boys went to bathing places near the foot of Hills in the canal, between 6.30 and 8. When once on, no boy was allowed to go off Hills, except Praefects, and any boy they liked to "take off" to walk with them.'

A little later, the Hills procedure consisted of: (1) Morning Hills on remedies and whole holidays. (2) Middle (or Afternoon) Hills from 2 or 2.30 to 3.45, on whole and half-remedies and holidays. The whole school assembled at On Place, where the Praefect of Hall took names-calling, and then conducted the procession two-and-two along the towpath, up Hills to Trench, where they separated to do as they pleased provided they remained within Trench. Later, the dispersal point was Tunbridge. Praefects often gave Inferiors leave to come from Hills with them for grubbing, badger-baiting, bathing or 'getting a rise out of the watermen'. (3) Underhills or Evening Hills was from 6.30 to 7.45 every day except Sundays in the summer, from the end of May when bathing leave came down; and there was bathing at Pot, Tunbridge and other places.

In 1859 Hills ceased to be compulsory, though some football was played there to 1860. In 1860 Morning Hills was abolished. Junior Match (College vs Commoners, cricket), was played on Hills to 1866. In 1867 it was enacted that boys could return from Middle Hills at any time up to 5 p.m. In 1868 the ancient custom of going up Hills was abolished altogether.

At that date over a hundred beech trees were still standing in Clump.

From 1868 onwards the school's attitude to Hills was rather one of 'dog in the manger': though they had used it for three centuries it was no longer needed, yet they resented any trespassers there. In 1878 a tenant tried to fence off Hills, and as a retort the boys invented elaborate initiation ceremonies, called 'doing Hills' [see **Hills, to do**], to which all new boys were subjected: partly to bewilder them, but also to show that the school still needed Hills. The ceremonies included 'tolling Labyrinth': but this, as always, was so dull that somebody inserted a false cut, thereby turning it from a race into a real puzzle. When in 1894 access to Hills was again threatened, Fearon revived Morning Hills in token form, and this continued till 1922 and probably long after. (See **Morning Hills**.)

Clump has continued, since 1460, to be a wasting asset. In 1897, fifty trees, fir and beech, were added. In 1917 only fifty-five trees, mostly beech, survived. By 1924 they had dwindled to forty-five, all beech, and a belt of beech was planted round the old clump.

Hills   a very bad notion in College (1920) for Junior Game, the derivation being: Ju.Ga., i.e. juga (yokes or ridges).

Hills Rolls   three lists of Commoners who had leave from Hills, made out by a junior, signed by the Commoner Praefect in course, and presented to the Headmaster, Second Master and Praefect of Hall (1868). Long since obsolete.

Hills, to do   access to Hills being threatened by a tenant in 1878 (see above), the boys invented elaborate initiation ceremonies for new boys, which they had to undergo on the second day of term (in College), or the first or second Sunday of the term (in Commoners), after lunch. The ceremonies were meaningless, and designed only to demonstrate to (1) the public, that the boys still used Hills, and (2) the new boys, that Hills was a mystical ingredient in the school's way of life.

The new boy was escorted by his Pater or teejay. In College, the second junior Praefect (1900), or the two junior Praefects (1920), attended to ensure fair play and adherence to tradition. The ceremonies varied from house to house, and with succeeding generations, and included: (1) to walk across First Pot and back, on a 6-inch [15-cm] beam, with deep water on the north and a fall on the south.

It was recorded in 1920 that only one man had ever fallen in. (2) to climb up Chalk Pit (mercifully obsolete by 1917). (3) to take a stone from Chalk Pit and hold it firmly, pending further instructions. (4) to run up the slope from the lip of Chalk Pit till he can see the tops of the trees in Clump, shout 'Feathers', and fall on his face. (5) to walk blindfold through Clump (1892), or to be blindfold in the middle of Clump and walk out of it (1920). (6) to toll Labyrinth, gown and top-hat off, waistcoat on (1920), from the centre to the outside. It has one branching of the ways, one leading out, the other a cul-de-sac. The Paters of the last two men had to toll it afterwards. (7) to toll round Trench (obsolete in College by 1917). (8) to run down the face of Trench at Domum Cross with his hands behind his back, put his stone (see 3) in Domum Cross, kneel down and kiss the cross. (9) to toll from Trench to Arethusa, pluck a twig, and return (obsolete in College by 1917).

Hill times   the times for going on Hills. In use 1820–68.

Hinkers   Mr A. Hinxman, College hairdresser (1920), who had a shop in Jewry Street. He came to cut hair in IVth Chamber from 8.30 to 9.15 on Mondays, Tuesdays and Wednesdays. **Hinkers' chair** was a hard chair with arms, in which his clients sat, painted on the back with 'A. Hinxman, Hairdresser'; greatly in demand when Hinkers was not using it. **Hinkers in B flat**: in performance of his duties, Hinkers was often afflicted with internal rumblings.

hirk a ball, to   to aim a kick at a football in canvas and miss it, so that it spins off the side of the foot and goes behind the player (1920). Probably derived from 'hark back', a cry to hounds which have lost the scent, directing them to retrace their steps and recover it; from Old English *harken* (listen, pay attention).

hiss   the warning given by the junior set to watch for the approach of masters at the beginning of School-time. The hiss was taken up by others in the body of School, and a general alarm thus given. From 1831; but long obsolete.

hit round, to   to return the service, in fives: a hit round had to hit the side wall first and then the front wall, except at 'game ball', when it might be hit straight on to the front wall (1920).

Hochstapler   the name of a famous German racehorse in about 1890. Hence: (1) the horse that drew the mowing machine in Meads and New Field (1890–1920). (2) his stable at the west end of Trees in Lavender Meads, and the cricket pitch near it. The stable vanished long ago, but the name lingered in the site. Thus, the passage leading from it to Kingsgate Street was Hochstapler Passage, and the gate at the end of it Hochstapler Gate.

Hockley   the golf course over Twyford Downs, used by men in the school when the School Golf Course on Teg Down was abandoned. Men who had special leave or were invited by a Don might play there (1920). In 1926 two Dons, Murray Hicks and Maurice Platnauer, bought Hockley to save it from other uses, and (later) in 1955 gave it to the school.

hold down, to   to hold the head in a convenient postition for receiving a clo (q.v.); long since obsolete.

hollis   an oval pebble, suitable for throwing, as distinct from a rock (a large stone); recorded from 1831. Said to be from a boy named Hollis. A Thomas Hollist was admitted 1747, and a Joseph Hollis in 1777. George Parry Hollis (dmitted 1809) and Robert Pelham Hollis (admitted 1829) were both of St Thomas, Winchester, and may be connected with the Hollis living in Hollis' House, later named Gattrell's, which stood behind College Mill. One of the requirements for 'being a Wykehamist' (q.v.) was to 'splice [throw] a hollis over Mill'. This was the only context in which a pebble was so called, and the phrase may be a corruption of 'splice at Hollis' over Mill'.

Holy Poker   a tall staff of dark wood about 6 feet [1.8 m] high with a head of light wood, beautifully carved with the school arms, surmounted by a small cross in silver. Bearing this staff, Johnny Bishop used to conduct the Warden, whenever in residence, from his Lodging to his seat in Chapel (1920). Lord Selborne revived this custom. Parker Smith eschewed it, because of his undignified shape.

Holy Water Stone   a small stone of indeterminate shape projecting from the wall under Outer Gate, opposite Porter's Lodge. A misnomer: dating from 1868, if not earlier, the stone was probably the remains of a cresset (primitive lamp) or a stand for a lantern.

Honey   caretaker of Museum and Photographic Society's rooms (1920). In answer to the cry 'Honey!' he appeared with hypo ready mixed at threepence the dish. He was also in charge of lanterns for slides. In private life Honey was a vegetable prizeman.

Honours Course   the senior of the three Praefects in course each week in Old Commoners (to 1842) was only in honorary course, or honours course; the two junior Praefects performed all duties, including names-calling, reporting offenders and preserving quiet. Nevertheless he obtained exemption from tasks and other duties which Praefects in course were always granted.

Hopper's   I House: Sunnyside. The original House Don, E. J. Turner (1869– 1903) was called 'The Hopper'.

Horlickers   Horlick's malted milk tablets, a great stand-by during the First World War.

Hot (at football)

horn of plenty   a cream-horn, on sale down shops (1920). Named from the cornucopia of the classics.

horse-boxes, or **loose-boxes**, or **rabbit-hutches**   a small enclosure below and to the eastward of the pews where Choir sat on Cathedral Sundays. With high sides, and no book-rest to lean on, it contained three narrow pews one behind the other, where junior members of VIth Book were obliged to sit. A most unpopular seat (1920).

Hostiarius   incorrect form of Ostiarius, the official title of the Second Master.

hot   (1) the equivalent of a rugby scrum at Winchester football. In the Twenty-two and Twenty-two games (1831–43) a hot took place whenever the ball went out. Retrieved, the ball was placed between the two sides, who gathered round with heads down and pushed, with the object of carrying the ball through their opponents. This was called a 'hotting game'. In 1880 a match always opened with a hot, which in XVs was three rows of three men, and in VIs one row of three. There was also a hot whenever the ball went out of canvas. The two back rows started with heads down but the front row had to keep theirs up until the ball was put in by the hot-watch (later by the referee). In 1921 the rule for 'heads down' was introduced, enabling the front row to start with heads down also. (2) any jostle or crowd. (3) as a verb, hot means (a) to hot at football. (b) push, shove, crowd. (3) to move (transitive and intransitive): e.g. hot up, hot down, hot along.

   The word may be conected with: (1) huddle, via Old English *hoderen*, from Anglo-Saxon *hydan* (cover, hide). (2) Dutch *hoetelen* (to bungle). (3) Old English *hotte* (a square basket slung on the back for carrying turf, slates, etc.). Hence in dialect a hot of muck or stones is a heap carelessly put up. A hotload (heap of manure) refers to its temperature: it would not have been carried on the back. In North Country dialect, people huddling together are said to be 'all in a hott'.

hot end   a half-burnt stick from a faggot, with one end red-hot (1836–43); long obsolete. See **tin gloves**.

hot plate   a covered dish of sausages, eggs, potatoes, peas, etc., ordered from School Shop and sent up for tea as a luxury (1920).

hot roll   (1) This was originally a diagram made out by the Captain of VI to show the position of each player in the hot (and elsewhere on the field) in XVs and VIs. It was held up to view by a junior on Quarter-Deck (q.v.) before morning chapel on the day of the match. By 1900 it had become a list of the team inscribed on some pictorial background such as the sails of a square-rigged ship. By 1917 the hot roll was a team banner, about 3 by 2 feet [0.9 by 0.6 m], drawn by a boy, showing College (or Commoners or O.T.H.) XV (or VI) symbolically triumphing over its two rivals. The captain, prominent players and referees were caricatured, and the roll of names added. Subjects chosen c. 1920, for example, were: Laocoon in Commoner VI attire, with two sons in Commoner and Houses XV costume, struggling against a blue and white serpent; Cinderella trying on the slipper; the Judgment of Paris. Hot rolls were then exhibited in Wells' window, finally passing into the possession of the Captains of VI. They were also made for College Chamber Sixes (see also Thule).
   (2) It also meant a roll put up in books-chambers or Toy-time with the ink still wet. The penalty (1920), threatened but never imposed, was a choice between (a) eating the roll dipped in Funkey grease (cf. **buttered roll**); (b) drinking a conduit full of soap and water.

hot up, to   if a man failed to get his remove but was thought worthy of it, the Headmaster could hot him up to the division above at the beginning of the next term. Men could also be hotted up by the Headmaster after monthly, or at any time during the half (1892). By 1917 it meant a charity remove. The words are also used as a noun: 'to raise a hot-up'.

hot-watch, or **hot-watcher**   see **football**.

hour   any school period (except Morning Lines), whether in books-chambers or up to books, lasting an hour or less. School Times, c. 1838, were: (1) *Common Time in the Short Half (Sep.–Dec.)* morning: Mon. and Wed. to Sat., 7.30–8.30. middle: Mon., Wed., Thu., Sat., 9.30–12; Fri., 9.30–11. evening: Sun., 4–5; Mon., 4–6; Wed., Fri., 2–6; Sat., 2–5. Tuesday was a remedy: Thursday a half-remedy. (2) *Common Time in the·Long Half (1 Feb.–15 Mar.)* morning: Mon. and Wed. to Sat., 7.30–8.30. middle: as under (1). evening: Sun., 4–5.

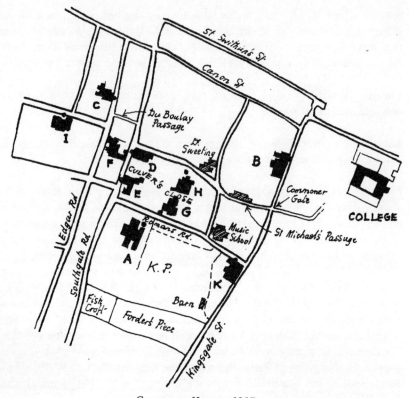

Commoner Houses, 1917

Mon., Wed., Fri., 2–6. Sat., 2–5. Tuesday was a remedy: Thursday a half-remedy. (3) *Easter Time in the Long Half (15 Mar.–30 Apr.)* as in Common Time. (4) *Cloister Time (May–July)* morning: Mon., Wed., Fri., Sat., 7.30–8.30. middle: Mon., Wed., Sat., 9.30–12. evening: Sun., 4–5, 6.30–8.15. Mon., Wed., Fri., 2–6, with a quarter of an hour for beavers. Sat., 2–5. Tuesday and Thursday, remedies.

In 1892, in the morning, originally called Middle School, there were 1st, 2nd and 3rd or Last hours: in the afternoon there were also three hours, except in Cloister Time, when there were four hours in Middle and three in Afternoon School.

In 1920 there were only two hours in the afternoon.

'Hour!'   (1) called by the First Junior in course at the beginning of Toy-time in College (1920), after which he went to raise leave off Toy-time from the Praefect in course for those who needed it. (2) called by the names-docker at the end of a game of Winchester football (from 1880); always followed, in College (1920) by cries of 'After you', for bidets. (3) see also **Peal**.

House Grub   the Notion (1900) for House Supper, q.v.

House Roll   a printed list of names of the men in a House, in Short Roll order. used for names-calling, etc. cf. College Roll.

Houses   the ten Commoner boarding-houses instituted between 1859 and 1905. Rather confusingly, they are divided in Short Half (for the purposes of Winchester football) into: 'Houses' (or Old Tutors' Houses, or O.T.H.), A, B, C, F and I; 'Commoners', D, E, G, H and K. College East and College West counted as two houses for games, O.T.C., etc., bringing the total to twelve.

The Houses were founded in the following order:

- In September 1859, Rev. H. J. Wickham, formerly a Commoner Tutor, established the first Tutor's House, A, or Old Chernocke House, in St Thomas Street, with four Commoners, one of whom had been in Commoners for a year and a half.
- In September 1860, Rev. H. E. Moberly established the second House, B, in Kingsgate Street.
- In January 1862, Rev. J. T. H. du Boulay established the third House, C, in Cheesehill Street, moving in May 1863 to Southgate Hill House.
- In January 1868, two new Houses were opened: D, in Kingsgate Street, by Rev. W. A. Fearon; E, in Cheesehill Street, by F. Morshead.
- In September 1869, New Commoners were abolished, the men being dispersed into D and E, which both moved into Culver Close, and three new houses: G, in Culver Close, Rev. E. W. Sergeant; H, in Culver Close, Rev. J. T. Bramston; and F, in Southgate Road, Rev. C. H. Hawkins.
- In September 1869, E. J. Turner opened the ninth house, I, in Painter's Fields.
- In September 1905, R. D. Beloe opened the tenth house, K, in Kingsgate Park.

Up to the end of 1867 the divisions of the school were simply College and Commoners. From January 1868 they were College, Commoners, and A, B, D, D, E. Since September 1869 they have been College, Commoners (that is, the four in Culver Close [D, E, G, H; and K later]), and Houses (A, B, C, F, I).

The resultant *list of Houses* is as follows.

	usual name	previous or alternative name
A Chernocke House	Furley's	Beetle's
B 69, Kingsgate Street	Toye's	Moberly's, Fort's
C Southgate Hiill	Cook's	Du Boulay's
D Culver House	Kenny's	Fearon's
E Southgate Road	Freddy's	Morshead's
F Southgate House	Chawker's	Hawkin's
G Culver Lea	Phil's	Sergeant's
H Culvers Close	Trant's	Bramston's, Rootite's
I Sunnyside	Hopper's	Turner's
K Kingsgate House	Beloe's	

Members of the Houses were called Furleyites, Toyeites, Trantites, etc.

House shirk   the failure of an entire House to turn up at Chapel or Morning Lines (from 1900).

House Supper   a break-up supper given at the end of Cloister Time by each House Don to his House. The House Don, all members of the House, and a few important men from other Houses attended. There were speeches and music.

house tie   given for prowess at games. Each House, and both sections of College, had two (1920): one with broad stripes of even width, called a crockets tie, being awarded for cricket; the other, with some stripes very narrow and others very broad, for all-round merit, called a full house-tie. There was no special tie for soccer or Our Game. Senior House-Tie was the man in the house who had had the full house-tie longest; 'crockets-tie' was also used personally like this. An Inferior with a house-tie could wear it once a fortnight (see **cud tie**).

housle, houstle, to (pronounced houzle)   to hustle. In use 1836–72; obsolete by 1890. cf. roush for rush: some dialects lengthen 'u' to 'ou' in this way: e.g. doust (dust), rowsty (rusty).

huff   strong ale brewed in College at Audit time. In many Colleges (e.g. All Souls) the auditors were plied with strong ale to keep them in good humour. In use 1831–60: long since obsolete. Occurs in dialect as noun, adjective and verb, with the basic meaning of well up, puff up, rise in baking, and still means strong beer: huff-cap (1577) or hufcap (1579) used for strong ale may mean it was strong enough to lift the cap off your head. In origin it is an onomatopoeic word for hard breathing: cf. gasper, for a strong cigarette.

humb, to be in a   to be angry (1920). Thackeray (c. 1834) used 'to hump' transitively in this sense, and today 'it gives me the hump' is standard slang. **to raise a hump off** meant to offend (1920).

husky   gooseberry fool with the husks in, as distinct from non-husky (1836 only).

Illumina (pronounced Illuminā)   on the last Sunday night in Short Half, before Grass Court wall was removed and Fives Courts built (1862), candles were put in the temples along the wall opposite Walford's. The custom was maintained by Commoners until they moved in 1869, and then inherited by College juniors, who (1920) had to save all tolly-ends through Short Half, and on the last night put them in the temples all round Meads and light them. It was a beautiful sight. A bonfire was lit near Ball Court, round which 'Domum' was sung (1880), and anyone who felt inclined strolled in Meads to see the display.

imita (promounced imitā)   an imitation (noun) or to imitate the action or diction of some well-known character or Don (verb), especially the Headman (1920).

imposition   a task to learn or write out for some neglect of duty (1838). This is standard English. By 1868 it had become impos; then cropple.

indigna (pronounced indignā)   a complaint (noun), to grumble plaintively, 'hold forth' about a grievance (verb) (1920). From indignation.

Inferior   any member of the school who was not a Praefect. Used in print from 1820; in its Latin form *Inferiores* it is found in Christopher Johnson's *Themes* (c. 1563).

Informator   the official Latin title of the Headmaster. He was originally called *Ludimagister* (games master!), [from Latin *ludus* (school, game)]. *Informator* does not mean he reported boys to the Warden, but that he gave form to their intellects, the true meaning of the Latin *informare*.

infra (pronounced infrā)   beneath one's dignity. From *infra dignitatem*; in standard English, infra-dig. Recorded from 1856: e.g. 'that would be infra' (I wouldn't do it). By 1920 it could be used both of the thing scorned, and of the scorner: to be infra meant to be scornful, aloof, offhand: to be infra to, meant to ignore a person or thing, to snub.

In Loco (pronounced Lōco)   the senior VIth Book Inferior in a College Chamber (1920). He was often a Tolly-keeper and had B after his name in bidet roll. One of the two In Locos in each downstairs Chamber had to supervise the making and pouring out of Praefects' teas, sweat juniors to make tea, and keep Chamber Tick accounts.

It is pronounced with a long o, though it should really be a short one. Some suggested derivations were that he was *in loco* (in the place of) *Praefectorum*, the Praefects, on whose behalf he performed; *in loco parentis* – but this was not quite his stance; or *in loco Diaboli* (the Devil) – a poignant attempt by some down-trodden junior. He was, in fact, *in loco Custodis Candelarum* (deputising for a Tolly-keeper), and this title occurs in full in older Chamber Rolls. Originally there was one Tolly-keeper to each Chamber. When the number was reduced, Chambers with no Tolly-keeper had an 'in loco' instead. cf. 'locum' (for *locum tenens*) in the medical profession.

inners   yellow wash-leather gloves worn inside fives gloves or wicket-keeping gloves (1920).

Inspeccer   General Inspection of the Officers Training Corps by a general, sometimes the father of a man in the school. The Rifles lent their band, which always played 'Toll for the Brave', and the two corps banners were set out. There were several marches-past, and general-salutes. The Great Man then walked round, talked to the very tiny men, and afterwards harangued us on an army career, and how the O.T.C. had won the War. It involved no competi or pot, but all uniform had to be spotless (1920). This colourful ceremony was later, to our loss, merged with Drill Pot.

[**Ja Ra**   G. H. Ridding: see **Peg**.]

jack/Jack and **black jack/Black Jack**   (1) the large leather can in which beer was served in College. (2) nickname of the Rev. Frederick Wickham, Commoner Tutor 1832–7, Second Master 1845–62. He was son of W. N. Wickham, school doctor for many years, after whom Wickham's in Old Commoners was named, as he lived there.

Jacker, the   H. A. Jackson (C 1898–1903), Sen.Co.Prae. Severely wounded in the First World War, he was taken prisoner and badly treated by the Germans, whom he detested. Don 1908–47; House Don of B 1921–45. An authority on Our Game, and an enthusiastic player (1920). Joint Editor of the *Winchester College Register* 1901–46.

Jack's Hags, or **Jacob's Harem**   the poor women who came to get broken meats from College Hall (1920). Originally it was put in Tub. After Waterloo, most of the boiled beef provided at lunch was given to French prisoners and, when these disappeared, to twenty-four old women who weeded the courts in College (1820–8). A group of them are shown in a picture of Outer Court in the *Illustrated London News* of 1893. In 1920 sundry old women used to come to collect broken meats from Hall, but they did no weeding. The name is from Jack (Rev. F. Wickham, Second Master 1845–62) and also from Jacob, who in Genesis 35.22–6 had issue by two wives and two handmaidens.

Jacob's ladder   the footbridge leading over the Great Western Railway line, from Domum Cottage to Portsmouth Road (1920). In Genesis 28.10–22 Jacob had a vision of a ladder leading to heaven.

Jambi (pronounced Jambī)   Greek Iambics, set as a task. To raise jambi was to win the Iambics Medal Task (1920).

'**Jam Lucis**' (pronounced Jam Lusis)   'Jam lucis orto sidere', the Latin *Hymnus matutinus* (morning hymn). No. 8 in the Hymnarium of 1910, no. 9 in 1928.

Noted as possibly fifth century, and sometimes said to have been written by Ambrose (340–97) in Latin from a Greek original. The words are obviously ancient. In c. 1674 Bishop Ken translated them into the English verses appearing as Hymn no. 1 in *Hymns Ancient and Modern*. The tune we used was by J. Bishop (1665–1737). Long ago, it was sung at circum (q.v.). Still sung often in Chapel and Chantry, it was sung twice a year at Morning Hills (1920). New men were expected (1920) to know that 'mundi' in verse 4 meant 'clean': not 'of the world'.

Jane Austen   a little old lady, name unknown, who lived (1920) in the house in College Street where Jane Austen had died in 1817.

jaw   loud talk, a scolding, a scrape. **to make a jaw** was to talk loudly; to **get into a jaw** was to be involved in a row (1838); **to jaw** (1880) meant to preach or give advice too weightily or too often. This is standard slang.

jawster   one given to profuse or tedious speech; a word fabricated Wiccamically from 'jaw'. To cut short an argument one was likely to lose, one called the other man a jawster. So used from 1831; obsolete by 1914.

Jemima's   a long building on the far side of Scards from Old Barge (1892); long since forgotten. Who was Jemima?

Jeroboam   a double battling. This occurred when the Aul.Prae. had not given out battlings on the previous Saturday, and gave two the following week. A treble battling was a Rehoboam (1920) from the story in II Chronicles 10.10–11, though it is not really a parallel.

jersey   a woven woollen shirt, white for cricket, blue and red for football (1838–68). Houses originally wore white football jerseys with green round the neck, but in 1870 were wearing red and blue. By 1880 the jersey was a thin, tight-fitting cotton vest used primarily for football. In practice games, to distinguish the opposing sides College wore white and red-and-white striped jerseys; Commoners and Houses wore white and blue-and-white stripes. This was so in 1917, but they were called zephyrs.
    In standard English, fine woollen yarn and a type of vest made from it were called jersey, after the island where it was originally knitted. Mary Queen of Scots wore a jarzie (1587); Jersey-stockings are mentioned in 1609, jarsies in 1657: and coloured house jerseys in *Tom Brown's School Days* (c. 1835).

jig   originally, a swindler, or a snob; from 1850, a clever person. In Commoners (1868) it meant one who was 'a swell' (good) at anything. It is one of those popular words which can mean almost anything the user desires. Outside Winchester, it is used more of things than people: and appears in dialect, mainly north Country, in the forms jig, jigg, gig, geeg, jeeg and giggum, with these trends of meaning: (1) a lively song or dance. (2) fun, frolic, joke, jest, taunt, or an object of sport. (3) an ingenious device, tool, or contrivance (examples occur in 1634 and 1652). (4) a swindle or trick: thus giggie (full of tricks) and jiggle (to swindle). From Old French *gigue* (a fiddle, or dance).

jiggish   clever. Recorded from 1856; from jig (q.v.).

Jobags   H. W. B. Joseph (Coll. 1880–5), Fellow and Philosophy Tutor of New College, Fellow of Winchester. He was often a Poser for New College exam (1920).

Job's Court   a small court in the Warden's Lodging, entered by a door near Middle Gate. Recorded from 1831; still so called in 1922. Named after Job's Chamber, a room in the Lodging, where Senior Fardel in Election Week used to go to translate part of the book of Job into Latin. Job's Court led to it.

Jock   Miss Wellsman's white Aberdeen at Sick House (c. 1920): a cheerful little dog, and a great favourite when one was continent.

jockey, to   (1) to get above somebody in cuse, or up to books; so used 1831–1900. (2) to engage or secure in advance (e.g. a seat, or a fives court), to bespeak, to 'bag' (as opposite of 'finge'); so used from 1838 to the present day. (3) to appropriate, steal; so used from 1850 to the present day. It is turf slang, meaning to get the better of or cheat (appearing as early as 1685): from Jockey, diminutive of Jock, meaning a Scot, strolling minstrel, groom, horse-dealer, cheat.

jockey not   the Commoner equivalent of 'finge', i.e. 'bags I not'. In use from 1856.

jockey up   to gain a place up to books. The opposite of 'lose down', it was in use from 1856.

Joel   College Under-Porter, who was always called after a minor prophet in strict rotation (1920). He rang First Peal and all bells for Chapel, turned on the lamps in Chamber Court and Meads, locked various gates at night, and locked Chambers at 9.30, having turned off the electricity mains in College. He might be summoned with Chamber keys by anyone wanting to get anything from a downstairs Chamber, till about 10.15, by a cry of 'JO-EL' through the round hole in Middle Gate. His name (1920) was Rawlins, and he kept goats and ducks in the garden of his cottage just south of College Mill, on the tongue of land between the two arms of Logie. The cottage, previously called Gattrell's or Hollis's, was called Joel's House (1920). The Under-Porter in 1836, Mansfield tells us, was Obadiah. He was succeeded by Amos. Then Joel succeeded Amos. Thus the wheel turns its circle.

joram

John Des (pronounced Dës)   white unruled paper, about 4 by 7 inches [10 by 17.5 cm]. It was introduced by John Desborough Walford, known as John Des, Mathematical Don 1834–73, Assistant Bursar 1854–76, co-founder of SROGUS. See **Walford's**.

Johnny Bishop   the Head Porter of College (1920). His real name was Henry Bishop. His father had been a Querister. His main functions were: (1) stamping and posting letters twice a day; receiving registered parcels; paying for luggage, etc. See **Gate**. (2) showing visitors over College: a valuable source of revenue in tips. (3) being verger, churchwarden and sidesman to the school in Chapel and Cathedral. He sat in the last row on the left of Chapel; turned the lights off and on; had charge of the Communion plate; conducted the Warden into Chapel with the Holy Poker. He was a pillar of strength to the Cap.Praes. at all times, especially at Confirma. He wore a velvet-edged gown. Though on the surface obsequious, he was good at heart, very efficient, and devoted to Winchester and its traditions.

joram, jorum   a quart [1.14 l] can or tankard, of pewter or tin, of peculiar shape, in which beer was served in Commoners (1831–6); a leaden drinking pot holding from a pint [570 ml] to a quart (1838); a pewter beer mug or jug (1868–1900). Now obsolete. In dialect it is a large jug, pitcher, bowl or dish for holding liquids, and was in use in 1780. Possibly from jordan, an old word for an earthen pot, used by Chaucer (c. 1380), abbreviated form jordan-bottle, in which pilgrims brought home water from the River Jordan. But the Winchester word might have a different origin, from one of the Jorams in the Old Testament: e.g. Joram son of Toi, who brought vessels of silver, gold and brass as a peace offering to King David (II Samuel 8.10.).

Jordan   a wall about 5 feet [1.5 m] high screening Through First from the door of First Chamber; also the gutter beside it, which carried rainwater down to a drain (1920). Named from the hymn 'There is a Land of Pure Delight', which contains the words '. . . old Canaan stood, while Jordan rolled between'.

jouns   tin cans for beer. This word occurs once only, in a Commoner word-book of 1880–4, and is almost certainly a miscopying of 'jorums' by a new boy.

journey dibs

journey dibs   money for travelling given out by the Housemaster on the last day of term, or before leave-out days. Thus used from 1892; called journey money in 1880. See **dibs**.

jubilee   a pleasant time, when there were no lessons or fagging. Thus used 1831–1900, but obsolete by 1914. Similarly used in standard English for rejoicing or celebration: there is an example in Dryden (late seventeenth century). Surprisingly, jubilee is not from Latin *jubilare* (to rejoice), but from Hebrew *yobel* (the blast of a trumpet announcing the fiftieth year or jubilee ordained in Leviticus 25.11); hence a celebration of fifty years of life (Fletcher, c. 1618), [reign] (Queen Victoria's Golden Jubilee), etc.

Judges' half-rem   an extra half-rem given about twice a year 'at the request of His Majesty's Judges of Assize'. When they arrived at Winchester on circuit, the Aul.Prae. wrote them a letter in Latin enquiring if they would ask for a half-rem, and they then asked the Headmaster for one. They usually invited senior men to breakfast in the Judge's Lodging, opposite the Deanery (1920).

junior   (1) the younger of a pair. Senior and Junior were used (1920) to distinguish two men with the same surname, and the use was extended to other pairs of comparable objects, such as trees, ends of tables and so on. 'Tight junior' meant the lowest of all. Major and Minor had also been used up to the end of the fifteenth century, concurrently with senior and junior, but the latter then succeeded the former. (2) every Inferior who was liable to be fagged or sweated. In 1836 in College this included all except the seven Candle-keepers and the Senior Inferior. Fag was used as a noun only with a qualifying word, e.g. breakfast fag. In Commoners in 1868, juniors were all Inferiors below Junior Div Senior Part. By 1917 junior meant anyone who could be sweated. (3) a diving board in Gunner's Hole (1920). See **Senior**.

'Junior!'   shouted by Praefects in College (1838) and in some Houses (1869) when they needed a junior to do something for them. 'Here!' was used in Old and New Commoners and other Houses. In College (1920) the twenty junior men ran to calls of 'Junior!', the last one or two to arrive being given the job.

Junior, First, Second and Third   the most junior, junior but one and junior but two in each upstairs Chamber in College. (See **Chamber Roll**.) Their duties

(1920) were as follows. (1) to wake everybody in the morning (see **Peal**). (2) to set up cold bidets. (3) at night, to light the fire, light Funkey, and set up hot bidets. (4) to keep newspaper upstairs, and provide it in large quantity on conduits for packing on the last day of the half. (5) to keep matches. (6) to fill Chamber Can after breakfast and at night. (7) to keep the Chamber well supplied with pint-pots, jockeying them from other chambers if necessary (this was always called 'to make pint-pots'): penalty, if nailed, a spanking. (8) in Short Half, to collect tolly-ends, and set these out in the temples at Illumina and light them. If in course downstairs, he had also: (9) to sweep the Chamber a quarter of an hour before Toy-time, except in Cloister Time, taking care not to sweep dust, but only paper and rubbish. (See **College waistcoat**.) (10) to sweat washers-up if Praefects had had tea in the Chamber. First Juniors in course could not be sweated to wash up. In 1921 a new law was made that washing-up should be done by juniors in their own Chambers, and sweating should cease. (11) to call 'Hour!' (q.v.), and raise leave off Toy-time for such as needed it. First Juniors also had (12) to raise leave continent for men in their Chamber (see **leave continent**), go down to Sick House after every meal to take letters, and see if they wanted anything. (13) to keep a ready supply of Long Paper, John Des and half-vessels, an india-rubber and a fill-up. *The Second Junior*, upstairs: (1) to light Bill Brighter for the Senior Praefect to dress by in the morning. (2) to see to all upstairs washing-up. If in course downstairs: (3) to mop Quarter-Deck with the mop kept in pot-cupboard, moistened at Chamber Court Conduit. There was no mopping in VIIth and Thule, which had fenders over Quarter-Deck. In 1919 mopping was abolished. (4) to take letters for stamping and posting to Porter's Lodge, in the evening: on weekdays at 8.30, on Sundays at 7.30, 8.0 and 8.30. He went to each toys and said: 'Letters?' (5) in Mansfield's day (1836), to be in charge of crockery; he had to produce pint-cups whenever demanded. *The Third Junior* had no official duties.

Junior College   the second fives-court on the left as one entered Old Fives Courts (1920).

Junior Commoner   the first fives-court on the right as one entered Old Fives Courts (1920).

Junior Conduit   in New Commoners (1868), next to Brewery, and opposite Fives Courts.

Junior End   the westernmost table on the north side of College Hall, where the New Roll and some of the Old Roll sat (1920). The carved shield on the panelling over Junior End was put up by a regiment that was quartered in College on holiday during the First World War.

Junior Game   one of College's only two canvases (1920): Canvas and Junior Game. The latter was in the south-west corner of Meads, running parallel to the wall of Sick House garden. Those not among the thirty men chosen for Canvas played in Junior Game.

Junior House   a junior house match, or the team playing in it. The meaning varied with the period, and the season; e.g.: (1) (before 1890) a house cricket XI, of men not playing in Lords, or in Senior or Middle Matches. The houses played each other on remedies and half-remedies before Eton match. (2) (after 1890) a house cricket XI of men not playing in Senior House; as Toye Cup occupied the time before Eton match, Junior House only took place after it. (3) (before 1917) inter-house matches at Winchester football between XVs and VIs. There were usually eight, nine, or ten players a side, drawn from those who had not played in canvas.

Junior-Junior, or **Jun-Jun** (pronounced Jŭn-Jŭn)   (1) the most junior game of all. Here again the meaning varied. In 1900 it meant a cricket XI of new men and old stagers who had to turn out on every day when the house was playing Toye Cup, up to Eton Match. By 1917 the old stagers had faded out, and Jun-Jun was the junior riff-raff, playing compulsory cricket. It could also mean a similar pair of XIs playing soccer. (2) a diving board at Gunner's Hole. See **Senior**.

Junior Match   a cricket match played before Easter between College and Commoners. Until 1867 it took place on Hills, near Clump. The XIs were composed of men not in Senior or Middle Match. After the separation of Houses and Commoners in 1869 there were three contests, until matches were abolished and replaced by Clubs.

Junior Mess   the six Junior Praefects in New Commoners who ate together at meals (1868).

Junior Part, or **J.P.**   Junior Part of Vth Book, consisting (1920) of J.P.1 and J.P.2, the two junior divs in the school.

Junior Part Cloisters   the cloisters on the north side of Flint Court.

Junior Schools   a fives doubles competition, open to all men under 16, held in Common Time (1920).

'Junket!'   an exclamation of self-congratulation or gloating, especially in the phrase 'junket over you', meaning 'I exult over you', 'I would not be in your shoes'. In use from 1831, but rare by 1922. Named from junket (a delicacy, sweet dish, feast, or treat), derived from French *jonchée* (a cream cheese made in a rush basket or *jonchière* which in turn comes from Latin *juncus*, a rush); so, juncate in Spenser (c. 1595), junket (a sweetmeat) in Milton (c. 1632). As a verb, to junket means to feast, make merry: so, iunket in Purchas (1613);

juncketting (1630); junketings (1712); junket with (in Swift): to junket (to treat), late eighteenth century.

Jun-Jun　see **Junior-Junior**.

Jupiter　(1) 'a notorious rascal at St Cross, long since defunct, who has been a Notion from time immemorial'. Recorded 1868; still current 1922. He must either have been elderly when he first became a Notion, the name being drawn from the phrase 'as old as Jupiter', [or perhaps from his build, as with Henry 'Jupiter' Thompson of St John's College, Cambridge (see C. A. Bristed, *Five Years in an English University*, 1852, p. 145)]. (2) the Captain of Boat Club (1920).

Jupiter on Olympus　a Notion of uncertain meaning. Mount Olympus was a wooden cowl on a building called Jemima's on the far side of Scard's Wharf from Old Barge. It was also the name for Boat Club foricas.

[**K.C.B.**   see **bidet roll**.]

keep in balls, to   when a ball was kicked out of canvas, there were juniors outside to throw it back (1868). This was called watching-out from c. 1890.

keep toys, to   the Praefect in course in a Commoner house 'kept toys', i.e. was on duty in Toy-time, maintaining order, giving leave out of place, leave to put up a roll, and leave to go out of Hall. If unable to keep toys himself, he had to find a substitute.

Ken   an upstairs College Chamber; see **Chambers.**

Kenny's   D House: Culver House. Original House Don, Rev. W. A. Fearon (1868–82). His successor, T. Kensington (1882–1904), was called the Kenny.

kept   'a boy was said to be kept when he had done something wrong, and was not allowed to go home at the same time as the other boys: in that case he lived at Sick House' (1838). Detention in the holidays is attested as early as 1682: but the punishment, and the notion, are long since obsolete. See **Domum.**

kick   the First, Second and Last Behinds at Winchester football are called kicks. See also **kick, kicking.**

kick, kicking   a modified form of Winchester football, played two a side, for practice in kicking. Played by Commoners in canvas or yard; by College (1920) in canvas or on Ball Court. In College the rules of 'ropes', 'post' and 'behind' held good. If the ball was kicked out, a 'mader' (q.v.) was taken.

kicking in   when a game of Winchester football was played between ropes, but with no canvas, about forty juniors stood outside ropes at regular intervals, and when the ball went outside ropes they had to kick it back, at the place it came out (1836). This ceased in 1843 when canvas was first erected.

kick off, to   to punt at Winchester football after getting a catch, or losing a schitt, gowner, or goal: also used as a noun. By 1917 this was called a bust, or bust-off.

kick out, to   to kick the ball out over canvas.

kick over, kick up, to   at Winchester football, to kick the ball high in the air, over the heads of the other side, when it was rolling along or lying still: considered unfair if done on purpose (1836–8). By 1900 there was a rule against it: to kick a ball over the height of a man's shoulder when it was still or rolling only very slightly, was a breach of the rule, as was kicking an 'own side' ball (i.e. one last touched by one of the same side) over that height. The penalty was a hot, taken a post back from the place where the offence occurred. **Kick-up** was also used as a noun (1892).

kid cheese: a Commoner Notion 1831–92 was 'hard kid' (hard cheese, hard luck). Possible derivations (1892) were: (1) originally for goat's cheese. (2) kit (a rush basket), perhaps the type in which cream cheese was made. cf. junket. (3) kit (cement, putty), from Anglo-Saxon *cwidu* (gum). (4) kid, kit (a small tub in which sailors receive their food). (5) kid, past participle of kithen, from Anglo-Saxon *cythan* (to make known): i.e. well-known. cf. cud. (6) the name of a grocer supplying it?

kill, to   to beat a boy (1838): to hurt severely, put out of action, overcome (1856). Long since obsolete. Originally it merely meant to strike, from Icelandic *kolla* (to hit on the head); in Ireland (1800) it bore our meaning, e.g. 'kilt and lying for dead'. We may have ironically used it for beating on the strength of Latin *caedo* (beat or kill).

kind   small, quaint, attractive, amusing (e.g. a kitten), especially in the exclamation 'Too kind!' (pronounced t'kind). Much in vogue 1917–18, advantage being taken of Milton's hymn 'Let Us with a Gladsome Mind', by singing in the next line 'praise the Lord, for he's too kind'. It may perhaps be an adaptation of the rustic use of kind for congenial, suitable, advantageous: e.g. 'kind weather', a horse that is 'kind' in harness, or a certain type of hay being 'kindest for sheep'.

King's daughter   a roly-poly with jam in the middle, sometimes served in College Hall. From Psalm, 45.13: 'the King's daughter is all glorious within'.

Kingsgate Street   (1) Kingsgate Street(!). (2) the Toye Pot pitch in the extreme south-west corner of Bull's Drove, which ran alongside Kingsgate Street.

Kitchen   College Kitchen, between Trusty Sweater's Hole and the store-room by the stairs leading up to the rooms of College Tutor. It originally extended from Hall Stairs to the above store-room, but its original proportions have been spoiled by building Trusty Sweater's Hole and Organ Room into its southern end. It reaches to the roof, and includes the kitchen proper and ancillary offices.

knout   a ball of wax-paper tied to a string and used in New Commoners by spree men and Course-keepers for chastisement. Recorded 1856–68; long since forgotten. It is a Russian word, *knutu* (a scourge); Icelandic *knutr* (a knot) is from the same root.

knuckle down   to kneel down. Recorded 1856–84; obsolete by 1914. The noun knuckle is from an Anglo-Saxon root meaning a little knob formed by bending a joint in a limb or a plant. We have knokylle bone of a leg (1440), knockles (for knees) (1584), a joint in a plant (c. 1620), a knuckle of veal (1632), vertebrae (1677), protuberances on the spines of books (1752). It is still used of the knee-joint of animals and the finger-joint of humans. To knuckle down is a phrase borrowed from marbles, meaning to hold the knuckles on the ground, which made it impossible to hunch too close to the mark; thus used by Cowper (1785). It came to mean bending to a task, submitting (cf. knuckle under). See also **finge**, another word derived from marbles.

knuckle-down hot, or **down hot**   at the beginning of each half-hour at football, instead of hotting ordinarily the players used to kneel down and hot (1868). By 1892 this was non-licet, and when a man touched the ground with his knee or body, he had to call 'Down', and his side gave ground to allow him to rise or be pulled out. But the notion survived to 1920 in a 'down hot' (q.v.).

K.P. or **Kingsgate Park**   bounded on the north-west by Furley's, south-west by Fishcroft, south-east by Forder's Piece and Barn, north-east by Beloe's, north by Romans Road (1920). In Short Half it contained a Middle Game Commoner canvas; in Common Time, an Ellis Pot ground on Fishcroft (q.v.) and a Jun-Jun on the site of canvas; in Cloister Time, three crockets pitches: (1) a Hopper Pot pitch called 'Barn' in the middle. (2) a Toye Pot pitch called 'Romans Road' along the north side. (3) a Jun-Jun pitch called 'Fishcroft' on the Fishcroft soccer ground (1920).

Ktema Book   a VIth Book lines (repetition) book. From the Greek words κτῆμα ἐς ἀεί (a possession for ever) which owners of Ktema Books have written on the fly-leaf of their copy from 1878, if not earlier. [The Greek phrase is used by Thucydides at the beginning of his *Histories*; the Latin equivalent is Horace's *monumentum aere perennius*.]

kuse   a misspelling of cuse (q.v.).

La Croix (pronounced La Croyks) Octavius La Croix, known as Octo, a pastry-cook with premises at no. 8 College Street (the house where Jane Austen died). A most important institution, especially to Commoners, c. 1835–55.

Labyrinth the maze cut in the turf on the summit of Hills. See **Hills**.

landies gaiters (1831); from Landy & Currell, who supplied them.

Late Chapel Morning Lines were sometimes discontinued in the depth of winter, in which case Chapel was at 7.30 instead of 7 (c. 1880).

Late Leave on a Leave-Out Day everyone had to be back in their House by 9 in Cloister Time, or 8 in the other two halves, unless they had obtained Late Leave, signed by their Housemaster and counter-signed by the Headmaster (from c. 1892).

launch, to to take hold of the two corners of a mattress, which projected below the end of the bed, and drag it and its occupant, bedclothes and all, on the floor. This was a pastime of 1831–92; obsolete by 1914.

Laurels the trees which grew opposite Studies in Moberly's Court in New Commoners (18678).

Lavender Meads the field south of Meads Wall, separated from New Field by a row of trees. Derived from Old English *lavender* (launderer or laundress), and Latin *lavandarius/lavandaria*. It was where the washerwomen, perhaps from the adjoining Convent of St Swithun, did their work. cf. Le Côtil de la Lavanderie, in St Martin's parish, Jersey.

Laverty a very fine carpenter, named James Laverty, who was an instructor at Mill (1920). He had a workshop in St Swithun's Street, and an antique shop next to King's Gate, opposite which he lived.

'Lawful time!' called by the Praefect in course (1880), by the Second Junior in course (up to 1917), in College, when Toy-time was over and men might leave their toys.

leave continent   before anyone could go continent in New Commoners (1868), he had to get leave from the Headmaster. The rules for this in College (1920) were that leave continent had to be raised directly a man went continent: if he was an Officer, by his writer; a Praefect, by his valet; an Inferior, by the First Junior in his upstairs Chamber; a First Junior, by his Second Junior. It had to be raised from: (1) the senior Praefect of the upstairs Chamber. (2) the Praefect of Chapel in course (which of the two could be ascertained from either of the Chapel writers). (3) the Aul.Prae. (4) the Second Master. To each of the above was said: 'May I have leave continent for Smith?' If Smith was in Senior Div, the man raising leave also had to go to (5) the Headmaster, and say: 'Smith has gone continent.'

leave from Chapel   permission from the headmaster to be absent from Chapel, in New Commoners (1868).

leave from Hills   four senior Praefects, four senior Inferiors, those who drilled, learned drawing, etc., had permission to stay off Hills, in New Commoners (1868).

leave from lessons   permission for a boy who was continent not to do lessons, without which he had to write out the lessons he missed, in New Commoners (1868).

leave off Morning Lines   if a College man felt ill in the early morning when he was called, he might ask the First Junior to raise leave off Morning Lines for him from the Second Master (1920).

leave off Toy-time   if a College man was going to be absent from the beginning of Toy-time, or the whole of it, he had to tell the First Junior in course to raise him leave off Toy-time. This the First Junior did, from the Praefect in course, as soon as he had called 'Hour!' (1920).

leave on   permission to remain in the school after the proper time for superannuation. Recorded 1900; obsolete by 1914.

leave-out   in College (1838) on a saint's day, any boy who had friends in Winchester or not more than 10 miles [16 km] away to invite him out, might

launch

have leave out of College. If his friends lived more than 4 miles out [6.4 km] he could go to them directly after morning chapel; if less than 4 miles, at 12 o'clock; if in the town, at 2 o'clock. In every case he had to wait till the roll was down. Boys who had early and 12 o'clock leave-out, did not have to return to College till 9 in the evening. Those with 2 o'clock leave-out had to be in for Toy-time in winter. But in summer every boy with leave-out could stay out till 9 o'clock.

In New Commoners (1868) there was leave-out every day 12–1 and 2–3, during which times boys could go anywhere in the country, but to shops only 12–1. On half-rem days in summer there was leave-out 2–5 (when there was names-calling) and again 5–6. In winter, leave-out was 2.30–5, and later on only till 4.30. On Hatch Thokes, besides regular leave-out, there was leave-out 10–11; on remi days and leave-out days, 11–1. On leave-out days the usual leave-out was 12–7.30, but in summer from 12 to 8.45 (prayer time). On returning from leave-out, boys had to enter their names and times of arrival on a list in Bread Room.

In 1890, all red-letter saints' days were whole holidays, on which men could go for leave-out to their friends. The limit of distance was 60 miles [96.5 km], thus excluding London, for which special leave was necessary from the Headmaster. Men could start as early in the morning as they chose, unless they were going only a short distance, in which case they had to attend Chapel at 8.45 together with those not going for leave-out.

In 1907 there were usually three leave-out days each in Short Half and Cloister Time, and two in Common Time; on red-letter Saints' Days if convenient but not if they fell on a Sunday or within the first ten days of term. Everyone had to attend Chapel at 7.45 and names-calling at 8.30. Leave-out day ended at 9 p.m. in Cloister Time, and 8 p.m. in the other two halves.

In 1920, leave-out was given (1) on leave-out days and whole rems. (2) to friends up town for meals on Sunday. (3) to one's pitch-up, if 'down'.

leave out of Chambers   had to be raised by Inferiors in College (1920) from a Praefect or the senior Inferior present, if they wanted to leave their upstairs Chamber once they had gone into it at night; not necessary for going to bidet room.

leave out of College   to be raised by Inferiors (1920) who wished to go out of College, i.e. Middle Gate, after lock-up; given by any Praefect.

leave out of Hall   in New Commoners (1868) at the end of breakfast (8.20) and of tea (6.20), the senior Inferior walked towards the Tutor in course for leave out of Hall, which the Tutor gave by nodding: after which, but not before, anyone might go out of Hall.

leave out of place   to be obtained from the Praefect keeping toys in Commoners, by anyone wishing to leave his toys or Middle Desk. He was allowed to walk about and talk to anyone so long as he did not make too much noise. The rules on this subject varied from House to House (1900).

Leave-out Roll   a list of boys who had leave-out on a saint's day (1836). In 1838 the procedure was for the Warden to send down a roll of boys granted leave-out. Opposite each name was that of the person he was going to dine with. By 1900 this roll showed each man's destination and the time of his train. It was sent round a few days before Leave-out day, and the Housemaster had to pass it as correct.

leave to sweat the Old Roll   when all the New Roll was already sweated (but see Junior, First: 10), the First Junior in course in College could raise leave from a Praefect in his Chamber to sweat the Old Roll. This was generally raised up in Hall at tea. As a last resort, VIth Book Inferiors might be sweated, but at one's peril (1920).

leave up into Chamber, leave up in College   had to be raised from a Praefect in his Chamber by any junior wishing to go upstairs in the daytime; in force in 1920, but lapsed later.

leave up Town   to be raised from his House Don by anyone who wanted to go up Town to buy something, have his watch mended and so on: this could be raised any day after lunch, and from 12 to 1 on Tuesdays and Thursdays (1920).

leaving sport   see **sport**.

Let us now praise famous men   these words (the opening of Ecclesiasticus 44, always read as a lesson on Hatch Thoke) were the Notion for either: (1) the corbels, carved in the shape of heads, supporting the roof beams of College Hall; or (2) the framed oil portraits of benefactors and benefactresses which used to hang on the panelling above Dais but were removed to the Warden's Lodging in 1920. There was always controversy as to which of these the Notion meant: perhaps it was the former, as being the less obvious (1920).

Library   (1) College Praefects' Library. It was in Walford's, next to old IVth Book, on the west of School Court. Built in 1833, it was removed in Long Half 1871. (2) College War Memorial Library. See **Election Chamber**. (3) Commoner Praefects' Library, in New Commoners, between Old German Room and Norris' Room. It was built in 1842; converted to other uses in 1869. (4) Continent Room Library. This was a small bookcase or shelves in continent room in the various Houses. (5) House Library. Each House had a library of its own, maintained by House subscriptions. (6) Moberly Library (q.v.). (7) Warden and Fellows' Library. Containing valuable books, rare manuscripts, and the Founder's ring, this library was established in the upper and lower rooms of Fromond's chantry in 1629, remaining in the lower room till 1875. The books were then taken to College Tutor's rooms and elsewhere, being finally assembled in the Warden's Lodging in 1908. A few of the larger books were overlooked, remaining in the upper room of Chantry till 1924.

library fags   juniors who kept Commoner Praefects' library in order: they got off all sweat (1868).

licet (pronounced lie-set)   permissible, allowed. From the Latin verb *licet* (it is permitted), used as an adjective. Recorded from 1856, but probably much older. For the opposite, see **non-licet**.

lick, to   to beat a boy. Standard slang, recorded as a Notion from 1820; obsolete by 1917.

lift   a kick-up, at Winchester football (1868). It meant to lift the ball, to make it rise well off the ground in a flyer (1892); obsolete by 1917.

Linen Gallery   a room in New Commoners, 1842–69, which later formed part of Moberly Library. Below it was Commoner Tutors' Room, later converted to Dons' Common Room. Linen Gallery included Hag's Room, Lower Continent Room, and Gallery Nymphs' Sitting Rooms.

Linen Room   (1) a room in Linen Gallery in New Commoners (1842–69), where linen was kept. (2) another name for IIIrd Chamber downstairs (see Chambers) where laundry was sorted and mended by Mrs Rolf (1920).

lines   (1) repetition, Latin or English, up to books (1920). (2) lines set, to be repeated or written out, as a cropple by a Don or Praefect (1920).

Little Benjamin   a ruler (1892). Derived from Psalm 68.27: 'there is little Benjamin, [with] their ruler'.

Little Lion, the   a name for R. L. A. Du Pontet, Don 1892–1926. Taken from Hilaire Belloc's *Ruthless Rhymes*:

> 'Ponto!', he cried, and Ponto came,
> For Ponto was the lion's name.

liver and crow   liver and fat. Recorded 1838 only. Crow may be from Greek χρώς(flesh) or from a butcher's term for part of the intestines of a beast. A phrase in American slang, to eat crow (to swallow one's words), may be connected.

loather   one to be loathed. In use in 1856, and still current. In 1920 one could vent one's feelings by compiling a Loather Roll, i.e. a list of men in the House or the school, in order of nastiness. In standard English, loather would mean one who loathes, but at Winchester such words could have passive meaning: e.g. disguster (a disgusting person), revolter (a revolting one).

lob   a yorker, at cricket: or a tice, as it used to be called (abbreviation for entice). It could be delivered by a fast round-hand bowler (1836). In use in 1884; long since obsolete. In standard English a lob is a slow underhand ball at cricket, or a tennis ball lofted high above the opponent's head; from Welsh *llob* (a clumsy fellow, a lout). The only explanation of our use is that the yorker entices batsmen as effectively as lobs.

lob, to   (1) to bowl yorkers; long since obsolete. (2) to weep, an abbreviation for lobster (q.v.); still used 1920.

lobster, to abbreviated to **lob**   to weep, to cry. Recorded from 1831; surviving 1920 as lob. Probably from Anglo-Saxon *hlowan* (to bellow like a cow), which survives in standard English as low, and in dialects: in Hampshire there is louster, lowster (to make an unwelcome noise, such as sudden, loud, clumsy, or rattling sounds); in other South of England dialects, lowster has wider meanings, such as bustling, scrambling noisily about, scrabbling, roaming and dawdling about. It is also used as a noun for noise or commotion.

Lockback, a **Lockback Holiday**   a holiday or remedy on which, owing to inclement weather or other cause, boys were kept back from going on Hills. They stayed instead in School Court. Gate was locked, and College and Commoners remained on the School side of Gate (VIIth Chamber Passage). Recorded from 1831; obsolete by 1860.

Locks and Keys   a Commoner Peal. See **Peal**.

Logie   a stream known in medieval times as Lort-burn (misread as Lock-burn), which served St Swithun's Monastery as an open sewer. North of College it divided into two branches: one serving as a sewer to the Sustern Spital, the Carmelite Friary and the western part of College; the other flowing past the east of College, operating College Mill, following round outside Meads Wall, and joining the first branch on the outside of Amen Corner.

The first branch was inadvertently blocked in 1842 when New Commoners was built, causing an outbreak of fever in 1846, but this was remedied, and the stream continued to drain New Commoners until its abolition in 1869. It is no longer visible, but its site runs under the terrace of Museum and past the east of Sick House.

The second branch, known as Mill Pond in 1900, and later as the Warden's Stream (it flows past the Warden's Garden), is still called Logie in College, and originally carried sewerage from the eastern part of College buildings. It no longer flows round to Amen Corner but, having joined another stream called Otterburn, flows along the east of New Field to what was known as Mill Pond, and gives its name Logie to the Jun-Jun cricket pitch there. The ball is sometimes hit from this pitch into Logie.

Lort-burn or Lorte-burn appears in the very early days of College, when its defilement by the monastery was a source of dispute, and in 1543 it is written Lot-bourne. There was a Lort-burn at Newcastle, and a Lort-gate at Beverley in the fourteenth century serving the same purpose. Lort is probably from medieval Latin *lurdus* (dirty), derived from Latin *luridus* (discoloured, yellow), whence English lurid and lourd (stupid).

The name Logie first appears in 1836, when it is simply defined as sewerage, and again in 1856. In 1880 it was spelt Logey stream; possibly from dialect log-burn (an open drain) or from Dutch *log* (a sluggish, stupid person), giving in English logger, logy, loggy (heavy, unwieldy) and loggerhead (a dolt).

The idea of fouled, sluggish water seems to be common to both lort and logie, though there is no etymological relationship between them.

Log Pond   a small shallow pond in the south-east corner of Meads, originally in the meadow of the Carmelite Friary which was added to Meads in 1548. It was connected with the second or eastern branch of Logie by a culvert in Meads Wall, and its depth varied with the height of that stream. It is mentioned merely as a sewer (1836) and connected with the first or western branch of Logie (1838). In 1839 the pond was reduced in size, and by 1868 was a small pool lying against Meads Wall near Telegraph (the cricket score-board). In 1880, when it was filled in, it was a small pond of dirty water. By 1892 the eastern branch of Logie had been diverted and Log Pond dried up. In 1907 it was described as a rubbish heap. In 1917 it was merely a depression in the ground, but memory of it was preserved in the phrase 'ad Stag (num Log)' in choice of direction of play in Canvas: and its position was marked by Log Pond Champions.

For its derivation, see **Logie**.

Log Pond Champions   three gargoyles' heads bult into Meads Wall above the site of Log Pond (not to be confused with Og, Gog and Magog). This part of the wall was built in 1548 from the masonry of St Elizabeth's College, and the heads must have come from those buildings. The term champions, from Latin *campus* (battle, duel), may have been chosen to describe the protective way in which these heads stare out over the pond: unless, that is, it was originally champian, from Latin *campania* (level country). Champian meant a squatter dislodged from open land by the enclosures of the fifteenth century. Meads Wall was such an enclosure, and the heads could have been imagined as evicted squatters.

London leave   given by the Headmaster to go to London on a leave-out day. It was given only when a man was going to his parents and then only once a half (1910).

long bat   (1) a wooden bat of the same style as a short bat but with an elongated handle. It was used for playing batters on Ball Court by College Praefects and Tolly-keepers only; Inferiors used the short bat (see **batters**). Commoners did not play long bat, and only their juniors played batters at all (1920). The long bat disappeared in 1927.

Mathew's poem (1647) hints at the use of such a bat in a kind of tennis on Hills, and T. A. Trollope (1820–8) describes it as of ash, a yard [0.9 m] long, with a round handle less than 1 inch [2.5 cm] in diameter: the handle grew thinner and wider, until 6 inches [15 cm] from the end it was an inch and a half [3.75 cm] wide and no thicker than half-a-crown: it then expanded and thickened into a head shaped like the ace of spades, 3 inches [7.5 cm] across and half an inch [1.25 cm] thick. The thin part was oiled well and could be bent back almost to the handle. The bat of 1920 was nowhere less than an inch [2.5 cm] thick, and far less pliant. (2) Long Bat: the game played with a long bat (1920). (3) a College competi (q.v.) (1920).

long box   a long deal box for holding bats, stumps and balls (1836), and fishing rods (1838); for holding the cricketing apparatus in each house and each division of College (1880). Obsolete by 1917.

Long Chapel   any Chapel, morning or evening, at which the whole of the service was said (1868–92). Obsolete by 1917.

long disper   part of a loin of mutton (1836); see **disper**.

long fork   a stick used as a toasting fork in College (1836–92). In 1917 it was a 5-foot [1.5-m] bamboo with a metal trident stuck in the end, enabling toasters to keep their distance when Simon and Jude was very hot.

Long Game   when there was no canvas, and all played together without changing into football clothes (1868). By 1880 it meant a game in which new men played on half-remedies and Saturdays in Short Half. A leading canvas man kicked on each side to teach the younger players. Obsolete by 1917.

Long Grass   all Meads except the paths and Turf (1836); the slope from Grass Court to Meads Wall, which was used for rounders, small football and junior bartering (1868); all uncut grass round Meads, Lavender Meads, etc. (1900). Obsolete by 1917.

Long half   the term which began in February and ended in the middle of July: divided into Common Time and Cloister Time in 1866.

Long John   an old bricklayer who had been in the service of College but was too old to work by 1842: see **Gurdler**. It was a common nickname in the past – cf. Long John Silver in Stevenson's *Treasure Island* (1883) – and Mansfield (1836) hints that it was hereditary.

Long Meads   (1) a field between Sick House and Commoners (1831–6), later thrown into Meads. (2) the time after dinner on early summer evenings before Underhills began (Evening Hills), when boys went into Meads instead of

Long Meads

Toy-time (1831) until 8.15, lock-up being at 8: or went on to Underhills (1836); or went into Meads to play cricket from 7.30 to 8, when Toy-time began (1880). By 1914 it meant the time between tea and lock-up on Sunday evenings in Cloister Time, when men might walk only in Meads or New Field. Obsolete by 1917.

long paper   foolscap (1856); of a bluish colour, used for writing tasks (1868); for writing impositions, etc. (1880); ruled or unruled (1880); ruled paper in sheets the size of a tug copy-book (1900); still used thus in 1920.

Long Roll   a list published in November giving the full names in Latin of the whole school body, including Queristers and those on Election and Exhibition Rolls. It was printed on one long narrow sheet and rolled up inside a cylindrical cardboard case, until 1914, when an elastic band was supplied instead. The earliest Long Roll extant is that for 1653, in manuscript.

Long Stinkers   a College toll (1920). See **tolls**.

Long Table   a Queristers' and Butlers' Notion (1920) for Middle End in College Hall; a bad notion for men in College.

Lords   the school cricket XI, called Lords Eleven (1838). The name is a survival of the time (1832–54) when we sent the XI up to Lord's to play Eton and Harrow there in July.

Lords Roll   a list of the XI chosen to represent Winchester in Eton match. In 1868 it used to be read out in School about a week before the match. By 1900 it was brought down on the balcony of Webbe (later Hunter) Tent a few days before the match by a Don whom the Captain of Lords invited to do so.

Lords Tree   a large tree near Senior Part Cloisters, just south of Flint Court, with an iron bench round its base. Only men on Lords Roll might sit beneath it. (Cut down in 1998.)

Louisa   a fruit shop at the corner of College Street and Kingsgate Street (1880).

loving-cup   two loving-cups circulated at Domum Dinner during the speeches: they were large two-handled cups of silver or silver-gilt, with a napkin slipped through one handle for wiping the rim after drinking. The ceremony was thus: the loving-cup reaches A, who stands up and receives it; B rises; they bow to each other; A says, 'Propino tibi, Domine, cum omnibus Wiccamicis', then sips; A wipes the cup and hands it to B, while they bow again; B receives it, and turns to C, who rises; they bow; etc. A remains standing until B has passed on the cup, so three men are always on their feet while the cup passes: an old custom to protect the drinker from a stab in the back (1920).

Lower Cloisters   see **Cloisters**.

luxer   a handsome fellow. In use 1831–92: long since obsolete. Lux (elegance) was standard English in 1650, but is so no longer: this is evidently a word peculiar to Winchester, derived from French *luxe*, Latin *luxus* (splendour). [Entirely unrelated is the use of 'Lux' by pupils of the Feinaiglian Institution, Dublin (1813–37), to refer to the school, housed in a building called 'Luxembourg'.]

mad angry. Recorded 1856; used in marginal notes to Statutes (1780); obsolete by 1900.

made beer College beer bottled with raisins, sugar, nutmeg and rice to make it 'up' (1836); warm spiced beer mixed in a cup with pounded white sugar, nutmeg and ginger, with more beer poured on top (1838); abolished 1866. The past participle here seems to mean made up from various ingredients, or home-made, as in a 'made dish', or (home-made) made wine.

made flyer see **flier**.

mader, or **made kick** one of the rules in the game of practice 'kicking' in Canvas or on Ball Court. This rule is an example of one made to allow for the fact that there were no hots in such games. When the ball was kicked out, instead of a hot taking place, the other side were allowed a mader, i.e. a bust with the foot not usually used (the left with most people) or, if preferred, a drop-kick with the usual foot. One could not score a goal off a mader.

major, minor see **junior**.

make, to (1) to appoint a Praefect (from 1856). (2) to appropriate (from 1836), especially of pint-pots in College (1920). In 1836 it was no crime to 'make' things supplied by College, such as stationery, knives, faggots, crockery, eatables.

  Although the second meaning was considered a conundrum in 1799, there is no mystery about it: standard English, in phrases like 'make harbour', 'make good'. 'make the grade', uses 'make' in the sense of achieve an object, and from this it was used to mean acquire: e.g. make money, make a fortune; 'make experience' occurs in 1589.

make tea, to in a Chamber (1920). During Hall a junior was sweated by the In Loco of a Chamber to make tea. He had to appear half an hour before the time of tea, bringing the food and milk from Foricas Table, and then proceeded, under the In Loco's directions, to cut bread, toast and butter it, put on the boiler, etc. At the end he was rewarded with a biscuit or a piece of cake.

malinger, to   to sham illness in order to shirk some duty or game. This is standard English, used at Winchester for a man going continent when in good health to avoid something unpleasant.

Malts   a Notion (1920), but the meaning is not recorded.

malt buns   in 1917, when good bread was scarce, a supper was provided in College Hall of cocoa, cheese and buns made of brown bread and malt, at 8.45 p.m. By 1920 the buns were of white bread. Long after the war, when the pictures in Hall were taken down for cleaning, several malt buns were found lodged behind them, proving their value as missiles.

Maltby   the prizes given by Dr Maltby, Bishop of Durham, during Long Half: two to Inferiors for speaking and composition, and four to Praefects for composition only. In 1880 Maltby was the prize given to the man who did the best verses in Senior Part.

Mammy Norton   the College Notion for Aunty Norton (q.v.) (1920).

man   a member of the school. Unknown before 1856, 'boy' being invariably used: in Commoners the normal word was 'fellow' until 1870. [In his *Winchester College* (1949), J. d'E. Firth referred (p. 213) to 'The Notion . . . which everybody knows, the use of "man" for "boy", [which] made Moberly laugh when he first heard it in the 'sixties'. A. K. Cook in *About Winchester College* (1917) reports (p. 107) that the change from 'boy' to 'man' in Aul.Prae.'s book occurred in 1867.] By 1960, 'man' could also mean a thing, as in 'man-of-war' in standard English. No special reason is known for this usage, unless it is in reference to the school motto 'Manners makyth man', claimed in 1836 to be the Founder's, but on what authority is not stated. On the cover of Wrench's book it reads 'Manare makythe man'. Whatever the origin of the motto it has unfairly encouraged people to expect more courtesy from Wykehamists than others. Actually 'manners' in this context is a translation of the Latin *mores* (way of life, character).

Mange Hospital   a name for German Room and Old German Room in New Commoners. They were fitted with toys, and Commoner Tutors took pupils there.

When Commoners dispersed in 1869 these rooms were put to other uses, and by 1890 had become Praefects' Common Room. The name may reflect the isolation there of the sick, e.g. cases of ringworm, in the past.

Manners makyth man   see **man**.

marbles   slabs of white, grey, or black stone, slate or marble, let into the walls of the seven old College Chambers, Ist to VIIth, with the names and dates of men who have been in College. The designs vary considerably. All marbles in VIth and some in VIIth were painted over in cream colour in the 1920s, and the inscriptions picked out in black, to make those Chambers lighter.

The earliest marbles made professionally by monumental masons date from about 1680: but there are earlier names carved in small panels in the surrounds of Chamber windows, especially in the west window of Ist, the window of IIIrd by Crustey's stoking-hole, and the north windows of IVth, Vth and VIth. Those on the staircase up to 10th are really on the north wall of IIIrd, the stairwell having been excised from the western end of that Chamber. There is an exhaustive list of marbles in 'Inscriptiones Wiccamicae'.

In the eighteenth century, almost everyone who could afford it had a marble put up when they left, and there are far more from this century than from others. By 1920 very few were being added. The rule then was that you could not have a marble unless you had left at least ten years earlier, and 'deserved well of the school'. Among recent marbles at that time were those of (IInd) A. H. A. Simcox, 1883–9 and (VIth) A. K. Cook and A. B. K. Cook; one with the names of five Aul.Praes killed in the First War; and (VIIth) C. S. Crossman, 'ultimus C.F. eo nomine electus, 1883'. Some marbles bore famous names: Thomas Arnold (IInd); Raymond Asquith (VIIth). Others were renowned for their strangeness: Cadwallader Coker (VIth). Furleys have some marbles, which they brought from Old Chernocke House. They call them 'tombstones'.

Mare, the   Mrs Du Pontet: of Swiss parentage [hence perhaps 'mare' from *mère*?]: mother of the Fillies: a dour, silent woman (1920).

Margaret   the fruit woman. In his journal for 6 May 1792, Sir John Dumaresq, scholar 1764–7, relates how he revisited Winchester and called on some of his 'old college acquaintances', including the College Porter, and Margaret the fruit woman. His cash account that day shows he gave Margaret half a crown.

Margot   a chamber-pot with a rim, but no handle, whose home was in 6th Chamber (1920). From Latin *margo* (a rim).

Master   the term of respect with which bargemen, farmers and labourers were always addressed by the boys. Recorded from 1836 but obsolete (alas) by 1892. It is quite common in Shakespeare as a deferential mode of address, and is still

Mate and Mate's Mate

applied to men at the head of their trade e.g. master baker, master builder, master parson; and it has long been tactful to assume that a man's rank is one higher than it is (by which convention, police constables are often addressed as 'Officer'). In the days when 'Master' was still in vogue, 'Sir' was reserved for gentlemen, who *ex hypothesi* had no trade, a distinction noted by a foreigner visiting England in 1782. Derived from Latin *magister* (director, teacher), corrupted later to Mister, and finally shorn to Mr.

Match: Senior, Middle and Junior   three cricket matches between College and Commoners, played on Hills near Clump until 1866, after which they were played on Turf. Soon afterwards Houses were separated from Commoners and took part in these cricket matches. They were eventually discontinued in favour of Clubs for the whole school.

Mate   an odd-job man about College (1920) named Cecil Offer, usually seen in company with Bendle, who addressed him as Mate.

Mate's Mate   a man working junior to Mate (1920), probably the same as Cyclops (q.v.). The original Mate's Mate died about 1914.

mathma (pronounced mathmā)   mathematics. In use from 1917, if not a good deal earlier.

matinée   a punishment (1920), generally for being late up to books, consisting in going to one's Div Don's house before Morning Lines and waking him.

Derived from French *matinée* (morning; hence an early performance at the theatre).

mat-money   sixpence, extorted from every Commoner by a Verger, for his seat in Cathedral (1868). Long (and happily) obsolete.

Meacher's Hatch   see **hatch**.

meader, or **meaders**   see **Meads cap.**

Meads   the playing fields south of College. Meads proper is the field immediately south of College, enclosed by Meads Wall on the south and east, by School on the north, and by Museum and Sick House on the west. To the south of Meads are Lavender Meads and New Field, and to the east of them are Water Meads.

   Meads proper was originally the *viridarium* (pleasure-garden) and *ambulatorium* (walking-round) of the monks of St Swithun's Priory, and William of Wykeham bought part of it as a southward extension of his College grounds. It became the playground of boys in College, and long ago Eton Match was played in Meads. In 1920, various cricket games, and all Fifteens and Sixes, were played in Meads. As its perimeter changed, there was a succession of gates leading into Meads, which will be found in this dictionary as they occur alphabetically; as will the many corners – Salve Diva Potens, Amen, Pen and Ink, Darius and Angelus.

   Meads is the Anglo-Saxon *māed* (a meadow) with the Wiccamical plural suffix -s. We find mede (1420), and Herrick uses mead (c. 1648), but by the time of Johnson's *Dictionary* the word had become mainly poetical. That has not prevented modern house-owners from calling their homes 'Kingsmead' or 'Little Mead' if there was a patch of grass in sight. Such names are a revival. At Winchester, the boys' field is still called by its medieval name, the mead, or, as they would have it, 'Meads'.

meads cap, meader or **meaders**   a cap so-called because at one time caps could be worn only in Meads, top-hats being used on all other occasions. In College such caps were of flannel, in Commoners of cloth, but they were seldom worn, men preferring to go bareheaded in Meads. By 1920 any cloth cap was known in College as a tug cap, and in Commoners as a meader, and both used the word meader for the blue-and-grey-striped flannel caps worn by all for crockets.

Meads Champions   two stone heads from St Elizabeth's College, built into Meads Wall on the Lavender Meads side, between Amen Corner and Meads Gate. cf. Log Pond Champions.

Meads Foricas   in the ground floor of College Mill, entered from Meads, the door being screened by a wall. Used by men who had not been in College two years. After lock-up, all could use Through First (1920).

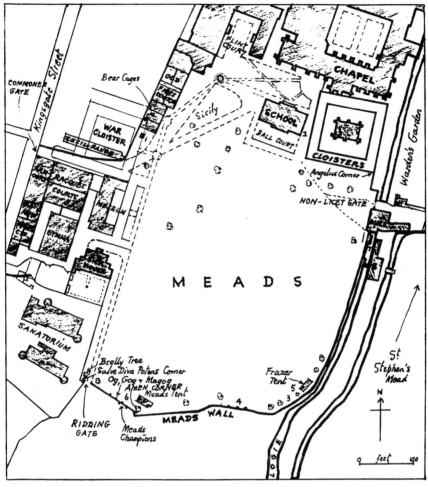

1. David's Kennel.
2. Good Friday Passage.
3. site of LOG POND.
4. Log Pond Champions.
5. Pen and Ink Corner.
6. Coxe's Wallow.
7. Meads Forices
8. Joel's House.

Meads and environs, 1922

Meads Gate (1) used originally for the gate leading into Meads from Kingsgate Street. (2) the gate in Salve Diva Potens Corner, in the south-west of Meads, leading to Lavender Meads and New Field. Originally called Ridding Gate, it bears an inscription to Dr Ridding as 'propagator finium nostrorum' (extender of our boundaries).

Meads Tent the old wooden pavilion in Meads, west of Amen Corner, originally used by Lords. In 1917 it was used by 2nd XI, Hopper Pot, or any other game playing there: being superseded by Frazer Tent, in memory of Jack Frazer, killed in 1927.

Meads Wall   (1) The stone wall enclosing Meads. It was built in three phases: 1398: from the west of College to Darius Corner, and diagonally to Log Pond. The only part of this now remaining is the wall between div rooms and War Cloister. 1402: from Log Pond to Cloisters and beyond. This is still *in situ*, being the tallest part of Meads Wall today. 1548: from Log Pond to Amen Corner, Kingsgate Street and Darius Corner. This was built of stones from St Elizabeth's College and is still *in situ* as far as Sick House wall. (2) the name of a cricket pitch. See **pitches**.

Measurement Room   the southernmost room on the top floor of the east wing of Flint Court (1920). Used originally for scientific measurements.

meatlessers   meatless dishes consisting of lentils and vegetables served for lunch in College Hall four days a week during the hardest years of the First World War (1917–18).

Medal Speaking   took place in School on the last day of Cloister Time at noon (changed in 1924 to before Domum Dinner), before an audience of pitch-up, Dons in full robes and men in the school. The Warden, sitting in the Headmaster's Chair with the Headmaster below him, distributed the medals and school prizes (not div books), with a handshake and a word or two to each winner. The winners of speeches recited them, and the winner of English Verse recited his poem. Winners were in evening dress.

In 1838 there were four medals given by the Queen to Praefects, two of gold for composition, two of silver for speaking.

The prizes given in 1922 were:

the King's Medals for:
    Latin or English Verse (alternate years)
    Latin Prose or English Essay (alternate years)
    Latin Speech
    English Speech
the Warden and Fellows' Prizes (of books) for:
    Greek Iambics
    English Verse or Prose
    Latin Prose or Verse
    Greek Prose
School Prizes:
    Moor-Stevens Prize
    Richardson Prize
    Senior Science Prize
    French Prize

Medes and Persians

German Prize
French Speech

Medal Tasks   the five compositions done in Senior Div in Common Time: (1) Greek Iambics (2) Greek Prose (3) Latin Verse (4) Latin Prose (5) English Essay. Nos. 1 and 2 always, and nos. 3, 4 and 5 every other year, got the Warden and Fellows' Prizes, of books. Nos. 3, 4 and 5 got a medal every other year (1920).

Medes and Persians (or **Pedes and Mersians**), **to give a man**   to jump on him when he was in bed. recorded 1838; still in use 1922. It was probably inspired by Daniel 5.25–8, where, at Belshazzar's feast, the word 'Upharsin' or 'Peres' is written by a hand 'over against the candlestick upon the plaister of the wall': and Daniel interprets the inscription as 'Thy kingdom is divided, and given to the Medes and Persians'. Alternatively, perhaps Pedes is from Latin *pedes* (feet).

Memorial Buildings, or **Museum**   erected 1893–7 from funds subscribed by the Wykehamical body, past and present, to commemorate the Quingentenary of College.

On the ground floor are laboratories for natural science, geology and photography; and Old Wykehamist Room, in which were displayed old Rolls, letters, medals and other Wiccamica: these were later removed to the room above Chantry. Old Wykehamist Room was used (1920) for the Headmaster's lantern lectures on Italian Art, and meetings of the Natural History and other societies. Portraits of distinguished Wykehamists hung on the walls.

On the first floor is a large exhibition room, running the full length of the building, and divided by four arches into two halls, devoted to Art and Science. In the Art Hall are plaster casts of famous Greek and Italian statues, and an oak table, 7 ½ by 3 feet [2.25 by 0.9 m] on the top of which is a carbon photo under glass of Michelangelo's paintings on the ceiling of the Sistine Chapel. There are also four oak portfolios containing reproductions of about 320 of the greatest pictures of the Venetian, Florentine, French, Spanish, English, German, Flemish and Dutch schools. Three similar portfolios contain architectural photographs of the pre-Norman, Norman, Early English, Decorated and Perpendicular styles. Archaeology is represented by a collection of pottery.

The main feature of the Science Hall is the collection of Hampshire birds, stretching the whole length of one wall, the gift of Dr Fearon, and one of the finest county collections in existence. There are also cases of geological and meteorological specimens, birds' eggs, butterflies and moths. The adjoining room is a drawing studio.

In the Tower, under the glass dome, is a landing, the walls of which are hung with casts and pictures of Italian Renaissance art. (The upper floor was connected to Dons Common Room in 1990.)

Memorial Gate   see **Bangy Gate**.

mention, to raise a   to be 'honourably mentioned' in a medal task or School Prize (1920). The Headmaster put up a roll on School Notice Board in this form:

Latin Verse, 1921

	Smith
proxime accessit:	Jones
hon.ment.:	Jackson

Mephistopheles   a lay-clerk from up Town who sang in Chapel Choir (1920). He had the aquiline features of a pantomime demon, a large flowing moustache, and a fruity bass voice which could sink to low D in the responses without trouble.

mess   a coterie sharing the same table and meal; and the meal itself. Once an important Notion, of varied meaning: (1) the Praefects' tables in College Hall were called Tub, Middle and Junior Mess, and the boys dining at each were also so named (1836). (2) in Chambers (1820), tea was called tea, or tea-mess. (3) a group of boys who breakfasted together was called a mess, with a distinguishing prefix, such as Deputy's Mess (1820). The same notion was used in New Commoners (1868). In Houses (1880), when a group of boys joined to share grub or a cargo, they were said to be 'eating messes'. (4) tea in Chambers in the evening (1838) was called mess, and any boy who got off Valet, made tea, coffee, or chocolate in his boiler between Evening Hall and Toy-time: this was called 'sporting mess'. See also **spree mess**. (5) mess could mean the remains of a joint of meat (1836). Mansfield uses it for the remains of a joint given by a Praefect to a junior, who was exempt from fagging as long as he was eating it.

A mess (a group of officers or others eating at the same table) is standard English; from Latin *missum* (a dish sent to the dining-table) and also from Old English *mese*, an Anglo-Saxon word (dinner) derived from Latin *mensa* (table): a meal sent to table.

mess cheese   in the early 1830s cheese was provided, with butter and bottled beer, as an alternative to tea and coffee when boys returned from Evening Hills: 'but the custom is exploded now' (1838).

mess things   a teapot, cup and saucer, sugar basin, cream jug, etc. (1838).

mess towel   every night the junior in chambers (1838) had to provide a towel to wipe up anything which was spilt, and to wipe out mess things. The notion was still in use in 1922 for the kitchen-cloths used by juniors for washing-up. Our mothers dutifully bought these dish-cloths and packed them in our school trunks. When unpacked at Winchester they became mess towels.

methla (pronounced methlā)   methylated spirit, used in cooking stoves (1920).

Michmash   on the first day of Cloister Time, Michmash took place on Ball Court pitch. It was a game of cricket, aimed at discovering who on the New Roll was any good. The sides consisted of half the New Roll each, led by the captains of College East and West cricket. Everyone was allowed to bat for ten minutes (1917). The custom lapsed in 1920.

  Michmash was a place north of Jerusalem where the Philistines had established a strong-point with an enormous garrison. By a daring manoeuvre, Jonathan and his armour-bearer commenced an attack, which turned to a rout, personally killing twenty of the enemy within half an acre [0.2 hectare] of ground (I Samuel 13.2–6, 14.1–14). It was an exhibition of youthful talent, which the captains may have had in mind when choosing this name; the Philistines being the insuperable hosts of Commoners: or the captains imagined themselves as the Hebrew champions, striving with the riff-raff lately admitted to College.

Micla (pronounced Miclā)   a Commoner notion for St Michael's Passage, leading from Culver's Close past St Michael's Church into Kingsgate Street opposite Commoner Gate. Recorded 1900; still in use 1922.

middle cut   a large thick slice out of the centre of a leg of mutton (see **disper**). This was a favourite cut, for which the 1836–8 recipe was: 'Wait till it is cold. Then cut gashes in it with a knife and put in them butter, mustard and pepper. Put it on a toasting fork, and hold it before the fire until both sides are well browned and the butter melted in. This makes an excellent piece of meat.'

Middle Desks   (1) four sets of double desks with forms on either side which ran across Hall in New Commoners (1842–69). (2) desks and forms for junior men in Mugging Halls in Commoners: their shape differed in the various houses (1892 on).

Middle End   the table in the south-west part of College Hall, opposite Junior End (1920).

Middle Game   a game played in canvas in order to give leading players a thoke. All regular canvas players took part, except the first six, their places being filled by men from Junior Game (1920).

Middle Gate

Middle Gate   the gateway between Outer Court and Chamber Court. In the tower above are three niches on either side containing statues: the centre niche has the Virgin and Child; the side niches, at a slightly lower level, hold the Angel Gabriel, and the Founder kneeling in prayer.

Middle House   (1) games played after Fifteens, in which only those who had never played in a Sixes' canvas might take part (1900). (2) inter-house competitions at cricket and soccer, instituted c. 1920.

Middle Match   a cricket match between College and Commoners, played by men who had not been in Senior Match. It usually took place in Meads on Ascension Day. After Houses were formed, there were three matches, until Matches were superseded by Clubs.

Middle Meads   time spent in Meads during the earlier part of Cloister Time, when lock-up was at 7.30 (1900); see **Long Meads**. Obsolete by 1917.

Middle Part   (of Vth Book) called Middle Part the Fifth until 1870: usually called M.P. in 1920, when it consisted of three divs with parallels, six in all. Sometimes M.P.1 had three parallels, in which case S.P.3 had only two.

Middle Part Cloisters   the doorway on the east side of Flint Court. There is no cloister here, but up to 1869, in New Commoners, there was a covered way round the court.

Middle Part note-book   see **note-books**.

Milk-Hole

Middlers Communion after morning chapel on certain Sundays, as distinct from Earliers (q.v.) (1920).

Middle Sands the pavement from Middle Gate to Chapel; see **Sands**.

Middle School school time between breakfast and dinner. Recorded 1860; obsolete by 1914.

Middle Toys three toys round chamber post in VIIth, used if College was overfull. They were not real toys, just tables and articles (1920).

Midnighters an emergency foricas off 12th bidet room next to Crutey's Hole (1920).

milk and bikkers biscuits and a glass of milk, served at Sick House between hours at 10 or 11, and taken by about half the men in College. For juniors it was a tonic, for senior men rather a luxury. Still so called in 1920, though the biscuits were stopped as a wartime economy and never re-started.

Milk Hole a deep hole in the river bed immediately below the lock-gates of First Pot, where the underlying chalk had been laid bare by the rush of water through Pot (1831). It was named from the whiteness of the chalk, or of the water foaming through Pot, and was a capital bathing-place, but dangerous for those who could not swim (1838). Obsolete by 1870.

milk jerries glass milk flasks sent up from School Shop for Chamber teas. Washers-up had to put them under Holy Water Stone at night, from which School Shop boy collected them (1920).

mill, to (1) to rag, fight, spar. This was Regency boxing slang; also used of cattle aimlessly gyrating when being herded. (2) of a ball (1920), to kick it out

mill

of canvas and over Meads Wall into Logie or Joel's garden. When this happened, 'Mill!' was shouted to the sixth watcher-out, who stood on a ladder leaning on top of the wall. He had to retrieve the ball and throw it back.

mill   a fight. In use since 1838, this was Regency boxing slang, used by Dickens.

Mill   (1) College Mill, disused. It abuts on Meads just south of Non-Licet Gate, and is entered by a balustraded ladder to the first floor. In 1922 it still contained the mill wheel and some of the apparatus, and was being used as a store-house for school chairs, which were brought down from it by a wooden chute. Mr J. D. Le Couteur and his glaziers used Mill as a workshop for mending Chapel glass, 1921–2. (2) School carpentry shop, in Kingsgate Street, nearly opposite Forder's Piece and just behind Stinks Buildings (1922). It was rebuilt in Forder's Piece c. 1925.

Mill Pond   a name for Logie, c. 1900, when it is described as a trout stream flowing through College Mill and Hammond's Mill.

Mint   the muniment room of College (mint is a corruption of muniment), which contained all the College deeds, records and accounts. Below it is Baptistery, and above it a room called Munimint. The ceiling of Mint is supported by four corbel heads, one of which is a contemporary portrait of the Founder. The room has been called by this name since 1868, if not earlier. This trio of rooms, Baptistery, Mint and Munimint, has sometimes been called Mint, Muniment Room and Bogey Hole.

mint julep   a spiced alcoholic drink with mint leaves standing in it, served on one day a year in a loving-cup in Hall: a sum of money having been left by a benefactor to provide this treat. It is also an American drink, made by pouring brandy on sugar and broken ice, and adding sprigs of mint. Mint is the Greek μίνθα, Latin *mentha* (mint); julep the Persian *julab* (a sweet drink), appearing as julap (1624) and julep (Milton, 1634).

Mirth and Funnypenny cf **Moral and Quackdonald** two very ephemeral notions of 1918, for J. d'E. Firth, B. C. Gybbon-Monypenny, W. J. C. Quarrell and A. J. Macdonald, all of them men in College between 1912 and 1920.

miserere seats eighteen oak miserere seats, part of the original furniture of Chapel, still survive in the choir stalls. Warden Nicholas removed them to Ante-Chapel in about 1690, and they were placed in their present position in 1875. As elsewhere in England, such a seat has a miniature seat on the underside, on which a man could prop himself during a tedious service; but if he dozed the seat might fall, and he with it. So called from the opening words of Psalm 51, 'Miserere mei, Deus' (Have mercy on me, O Lord), which was used in many types of service.

Misery Corner the corner of Trench nearest First Pot. From here 'the legendary author of Domum is said to have gazed on the scenes of his former joys'. This is apocryphal, and the name was no doubt chosen by weary juniors who had to run round the whole of Trench calling 'Domum', when it was time to go back to College.

Mission the Winchester College Mission in Rudmore, a suburb of Portsmouth. Praefects could stay a week-end there during term (1920), by arrangement, to see the Missions' work. The Missioner (1920) was Rev. E. de G. (Bertie) Lucas (G 1891–7), assisted by Rev. Walker, curate.

Mission Meeting on the first Saturday afternoon of Short Half and Common Time the Missioner addressed the school in School on the work of the Mission: an event much enjoyed by us (1920) as he enlivened his address with humorous anecdotes about Mrs Bumstead and other of his parishioners. Next day he preached in Chapel, and the collection was given to the Mission.

Mizmaze see **Hills** and **Labyrinth**.

Moab taken from Psalm 60.8: 'Moab is my wash-pot'. (1) College wash-house or conduit on the west of School Court, built c. 1838 in the range of new rooms established there. It was separated from Praefects' Library on the south by Good Friday Passage, and abutted on the south wall of New Commoners' Grubbing Hall when that was built in 1842. Moab was equipped with seven marble basins and had lockers all round the room. The entrance was in School Court. (2) a conduit on the wall of Cellar, facing School. (3) the conduit in some Houses. (4) a small conduit in Moberly Court (1880). cf. Edom and Little Benjamin.

Moabites, or **Harry Moabites** an 1868 Notion for boys in the Rev. H. E. Moberly's House (B).

Moberly Gate

Moberly Court, Moberly's Court, or **Gravel Court**   court created by Dr Moberly when he demolished Old Commoners and built New Commoners, 1839–42. It was bounded on the north by the Headmaster's House, south by Hat Place, east by Arcadia, west by Commoner Praefects' studies. When in 1869 New Commoners buildings were converted, these studies became div rooms.

Moberly Gate   the gate adjoining the Headmaster's House on the east, leading from College Street into Moberly Court. It was formerly called Commoner Gate.

Moberly Library, or **Mob.Lib.**   the school library, formed out of North Gallery and adjacent rooms in New Commoners. It was formally opened and named on Domum Day (26 July) 1870, in memory of Dr Moberly's Headmastership (1836–66). At the end of Common Time 1871, Dons and VIth Book were allowed to use the library, as were the rest of the school with certain resstrictions. It is above Common Rooms. Funds for its creation were provided by Old Wykehamists. The nucleus of the books came from College and Commoner Libaries. It was maintained by an annual grant from school funds, and a subscription from each House. In 1934 it was removed to Brewery.

It was important for juniors (1920) to know the rules of getting a book out of Mob.Lib., a thing they were often sent to do. This could be done after last hour on whole-school days, a quarter of an hour before Lock-up on half-rems, and after chapel on Saturdays. You found the book and asked Mob.Lib.Writer to enter it. If he was not there, you wrote name of book, author and borrower on a slip of paper and left it on his desk near the door. Books had to be returned to this desk before first hour in the morning.

Mob.Lib.Writer   the Writer of the Bib.Prae. His duties (1920) were: to be in Mob.Lib. at the above times to enter books borrowed in the ledger; to restore returned books to their shelves next morning; to extort a fine of sixpence from anyone failing to return a book next day. Mob.Lib.Writer could not be sweated to wash up on whole-school days.

mock trial   last held in 1917, in a downstairs Chamber in College after Preces. Praefects and senior men attended, refreshments were provided, and it was in essence a sport. In the last recorded instance, the case heard was *Rex* v. *Frank Carter* for the murder of Mr Du Pontet. Those with talent for mimicry took the roles of the Judge, Prosecution and Defence Counsel, Sherlock Holmes and other witnesses. It was great fun.

money   see **dibs**.

Money and Direction Rolls   a Commoner Peal (see **Peal**).

mons   a crowd or pile-up of people, from Latin **mons** (mountain, mass); also used as a verb, to crowd or push ('Don't mons!'), or to press or agitate for. In the evenings after tea (1892) there would arise a cry of 'Mons on', and anyone in hearing who wanted that kind of exercise would congregate and form a pile on top of some victim. [See also **Ponto mons**.]

Monthly   an examination of every div in the school except VIth Book, held personally by the Headmaster. It was originally held every month; later, in the middle of the half, after which half-term reports were sent home (1920). Monthlies took place every half for Middle and Junior Parts, but only in Short Half and Cloister Time for Senior Part. The Headmaster conducted the exam orally and on paper, on the classical and historical work which each div was doing. It was an excellent institution, which gave authenticity to his remarks in half-term reports.

Monty   see **Headmaster**.

Monty Fiasco   a terrace garden in front of the Headman's House, facing Moberly Court, and designed by Monty Rendall in Italian style, with fountains and 'putti' (cherubs) (1920). Named from Montefiascone, a town north-west of Rome.

Monty Pot   for Swimming Athla; see **Pots**.

mopping   see **Junior, First, Second**.

[**Moral and Quackdonald**   see **Mirth and Funnypenny**.]

Mordecai   the second senior butler in College Hall, at some remote period. The name was later used for anyone holding that office, though one of his successors was called More-than-most-Decai. This cheerful notion unfortunately lapsed in about 1915. Mordecai, a Jew of the captivity under Xerxes, took a post at court to be near his daughter Esther, and between them they prevented Haman from exterminating the Jews (see the Book of Esther). Our butler must have got this name either from his decayed appearance, or perhaps from having joined Hall staff to keep an eye on a Quirister relative: or from both.

more sack   'when one boy lies down and a number of boys get on him, one on top of another' (1838); later called a 'mons'. This is a strange phrase, of uncertain origin; suggestions are: (1) from the verb sack (to heap or pile by sackfuls), used by Peele (c. 1590): 'hath sack'd on me such hugy heaps of . . . sorrows'. (2) a reference to Shakespeare's *King Henry IV*, Part I (act II, scene iv) where Falstaff calls for repeated cups of sack: 2 gallons [9 l] are eventually consumed, which Prince Henry calls 'an intolerable deal of sack'. (3) a play on the word 'mons': 'Mountain' is wine made from grapes grown in the hills; sack is a white wine from Spain. (4) an echo of an old word of command for loading harquebuses: amorce is priming powder for this weapon, and hack, short for hackbut, was slang for harquebus. The order to load harquebuses may at one time have taken the form: 'Amorce hack'.

Morning Hills   In 1920, on the second morning of Short Half and Cloister Time, the whole school and some Dons went up Hills, where the Headmaster marshalled them in crescent formation just north-east of Clump. He and the Aul.Prae. stood with their backs to Clump and the Dons behind them, facing the school. Hats were removed. Dr Sweeting, Master of Music, blew on a pitch-pipe, and conducted a band of Queristers in the hymn 'Jam Lucis' (an innovation of Dr Fearon's), which was sung through, the school joining in. Hats were replaced. The Aul.Prae. then called a namers of the whole school by divs. Each man, as he answered 'Sum' to his name, walked past the Headman and Aul.Prae., raising his hat. As they came away, men went down, to their Houses, and breakfast. One could not go to Morning Hills without a socius, because in Tabula Legum it is written: 'sociati omnes incedunto'. See also **Hills**.

Morning Lines   the school time between 7 and 7.30 a.m. (1868) or 7.45 (1892), when Chapel bells began. It was so called because lines varying from 15 to 50 (1868), or 10 to 30 (1892), were repeated every morning during this time. In VIth Book there was repetition of lines at this time on four mornings a week (1892), three (1907), two (1920). By 1917 Morning Lines meant any work up to books before breakfast.

Moses and Aaron   a wooden shield at gutter level on Old Tent displaying College arms, of the design in vogue at the end of the nineteenth century: viz. College arms impaled with those of the see, keys and a sword. The shield was held erect by a bracket on the sloping roof. In Cloister Time 1923 it was removed, and two plain shields substituted, with general disapproval. It was customary in a Notions examina to be asked: 'Which is Moses?' The correct answer was: 'The one that isn't Aaron', and vice versa.

Mother Gumbrell   (usually pronounced Grumble) a tall, austere woman in charge of Sick House, c. 1820–8. Her husband, Dicky Gumbrell, ex-butler to

Moses and Aaron

Dean Ogle, was allowed to reside with her there. A predecessor of Mrs Gumbrell in the period 1764–7 was 'Mrs Williams at the Sick House', named among his old college acquaintances by Sir John Dumaresq, scholar during those years, in his journal for 6 May 1792, when he revisited College. His cash account shows he gave five shillings to 'old Mrs. Williams at sick House'. In Mansfield's day, the nurse at Sick House was **Mother Maskell**, who provided tea which the fags brought.

mottoes   when a Medal task was shown up, a motto was written on it instead of the author's name. Some examples, c. 1920, are 'In vino veritas', by Igor Vinogradoff, known as Vino; or 'Monte viget platanus, sed quercus proxima ponto', which contained veiled references to Monty, Platnauer, Quirk and Du Pontet, and was pronounced by the Headmaster to be 'banausic'. R. W. M. Atkin (E) showed up his task without a motto, and the ingenious classicus M. H. Brown added one of his own invention, reading: 'I am as ugly as a bear'. Naturally, in identifying the author, the Headmaster enquired: 'Who is as ugly as a bear?'

Mount Olympus   a wooden vane or cowl, shaped like a rounded pigeon-house. It was on the top of a building in Tempe (1868), of an old house on the left bank of River between Redbridge and Boat-house, which had fallen down by 1880, and of a building on Scards wharf (1892). Obsolete by 1917.

mouse-digger   a miniature pickaxe used by amateur geologists for digging fossils in Chalk Pit, and by naturalists for unearthing field-mice, which were brought home and kept in cages. It was wrongly supposed to have been introduced by the naturalist F. T. Buckland (Coll. 1839–44), later Dean of Westminster. Recorded from 1820; obsolete by 1914.

Mudie books   books hired from Mudie's lending library for Mob.Lib. by the Bib.Prae., who ordered them about three times a half from suggestions collected in College (1920).

mug, to   (1) to work (at lessons), work at, work up, work hard. (2) to study, pay great attention to, imitate another boy, e.g. by wearing similar clothes. (3)

mouse-digger

to bestow pains, e.g. on one's dress or hair; carefully brushed and greased hair was 'mugged hair'. (4) to tidy up, ornament, beautify: e.g. one's toys. (5) to clean and oil a bat: hence batmugger is an instrument for oiling bats. The above used are recorded from 1831, and many of them are still current. In the 1960s, mug could also mean (6) to work (intrans.): e.g. 'My watch doesn't mug.' 'Mug' is from smug (cf. puke for spuke) past participle passive of Anglo-Saxon *smeagan* (to meditate, study) and means that which is studied, hence neat or spruce. It was so used by Shakespeare in 1598 and there was another example in 1682. Today smug means prim, self-satisfied. To smug was also a verb in standard English, meaning to take trouble over, beautify; in an example from 1621 we have 'a young man . . . smugs himself up'. The 's' was then dropped and in modern standard English to mug up means to work up a subject of study; or, in theatrical slang, to make up the face.

mugging (1) work, study; still in use. (2) material used to adorn a toys; obsolete by 1917.

Mugging Hall (1) in New Commoners (1842–69), it was on the ground floor on the east of Flint Court, under East Hall, and in it all boys who had no study sat in Toy-time. Down each side were toys, and Middle Desks ran in four rows across. On one side was a large space. At each end were three pigeon-holes occupied by the six seniors who had no studies. (2) in each of the Houses there are one or more halls where men prepare work and spend their time indoors. Toys line the sides, and there are usually Middle Desks in the centre of the room.

mugster a diligent boy. One who works. This was in use from 1838; not standard English.

Munimint see **Mint**.

[**Museum** see **Memorial Buildings**.]

Music School erected in 1906 west of St Michael's Church. It contains a large concert hall, and a series of practising rooms.

Mugging Hall (toy-time)

Mushri   the language of E. D. A. (Doidge) Morshead, or 'The Mush', who was scholar 1861–7: Don 1872–1903: Div Don of VIth Book Junior Div for many years, and a famous translator of Greek plays. Under the title *The Mushri Dictionary* some of his div published a glossary of his language and usages, which were very extraordinary. Scarce, and hardly ever seen now, this book is full of fun. There is a copy in Mob.Lib. The word best known in it to modern Wykehamists is in the addenda: it is 'Attarambamph', an exclamation. [The book has been reprinted with an introduction and appendices: C. A. Stray (ed.) *The Mushri-English Pronouncing Dictionary*, 1996.]

Mushroom, the   the Mush's div room, known as Frank Carter's in 1920.

mustard-and-pepper-keeper   a piece of patronage in the gift of the Praefect of Hall, resembling bread-picker in Commoners, which exempted the holder from fagging at games, i.e. watching out at cricket and fives, and kicking in at football. His only duties were to keep Praefects' subscriptions, and pepper, the money for which was given to him by subscription-keeper. It was in use 1831–43; long since obsolete.

muttoner   a blow from a cricket ball on the knuckles, the bat being at the time clasped by them (1831–84): or a blow from anything on the body. In standard

muttoner

slang this word means a roué. Our word contains the idea that the blow exposed raw flesh or fell on a knuckle or joint, making it resemble a joint of mutton.

muzzler   a blow on the nose. Recorded 1892; obsolete by 1914. Derived from muzzle (the mouth and nose of an animal) and the verb to muzzle: to put a muzzle on an animal, to silence a person.

My Garden   the Warden's Garden. It was so called because in notices and conversation (1920) Monty Rendall often said: 'The Warden's Garden, my garden.'

nail the central sconce, fixed in the panelling at the east and west ends of School. A boy who had committed some unusually disgraceful offence, or was detected in a lie, was ordered to 'stand up under the nail', i.e. on Junior Row, under the sconce, during the whole of school time. At the close of it he received a bibler (1831–43).

nail, to (1) to catch or detect in some misdeed: e.g. 'I was nailed shirking up Town', 'tight nailed'. Thus Goldsmith (1766) uses it in the sense of exposing in an error; and in standard slang, it derives from nailing a false coin to the counter. Our use is in line with this, with perhaps a tinge of the sconce implication as well. (2) to engage or impress for some duty, or for fagging of a Praefect. At the end of the nineteenth century there was a special kind of nailing, to obtain watchers-out for irregular hours, at the end of Short Half and Cloister Time when regular watching-out had stopped. There were strict rules to be observed by the man who was nailing: he might nail only for a Co.Prae.; he might not nail earlier than the morning of the day when watchers-out were required; he might not nail men in his own house, men in his own division, men who had been in the school more than two years, men under cover, such as a house, doorway or projecting roof, or men who were sweating for some other Praefect; he might not nail to the north of St Swithun's Arch, to the south of Romans Road, or New Field Gate, or to the east of Non-Licet Gate. This form of nailing was abolished by School Committee in 1902. This use of nail is standard slang meaning to catch or secure by prompt action: it is used thus in *Pickwick Papers* (1837) and in 'nail a cab' in the *Ingoldsby Legends* (1840), the idea being to nail down to a bargain. (3) to join two men sociusing each other. Thus used 1914; obsolete by 1917. It was an extension of (2) above.

naked with one or more buttons of one's clothing undone (1920).

Namers, or **Names-calling** (1) in New Commoners (1868) the Praefect in course had to call names before meals and after leave-out in the afternoon, and in Long Meads when leave-out was over at 8 p.m. The names of those not answering the first time were called over again. (2) in Houses (c. 1892) there were namers up at House two or three times daily. (3) there were namers,

nail

called Bear's Namers, in Lavender Meads at 5 p.m. on Tuesdays and Thursdays in Cloister Time before Eton match (c. 1892). (4) in College (1920) there were namers on

half-rems: at Lock-up, from Hall Stairs
Sundays: at 8.30 a.m. up in Hall
        10.15 a.m. from under Middle Gate; after which men crowded round the Second Master to raise leave out to meals
        4.45 p.m. (4.30 on Cathedral Sundays) from Hall Stairs
every day in Cloister Time, from Hall Stairs at Lock-up.

Namers were read by the Aul.Prae. or next senior man present (see **Hall Writer**). When he had finished, the Second Master came down and read again the names of absentees. This was called second namers. Men who came in time for it, having missed first namers, had to answer their names with their gowns buttoned. The Second Master took the roll away for further reference.

names-docker a junior (usually the senior watcher-out) appointed to tick off the names of players in canvas as they came, shout 'All down' when they were all there, write the goals on the card, keep the time, and supervise the watchers-out. In summer, the names-docker supervised watching-out at nets (1920). Recorded from 1892.

Nebuchadnezzar the ventilator in the ceilings of Chambers on the top floor of College, opened and shut by a cord worked from the fireplace (1920). The wheezing and creaking made by this contraption may have suggested a primitive oriental band, such as performed for Nebuchadnezzar (with 'cornet, flute, harp, sackbut, psaltery, and dulcimer and all kinds of musick') in the tale of Shadrach, Meshach and Abed-nego, in Daniel 3.

Nestor a boy who was over 18, or too old for his position in the school, or known to be older than he looked. Recorded 1831–56: obsolete by 1914. It was from Nestor, King of Pylos in the Odyssey, who lived for three generations of men (90 years). His name passed into English as a symbol of the oldest and wisest man in a community. [cf. C.F.]

Nevi, Nevy (1) a well-known pastry-cook named Burton (1838). His aunt, with whom he lived, always called him Nephi or Nevy (for nephew). (2) nephew: see **pitch-up**.

new new potatoes, ordered in a hot plate from School Shop (1920).

New Barge, or **River** this separated from Old Barge at Seven Hatches and rejoined it at Whirlpool (1868). In origin this waterway is Bishop Godfrey de Lucy's ship-canal of 1195. See **Barge**.

New Bridge 'a part of the river near Domum Wharf and Commoners Field, where Commoners used to bathe: but as the windows of the owner of Domum Wharf looked that way, it was thought fit by Dr Moberly to stop bathing there' (1838). Alternatively, 'a bit of wall, or foundations of a new bridge on the right bank of New Barge, below Red Bridge and opposite Clark's garden' (1868).

New Chamber an upstairs Chamber in College, created from a complex of passages and small rooms in the southernmost wing of the Warden's Lodging, which projects into Logie. This was done in 1917, when College first took War Scholars and had not enough sleeping accommodation. It was approached by going through Ken and Rabbit Warren. In 1920 it contained the junior Senior Praefect in College, supplied from Vth, an In Loco, and one or two juniors, these being an overflow from VIIth. The Headmaster wished it called War Chamber, but New Chamber was its only name (cf. Forder's Piece). No doubt the Founder encountered similar obstinacy about the name of his New College in Oxford.

New College (1) the Coll.B.V.M.Winton in Oxford. (2) the examina at the end of Short Half, on the results of which about five Scholarships and two Exhibitions at New College were awarded. It also took the place of div examinas for Senior Div. It differed from Goddard by the addition of an English Essay, and the absence of General Books.

New College Roll the list of men, issued by the Posers, who had been awarded Scholarships and Exhibitions at New College.

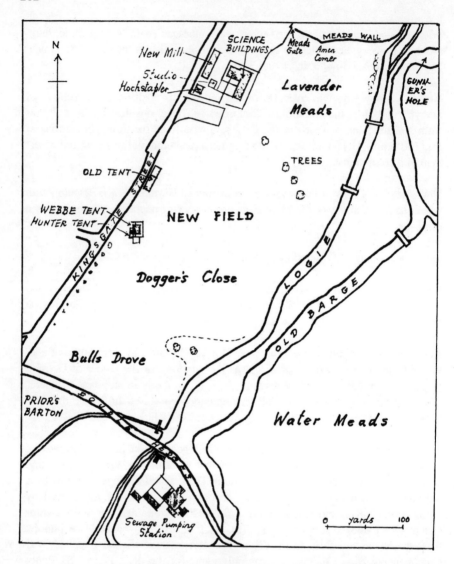

New Field

New Field the area of playing fields between Lavender Meads and Dogger's Close, opened in the winter of 1869, mainly owing to the enterprise and generosity of Dr Ridding: in whose memory the staff made valiant efforts to get it called Ridding New Field, Ridding Field, or Riddings. But after the contrary manner of boys, it was invariably called New Field, and by 1917 this name was applied to the whole expanse between Meads Wall and Double Hedges.

New Roll men who had come into College on the latest Election Roll, as distinct from the Old Roll, those of the previous year (1920).

New School   see **Walford's.**

nicknames

Some nicknames of the 1917–22 period

H. S. Altham	Harry, Harry Altham
H. Aris	the Hake, the Haddock
G. H. Blore	Georgie Blore
A. F. Booth	Piggy Booth
A. E. Broomfield	the Broomer, Broomers, Brummers
F. Carter	Frank
Miss Carter	May, May Carter
H. Chitty	Herbert Chitty
W. S. Cowland	Wally, Wally Cowland
W. B. Croft	the Bleeder
F. P. David	Ping, Fritz
R. P. Davidson	Little Davidson, Pyrrhus, Pringle
M. S. Dimsdale	Dimmers
C. V. Durell	Clem, the Tout
W. A. Fearon	the Bear
J. S. Furley	Sam Furley
J. A. Fort	James Fort
L. L. Garbutt	Larder, Gurbs
F. W. Goddard	Little Goddard
H. J. Hardy	Little Hardy
F. M. Hicks	Murray
R. L. G. Irving	Fang, Little Fang, Twitch
H. A. Jackson	the Jacker
J. D. Le Couteur	Wally, Wally Tooker
C. W. Little	Charles Little
S. A. MacDowall	Guts, Sid
L. M. Milne-Thompson	Milners, L-Msquared-T
W. D. Munro	the Munner
J. W. Parr	Jack Parr
J. L. R. Pastfield	Pasters
M. Platnauer	Plat, Plats
R. Quirk	Bobby Quirk, Bobby Q.
R. L. A. Du Pontet	Ponto, the Little Lion
M. J. Rendall	Monty, Push, the Head Man, the HM
C. E. Robinson	the Beast, the Bin, the Bince
M. Robertson	the Bobber, the Hoover
W. A. Spooner (Warden New Coll.)	the Spoo
H. C. Steel	Polly Steel

E. E. B. Stephens	Nen Stuggins
J. M. Sing	Little Sing
C. H. Thompson	Owl Thompson
J. A. K. Thomson	Little Thomson
H. E. G. Tyndale	Harry Tyndale
A. T. P. Williams	Bill, History Bill, the Second Man
A. E. Wilson	Archie, Archie Wilson
E. R. Wilson	Rockley, Rockley Wilson

nihil ad rem   nothing to the purpose. Used by masters (1838) in comment on verses or composition. By 1856 it had come to mean unaware, unconscious, vague, especially of an innocent expression on the face: e.g. 'he sported a nihil ad rem duck'. Obsolete by 1900. Used in standard English for anything irrelevant.

Nipperkin, the (occasionally **Nibbikin**)   a stone jug for beer, of which there was one in each College Chamber. In 1820–8 T. A. Trollope called it 'huge': and it was the duty of bedmakers to bring it in each evening, 'to last for all night'. In 1831–43 it was 'large'. By 1856 it was 'small', and served between meals, tea having been introduced in about 1845. Originally, no doubt, the nipperkin was a large jug, and the name was chosen humorously as being the smallest measure for spirits (one-eighth of a pint, [70 ml]) and is thus used by Scott (1822–4). But in the past it had meant something larger, as is seen from a reference (c. 1690) to snoozing over a 'nipperkin of Schiedam' and a 'penny Nipperkin of Molasses Ale' (c. 1710). The name comes from nip (sip, dram), appearing as nipper (1848), with -kin added for diminution.

Nomina (pronounced **Nominā**) or **Headmaster's Nomination**   The Headmaster could nominate boys, who did well in Eleckers but failed to get on to the Roll, for vacancies in Commoners, in preference to those who had simply done the Entrance Exam (1920).

non-husky   gooseberry fool without the husks (1836). Long since obsolete. cf. **husky**.

non-licet   (adj). From Latin *licet* (it is permitted); thus its opposite: not allowed, illegal, unwiccamical.

Non-Licet Gate   the large gate in the east wall of Meads, leading out past College Mill to St Stephen's meadow and College Walk. It was probably used originally as the shortest way out to Hills, but closed when it was found to be too far from supervision (1831). By 1892 it was permanently shut, except in Cloister Time after bathing leave had come down, and then only at times when bathing was officially licet. Its name means the Forbidden Gate. There is a tradition, recorded from 1831, that a boy expelled from College had to leave that way,

Non-Licet Gate

but no instance of this was ever quoted. The story could have arisen during a mass expulsion after one of the rebellions, the authorities ejecting rebels by the postern gate to avoid arousing the sympathy of the townsfolk. The further legend that the clothes of the expelled were handed over the gate on a long-fork is a mere embellishment arising from Horace's 'naturam expelles furca' (see **firk**), but colour may have been lent to it on some occasion when such a manoeuvre was necessary to avoid infection.

Non-Licet Passage, or **The Weirs**   the broad riverside walk round the wall of Wolvesey from Foster's Corner to the Soke Bridge; out of bounds for men in the school (1892), unless they had raised leave up Town (1920).

Norris' Room   in New Commoners (1842–69) between Commoner Praefects' Library and West Hall stairs. There were boxes in it for Tutors' House men to keep books in (1868). It takes its name from Norris the hairdresser, who used to cut hair there.

Northalls   tailors in Kingsgate Street: the predecessors of Gard. In 1920 College men declared that the legend painted on his windows was: 'R. H. Northall. Tailor to the Gentlemen and Commoners of Winchester College.' A libel. There was no 'and'.*

North Gallery   over Linen Gallery in New Commoners (1842–69).

North-West Passage   the passage leading from Chamber Court to Thule Chamber, which was added in 1906. It was in the north-west corner of Chamber Court: hence the name, which echoes that of the long-sought sea-passage round the north of America (1920).

note-books   types in use c. 1900–20 were:

---

* The premises are now occupied by B House Library (1998).

Du Boulay: a small notebook with red (later variegated) paper covers: introduced by Rev. J. T. H. Du Boulay, Don 1862–93.
VIth Book: a large book half-bound in white vellum.
Senior Part: a large book with blue cardboard covers.
Middle Part: a large book with stiff black paper covers.

Notice Boards   the School Notice Boards in Junior Part Cloisters, or Hat Place.

Notion   (1) (as in standard English) an idea or belief (1880). (2) a word, phrase, person, place, or custom peculiar to Winchester (in fact, the subject-matter of this book). (3) (in some contexts) a privilege of certain boys in the school. For instance, in 1920, it was:

Praefect of Hall's Notion to wear a beard, and have a wife, though he never did either.
an Officer's Notion to sport velvet.
a Co.Prae.'s Notion to sport a rolled-up brolly, a silk hat-ribbon, and turned-down trousers.
a Praefects' and Tolly-keepers' notion to carry the gown; to wear hats in Chamber Court; to have sauce up in Hall; to walk down Middle Sands; to sport a cud tie: to wear a soft collar. (During the First World War, starch became expensive and soft collars were licet for all.)
a three-year Notion to wear brown shoes; to walk across Flint Court while men were up to books; to play fives in cut-shorts.
a two-year Notion to sport a roll (q.v.).
a one-year Notion to sport cud socks and handkerchief; to wear a butterfly collar on Sundays; to wear a black hatband or narrow house-ribbon (in College).
a Lords Notion to sit under Lords Tree; to go upstairs in Webbe Tent; to put on your pads by School Nets; to wear a VIs blazer for Hopper Pot (VIs blazers were abolished in 1921).
a second XI Notion to keep your pads, etc. in Old Tent.
a VIs Notion to wear blue cut-shorts.
to wear white fives-shoes was a XVs', Flannels', Praefects' and Tolly-keepers' Notion, and in Commoners a three-year Notion. And so on.

The word 'Notion' came into fashion c. 1850, and may owe something to Bunyan's phrase in *Pilgrim's Progress* (1678): 'They are for holding their notions, though all other men be against them' (p. 165). [See the discussion in the Editor's Introduction.]

Notion book   any book of Notions: called 'word-book' till c. 1870. [See the Editor's Introduction.]

Notions examina   [see the Author's Introduction.]

nuces an attempt to put toys into Latin: from Latin *nuces* (nuts): *nuces relinquere* (to put away childish things). Used in College Chamber Rolls in the phrase 'qui has nuces habebat' (who occupied this toys).

Nutley's Hole the small sweater's hole or room off 8th bidet room: or the stoking room next to Foricas Table. Nutley was chamberman on 8th staircase c. 1920.

Oath, or **College Oath** (q.v.) every year on the last Saturday of Standing-up Week, every College boy who was 15 years of age and had not yet taken the College Oath, had to do so. It was read out in Latin by the College Steward and the boys signified their assent. The Oath bound them to uphold and defend the College, and not do anything to injure it and its revenues, divulge what went on within it, or look down on a scholar of inferior social status. In 1820–8 it was regarded with much awe, and it is related that Warden Huntingford, in administering it, used to insist that revenue be pronounced revēnue. By 1843 it had become meaningless and was discontinued soon after.

Obit see **Founder's Com. and Ob, Hatch Thoke, Amen chapel**.

Octo Octavius La Croix, well-known pastry-cook at no. 8 College Street; see **La Croix**.

off-bat point, at cricket. In use 1836–92; obsolete by 1900. The usage is peculiar to Winchester. In Nyren's *Young Cricketer's Tutor* (1833) this position in the field is called 'the point of the bat' or 'the point': this may have become point-of-bat, or off-bat.

Officers the five Senior College Praefects. In former times they held the offices of Praefect of Hall, Chapel (2), Cloisters and Tub; latterly, Praefect of Hall, Chapel (2), School and Library. They are not mentioned in the Statutes, but in Mathew's description of 1647 they seem well established. Their order of precedence varied from time to time.

(1) Praefect of Hall (Aulae Praefectus, or Aul.Prae.) was the senior Officer, and regarded as head of the school, though not always the senior in VIth Book. He was responsible for the conduct of the boys out of school, and his duties and privileges were numerous (1838). He had to take the boys to Hills and Cathedral; prevent them from smoking and sherking out; see that they all went up into Hall for Middle Hall at 1.15; and keep order in Hall (1838). He received a stipend of about £60 per annum (1838). In 1917 he discharged the multifarious duties of head of the school, including asking the Headmaster for half-rems, and represented the school on all important occasions.

(2) and (3) Praefects of Chapel, Senior and Junior (Capellae Praefecti, or Cap.Prae.), formerly called Templi Praefecti. They called names in Chapel in alternate weeks, and reported absentees to the master. If the Aul.Prae. was continent, the Cap.Prae. in course acted for him (1836–8). Latterly, they arranged where men were to sit in Chapel and Chantry, and received the rolls of each row from Dons and Co.Praes as men went out of Chapel. They sat on either side of Chapel door, and when the school attended Cathedral they sat on either side of the Choir gates. They also received a stipend.

(4a) Praefect of Cloister: when Cloisters was used for teaching and recreation, he was responsible for good order and discipline there. When School was built, Cloisters ceased to be used, and his office lapsed, being replaced by that of (4b).

(4b) Praefect of School (Scholae Praefectus, or Schol.Prae.) had formerly to keep School in repair, have the windows mended, conduct Preces in School at the end of whole-school days and hire chairs for concerts and lectures. He had to light School and New School (1838). His salary was about £50 per annum (1838). By 1917 his only duties were to make all arrangements for concerts and lectures in School, and keep order before, during and after them. In Mansfield's day, Praefect of School had once a year to renew the cushions of the Masters' seats.

(5a) Praefect of Tub (Ollae Praefectus, or Oll.Prae.), under the direction of the Stewards, had to supervise the distribution of food in College Hall: and to see that the broken meats thrown into Tub were properly divided amongst the poor. When dinner ceased to be at 6 p.m. in 1837, his office was abolished, and its place taken by that of (5b).

(5b) Praefect of Library (Bibliothecae Praefectus, or Bib.Prae.) was in charge of College Praefects' Library up to 1870, when Moberly Library was opened and he took charge of that. His stipend in 1838 was about £20 per annum.

Officers' Bat   see **College competis**.

Officers' Field   the second field from Half-Mile Road in the direction of St Cross, abutting on the Southampton Road. It was used by the Greenjackets, the cricket club of the 60th Rifles and Rifle Brigade, whose depot is in Winchester: and they used to lend it to the school every Common Time for the finish of Steeplechase (1900).

Officer's gown   worn by the five Officers. It had velvet round the collar, outside and in, and a half-inch [12.5 mm] edging of velvet from the collar down the front of the gown to the feet (1922).

Og, Gog and Magog   three heads built into Meads Wall on the Meads side, near Amen Corner. Like Meads Champions and Log Pond Champions, they come from St Elizabeth's College, demolished in 1548. The name is inspired by Gog and Magog, the two famous effigies in London's Guildhall, which were named after either Gog, ruler of the land of Magog (Ezekiel 38.2) or the two tribes Gog and Magog (Revelation 20.8), with Og, King of Bashan, added for good measure (Deuteronomy 3.11).

oik   an urchin, especially in the phrase 'Town oiks'. It was a corruption of 'boy': cf. oy, with the same meaning, at Charterhouse (1920).

oil, to   (1) to act subtly, insinuatingly, in a manner designed to escape notice, e.g. 'he oiled into the room'. Thus, to oil up to means to ingratiate oneself with (1914 on). (2) to avoid, shirk: especially of cowardice at football: e.g. 'to oil a plant': used also as a noun in this sense, when an oil means a shirking, a lack of courage (1914 on). In other schools the word is used of varieties of mean action, e.g. at Rugby it means to cheat up to books.

Oiliers, Oilyers (**Oily Hatch** in Commoners)   the branch of School Shop which used to open in Cloister Time in Old Tent, where there was a serving-hatch for that purpose (1920). The name was perhaps the nickname of someone serving there, or a reference to the presence there of bat and machine oil, or a nuance that visits there by people supposed to be playing cricket were clandestine.

oily frommers   a behind at Our Game kicked straight forward for less than one post, thus giving time for the ups to gather round and block a kick at goal. This was done only by a losing side, and was made illegal in 1920. It was oily because unsporting: 'frommers' may perhaps be owed to the preposition from.

Old Barge   the Itchen proper; see **Barge**.

Old Bridge   a red bridge between Black Bridge and Boat-house (1892).

Old Fives Courts   see **Fives Courts**.

Old German Room,   in New Commoners (1842–69). See **Edward Wickham's**.

Old Piece   Mr S. A. McDowall's unfilial name for his father, who was to be seen shuffling about the vicinity of College, c. 1920.

Old Roll   see **New Roll**.

Old Tent   (1) the Victorian-style cricket pavilion on the western edge of New Field, over which are the arms Moses and Aaron. It was chiefly used for storing sawdust and footballs (1900), or for assorted games equipment (1920). (2) the name of the Hopper Pot pitch there.

Old Tutors' Houses, or **O.T.H.**   see **Houses**.

Old Wykehamist Room   see **Memorial Buildings**.

Oliver's Battery

Oliver's Battery a small earthwork on a spur of the downs facing Hills, just east of the Romsey Road and a mile [1.6 km] out of Winton: a well-known landmark. It was named, probably wrongly, after Oliver Cromwell: but it might be the fort or 'great sconce' used by Lord Hopton before the battle of Cheriton (1644). The site is covered with firs. Noted as a Notion from 1838 on.

Olympus see **Mount Olympus** and **Jupiter**.

'On!' (1) the order to start, given to the school procession by the Praefect of Hall in going to or from Hills or Cathedral. In Commoners (1868–84) it was given by the Praefect in course, and included going in line to Chapel. When the procession moved off it was called 'going on'. Recorded from 1831; obsolete by 1869. (2) a master was said to be 'On' when he was known to be likely to come to inspect Hills: e.g. 'Wordsworth on'. Recorded from 1836; obsolete by 1869. Similarly, 'I'm **on** basket' or '**On** plates' were excuses given by Queristers who were being called to do a job and who had already been detailed to take the basket of plates down to Kitchen (1920).

On Place (1) the gate in School Court leading to VIIth Chamber Passage at which the boys assembled before going to Chapel, Cathedral, or Hills (i.e. the places where 'on' was called). Obsolete by 1869. (2) a stile between the foot of Hills and Tunbridge at which boys dispersed when they came on Hills, and reassembled to return from Hills. Obsolete by 1869.

open cesspool an open jam-tart, served once a week in College Hall (1920).

'O Quanta' the hymn 'O quanta, qualia sunt ista Sabbata', no. 230 in the Hymnarium (1910 edn), no. 205 (1928 edn): a favourite Saturday evening hymn in Chapel and Preces: words by Peter Abelard (1079–1142), melody from Hymnal Noted (1856). It appears in English in *Hymns Ancient and Modern*, no. 235: 'Oh What the Joy and the Glory Must Be'. Beware of the following traps for the translator: *iugis, iuges* (continuous); *cantica Sion* (songs of Sion); *iubili* (songs).

Orderly Room the headquarters of the Rifle Corps, later the Officers Training Corps, later still the Junior Training Corps. It was over Commoner Gate.

'Order your name'   the command given to a delinquent in School by a Master, to give in his name for punishment. For minor offences, such as making a noise, not knowing the lesson, or neglect of some duty, the offender gave in his name to the Ostiarius, who wrote the particulars on a roll in this form:

> 'Brown.
>> jussu Domini Jones tibi detuli.
>>> sgd. A.Smith,
>>>> Ostiarius.'

At the end of school the Ostiarius took the roll up to the Headmaster or Second Master, and the offender got an imposition or a scrubbing. For graver offences ('if a boy is nailed in a lie, smoking, the sherking out &c., he is sure of a bibler' [1838]), the offender was told to order his name to the Bible Clerk. In such cases he received a bibler, attended by the Ostiarius and Bible Clerk. A name could also be ordered for offences outside School, i.e. in College or in Commoners: in such cases the offender gave in his name to the Ostiarius (College) or the Praefect in course (Commoners).

These formalities are recorded from 1831, but are a great deal older, for Mathew's poem (1645) describes how the names of obstreperous boys are entered on a paper which is handed to a master, who corrected all shortcomings with a quadripartite rod. The system continued till 1869, when work was done in classrooms instead of School. But the phrase 'to order a [boy's] name' was still current in 1922, for the rare occasions when a Don handed a man up to the Headmaster for a grave offence up to books, such as cheating.

Organ and Bellows   an irreverent, but popular, notion of the Warden and Fellows (1920).

Organ Room   a room on the north of Hall stairs in College, where Queristers practised and the Glee Club met (1868). In 1920 Queristers still practised there, and it contained a piano for general use in College and the head of a lift by which food was sent up from Kitchen.

Ostiarius   [a title with two meanings.]

(1) A College Praefect, in full power, was appointed by the day in rotation, to keep order in School, collect the vulguses, prevent boys from sherking out, ensure that there was no noise, particularly on the part of those entering and leaving by the door of School. On his scob were engraved the words: τῷ ἀεὶ θυρωρῷ (for the doorkeeper, for the time being). He had consolations: he was excused going up to books (1831–60); Wednesday's Ostiarius got off Prose Task; Friday's, off Verse Task (1838). The office of Ostiarius was important in the eighteenth century: in marginal notes to the Statutes (c. 1783) the Praefects decided that Founder's Com should be an Ostearius (*sic*) day, but Founder's Ob should not. The notes hint that the same boy was sometime Bible Clerk and Ostiarius concurrently, and that if

Outer Gate

he changed his week as Bible Clerk he could not be Ostiarius during that week unless he served each day of it as Ostiarius. But the entry is obscure.

In about 1800 the office of Ostiarius seems to have lapsed, but in 1866 Dr Moberly revived it, on account of the greatly increased number of boys in School. In 1868 there was a Commoner Ostiarius who attended to comings and goings in New Commoners. When, in 1869, School was no longer used for teaching, Ostiarius was out of a job, but it is recorded (1880–4) that he still existed; he had to look after School and open the door for any Master who wanted to enter.

(2) Ostiarius, or Hostiarius, was the official title of the Second Master. In the early Church the Ostiarius (Ostiary) was the church door-keeper, and in medieval times the porter of a monastery: Latin *ostiarius* (door-keeper), from *ostium* (door). In the course of his duties the door-keeper received subordinate persons, and passed them on to men of consequence. He thus became a hostiarius, hussher, or usher (assistant to a schoolmaster). This derivation applies equally to boy door-keepers in School, and to the Headmaster's understudy, the Second Master.

O.T.H.   Old Tutors' Houses. Synonymous with Houses (q.v.), but used only in connection with Our Game: e.g. O.T.H. XV Roll, not Houses XV Roll (1920).

Otterburn   Otter Brook, a stream flowing from New Barge by Black Bridge, along College Walk to Mill. It was a Notion (1900) that if a boy who had been less than three years in the school walked along the edge of this brook, he could be hotted in by a senior boy who was not in the same House or Divison. This survived in College (1917) as one of the qualifications for 'being a Wykehamist' (q.v.).

Our Game   Winchester football, as distinct from soccer (1920).

Outer Court   the court between Arcadia and the Warden's Lodging.

Outer Gate   the gate leading into Outer Court from College Street, under Bursary. Above the gateway is a statue of the Virgin and Child, which has survived the iconoclastic hazards of the past. The two Bursary windows on each side were formerly oriels. Below, the moulding of the arch terminates in two busts, probably of King Richard II and the Founder, but they are too mutilated for identification.

Outers   for Out-of-schools: mathematical homework, set to be done in writing before the next mathma hour up to books.

own side   it is against the rules of Our Game to kick a ball last kicked by a man on your own side, unless it had come back behind the point where he kicked it. If it has, it may be kicked (but not kicked up), and is then known as an own-side kick.

Packing up   see **Peal, Commoner**.

pandemonium   a harmonium used in College Preces for the hymn on Sundays, half-rems and Saturdays, unless there was someone in College who played the organ (1920).

panels   the two sliding panels in a College toys and the recess behind them, in which paper, ink and personal things were kept (1920).

Pantry   a room in Linen Gallery in New Commoners (1842–69) opposite Gate, which served as a pantry to Hag and Continent Rooms, etc.

paper   several types were used in the school (1920):

long paper: ruled paper in double sheets, the size of a tug copy-book.
John Des: unruled paper in single sheets, about 4 by 7 inches [10 by 17.5 cm] (introduced by John Desborough Walford, mathematical don 1834–73).
Army Class paper: same as above, only about 6 by 10 inches [15 by 25 cm].
foolscap: for Medal Tasks: the same size as Army Class, but in double sheets, ruled.
Godder block: or Godfrey block: unruled paper in blocks about 5 by 7 inches [12.5 by 17.5 cm] (introduced by C. Godfrey, senior Mathematical Master 1899–1905).
David block: ruled paper in blocks about 2 by 6 inches [5 by 15 cm] (invented by Mr F. P. David for one-word questions (Don 1899–1931).
examina paper: ordinary school paper, ruled and margined.

paper-case   a portfolio or blotting book (1838); called a papulase (1892). Paper-case is standard English for a box holding writing materials and paper; papulase must be a facetious version of this. the nearest word in English is papulose (covered with pimples). Both were obsolete by 1917.

Paradise   a small clump of trees in Outer Court facing the Warden's Lodging and backing on the wall built in 1663 to screen the stables. The trees were pollard limes, replaced in 1921 by Siberian crabs. The lion's head in the wall is said to be the emblem of St Elizabeth of Hungary, and to come from the College dedicated to her which was destroyed c. 1547. On the other side of the wall was the Second Master's rose garden (1920). In the rockery in front of the trees two small medieval statues were found in 1920 and deposited in the Warden's Lodging.

The clump is referred to as Paradise from 1831 onwards: from Greek παράδεισος (a park), used in the Septuagint for the Garden of Eden, and by Evelyn (1645) for a park. There may have been a garden there originally. In 1868–84 it was called Paradise Regained, after Milton's poem, to distinguish it from a similar clump on an island in Logie near the bridge in College Street, named Paradise Lost because College no longer had it. These Notions, which survived to 1922, were sometimes transposed.

Parallel   see **div**.

Parker's Gallop   (1) on Senior Steeplecha course. It was a high ridge of downland, curving round from Longwood Warren into Bloody Lane: a long, tiring and usually wind-swept stretch, probably named after a farmer or landowner. (2) the passage between the Warden's bedroom and foricas. This notion arose from a brilliant suggestion by a new man in a Notions examina. J. Parker Smith was Warden 1915–20.

Part   see **div**.

Party Rolls   a Commoner Peal; see **Peal**. Party rolls containing the names of groups of boys who had agreed to travel home in the same coach.

pass   when a football crossed the goal line without the 'Goal' or any of the side touching it. See **schitt** and **goal**. Introduced c. 1840, this word was long since disused.

pass out, to   to pass a swimming test at Gunner's Hole. All new men had to do this as soon as possible, as a mark was taken off in Swimming Athla from each House's total for each man not passed out. It was done under the supervision of certain Dons and consisted in swimming from the broad diving-board up to the roush board and back (1917).

pass through a Chamber, to   everyone who went through an upstairs Chamber in College at night on his way to another was expected, in courtesy, to ask the senior man present: 'May I pass through [or go through] this Chamber please?' He then shook hands with and said good-night to everyone in the Chamber, in bed or up.

There were no passages giving access to sleeping Chambers. To go from 8th to 12th on the top floor, one crossed 8th landing, passed through 9th, through the swing door to 11th, through 11th and across 12th landing to 12th. On the middle

Pauls

floor one could go from 7th, across the landing, through 6th, through the swing door to Ken, and thence either through Rabbit Warren to New Chamber, or across 10th landing into 10th.

Pater   (1) father. (2) the equivalent of teejay in Commoners. He was the junior appointed to look after a new man during his first fortnight, show him the ropes, teach him Notions and duties, and take him to Amphitheatre and Third Pot. At the end of which, his Son sported him down shops (1920).

Pater Noster Cupboard   the lockers up to the right of stove in School, where newspapers, candles, etc., were kept (1868–84). Perhaps fishing-tackle was kept there also. Izaak Walton (1653) recommends the Pater-noster line, a fishing-line to which hooks and lead beads were attached at intervals, making it resemble a rosary [which was also known as a] paternoster. Walton fished the Itchen.

Path   the Jun-Jun cricket pitch just south of Meads Wall. The queristers, who had half-rems on Wednesday and Saturday, played here (1920).

Pathéphone   a gramophone, the property of the school, used by Mr Du Pontet to illustrate French pronunciation up to books, and for coaching for French Speech. The most famous records were 'Le Bourgeois Gentilhomme', 'Le Héron' and 'La Vase Brisée' (1920).

patheticers   a grumble or an indigna in which someone tried to attract sympathy by representing himself as ill-used. The habit was not encouraged (1920).

patrol jacket, or **blue patrol**   a dark blue jacket of coarse cloth and white-metal buttons, and stripes (if any) in silver braid, worn at Camp with a slouch hat and greyers as undress uniform. Most schools had no undress uniform, and thought this an affectation, but the Win.Coll. Officers Training Corps looked smart in it (1920).

Pauls   a mill immediately above Black Bridge, and the area of water adjoining it. In 1838 it belonged to 'Paul the Miller, an inveterate enemy of College and Commoners'. Recorded to 1872; long since obsolete.

Pawson's Place   the foricas behind Webbe Tent. Named from A. G. Pawson (B 1901–7), Captain of Lords for two years.

pax   an intimate or particular friend. Recorded 1831–92; obsolete by 1914. Two derivations are suggested: (1) in the early Church, Communion began with a kiss of peace between the faithful. In the thirteenth century this was superseded by the priest's and congregation's kissing a tablet known as a pax. (2) a pack was an unlawful confederacy, e.g. a pack of thieves, the verb to pack, coming either from Anglo-Saxon *paecan* (to deceive) or Latin *pangere* (to fasten; whence *pactum*, agreement); so Shakespeare (1605), 'packs and sects'. The word is now neutral: e.g. pack of hounds, or pack of cards. The verb occurs in Shakespeare (1594), 'go pack with him': and in Scotch the adjective, 'unco pack and thick thegither'. The second seems the more likely derivation: unless pax merely means someone you have pax (peace) with.

'Pax!'   peace, truce, silence, enough, hands off! so, have pax (make friends, make up a quarrel). Recorded 1831–60; obsolete by 1890. It is standard schoolboy slang, direct from Latin *pax* (peace): common in Terence and Plautus, e.g. 'Pax! abi!' (peace, be gone!): and the early Christian salutation 'pax vobiscum' (peace be unto you).

Peal, Peals, Pealings   (1) Peals were rung on Chapel bells, to wake the boys and get them into Chapel. *First Peal* was the first morning bell, which rang an hour before Chapel in summer, and three-quarters of an hour before in winter (1838). At York Minster the Prima Pulsatio was for Matins and continued for as long as it took to say them (1294), and the same was true of Southwell (1497). Our First Peal, still so called in 1922, was simply to wake us up. *Second Peal* rang during the quarter-hour before boys went into Chapel: called by Commoners 'Bells go'. These names did not survive. Other peals were rung for various services; see **Bells**. The last peal of the day was one of seventy notes, to summon the seventy scholars to Preces.

(2) Peals thus came, in Commoners, to mean calls backed up in Galleries in the morning by two juniors, called Senior and Junior Peals, to inform others of the time (1856 on): known in College (1920) as 'Calling'. The calls were:

(a) in New Commoners (1868)
(i) *in early chapel time*
6.15 a.m. 'First Peal', by Junior Peals, when bells ring singly.
6.45 a.m. 'Bells go', by Junior Peals, when bells go together for Chapel.
6.55 a.m. 'Gates', by Senior Peals, when bells go single.
6.58 a.,m. 'Moberly through', when Dr Moberly entered Chapel (obsolete by 1867).
7.00 a.m. 'Bells down', by Junior Peals, when bells stopped (obsolete by 1868).

(ii) *in late chapel time*

all the above peals, backed up half an hour later.

(iii) *on Sundays*

7.00 a.m. 'First Peal'.

7.30 a.m. 'Half-Hour', by Junior Peals.

7.45 a.m. 'Bells go rotten', ditto.

7.50 a.m. 'Bells go double', ditto.

7.55 a.m. 'Gates', by Senior Peals.

8.00 a.m. 'Hour', by Junior Peals, on saint's days.

9.00 a.m. 'Hatch', by Junior Peals, on Hatch Thoke.

(b) in College, c. 1868, similar calls were given, three times in succession.

(c) when Commoners moved into Houses (1869), and the wind was in the wrong quarter, Chapel bells were not always clearly audible, and juniors (or Peals Callers) called the time every five minutes for the quarter-hour before Chapel:

'Quarter'

'ten to Half-Hour'

'five to Half-Hour'

'Half-Hour'

or similarly, leading up to 'Three-Quarters', or 'Hour'

(d) in College (1920) the First Junior in each Chamber gave similar calls:

'Quarter'	'Three-Quarters'
'five past Quarter'	'five past Three-Quarters'
'five to Half-Hour'	'five to Hour'
'Half-Hour'	'Hour'

(3) organised cheers, or chanted phrases, were 'pealed', backed up, or performed in College or Commoners on special occasions: of the same nature as the modern 'Three cheers for So-and-so', but more complicated and lasting longer. They were a regular and important event between 1831 and 1843, but obsolete by 1870. There were several types.

Type (a) was to celebrate the winning of a prize like the Heathcote by a scholar or Commoner: thus: 'Heathcote in College (or Commoners), Hip, hip, hurrah!' This went on for about a quarter of an hour.

Type (b) were Commoner Peals, to celebrate the approaching end of Long Half (and possibly Short Half also). There were two sets of these. Each set contained three Peals, a week elapsing between one Peal and the next. Each Peal began with 'Once, twice, thrice', and was repeated three times. One boy started, and the others joined in. The words referred to progressive preparations for going home. The two sets of Peals were:

(i) on the last three Fridays, after breakfast, when the Tutors had gone out of Hall, the boys remained and pealed the following Peals:

- *on the last Friday but two*, the Peal was 'Locks and Keys' (i.e. of boxes and rooms).
- *on the last Friday but one*, the Peal was 'Boots and Leathers' (i.e. boots and leggings, or stirrup-leathers: cf. the cavalry order 'Boot and saddle').

• *on the last Friday*, the Peal was 'Gomer Hats', or 'Gomers and Hats' (i.e. beaver and other home-going hats, as distinct from the school top-hat).

When each Peal was over, Sticking-up took place, i.e. an unpopular boy chosen by Junior Mess was stuck-up and pelted with pontos.
(ii) on the last three Sundays, immediately after dinner in Hall, when Tutors had gone out, the boys pealed:

• *on the last Sunday but two*, the Peal was 'Party Rolls' (i.e. rolls submitted to the Doctor (Headmaster) in coaching days to show the parties which boys had made up among themselves for each coach: the object being to prevent their going home by post-chaise or on horseback.) Railways having superseded coaches by c. 1850, this Peal lost its point, but lingered on in New Commoners to 1868.

• *on the last Sunday but one*, the Peal was 'Money and Direction Rolls' (to remind each boy to write on a vessel of paper the amount of journey money he needed and his destination, and put it on the desk of the Senior Commoner Praefect. By 1868 the vessel showed journey money, residence of parent, time of train and amount of luggage, and had to be put up in the study of the second Senior Praefect). The Peal ceased in 1869, but the rolls continued in various Houses.

• *on the last Sunday*, the Peal was 'Packing up' (a reminder to get on with packing).

On each occasion the Tutor whose turn it was to come into Hall was clapped or hissed, according to his popularity or otherwise (1838). By 1868 the day had been changed from Sunday to Tuesday, and the order of the Peals was different. The entire tradition is long since dead.

Type (c) was Cloister pealing. On the first Middle School in Cloister Time, 'Cloisters' (q.v.), standing up at books, pealed all College Praefects not in full power, and all Commoner Praefects. These Peals, composed by the Senior Candle-keeper and the Course-keeper, were epigrammatic comments on the Praefect's appearance, character and idiosyncrasies, in Greek, Latin and English, chanted three times in succession. The pealing went on until a master came into School.

The whole episode was licensed impertinence, and arose from the boys' knowledge of the Roman feast of Saturnalia, when slaves were allowed to ridicule their masters and speak freely on any subject: schools also were closed. It was a democratic bastion against extreme autocracy. This kind of pealing was abolished in 1841.

Interesting examples of such Peals are preserved for the period 1838–43; and we are told that the Peal was sometimes stressed by repeating the boy's name three times at the end of it: (1) a Peal on a Commoner Praefect named Brown:

Blacking your brushes we don't wish to enforce:
you're a dam'd good Praefect, but rather too coarse.

(2) a Peal on a College Praefect who had an auction sale of personal effects as a method of 'raising the wind':

> When next you have an auction, let Commoners know.

(3) a Peal on the same boy, who used to wear an old pair of fustians as he could not afford new trousers:

> When you have done with the fustians, send them to the hammer.

(4) a Peal on a Commoner Praefect who was addicted to lying: a complimentary line was added to the first, no doubt to avoid reprisals:

> Parker is a rum one for conscience and lies.
> Parker is a jolly Conservative trump.'

(5) a Peal on a College boy whose home was Liverpool. Owing to exceptional brains he soon rose to be a Praefect: having had but little fagging on this account, he tended to give himself airs which fagging would have corrected: he was also rather dressy:

> 'Singing, stanging Liverpool swell:
> If you had any fagging you would not be so sprea.'

This is probably J. C. Prince (Coll. 1838–42), who came from Liverpool. To stang seems to mean to make a culprit ride on a stang (pole), a penalty inflicted at Cambridge c. 1777 for missing chapel. (6) a Peal on a Commoner Praefect who was uncommonly slow in all his actions:

> 'unfortunate goat thinks it fast to be slow'.

The goat was possibly J. Capel (Comm. 1838–42), *capella* being Latin for a she-goat.
   To 'peal' is from the Old English word *apel* (a call in hunting music, or chimes: from French *appeler*, Latin *appellare*, 'to call by name'): and came to mean to assail with noise, the sense given in Johnson's *Dictionary* (1755). Milton (c. 1655) speaks of a person's ear being pealed by a loud noise. A peal is such a noise, and is appropriate to the clang of bells, of which we still use it. But meaning (3) above, that of cheers, chants and calls, no longer survives, though standard English still uses a peal of laughter, thunder or gun-fire.

Peat and Repeat   names suggested (1920) for the children of Rev. A. T. P. Williams and Mrs Williams, should they have had any. His third name was Petre.

[Pedes and Mersians   see **Medes and Persians**.]

[Peg, the   G. H. Ridding, Headmaster 1867–84 (cf. **Ja Ra**). The nickname comes from an incident described by Lady Laura Ridding in her memoir of her husband. A victorious Wykehamist tennis team arrived back in College late at night from Wimbledon, bearing the Ashburton Shield. They were met by a delighted Ridding, who told them the library (where the shield they had won would normally be displayed) was locked, and asked, '"Will you allow me to be Peg for tonight?" "Three cheers for the Peg" was shouted in reply. And henceforth he added the name of The Peg to Ja Ra.' (Quoted from Lady Laura's memoir by Firth, p. 174)]

Peggy　the wife of Rev. S. A. McDowall (1920).

Pempe　πέμπε μωρὸν προτέρῳ (often misquoted as πρότερον): Greek, meaning 'send the fool forward'. A trick was practised on new boys when they came into School for the first time. A boy went up to one of them and asked if he had got a book called a Pempe: when he answered that he had not, he was told that if he did not get one before the master came in he would be flogged. The new boy asked his questioner if he could lend him one, but the latter made some excuse, directing him to another boy, who referred him to another: and so on round School until someone told him the trick. Recorded from 1831, with explanation. In 1892, in an effort to preserve the secret, it is defined as 'a necessity for all new men'. By 1920 the secret was out, but Paters and Sons still kept up the pretence.

Pen and Ink Corner　the south-east corner of Meads Wall, between Log Pond and Amen Corner. The name was not recorded before 1880, when it is derived from a boy named Penrose who began to carve his name there; after cutting PEN he was called indoors, and returned to find INK had been added. There is no Penrose in the lists of the time, but there is a T. A. Penruddocke (Comm. 1848–?54) with whom the story might have originated. If a subtler explanation is required, there was a culvert from Log Pond through Meads Wall near this corner, and if the name is an ancient one, it might derive from the old word pen (pipe, conduit), or a word pen, now lost, from Latin *penna* (feather) in the sense of a bucket on a water-wheel: and ink can mean the socket of a mill-spindle. The two together might point to relics of a water-mill in the Lorte-burn.

percher　a cross marked thus ———+ against the name of a boy who was absent from Chapel or Hills without leave; had not done his verse of prose task or vulgus; or neglected some part of his duty. If put by a master in the margin of a task or gags, it indicated gross error. Recorded from 1831; long since obsolete. Its unusual length and horizontal position resemble a bird's perch, from French *perchoir*, Latin *pertica* (long pole), and percher no doubt simply means a thing to perch on. The word appears c. 1375, and as pearcher (1577), for various types of long candle or the bars they were fixed in; and in dialect it can mean long timbers of various kinds.

　　There is a North Country verb to perch (to examine and pass cloth for the looms), and 'stand the perk' means to stand examination of character. Our percher, if derived from this, would mean a mark of disapproval in a list of names. But this may be rather far-fetched.

perfect of all the Praefect of Hall, a notion originating with Mammy Norton (q.v.) (1920).

Peter College cat: a black tom, called vociferously across Chamber Court by his mistress, College Cook (1920).

Phil's G House: Culver Lea. First House Don, Rev. E. W. Sergeant; named after his successor, Mr C. B. Phillips (1883–95), known as the Phil.

Phil Wells proprietor of the school bookshop, Messrs P. & G. Wells, in College Street. He also arranged for the printing of the *Wykehamist*, and the Editor saw a good deal of him. A man of truculent manner, he lived at Sutton Scotney, and had a daughter (Margot) and a son (Young Wells, an Old Rugbeian), both of whom helped in the shop (1920).

Phoebe a damsel who served in School Shop and Oiliers (1920): it was probably her real name.

pi virtuous, sanctimonious, tame; also occurring in pi-jaw (a moral lecture). An abbreviation of pious, this was standard slang.

pi-chapel a service at 8.45 on Friday evening, in preparation for Holy Communion; seldom held (1920).

pig, to, pigging a College custom (1831–43) designed to secure greater warmth at night. The boys in a Chamber took their bedding from the bedsteads and laid it round the fire in a semicircle, feet inwards. Lighting half-faggot, they got into bed and slept in comfort. Pigging was usually practised on the night before Hatch Thoke, or some other day when early rising was unnecessary. The bedding was laid out at 11 or 12 o'clock, when there was little risk of a master coming about.

To pig is standard English for to litter: boys pigging would have resembled a litter of piglets. Macaulay (c. 1850) speaks of a dozen men pigging together in a confined space: and 'to pig it' originally meant to huddle like pigs.

pigeon-holes (1) a space in the Under-Toys in College, like a pigeon's hole, used for keeping papers, etc. (1838). (2) three recesses at either end of Mugging Hall in New Commoners (1842–69), each about as large as two toys: they were used by seniors who had no studies.

pinnacles thirteen pinnacles in which the panelling above Dais in College Hall terminates. One was asked their number in Notions examina (1920).

pint-pot, or **pint-cup** china mugs holding about half a pint [285 ml]; originally they were larger. Each upstairs Chamber in College had about six, on top of

Conduits, and it was the First Junior's duty to maintain the supply: if necessary, he could make (q.v.) pint-pots. Pint-pots in 6th had a green rim, and were therefore virtually unmakeable. Used primarily as tooth-glasses, they came in handy when there was cocoa or lemonade up in Chambers (1920).

pitches   (c. 1920) *Our Game pitches*: see *canvas*.

Soccer pitches:
(1) School Game Bull's Drove (in 1910 it was in Lavender Meads, and it and
                              Chawker Pot were sometimes played on the Town ground
                              at Bar End).
(2) Chawker Pot   Webbe Tent (east of Webbe Tent).
                  Dogger's Close (south of Webbe Tent).
                  Bull's Drove (School Game ground).
(3) Ellis Pot   Logie (parallel to Logie, south of Trees).
                  Trees (Lavender Meads, north of Trees).
                  Fishcroft (in K.P. see Fishcroft); in 1910, Ellis Pot grounds
                  were: Logie, Bull's Drove, Kingsgate and Webbe Tent.
(4) Jun-Jun   K.P. (on Middle Game canvas).
Crockets pitches:
(1) Lords   Webbe Tent (pitch north and south).
(2) Second XI   Meads Tent
(3) Senior Club   Meads Tent
(4) Hopper Pot   Webbe Tent (pitch east and west).
                  Old Tent (between Trees and Webbe Tent pitch)
                  Dogger's Close (east of Houses canvas)
                  Ball Court (between Ball Court and Senior Club)
                  Senior Club (Meads Tent).
                  Barn (the eastern half of K.P.).
(5) Toye Pot and Mellish Pot
                  Hochstapler (in front of Museum).
                  Meads Wall (east and south of Amen Corner).
                  Trees (between Trees and Meads Wall).
                  Kingsgate Street (q.v.).
                  Romans Road (north side of K.P. parallel to Romans
                  Road).
                  Fishcroft (same as Ellis Pot ground).
(6) Jun-Jun   Logie (east of Dogger's Close pitch).
                  Path (q.v.).
(In 1910, the last two were Toye and Mellish Pot pitches. Ball Court was a Middle A pitch, Dogger's Close a Middle B, and Trees a Junior Club pitch.)

pitch-up   (1) a knot of people, circle of friends, set of men or things, a boy's ordinary companions, or a party made up for a special purpose, e.g. a game of fives. To pitch up with was to associate with. Recorded from 1831; obsolete by 1917. (2) one's family or relations, including Pater, Mater, Frater, Soror, Nunky, Nevy.

In Hampshire and Isle of Wight dialect, a person's pitch-up are his normal associates: to pitch up means to stop, stand and talk with. In standard slang, 'So-and-so pitched up' means he happened upon a group of people, stopped and joined them. So at Winchester it meant the group of men one normally stood about and conversed with: and from that, one's family, with whom one stood and talked during their visits, while waiting for Chapel, and so on. This usage is akin to the standard English 'pitch upon' (light upon, choose): and 'pick up', of an acquaintance. Pitch and pick are from an Anglo-Saxon root meaning pick or peck.

place   a College Praefect's toys was called his place (1920). It was not shut in like a toys, but lay across one of the window embrasures of the Chamber, with a slab (q.v.) built into the masonry, and tables and bookshelves arranged at the side according to his taste. **Plague Pits** see **Death Pits**.

Plank Bridge   the bridge across New Barge between Old Bridge and Boat-house.

plant (1831 to present day), or **planter** (1836–43)   a blow from a football kicked straight into someone's face or stomach. When A kicks the ball, and an opponent B receives it full-pitch on part of his body, B is said to 'raise a plant', and A is said to 'plant' B. Plant occurs in standard English phrases implying an attack or blow aimed at an opponent: to plant a cannon is to direct its aim; an assailant may plant a blow between a man's eyes, or a stick on his back. Hence plant may mean figuratively to mark a victim down for plunder, and a plant is standard slang for a conspiracy or 'frame-up'.

Platform   level ground on the summit of Hills where Labyrinth was cut, and where names-calling was held at Morning Hills. Recorded 1868–1907; obsolete by 1917.

pledge, to   to give or lend to someone. Recorded 1856–1900; obsolete by 1917. It was evidently from 'Pledge you' (q.v.).

'Pledge you!'   an exclamation meaning: pass me, lend me, give me, after you with! It was used by a boy who wished to secure the bob or joram of beer as it passed round Hall; used of other things also, e.g. 'pledge you with that book', or 'with that newspaper', or 'pledge you your baker'. In use 1831–1900; obsolete by 1914.

It is the survival of some ancient etiquette of drinking: there are two theories: (1) A invites B to drink, himself first tasting the cup before handing it to B, as a pledge of good faith, and a guarantee against poison: saying, as he does so, 'I pledge you' (I promise it is all right). Hence it comes to mean to drink to the health of. (2) An explanation as old as 1617 is that this is an old custom brought to England by the Danes. A drinks to B, who says: 'Drink, I will pledge you' (I guarantee none will harm you). Thus Cowley (c. 1665), 'Pledge me, my friend'; and Cotton (1676), 'I'll pledge you, Sir'. The Wiccamical sense of 'after you with' implies that the speaker hopes to get the drink next, and our phrase may well be an abbreviation of 'Drink, I will pledge you', uttered by the third member of any trio at the passing of the loving-cup in College Hall (see **loving-cup**). A and B are standing: A drinks to B, whose back is unprotected, so he looks to C, who also stands, and says 'Drink on, I will pledge you'. D then protects C. In each case the next man down the line pledges the safety of the drinker, while looking forward to the drink himself. Thus his guarantee contains an element of 'hurry up, and let me have some'.

Ploughs   three ploughed fields known as First, Second and Third Plough, which were crossed by the original Steeplechase course (1900). 'The Plough' was still used (1920) for fields on Junior Steeplechase course. [cf. 'Agar's Plough' at Eton.]

ponto   a ball of hot new bread, usually the inside of a sines, kneaded up and squeezed in a towel till it became hard. This was a common missile of attack, used particularly at Sticking-up (q.v.) Recorded 1831–1900; obsolete by 1917.
   In West Country dialect, ponted or punted, of decaying food, means indented; of an apple, bruised. Ponto might thus mean kneaded bread, or it might come from Spanish *punto*, Latin *punctum* (as point or hit in fencing), used in duelling scenes by Shakespeare (1591) and Ben Jonson (1598).

Ponto, or the Little Lion   see **Little Lion**. Mr R. L. A. Du Pontet. He taught French, and took Senior Div for entries. He was very small, had a beard, was sometimes brocked, but could be fierce on occasion (1920). It is related that when serving in the Officers Training Corps and wishing to effect an about-turn, he said: 'Winchester, turn round!' See also the **Mare**, and the **Fillies**.

Ponto mons   to close in on Ponto on his little dais in his div room by jumping the desks forward inch by inch, until he was quite hemmed in (1920).

Ponto's Wallow   some muddy place, exact whereabouts not recorded: on the analogy of Coxe's Wallow (q.v.).

pont-up   a variant of pitch-up, arising from a mistaken attempt by the pitch-up of C. F. C. Hawkes to use local idiom (1920); a good example of the creation of a Notion by a mistake.

poon, to   to prop up the piece of furniture with a wedge (a poon) under the leg (from 1856). Originally to poon seems to have meant to be unsteady, and you propped up the leg that pooned. In dialect to poon can mean to kick, i.e. to raise one foot off the ground. A pan or pon is a piece of timber wedged in to support the roof of a house under construction, and the verb to poon means to fit in or join together. Poon-wood is a commercial term for a type of Malayan timber ideal for ships' spars on account of its straight grain, lightness and strength. Perhaps our word originally meant to have one leg off the ground (of a table), and was then applied to the prop by someone with a knowledge of building or shipbuilding.

porges, or **small porges**   small squares of fried bread served in College Hall with soup once a week. They began in 1919. Small Porges is a monster in Kipling's *Just So Stories*, who rose out of the sea. [The name porgy is used for several different kinds of fish, including sea bream (*OED*). A popular ballad quoted by Jane Grigson in her *Fish Cookery* (Harmondsworth: Penguin 1975, p. 141) begins:

> My father was keeper of the Eddystone Light,
> Who slept with a mermaid one fine night,
> And of that union there came three –
> A porpoise, a porgy, and the other was me.]

Porter   there were two College Porters, whose duty is recorded from 1838 onwards as being to lock and unlock gates at the proper times, and to show visitors over College. The Senior Porter lived in College c. 1900, but by 1917 lived up Town and spent the day in College. The Under-Porter, called by the name of one of the minor prophets, lived in the house behind Non-Licet Gate, c. 1920. In Mansfield's day (1836–42) College Porter was Poole, and the Under Porter was Obadiah. In 1917–22 they were Bishop and Joel. A fresco and verses on the wall of Porter's Lodge show that at one time the Porter was named Locke. There was also a Commoner Porter (c. 1890; obsolete by 1917) who looked after Classrooms and brought round Chapel, Chantry and continent rolls, and carried messages for dons.

The derivation is from Latin *portarius* (gatekeeper), *porta* (gate), which gave portour in Chaucer (c. 1375).

Porter's Lodge   on the west of Outer Gate. In College archives it is called 'barbaria' or 'domus barbitonsoris', as the Porter used also to be the barber.

Posers   examiners: especially the two Fellows of New College, called Senior and Junior Poser, who came down at the end of Short Half for the Electio ad Oxon. Formerly they came early in July, resting overnight at Newbury. The word was also used for the examiners in the elections to Winchester, and is still used at Eton.

It occurs as oppositors (1574), apposers (1605) and opposers in endorsements of recommendations of candidates for Winton election. Chaucer (c. 1390) uses apposen for to question, and opposed for cross-examined. In 1440 appose, posyn, posen were synonyms for examine; in 1536 aponent, for questioning; c. 1550, to

Pot

appose one, for to test his learning. Bacon (c. 1600) uses poser for examiner, opposed for cross-questioned. In Scotland (1631), pose was question, and posed questioned. Evelyn (1661) uses posers for university examiners of Westminster scholars.

Old and modern French have *poser* (to question), and Italian has *posare*, *pausare*. It is standard English to say 'I will pose you a question', or 'That's a regular poser'. The basic idea of the word is that of a viva-voce examination conducted by learned men facing (oppositi) the candidate across a table.

'Post!'   the cry backed up when the ball is supposed to have passed over the post on worms (1892).

Pot   (1) Pot meant one of the locks on New Barge, the canal between Winchester and Southampton. The name was most commonly used for the lock at the foot of Hills, also called First Pot, above which the school had boating rights. It was a favourite bathing-place for the boys (1838), until the canal was disused and the locks abandoned. Second and Third Pot were further downstream.

See also **doing Hills**, and to be a **Wykehamist**.

Pot is used in English for a deep circular hole, e.g. a pot-hole in a road. In 1375 the holes [that had been] dug by Bruce at Bannockburn [1314] were called pottis. The word pot is common in the North Country for deep holes filled with water, e.g. peat pots, where peat has been dug out, and cavities in riverbeds caused by the eddies of the stream.

(2) It also meant a challenge cup. In 1920 these were:

Beloe Pot	house teams of five: Junior Steeplechase
Burne Pot	inter-house fours: rowing

Chawker Pot	house first XIs: soccer
Company Pot	individual open: shooting
Drill Pot	house squads: Officers Training Corps
Eldon Pot	middle house XIs: cricket (originally golf)
Ellis Pot	under-16 house XIs: soccer (originally tug-of-war)
Finch Pot	open pairs: rowing
Flower Pot	middle house XIs: soccer (originally golf)
Fresher Pot	College, Commoners and Houses IVs: rowing
Freshfield Cup	see **Fresher Pot**
Greenjacket Pot	inter-school athla at Camp
Hawkins Cup	see Chawker Pot
Hewer Pot	under-17 inter-house IVs: rowing
Hewett Cup	see **Hewer Pot**
Hopper Pot	house first XIs: cricket
House Pot	inter-house teams of four: shooting
Hunter Pot	Marlborough vs Winchester: shooting VIIIs
Indian Wykehamists Pot	Coll. Commoners and Houses: shooting IVs
Melhuish Cup	or **Mellish Pot**: house 2nd XIs: cricket
Monty Pot	inter-house swimming athla: unlimited numbers
Recruit Pot	prize to the runner-up in Drill Pot
Recruit Pot	best squad of house recruits (originally Morris Tube)
Rendall Cup	see **Monty Pot**
Steel Pot	Wellington vs Winchester: shooting VIIIs
Steeplecha Pot	house teams of eight: Senior Steeplechase
Tank Pot	inter-house: efficiency in Camp
Taylor Pot	inter-house: aggregate of marks in athla
Thornton Cups	see **Thorntons**
Thorntons	inter-house fives doubles: one or more pairs
Toye Pot	under-16 house XIs: cricket
Turner Cup	see **Hopper Pot**
Turner Pot	house teams of three: gymna
Watney Cup	see **Watneys**
Watneys	open singles: fives
Wigram Cups	see **Wigrams**
Wigrams	inter-house pairs: racquets
Wilson Pot	open singles: racquets

Pot Cad   the owner and workman employed at the sawmill at Pot. Recorded 1868–84; long since obsolete.

Pot Cupboard   a shelved cupboard in each upstairs and downstairs Chamber in College, near the door, in which tea-things and provisions were kept (1920). Originally pot cupboards were low cupboards under the window in downstairs sleeping Chambers, in which chamber-pots were kept, and washed out by the junior each morning.

Pot Gate   the lock gates of First Pot, long since removed.

Pot House   a large black shed beside First Pot, containing the apparatus for the sawmill there; long since demolished.

pot-houser   a purl into First Pot from the roof of Pot House. It was dangerous, and required good nerve; long since obsolete.

Praefects   the senior boys in the school, to whom authority was delegated over their juniors. They were instituted by William of Wykeham, in imitation of the system at Oxford, 'to superintend the studies of their chamber-fellows, and diligently to oversee them and, when called upon, truly to certify and inform the Warden, Sub-Warden and Master Teacher of their morals, behaviour and advancement in learning from time to time'.

The Founder appointed eighteen Praefects, probably on the basis of three to each of the six Chambers, and there are eighteen College Praefects today. Originally they only informed the authorities of misdeeds, and had no power to administer punishment themselves. Later on, the ten senior Praefects were invested with full power, and took the office of Bible Clerk in rotation. Half-way through the eighteenth century, when the foundation of Commoners made the Headmaster's jurisdiction more remote, fagging and tunding were added to a Praefect's privileges, and by 1836–8 full-power Praefects could fag juniors 'anywhere and everywhere'. The eight Praefects not in full power, known as Bluchers (1868), could fag only on Chamber side, not School side, of Gate, but nevertheless did so (1836).

The five Senior Praefects in College had offices assigned to them and were later called Officers (q.v.). Each Praefect had boys assigned to him as pupils, and they paid him one guinea a half (1836), but the payment was later reversed (see **pupil**).

In the Victorian period, when the billycock was in fashion, Praefects had the right to wear cowshooters (q.v.), to distinguish them from Inferiors.

In Old and New Commoners there were originally eight Praefects, increased to twelve after 1829. When they dispersed to Houses, in 1869, there were from three to six Praefects per House, and those in VIth Book were invested with full power over all Commoners, and called Commoner Praefects, Co.Praes. Those not in VIth Book were called House Praefects (originally Dom.Praes), as their authority was limited to their own House.

Praefects were appointed by the Headmaster, with the following formulae:

'Praeficio te Aulae (Capellae, Scolae, Bibliothecae)', for the five Officers.
'Esto plena potestate Praefectus', for the ten senior College Praefects.
'Praeficio te tuis sociis concameralibus', for the eight junior College Praefects.
'Praeficio te tuis sociis commensalibus', for all Commoner Praefects.

The title Praefect was in use by 1550 if not earlier. But concurrent with it is the title *Praepostor*, appearing as Prepositore (1519), Praepositor (1776), and disappearing at the end of the eighteenth century, except in the phrase 'the Praepostors' duty' used in asking for remission from lessons (a remedy). It occurs in College registers, and survives at Eton, having probably been taken there when Eton was founded from Winchester. [Praeposter was the formal title at Shrewsbury.] It seems to describe a boy's function of supervising the studies of his juniors, as distinct from his administrative status as Praefect. In 1519 Horman says: 'I am Prepositore of my boke'. But the phrase in Mathew's poem (1647), 'tres Praefecti praeponuntur in una Camera', shows that the words were synonyms, and the repetition of 'praefectus' in the poem indicates that it was already the commoner word of the two.

Praefectitis a disease to which men recently made Praefects were particularly susceptible: the symptoms were a swollen head and officious behaviour (1920).

Praefect of Chapel see **Officers**.

Praefect of Cloisters see **Officers**.

Praefect of foricas see **For.Prae**.

Praefect of Hall, Library, School, Tub see **Officers**.

Praefect of worship Praefect of Chapel: a skit on the Headmaster's habit of referring to Chapel as 'yer morning worship', 'yer evening worship' (1920).

Praefects' Common Room on the west of Hat Place, opposite Dons' Common Room: a room set aside for the use of College and Commoner Praefects.

Praefects' foricas usually known as Through First. It might be used by all except men under two years, and by them also after Lock-up (1920).

Praefects' Notion see **Notion**.

Praefects' photo (College) taken in Cloisters after College photo, and followed by Officers' photo (1920).

Praefects' Rolls used for calling names in Commoners prior to 1869, these were similar to the House Rolls which succeeded them, i.e. a printed list pasted on cardboard.

Praepostor a Praefect, in his capacity of supervisor of studies of his juniors: in use from c. 1519 to the end of the eighteenth century. It survived (1920) only in the formula used by the Aul.Prae. when asking for a half-rem. See **Praefect** and **remedy**.

Preces (pronounced prēcēs, preesees)   prayers (from the Latin) (1) prayers for the whole school took place in School up to 1869 at the end of a whole-school day. The Praefect of School stood up to books by the Headmaster's chair and read prayers. Boys stood around according to their places in the school. Some Div Dons carried on this tradition by reading prayers at the end of afternoon school, but it has long since lapsed.

(2) Up to 1869, prayers were read in New Commoners at 8.45 p.m. in Mugging Hall by Tutor, and afterwards namers were called. Boys knelt at their toys or desks.

(3) Prayers were said in Commoner Houses. In winter, when Morning Lines stopped, there were Preces in each House before breakfast at 8 o'clock. And every evening, at the end of Toy-time, the House Don read Preces in Hall, men remaining at their toys or Middle Desks.

(4) College Preces (1920) were at 9 p.m. After Hour had struck, the bell rang seventy times, and all Inferiors had to be in Chapel before bells went down. Chapel Writer stood at the door calling out the number of the hymn at intervals, on half-rems, saints' days, Saturdays and Sundays: finally telling it to the Second Master, behind whom he shut the door and came up to his place. When there was no hymn, the Second Master read a short lesson.

College sat in Choir, Praefects in stalls, the Second Master in the Warden's seat, Cap.Praes in the second row of the nave on either side. When Preces was over, College filed out, led by the Second Master and the Cap. Praes, this trio standing at the door while the Cap.Prae. in course called a namers. Out in Chamber Court, men shook hands and said good-night to their friends: the Second Master and Aul.Prae. strolled across to the door of VIth (which was also the approach to the Second Master's staircase) and stood there with other men of consequence for a few minutes, mulling over the day's events. And so to bed.

(5) Private prayers were said at bed-time. In College, everyone knelt at his bedside for a few moments before getting into bed. In Commoner Houses (1892), at a convenient moment, the Praefect of a Gallery called 'Preces', and there was silence for private prayer.

Preces book   a prayer-book.

precify   to pray. A Commoner Notion (1900); obsolete by 1914.

Preffy   a Praefect. A Commoner Notion (1920): a bad notion in College.

preke   to pray. Used from c. 1900. Not standard English: from Latin *precari* (pray).

prike   a borer in a knife, something to make a hole with, an ingenious device, a stratagem, something up your sleeve. Surprisingly, it was first recorded in 1917. This is the medieval form of prick, pricker (any slender pointed instrument, skewer, or goad). New College Bursars' Rolls (fifteenth-century) have a 'fire-prike'; (poker or fire-iron).

Prince of Princes the captain of racquets (1920).

Prince's Racquets pair. The annual Public Schools competition was formerly played at Prince's Club, later at Queen's Club. They wore a Second XI blazer with crossed racquets on the pocket, and a dark blue cap with white edge and white crossed racquets.

prix (pronounced as spelt) any prize (1920).

prixless priceless, splendid (1920).

proclama (pronounced proclamā) a proclamation issued by Praefects in New Commoners, after Preces, in Mugging Hall, by a boy standing on Middle Desks. After 1869 it meant a similar announcement in a House, by a Praefect himself, or through a junior. But it was more usual to write it on a notice on House Notice Board.

prose, to to lecture, make a long-winded speech. Recorded 1836–1900; obsolete by 1914. This is standard English for writing or talking in a tedious manner. It was also used at Winton as a noun, meaning a lecture or boring speech; it does not occur thus in standard English, but the adjective prosy is familiar. Prose, in use since Chaucer, is normal speech as distinct from verse: from Latin *prorsa oratio* (straightforward speech).

prose task a piece of Latin composition, which all boys had to do once a week (1836).

pruff hardy, tough, sturdy, insensible to pain, not easily hurt, not susceptible to entreaty, obstinate. So used 1831–1900, but obsolete by 1914. This is a dialect survival of *prouff*, the Old English form of proof (power of resistance). cf. Welsh *prawf* (unyielding). Sidney (1590) says: 'men of great proof in wars'; Shakespeare uses proof of a coat (1593), and speaks of 'fathers of war proof' (1599); Milton (1671), 'proof against temptation'; Bunyan uses it of armour (1678). It survives in waterproof, fireproof, etc. It comes from Latin *probare* (to prove).

Prunt's pincushions a Commoner Notion (1920), but for what?

Pseudo-Good Friday Passage the passage between School and Cloisters, sometimes called Good Friday Passage (q.v.). The prefix pseudo-, from Greek ψεῦδος (falsehood), is added as it is not the original passage of that name.

Pseudo-T, or **Pseudo-Telegraph Hill**   so called as it was not Telegraph Hill proper: cf. Good Friday Passage. A shoulder of the downs on the north of the Portsmouth Road, about one and a half miles [2.4 km] out of Winton, with a flagstaff on it. About half a mile [0.8 km] to the west of it, just off the road, was the start of Senior Steeplechase course. From the start one went up over the hill past the flagstaff.

pudding   an inferior kind of ball used by Commoners for games in Grass Court, until that court vanished in 1871. The name was then transferred to any cricket ball that had grown soft through usage. Obsolete by 1914.

pulpiteers   the name given to Book and Senior Part V when they went up to books together in Cloister Time to the Headmaster in School for two hours' translation. VIth Book gave the construe first, and then Senior Part. [Pulpiteers was discontinued c. 1862; W. A. Fearon tried in vain to revive it when he became Headmaster in 1884.] It was named from the rostrum (pulpit) erected in VIIth Chamber for this purpose (the original school-room) and mentioned by Mathew 1647: 'erigitur rostrum quo declamare solemus'. In 1687 the rostrum was moved to the new 'School'.

Pulver's Dust Hole   a hollow under the Headmaster's chair in School, to which access was gained by removing a defective board. Here boys used to store all kinds of articles both legal and illegal, e.g. a gun (referred to in a letter from Newdigate Poyntz [Comm. 1856] to the Sen.Co.Prae. in 1921). cf. Fletcher's Dust Hole. The name was perhaps from Purver (q.v.), an old man who cleaned School; or from Latin *pulvis* (dust); or had something to do with Pulver-Wednesday (Ash Wednesday); or was from pulverain (a horn for fine priming powder; cf. amorce (priming powder) under 'more sack').

Punch   Dr Richards, physician to some of the Commoner Houses (1920).

pupil   (1) up to 1869 the two Commoner Tutors divided the Inferiors between them as pupils, looking over their compositions and helping them with their work. (2) each of the ten senior Praefects in College looked after the work of one or more juniors, who were called his pupils. For each pupil he received £1 per annum from College (1868), later reduced to fifteen shillings (1900 onwards).

purl (and older form **purler**)   a dive into the water (1831 on), also a fall (1838); to purl (to dive into the water head-first) from a bank, boat, or bridge (1838 on). Special feats of diving were a gater, pot-houser and top-poster (q.v.). It could also mean to trip a boy up (1838). Purl was still in use in 1922 for a dive, and to dive.

Pirler or purler is common dialect for a toss from a horse: an Oxfordshire farmer once said to me: 'My horse slipped and we came such a purler.' It comes from the Old English verb *purl, pirl*, with the intransitive meanings of swirl, curl (as of breath or steam to the sky): so Shakespeare (1594), Dekker (1602). It was used of wind by Chapman (1631): to spin like a top, turn somersault, go head-first. Used transitively it means to whirl about (as of wind whirling a snowdrift), upset, unhorse (at hunting).

Purver   an old man who had been in service of College a long time (1838): he cleaned Hall and School and lighted the fires there, and cleaned trenchers. He is perhaps the eponymous hero of Pulver's Dust Hole (q.v.). See also **Long John**.

Push (pronounced Püsh)   a name for Monty Rendall; see **Headmaster**.

push (pronounced pūsh)   a clique of people who always went about together. School Push were the athletes and great men who stood in groups in Flint Court, chatting: a name invented by men not in it (1920). Derived from pushing (giving oneself airs).

pussy   the long white knitted scarves, with three bands of blue (or red or brown) at each end, worn by XVs and dress. They were crossed on the chest, passed round to the back and crossed again, and then fastened in front with the ends falling between the legs (1900 on). The name indicates softness, but actually the wool became harsh after many washes.

put in balls, to   to kick in balls (1868).

put on, to   see **go on**.

Quadrangle　the name for Chamber Court, 1838–68.

Quarter-Deck　(1) the steps around stove in School (1868). (2) the stone steps outside School (1900 on). Here hot rolls (q.v.) were held up, and brought down. (3) the stone slab before the fireplace in each College Chamber (1838 on). The quarter-deck in a man-of-war was the officers' promenade.

quarter of paper　a quarter of a sheet of foolscap (1836), of long paper (1838–1900), on which the prose and verse tasks were always written (1836). Obsolete by 1914.

Querister, Quirister　one of the sixteen Choristers admitted 'by way of charity' to the foundation of Winchester College, whose duties were to sing in Chapel and wait in College Hall. In return they received free education.

　In 1820–8 they were twelve in number, and had nothing to do with the choral service, their main functions being to carry dispers into Hall and act as messengers to the scholars. They wore a livery, which in 1868–1900 was grey and said to have been given by John Fromond; in 1910, said to be chosen by the Warden in office. In 1920 it was dark blue stockings, knickerbockers, Norfolk jacket and full peaked cap with a red rose badge. They were formerly housed in the room between VIth Chamber and kitchen, later used as a cellar; moving from there to a school-house of their own at the junction of Kingsgate Street and St Michael's Passage. At one time they used to make the Fellows' beds and dine off the remains of Fellows' dinners. Mansfield says that the Queristers never sang, but waited on boys in Hall and Chambers till 7 p.m., and ran errands for them in town. They wore chocolate-coloured tail-coats and trousers with metal buttons.

　They were eligible for election to College. They appear in Long Roll as Secunda Classis.

　Querister is an ancient word which has hardly changed in 600 years. In 1347 St Paul's Church had querestes, queristres, or choristae. In 1447 another London Church had queristers; the document that mentioned them was written by a Wykehamist. In 1552 York had queresters. Quiristers are mentioned in 1601 and 1638, by Ford (1629), and by James Thomson (1728). The name comes from Old English *quire* (choir), latin *chorus*, Greek χόρος (dance, chorus).

'**Querister!**' call by Praefects and Tolly-keepers in Hall when they required the services of a Querister. Inferiors had to call the name – 'Sparkes!', 'Trask!', 'Plaisted!', Dowdeswell!', etc. (1920).

Querister Don known to the Queristers (1920) as Rumblebelly, was the Master of Queristers and supervised all their work and play. His name was Williams, and he appeared as Dnus Williams on Long Roll. He had a short, squat figure, glasses and a walrus moustache: and sang in Chapel Choir. No one but he might beat a Querister. Queristers were occasionally handed up to him by men in College for inefficiency or impertinence.

Querister game played in VIIth by two persons standing on Quarter-Deck and throwing up a ball against the wall above Half-Faggot, and trying to make the opponent miss catching it by making it drop on the extreme edge of the pent-house. A shot which hit neither the wall nor the pent-house did not count. A good game, but inclined to give one a stiff neck, it was supposed to be a queristerish sort of sport, but no one ever saw them playing it (1920).

Querister Palace a red-brick house in Kingsgate Street nearly opposite Commoner Gate, where the Queristers lived in the charge of Querister Don, and learned lessons, music, etc. (1920).

quill, to to curry favour with anyone (from 1836), to please (from 1860). To quill or raise a quill/quills off was to ingratiate oneself, flatter, cause pleasure to (1920); to be quilled was to be pleased. It came from the Devon dialect quill (the faucet of a cask): to quill was to tap liquor and hence to ply Parliamentary electors with drink; quilling is so used in 1806. Thus, metaphorically, it came to mean currying favour. In standard English a quill is something slender and hollow, a stalk, a pan-pipe, the central spine of a goose-feather, and hence a pen, the spines of a porcupine: and though in dialect the word is used for a barrel-tap, the basic meaning is evidently a tube of smaller calibre than a tap, such as the straw through which iced drinks used to be taken.
  Etymologists hover between a derivation from an Old English word *quylle* (a stalk) and Latin *calamus* (a reed); or *quille* (Old French) with *kegil* (Old German), meaning something slender but solid, like a peg or a ninepin. Possibly both are right, representing as they do the illicit way of drawing liquor through an almost invisible hole, in contrast to the approved exit through a half-inch tap. In the old colonial days in Africa, thirsty transport-riders would bore holes with a gimlet in casks they carried, insert a straw, draw their requirement, and bung the hole with a peg. At the end of a long journey, it is said, the inside of an almost empty cask looked like a porcupine's back. This technique would have been learned in England, and dates back, no doubt, to the days when votes could be won by illicit draughts from a cask, obtained by inserting a quill and then plugging the hole with a quill: a background that accords closely with the Wiccamical use of quill, namely to ingratiate oneself with another by underhand methods.

quilling   pleasing; see **quill**. Not standard English.

quilster, quillster   one who curries favour, a flatterer, a toady. Recorded 1856; obsolete by 1914. The Wiccamical equivalent of English slang, quiller (who who sucks expertly through a quill): hence a parasite or one who, in English slang, 'sucks up' to somebody.

Quork, or Alexandra the Quork   a mythical creature, perhaps of the species stork, created in Wiccamical minds (1920) when Mr S. A. McDowall, hurrying through the prayer for the Royal Family, slipped the clutch [and with it '-een Mother, Edward, Prince of Wales and Albert, Duke of Y-'] and said '. . . Alexandra the Qu-ork . . .'

rabbiter a blow on the back of the neck with the edge of the open palm. Recorded 1831–1900; fortunately obsolete by 1914. This is the death-blow used by keepers on rabbits, and can be lethal to human beings.

Rabbit Warren a dark recess between Ken and New Chamber, containing coat-pegs, discarded gowns and hat-boxes. It was probably once a passage to the little projecting room off New Chamber and leading to the Warden's Lodging (1920).

rack a disper consisting of a bone from a neck or loin of mutton: a cut from the neck or scrag of mutton (from 1836). In dialect, rack is the neck of mutton (or pork), used by Middleton (1630); Johnson's *Dictionary* (1755) mentions it as a neck of mutton cut for the table. Derived from Anglo-Saxon *hreacca* (the back of the head).

Railway Bridge the long diving board at Gunner's Hole, between the entrance and the diving stages, to be taken at a run (1920).

Railway Society a dedicated coterie of men, led by H. D. E. Rokeby (Coll. 1917–23), who took the *Railway Magazine* and knew Bradshaw from cover to cover.

raise, to (1) to make angry (1914 on). cf. 'get a rise out of'. (2) to get or win, in every sort of context (1900 on):

to raise books: to win the div prize, or get the highest score at cricket.
to raise leave: to get permission.
to raise a hump: to offend, make angry.
to raise a plant: to run towards a ball which is being kicked, and receive it on part of one's body.
to raise a quill: to please, curry favour with.
to raise a remove: to get moved up into the next form.

ramrod, ramroder, raymonder a ball bowled underhand at cricket in a series of hops along the ground; in standard slang a 'sneak'. Recorded 1831–92;

obsolete by 1914. It is said to be from one Raymond, of whom nothing else is recorded except that he bowled thus: possibly H. B. Raymond-Barker, Captain of Lords 1839. There was a Raymond's shop up Town in 1836.

rapped out, to be   when a boy was wanted during School time, the Porter rapped the knocker on the door of School. The Ostiarius answered the door, and sent out the required boy, having asked leave from the senior master in School (1838).

Rat, the   Miss Lee: sister (?) of Warden G. B. Lee (1861–1903). Her large Wiccamical acquaintance usually included some men in the school, whom she asked to tea (1920).

Rat Williams   in Mansfield's day, a College chamberman who did a rat-tat on the door to awaken the Junior in Chambers.

Reach   the straight stretch of River between Tunbridge and Birley's Corner.

reader   an office in the gift of every College Praefect in Senior Fardel, which excused the holder from watching-out at cricket: his duty was to read aloud the translation of any book his master was cramming for New College Election. Recorded 1836 only; long since obsolete.

reading-board   (1) the under-lid of the scob, on which boys wrote (1838). (2) a long narrow deal board resting on two scobs, for the boy who sat between them to write on (1838).

reading-shelf   on the side of each bed in College there used to be a small shelf with a drawer, on which boys put their candles when sitting up in bed reading after Chapel: 'but one night Wordsworth came about when a boy was putting out his candle, a spark fell on the reading-shelf and Wordsworth, fearing that a bed might be set on fire, ordered them all to be demolished' (1836–8) [Charles Wordsworth was Second Master]. Mansfield (1836) describes it as a shelf for books and tollystick, fixed inside the canopy of the bed.

recess   any time when the school broke up early on account of illness. There was a recess of a month in 1840 'on account of the fever'. Recorded 1836–84; long since obsolete.

reck   a diving stage at Gunner's Hole; see **wreck**.

Red Bridge   a red-brick bridge over New Barge below Black Bridge (1868).

Registers   booklets of about thirty pages bound in paper, published in March, which gave an account of the school's doings for the past year, including cricket and football matches, rifle shooting and athletic sports. Superseded by the *Wykehamist* in 1866.

Rehoboam   a treble battling. cf. Jeroboam.

remedy, rem, remiday   a partial holiday from lessons. Originally there was always one remedy a week, and generally two, on which there were Morning Lines and Toy-time, but instead of being taught all morning and afternoon in School by masters, the boys had two hours books-chambers in School under the supervision of Praefects. There was no leave-out.

Later, every Tuesday (and often Thursday also) in Easter and Cloister Times were remedies, and the books-chambers were from 9 to 11. Later again, Thursday only in Cloister Time was a remedy. By 1914 such remedies were called whole remedies, and there was no work except Morning Lines and Toy-time.

By 1920 they were called whole rems, and there was Toy-time only. They were rare, Hatch Thoke being one of the regular ones, as was Ascension Day and, previously, Queen's Accession Day. Red-letter saints' days were remedies as far as work was concerned, but being leave-out days they were called the latter (1920).

A remedy was not a matter of course, but had to be requested from the Headmaster, as he was walking up and down Sands before morning chapel, by the Praefect of Hall, in the formula: 'The Praepostors' duty, and they would be obliged for a remedy' or 'for a half-remedy'. If the Headmaster intended to grant it, he gave the Praefect of Hall remedy ring (q.v.). As late as 1868 a reason for the remedy had to be given every Tuesday and Thursday.

There were also half-remedies, or half-rems, i.e. half-holidays with no work in the afternoon, for which the same request was needed. By 1890 they occurred automatically every Tuesday and Thursday. By 1917 work stopped at 12 on half-rems, and in Cloister Time Saturday was also a half-rem, work stopping at 12.45. By 1900 there were several extra half-rems, for which the Praefect of Hall also had to make his request:

a Judges' half-rem: given at the request of the Judges of Assize.
an extra half-rem: given about twice a half for some special event, e.g. an honour or appointment of an Old Wykehamist; birth of a baby of a member of the staff; etc.
a Choir half-rem: given to members of Chapel and Chantry Choirs once a half, to make up for the time they spent on choir-practice.

The origin of the word remedy is not 'quasi dies remissionis' or remi-day, but Latin *remedium* (cure), used for leisure as a restorative after study, and translated as 'remedy'. So used at Southwell Minster (1484), as remedyes at St Paul's School (1512), as remedy at Newark Grammar School (1530) and Durham (1593). At St Paul's and Newark there was the tradition of remedies being granted at the request of eminent persons, which survives at Winton in the custom of Judges on circuit asking for a half-remedy.

Remedy Ring

remedy hot   when a whole remedy was given, there was a stampede for the door of Good Friday Passage, some getting outside and some inside, the latter trying to prevent the former forcing their way in. The passage vanished in 1871, and the Notion with it.

Remedy Ring   a plain gold ring which the Doctor (Headmaster) always sent down on a remedy or half-remedy, with an inscription on it from Juvenal (Satire xi.208): 'COMMENDAT RARIOR USUS' (the less it is used, the better). It was given to the Praefect of Hall, who sent it to the Praefect of School, who returned it to the Doctor at Middle School next day (1838). At some stage in its journey (1868), the ring was carried by the Headmaster's Child (the boy who got books in Middle Part in the preceding Cloister Time). By 1900 the ring was used only for an extra remedy or half-remedy, the Aul.Prae. wearing it through the remedy and returning it to the Headmaster next morning.

The original ring was given by John Potenger, Headmaster 1642–53, and ingeniously inscribed by him with 'POTENtiam GERo feroque' (I display and bring authority). Quaere: where is Potenger's ring today? [Lost.]

remi (pronounced remī)   a remission from work: especially when a Don gave his div leave off morning lines. In use since 1856. cf. tui, for tuition.

remission   when a saint's day fell on a day previous to that on which a verse or prose task, or a vulgus, was due, the boys were excused from doing it, and there was said to be remission from it; also used generally for remission from anything (1836–8).

remove   a move up into the next div at the end of the half (1920).

Reservoir   a tank or pond (1868), or a spring (1900) on Twyford Downs. See **Shepherd's Well**.

resignation   a form of words sent in (1838) to the Warden by College boys when they left or resigned, on a sheet of letter paper, folded like a letter, and addressed to:

> *Viro Reverendo,*
>   R. S. Barter,
>   Winchester College.

Ego, Johannes Brown, omne jus quod habeo aut unquam habui in hoc
Collegio Beatae Mariae Winton prope Winton, aetate cogente [if over
18 years old; if not, he put *patre et matre* (or *custodibus*, or *parentibus*)
volentibus], *libenter resigno.*
[date]

results   the last hour of the half, during which Dons read out to their divisions
lists of marks, and particulars of removes and prizes (1900 on). Senior Div alone
had no results (1920).

Revolt   Volt and Revolt were the eldest and second sons of Rev. S. A.
McDowall, Science Don who taught, *inter alia*, about electricity (1920). Volt
was K. S. P. McDowall (H 1921–7).

revolter   a horrid or revolting man (1920). cf. loather. In standard English it
means a rebel.

Ridding Rield, Ridding New Field, Riddings   that part of New Field between
Lavender Meads and Dogger's Close: opened in the winter of 1869, mainly
owing to the efforts of Dr Ridding. Invariably called New Field (1920).

rile, to   to make angry. Recorded 1880, but is standard English.

River   the more usual name for New Barge, q.v.

Robbins   the well-known grey-headed bookseller in College Street (1820). He
took a young partner, Wheeler, c. 1828.

rock   a medium-sized stone, as distinct from a hollis (pebble). Old English: still
so used in North Carolina, Georgia and California.

Rockley   E. Rockley Wilson, Don 1903–46: captain of Cambridge cricket, and
in the Yorkshire XI: to Australia with the MCC 1920–1: joint editor of the
Register 1901–46. He always fingered his tie nervously when speakng to one.

rodmakers   the two junior College boys who had been in the school more than
one half had to make the bibling rods, i.e. to fasten the twigs into the handle: for
which service they got off all fagging from 8.30 to 9 a.m. (1838–68).

rods   (1) the bibling rods. These consisted of a beech handle 3 feet [0.9 m] long,
with four grooves, pencil thick and 3 inches [75 cm] long, cut in the end of it,
into which fitted four apple twigs 5 feet [1.5 m] long, which were bound into
the grooves with string. The twigs were sent up from Herefordshire in bundles.
They stood out about 1 foot [0.3 m] from each other. The rods were kept by
the Praefect of Hall in lockers at the west end of School and were never used

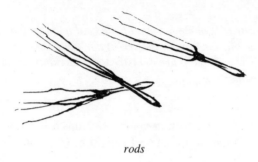

rods

twice (1820–38). (2) birches used in private whippings and kept by Commoner Steward (1868).

Roebuck an inn of that name just outside Winton on the Stockbridge Road, where much potato weeding and digging was done by men in the school towards the end of the First World War.

Roger (1) the person addressed in verse 5 of Domum: 'Heus! Rogere, fer caballos'. This was a College servant, Roger Oades, who kept foxes for the boys in 1658–9, and at Whitsun 1666 used to take food on pack-horses to the boys who had been sent to Talmage's farm at Crawley to avoid plague infection. (2) a young and disobedient black Aberdeen, successor to the defunct William of Wykeham (q.v.) in 1920. College men used to call Roger in Chamber Court, in imitation of the voice of his mistress, College Cook.

roke, to to stir liquids (1831–1900); to poke the fire (1856 on). Chaucer speaks of fire as 'y-reke' from old ashes; dialect, in Cumberland has 'wrok the fire'; in Devon, 'roking about in the muck': elsewhere, roake and rauk (to rake). To roak up can also mean to heap up; to rake a fire can mean to bank it up: these stem from Old English words *rukelen* (heap up), *ruken* (rake), *raken* (scratch), and others of similar sound such as rock or ruck, which together have given meanings such as shake, roll, stir liquids and scratch glass with a point. The easiest way out of this spider's web is to suppose that roke is an onomatopoeic word as old as the practice of poking the fire.

rokeby blancmange and jam, served once a week in College Hall: so called from its supposed resemblance to H. D. E. Rokeby (Coll. 1917–23).

roker a stick or other instrument for stirring or poking anything: recorded from 1831. Used for a poker from 1856, when a ruler was also called a flat-roker, because it was used for stirring egg-flip: a poker only (1920). In dialect a roker is a long hooked iron for riddling furnaces.

Roll a piece of paper with writing on it, usually a list of names: the word dating from a time when all writing was on a scroll of parchment. The Roll, *par*

Roll

excellence, was Election Roll to New College (1831), later called New College Roll, and Election Roll to Winton (1836), still called the Roll.

Other types of roll in common use were the lists of names: (1) for calling names, by a master or Praefect: e.g. the Praefects of Hall and Chapel, Commoner Praefects, or masters of divisions. These were usually mounted on squares of cardboard. In 1831, those used by masters were prepared by the classicus of each part. (2) of absentees on such occasions. (3) of delinquents awaiting punishment, handed to the master at the close of school by Bible Clerk or Ostiarius: 'carta est data deinde magistro' (1647: and so continuing to 1870).

Other rolls are dealt with alphabetically in this book: see **Chantry, Chapel, College, Fifteens, Flannel, Hills, hot, House, Leave-Out, Long, Lords, New, New College, Old, Praefects, Second XI** and **Sixes** Rolls.

roll, to put up a   when an Inferior in College wanted to leave the Chamber during Toy-time, he had to put a slip of paper in the following form on the washing-stool of the Praefect in course, provided there were not two rolls up at the same time (1838). The same procedure applied in New Commoners (1868) if a boy wanted to leave Hall or IVth Book. Having obtained Tutor's permission, he put the roll up on the end of Middle Desks. Only six rolls could be up at one time. This continued in Houses and College, and by 1900 applied to books-chambers also, a vessel of paper being used. One roll at a time was the

Twyman   veniam exeundi petit

maximum allowed. On his return the owner of the roll had to take it down, i.e. remove it.

By 1917 the rules on this subject in College were:

- in books-chambers (for men below VIth Book) and in Toy-time (for all Inferiors), anyone wanting to go out of the Chamber had to put on the toys of the Praefect in course (or failing him the senior Inferior present) a half-vessel bearing the formula 'veniam exeundi petit', and his name written on the left at right-angles. Tolly-keepers wrote their rolls on envelopes. The roll had to be written clearly, in ink, with no capitals except for the name, and no initials. It was non-licet to put up a hot roll (q.v.), i.e. a roll with the ink still wet, and there were penalties for so doing.
- Two rolls only might be put up by one person in one books-chambers or Toy-time, the first for a maximum of fifteen and the second for a maximum of five minutes. Not more than three rolls might be put up to a Praefect at once.
- No individuality might be shown in writing the roll. Once a spirited Inferior, at a time when Vth Chamber was in the hands of lax Praefects, put up a roll reading: 'Hawkes. obscoenitate praefectorum obstupefactus erumpit'. He was inevitably chastised. Hawkes [this was the archaeologist C. F. C. Hawkes] composed an equally impudent roll for use up to books, but I doubt if he was rash enough to use it. It read: 'Hostiarii veniae oblitus, tuam pariter exeundi spernit'.

In School in the old days the procedure was similar. Having obtained leave of the Ostiarius, the boy put up a roll in the following form on the master's desk, unless there were four rolls up already (1836–8). He could stay out for about a quarter of an hour, but it was common to stay out much longer, and boys used to go out to play fives or cricket. No boy could put up more than one roll in any School time. No roll could be put up during the first three-quarters of an hour, or 'when it wanted a quarter of an hour' to the end of School time (1838).

In 1868 leave had to be obtained from the Bible Clerk, and the roll was put on the steps of one of the masters' chairs. Praefects did not put up rolls, but 'scraped out' (q.v.).

The custom of putting up rolls during school hours lingered on, and in 1917 up to books one could write a roll in the above formula on any piece of paper and put it at the foot of the Div Don's table. But hardly anyone did.

Huntingford

Ostiarii venia potitus,
tuam pariter exeundi petit

roll, to sport a   to roll the gown tightly up from the bottom till it formed a sort of lifebelt round the waist. This was done in cold weather for kicking practice, or patting-up on Ball Court: but was a two-year Notion (1920).

Romans Road   the road leading west from Kingsgate Street past Beloe's, with K.P. on its south and Culver's Close on its north. Also the name of the Toye Pot pitch on the northern side of K.P. (1920).

Rootites   Trants, or members of H House. This name, obsolete by 1914, derived from the fact that at one time the Rev. J. Trant Bramston (the Trant) was known in certain quarters as 'the Root of All Evil'.

Ropes   a length of stout rope running down each side of canvas, about a yard inside the netting and 3 feet [0.9 m] from the ground, supported by strong posts at 10-yard [9-m] intervals. 'In Ropes' is between ropes and canvas.

'Ropes!'   called when the ball has been kicked from between ropes and canvas, or when the man kicking it is touching ropes: so as to warn him not to take a bust.

ropes-keeper   a man sitting at the end of ropes, just outside worms, to decide whether a ball has been kicked out of ropes or not. Obsolete by 1917.

rot   nonsense; e.g. what rot. To rot was to talk nonsense. National slang, but recorded as a Notion 1831–84.

rotten, bells go   i.e. intermittently. The phrase was used to describe the intermission after every two or three strokes in First Peal. Recorded 1831; still in use 1922. See **Peals**.

roush   a rush or charge by a man, a group of people, or water: especially for the aperture at the eastern end of Gunner's Hole, where the water enters with a rush. Recorded from 1836. It is the Wiccamical form of rush: cf. housle for hustle.

roush board   the duck-boarding over the roush in Gunner's Hole.

Rows   (1) the fixed benches at each end of School, called Senior, Middle and Junior Rows, Senior Row being in front. Recorded 1836–72. By 1890 only those at the west end survived. (2) the pews in Chapel and Chantry (1920).

rum   odd, strange. National slang, but recorded as a Notion 1838.

Rumblebelly   the Queristers' name for Querister Don, c. 1920.

run cloisters, to   to skip a div. It was defined (1831) as when a boy in Junior Part V got above so many Middle Part boys as to be put up into Senior Part at the beginning of the next half-year, without having been in Middle Part at all. Later examples were: (1868) from Junior Div Junior Part to Junior Div Middle Part, skipping Senior Div Junior Part; (1892) from Junior Div Middle Part to Senior Part, skipping Senior Div Middle Part. Obsolete by 1917.

This must date from a time when the divisions were strung out on the stone benches round Cloisters, and a boy who was moved up many places had literally to run the length of one of the sides of Cloisters.

rustic handle   a wooden handle, extemporised out of a stick from a faggot, stuck in a boiler when the proper iron handle had been knocked off. Recorded 1892: obsolete by 1917.

sack, to   to send; generally used of sending a junior on an errand. It was never used for expel, which is firk. In use since 1917, if not before: a specialised use of the Regency slang to sack, i.e. to give someone the sack or bag, and so to dismiss someone with all their goods and chattels.

sack for, to   to send for; especially used when a Praefect sent for someone in order to punish him.

[St Michael's Passage   see **Micla.**]

St Peter   see **Burgess, senior**

Salem   a small room off 8th bidet room to the south-east. In it (1920) were kept Bill Brighters, coal and funkeys by the chamberman: hence 'Light's abode, celestial Salem'. A mural inscription shows it was once used by Praefects as a sanctum: 'This Chamber, entitled SALEM, was first colonised by Mr. D. S. Margoliouth, then by R. H. Titherington, lastly by Mr. A. L. P. Tucker, who was assisted in the mural decorations by the following gentlemen: A. H. Cruickshank, P. M. Bigge, E. Clarke.' Margoliouth entered College in 1872 and Clarke left in 1881.

Salve Diva Potens Corner   in the south-west corner of Meads by Meads gate and Brolly Tree. On a stone just west of the gate are carved the words SĀLVĔ DĬVĀ PŌTĒNS in lettering of the first half of the nineteenth century, with false quantity marks over the four central syllables: the marks should be 'sālvē dīvă pŏtēns'. The words recall the opening line of Horace's Ode (1.3), 'Sic te diva potens Cypri', and are probably a memorial by his class-mates to a famous howler committed by a boy up to books.

Sanatorium   the College notion for the turreted red-brick building just beyond the south-west corner of Meads: for infectious cases. Commoners called it Sick House, and called Sick House 'College Sick House'. The bathrooms and lavatories are located in the turrets. The explanation of this (1920) was that the architect of the winning design for this building forgot to provide these facilities, and had to stick them on at the corners, disguised as towers. (It was converted into the Art School in 1985.)

sanctum   'a hidden place in the Under Toys used as a receptacle for things which a boy wishes to keep unseen' (1838 only). Standard English for a private room.

Sands   the flagstone pavement in Chamber Court along the north side of Chapel (1820–56): all the flagged areas in Chamber Court, Middle Sands being that running from Middle Gate to Chapel (from 1892). There are many possible derivations: (1) that the flagstones are of sandstone, or bedded in sand. (2) from the saints (cf. the Sans day Carol) in Chapel windows, under which the Headmaster used to pace to and fro, waiting to be asked for a remedy or leave continent (1836). (3) from Old English *sain*, derived from Anglo-Saxon *segnian*, Latin *signare* (to bless with the sign of the cross), from the attitude of the saints in these windows. (4) the invention of some humorist, who was late for Chapel, from 'now our sands are almost run' (Shakespeare's *Pericles*, act V, scene i), or from Psalm 119.25: 'my soul cleaveth unto the dust: quicken thou me' (adhaesit pavimento anima mea): *pavimentum* can mean pavement.

Sardine Tin   a name given to Eldon Pot, because D. R. Jardine, called Sardine by his enemies, was captain of Lords in 1919 when it was changed from a golf cup to one for Middle House cricket.

scadger   a rascal, ruffian. From Cornish dialect scadgan (a tramp or disreputable-looking fellow). In use 1836–60.

'Scaldings!'   a cry to warn others to get out of the way, as though something hot were being carried. It was a nautical exclamation, shouted by anyone carrying hot water or the like on deck: Smollett (1748) uses it of someone carrying boiled peas. In use 1831–1914; obsolete by 1917, though in 1914 'to keep scaldings' still meant to be on the look-out.

Scards   a wharf directly below and beyond Black Bridge, extending to Old Bridge: belonging (1868) to one Newton, successor to a man named Scard.

scheme   a primitive form of alarum devised by boys in College for waking themselves or a Praefect early in the morning, especially in the summer. Recorded from 1831, but obsolete long before 1917. Functure was known to burn an inch [25 mm] an hour. A boy wishing to wake up after, say, four hours' sleep cut off Functure 4 inches [10 cm] from the bottom, wrapped paper round the socket and tied a string round the paper. The other end of the string passed through the head of the sleeper's bed, or over a faggot stick placed over the head of the bed and resting on top of the toys on either side: and was tied to a hat-box, cup of water, heavy book, or 'a dozen or so large books tied up in a towel', which were suspended over the sleeper's head. In due course Functure burned down, the paper and string were severed, and the books fell on the sleeper. 'This scheme', says a writer of 1838, 'if set properly, never fails.' If a pint-cup of water was used instead of books, it was called a water-scheme (1836).

schitt a goal at football. It was superseded in 1860 by 'goal'.

In early Winchester football the goal was formed by two gowns (or coats if in Commoners) between which the last Behind stood. If the ball passed over his head or between his legs it was a 'goal' and scored three: over the gowns, a 'gowner' worth two: over the rest of worms, or between the goal and the last of the line of kickers-in, a 'schitt' worth one: in 1838 this was called a 'pass' (see **goal** and **pass**). When the whole of worms was made to count equally, every goal was a schitt.

First recorded 1836. As there is no record of how this word was pronounced, it is difficult to be sure of the derivation. Possibilities are: (1) it is a form of shute or shoot, a dialect name for the game of shovel-board, in which the object is to shove the counters beyond a certain line, and as near the end of the table as possible; (2) it is a form of skit, from Old English *skitten* (to leap aside or fly awry, hurry away): it appears as skyte in this sense in the Paston Letters (1424–1509) and as skit (1611): and survives in standard English as skitter (to skim over) and in dialect in skitter-brained, skitter-wit (giddy, hair-brained).

School the communal school-room, before the days of div rooms.

(1) The original School was underneath Hall, and part of it is now College VIIth Chamber, which was a bedroom from 1701 to 1875. It is one of the oldest school-rooms in England, and is described in Robert Mathew's poem 'De Collegiata Schola [Wicchamica]' of 1647. The ceiling and Hall above were supported by four wooden columns, only one of which is now left, facing the door. There were three windows on the south side, and in each of them were stone benches for the eighteen Praefects. These benches survive in two of the windows. The upper part of the third window now lights Seventh Chamber Passage, which was excised from the old school-room in 1687 to give access to the new School. In its original state, School measured 45 ½ by 28 ¾ feet [13.8 by 8.7 m] and was 15 1/4 feet [4.8 m] high.

On its north wall hung Tabula Legum, which Mathew calls 'the Rules of Quintilian'. On the west wall was Aut Disce board, and beneath it the rostrum 'in which we were wont to declaim'. In the south-west corner (assuming the new School was an exact copy of the old) was the Headmaster's chair, and the rest of the room was occupied by benches and scobs. At the east and west ends there were probably the Rows which were reproduced in the later School.

It is not known what happened to the Mappa Mundi, and the Rostrum, which did not appear in the new School.

(2) The present School is an example of Jacobean architecture which has been much admired. It was erected by subscription at a cost of £2,500, of which Warden Nicholas contributed £1,477. The architect is unknown, but Sir Christopher Wren may perhaps have designed it when preparing plans for the palace of Charles II at Winchester.

The present School

The foundation stone was laid in September 1683 and the building finished in June 1687. Internally School is 90 by 36 feet [27.4 by nearly 11 m] and about 30 feet [9.1 m] high. Over the entrance door is a statue of the Founder presented by Caius Gabriel Cibber, a Holstein sculptor, to procure admission of his son to College.

At the east end, facing Aut Disce board, is Tabula Legum, which in the 1917–22 period was above the entrance door, having been moved to make room for an organ. Beneath these devices the walls are panelled in black oak, on which former generations of Wykehamists have had their names carved. The ceiling rests on a cornice, round which are nine shields emblazoned with the arms of the chief contributors to the erection of School. Over the fireplace is the coat-of-arms of the Paulets, Marquises of Winchester (sable, 3 swords in pile, points in base, argent, pommelled and hilted or).

At the south-west corner is a triple seat, the centre seat for the Warden, on his right the Sub-Warden, on his left the Headmaster. At the north-west corner is the Second Master's chair, which stood originally in the south-east corner. Opposite it, and opposite the Warden's group of chairs, there were two lower chairs for the use of French masters and others, both now removed. At both ends of School were Rows, rising one above the other. Those at the west end remain, those at the east having been removed.

Down the length of School were four parallel rows of benches separated by three passages lengthwise, and intersected by transverse benches every 5 feet [1.5 m]. At the corners thus formed were placed scobs, between which sat College men, and in 1838 the area was called Scob Place. At the other side of the central passage, opposite the door, were the two Commoner tables down the centre. The Rows were divided from the rest of School by passages from north to south.

School was the school-room for the whole school until 1869 when New Commoners became classrooms. It was then used for concerts, lectures and examinations, the Electio ad Winton being held there: but the new Memorial hall now fulfils some of these functions.

School Cap   a possessor (1920) of one of the following caps: Sixes, Soccer XI, Lords, 2nd XI, Senior Club, Princes, Bisley and School IV. School caps in College were usually asked in Notions examina.

School Committee   a committee consisting of one Don, the Captains of Lords and VIs and three other members, elected by Co.Praes, one each from College, Commoners and Houses. They dealt with the financing and general administration of all games and athletics in the school.

School Court   between School and VIIth Chamber.

School exhibi (pronounced exhibī)   the first three men in Goddard, and often the senior scientist or historian in the school, making up the total to four men who were leaving, were awarded an exhibition of £50 a year at the university (1920).

School Game   (1) the senior soccer game, played on Bull's Drove nearly every day in Common Time. (2) a pick-up game of Lords and Second XI men occasionally played at the beginning of Cloister Time (1920).

'School in School'   when the whole school assembled in School to hear something of general import from the Headmaster: such as catapults, swearing, or tolling in Cathedral. The school was summoned by a notice put up by the Headmaster saying: 'I wish to see the School in "School" at 12'. (1920).

School nets   the five nets just south of Trees, used (1920) on whole-school days by Lords (1.45 to 2.45); Second XI and Senior Club men (2.45 to 3.45); Toye Pot men in the running for flannels (6.30 to 7.30). The skipper of Lords made up the nets, three men to each. The usual coaches (1920) were: in the 1st net, Ernie Hayes, the Pro; 2nd net, Harry Altham; 3rd net, Irving (sometimes); 5th net, Rockley Wilson.

School Push   see **push.**..

School Shop   a confectioner's shop on the corner of College and Kingsgate Streets, started by the school authorities in 1893 as a school 'grub' shop. Also called School Grubbers or New Shop (1900).

School Writer   writer to the Praefect of School. His duties were: (1) to go down to Sick House every day after breakfast, make out a roll of College men continent, and leave it in Praefects' Common Room, and to take up Miss Wellsman's note

Scob

on men continent to the Second Master. (2) to arrange with Honey for lanterns for lectures in School and Old Wykehamist Room (1920).

Science hut   an old wooden army hut with tin roof, bought after the First World War, and erected in 1921 on Kingsgate Street just east of Forder's Piece. It contained two extra lecture rooms for science.

Science Schools   see Stinks Buildings.

scob   a double-lidded oak box, set at the angles of the squares of wooden benches or scrubbing-forms in School. One lid was kept up as a screen and the other was used as a desk to write on. In the box beneath, books and personal property were kept. In this respect the scob corresponded with the modern schoolboy's playbox. Each College boy, and a few Commoner Praefects, had a scob and sat at it in School. The Praefect of Hall's scob was immediately to the right of the Headmaster's chair, next to which was the Praefect of Library's and then the Praefect of School's (1868).

The word is recorded from 1620, when J. Hutton on entering College received an account for three shillings and six pence for 'a scobb to hold his books'. When div rooms were provided in 1869, scobs were abolished, and by 1917 only one survived, in Porter's Lodge. The derivation is not box spelt backwards, though this was believed as early as 1836. Nor is it from the adjective squob (short and fat). It is probably transferred from the bench, Latin *scabellum*, French *escabeau*: cf. *flagellum* (flog): and for the change from 'a' to 'o', cf. strap, strop: chap, chop. It appears in the form cobb in 1612 for the chest in which song-books were kept in Salisbury Cathedral: and survives in Hampshire and Wiltshire dialect for a desk, an oak chest, or a dark cupboard.

The word may have received impetus in the alert minds of seventeenth-century Wykehamists from the abverb squab, for falling plump, falling with a crash, of which there is an example of 1692, where the eagle drops the tortoise 'squab' on a rock. The lids of scobs must often have fallen with a clang, and this adverb would be very appropriate to it. Adams, p.343, gives an engraving of a boy at his Scob, reproduced from p.11 of Wordsworth's 'College of St. Mary Winton'.

sconce   (1) a projecting candle-bracket fixed to a socket in a wall. In 1838 it is illustrated in this sketch, A being the socket, B the sconce and C the candle. At that time sconces were of brass and each boy had a pair fixed on each side of his under-toys instead of a candle. They were also used to light Chapel and School. In 1856 sconce could also mean a candlestick with a reflector, and in New Commoners (1868) these were of tin, and there was one to each room in Gallery. In 1890 it meant a branch candlestick. Now obsolete. (2) a nuisance, an obstacle. In the Marginal Notes to the Statutes (1780) a boy is described as a 'damd little sconce', in the sense of a hindrance or spoilsport. Also obsolete.

Whether noun or verb, sconce is an Old English word deriving ultimately from Latin *abscondere* (to hide), with a wide variety of meanings in which the idea of hiding is present: e.g. cover (hence obstruction, prevention, deprivation, forfeit, fine), shelter, screen (hence a dark lantern or candle-bracket with reflector), chimney-seat, defence, fort, helmet.

sconce

sconce, to   (1) to obstruct, get in the way of, supplant: especially of hindering a kick at football or a catch at cricket by getting in the performer's way. The use does not survive in standard English. (2) to deprive of: especially in the phrase 'to be sconced leave-out'. This is akin to the use of sconce for to fine or mulct, recognised by Dr Johnson (1755) and still surviving at Oxford, where to sconce a man in Hall is to penalise him (usually for talking shop) by making him drink a large flagon of beer without stopping, and if he fails, making him sport drinks to the whole table. It also survives in North Country dialect in the game of marbles, where sconce means to extract a forfeit. For other terms from marbles, cf. **finge** and **knuckle-down hot**.

score a person off, to   to get the better of, humiliate; e.g. 'that scores you off', 'score him off'. In vogue in 1917, either this is an inversion of the standard slang, 'to score off a person', or score is used in the sense of scratching off a list.

scourge, to   the word in use, 1820–8, for bibling by a master with rods. Flog, bible, tund and beat were not yet in fashion.

scrape out, to   when a Praefect wished to go out of School, instead of putting up a roll, he stood near the door by the Ostiarius' scob and scraped with his

scrape out

foot until he obtained a nod of permission from the senior master in School. Similarly, until 1869 in New Commoners, Praefects wishing to leave Hall during dinner used to scrape in their places until the Tutor nodded. Recorded from 1831.

Screen   the panelled wooden partition which separates the body of College Hall from Hatches.

scrubbing   a flogging of four cuts performed at scrubbing-forms with the vimen quadriferum (a bundle of birch-twigs), the offender's name having been ordered to the Ostiarius. The master administering punishment put on his cap and called the boy's name: the boy then walked up, threw his gown over his head and knelt down at the scrubbing-form, and the two juniors in College 'took him up'. It was also called a 'scratching' (1831–8). T. A. Trollope, in his memoirs (1820–8), calls them 'scourgings' of three strokes, not floggings, and does not mention bibling.

   From Anglo-Saxon *scrybb* (brushwood, shrub, scrub). To scrub in standard English is to scour with a brush of stiff bristles; in the North Country and Scotland a scrubber is a bundle of heather or twigs for cleaning cooking pots. Our notion is aligned with this, to scrub meaning to treat with a bundle of sticks.

scrubbing-forms   the transverse oak benches in School where a scrubbing (q.v.) was administered: described as near each of the two senior masters' chairs (1838), or to the left of the Second Master's chair (1892).

Scrutiny   an enquiry made, in accordance with the Statutes, on the first day of Election Week, by the Warden of New College and the Posers, of the seven seniors and seven juniors in College: they were asked if they had any complaint to make about conditions in College, the arrangements made for their comfort, and fagging. By 1838 only 'the juniors in Chambers' were called up for Scrutiny, and it is recorded that they usually complained, not of fagging or punishments, but of the butter, cheese, beer and potatoes. There was a similar Scrutiny by the Warden and Fellows of Winchester in Sealing Week.

This humane custom, recorded from 1831, has unfortunately been allowed to lapse: probably because schoolboys' code of honour prevented their ever complaining of ill-treatment.

Seagers   a pastry-cook's up Town where boys were not allowed to buy food, but often did (1917–22).

Sealing Days   the quarter-days, on which the Warden and Fellows used to seal the College leases, as required by the Statutes (R.xxxiii, 'of the Common Seal, the Chest and the Annual Inventory'). On Sealing Days the Praefect of Hall used to write a letter to the Senior Fellow, addressing it 'Seniori Soc. tradatur hoc', asking him to request a half-remedy, which was always granted as a matter of course. The death of the last Fellow of the old regime in 1893 put an end to this agreeable custom.

Sealing Week   the week at the beginning of December, in which the Thursday was a Hatch Thoke and the Friday was a Sealing Day. Sixes took place in this week. See **Founder's Com and Ob**. A Notion long since forgotten.

IInd Book   Queristers originally formed a div of the school, and still appear in Long Roll as Secunda Classis, though IVth and IIrd Book have long since vanished. In 1529 (see vulgus) IVth, IIIrd and IInd Books existed, but not Ist.
   Quaere: 'What was First Book, and why did it disappear so early?'

second edition   to have the toe-pan after another boy, and wash your feet in water he had used: 'always the case with juniors' (1838).

Second XI Roll   a roll brought down at the end of Cloister Time, giving the names of those who may wear Second XI colours (1920).

Second Junior   see **Junior, First, Second**.

Second Master, **Secondmaster**, or **Ostiarius**   usually called the Second Man (1920), on the analogy of Head Man for Headmaster. Next below the Headmaster on the staff and deputises for him if away: is also Housemaster of College, like the Master in College at Eton. The Second Master of 1917–22 interfered very little with what went on in College, except when anyone made excessive noise.
   Recent Second Masters were:

Rev. C. Wordsworth	1835–45
Rev. F. Wickham	1845–62
Rev. G. Ridding	1863–7
Rev. J. J. Hornby	1867–8
Rev. W. Awdry	1868–73
Rev. G. Richardson	1873–99

M. J. Rendall	1899–1911
J. A. Fort	1911–15
Rev. A. T. P. Williams	1916–24
Lt Col. R. M. Wright	1924–51

The **Second Master's House**   occupied the upper-floor rooms in the north-west corner of College.

Second Six   a match between College and Commoner Second Sixes, played on the day after Hatch Thoke (when Sixes were played): discontinued in 1867 on the separation of Commoners and Houses.

seething lake   a conduit of cold water drawn at Chamber Court Conduit and taken up to Chambers at night in Cloister Time (1917–22) for making lemonade in quantity. Perhaps a geography book phrase relating to geysers or the lake of pitch in Trinidad.

sellings   hard luck. An expression of sympathy (1838), especially in the exclamation 'much sellings', which was used if a boy had failed or been disappointed ('sold') in anything. Now obsolete: it is a Winton version of the standard slang 'to be sold', 'sold down the river', 'what a sell'.

semper   always (Latin). It was used instead of 'always' from 1836, but obsolete by 1917. Also used adjectivally, e.g. semper socius, semper tardy, semper continent, semper ex-trumps: see also semper leave and Semper Testis.

semper leave   permanent leave-off. Obtained (1838–68) by boys 'who are sickly sort of fellows' from the master, never to go on Hills: and from Senior Praefect, never to fag at games, which was called 'semper leave from games'.

Semper Testis   the perpetual witness. (1) College Steward, who was always present as witness at the swearing of College Oath. (2) anyone who invariably corroborated a statement, without regard to its accuracy. It is recorded (c. 1831) that a boy was called up to give testimony to Dr Williams in support of another's statement: and later the Doctor discovered to his indignation that the witness did not know what the matter was. Long since obsolete.

Senior   there were four diving stages between roush board and Railway Bridge in Gunner's Hole: the lowest was Junior-Junior; next, Junior; next, Senior; and the highest, Senior-Senior, or Senior Wreck.

Senior Club   the senior (pick-up) game of cricket when Lords were playing a match, played on 'Senior Club', i.e. Meads Tent pitch. By 1917 any club organisation there may once have been had disappeared from this game.

Senior Club cap dark blue and white, like College VI cap but with wider stripes. It was awarded up to 1919 to prominent cricketers who failed to get into Second XI, and could also be worn by men who had already been in Lords a year. Doubtless long since obsolete.

Senior College the first fives court on the left as one entered Old Fives Courts (1920).

Senior Commoner (1) the man in Commoners who was senior in Short Roll; not necessarily the Sen.Co.Prae. He was also called Senior Wreck (in College). (2) the far court on the right as one entered Old Fives Courts (1920).

Senior Co.Prae. the man appointed by the headmaster as Senior Commoner Praefect. He represented Commoners generally, and had sundry duties, including keeping Commoner Annals, giving out fives courts, etc. Recorded from 1880.

Senior Div Classroom the southernmost upstairs div room on the west wing of Flint Court; used by VIth Book, Senior Div (1920).

Senior Div table an octagonal table in the middle of Mob.Lib., which could be used only by men in Senior Div (1920).

Senior End the table on the south side of College Hall next to Dais. Senior Tolly-keeper sat at its head, and the other two Tolly-keepers beside him (1920).

Senior House cricket and football matches played between the first teams of the various Houses, including College East and West.

Senior Inferior the senior man in each house not a Praefect. At one time the four Senior Inferiors in Commoners had praefectorial rights, with certain clumsy restrictions: but complications arose, and in 1829 their powers were abolished.

Senior match a cricket match formerly played between the best XI of College and Commoners. Houses were added later. Recorded from 1868, but the notion must have existed earlier. Obsolete by 1914.

Senior Mess in New Commoners, the six Senior Praefects sat and messed together at breakfast and supper.

Senior Part the Senior Part of Vth Book, called 'Senior Part the Fifth' as late as 1872. In 1917 it was divided into Senior Part 1, 2, and 3, each with two parallels. Senior Part 3 sometimes had three parallels.

Senior Part Cloisters the covered portico in the south-west of Flint Court.

Seven Hatches

Senior Part note-book   see **note-book**.

Senior Part Order books   see **books**.

Senior Querister   the head querister, who was supposed to keep the others in order, but rarely did so (1920).

Senior Senior   see **Senior**.

Senior Tolly-keeper   the senior of the three Tolly-keepers. He was the senior Inferior in College and sat at the Head of Senior End (1920): see **to sport a baulk**. He came round at the beginning of the half to get votes for what newspapers College should take in. Every Chamber had *The Times*. *Punch* and the *Sphere* were also taken, and passed round from Chamber to Chamber.

Senior Wreck   see **senior** and **wreck**.

Sergeantites   the old name for Phils, or G House, after the first Housemaster, Rev. E. W. Sergeant (1869–82).

serges   rough trousers which had to be worn for football by everybody except men in XVs, VIs, or in dress, who wore cut shorts. Obsolete before 1890.

set on, to be   (1) 'to be called upon when up at Books to construe the lesson'. Recorded 1838–72; obsolete by 1890. (2) to be put on to bowl. Recorded 1868; obsolete by 1890.

set up, to   used 1917–22 for: (1) to put on its shelf in Hatch (of jampots, etc.). (2) to fill a bidet: see **First Junior**.

settler   a crushing retort, always relished by the boys. Two famous settlers were handed down orally to posterity: (1) in the rebellion of 1793, Warden Huntingford began an address to the rebels with 'Eloquar, an sileam?', to be cut short with the settler 'Silly ass'. (2) soon after the completion of New Commoners in 1842, a Commoner junior taunted a College junior with 'Well, charity boy' and was answered with, 'Well, wurkus.' The word is standard slang; forgotten by 1850. [Wurkus = workhouse.]

Seven hatches   seven hatches in a line, separating Old and New Barge, just below Black Bridge, opposite Scards, and noted (1838) as a favourite fishing ground. In 1875 the old hatches were replaced by new ones, and an eighth was added. By 1880 there were only five.

VIIth Chamber   see **School**.

VIIth-Chamberers   a Notion (1920) for occasions when all College assembled after Preces in VIIth, Juniors staying up, in order that the Second Master might speak to them about some matter of public interest: e.g. luggage arrangements, fire, stealing.

VIIth Chamber Passage   the passage leading from School Court into Chamber Court. It was excised from the old school-room (VIIth Chamber) when School was built.

share   a loaf given at meals to each man in College. By 1917 it was only part of a loaf: but a 'second share' could be obtained by asking Chandler the butler.

Shebe   see **Hebe**.

sheepwashing   (1) up to 1837 it was the custom to throw into deep water every boy who could not swim, but, it is noted, 'there were always good swimmers in the water to take them out before they were *quite* drowned: this was done annually on one particular day'. The custom was abandoned, but the word remained in use, with the meaning of throwing a boy into the water if he refused to purl in. (2) by 1892 it meant to drag a man out of bed to tub-room and throw him into a tub with his night-clothes on. Leave-out days and Hatch Thokes were generally chosen for this performance, as there were no Morning Lines or Chapel before breakfast. Long obsolete.

Shepherd's Well   a well or pond on the south-west edge of Twyford Downs. See **Reservoir**. First recorded 1868.

sherk   see **shirk**.

shig   a shilling. Recorded from 1836; obsolete by 1914.

shirk   a failure by a Don to appear up to books. If he was fifteen minutes late, the div 'raised a shirk', and could go away (1920).

shirk, to	spelt more correctly **sherk** till 1843. (1) to avoid, evade, leave undone, fail to appear at: e.g. to shirk Chapel. Used by Dickens (1852), and in Isle of Wight dialect to 'shirk off' (or out) of work; still used in standard English, e.g. to shirk responsibility. (2) to slink away, sneak off, go illicitly to: e.g. to shirk up Town. [At Eton, used to describe an informal mutual ignoring of each other's presence on forbidden ground by masters and boys.] It is either from provincial German *schirgen*, or from 'to shark' (to live on one's wits, play the adventurer).

shirk/sherk in, to	to enter the water timidly without purling, 'first putting in a foot to see if the water is cold'. Recorded from 1838: obsolete by 1914.

shirk/sherk out, to	of College or School, to go out without leave; 'both very common occurrences' (1838). Obsolete by 1914. It echoes the standard slang 'shark out' (slip out by a trick).

shirkster	a man who shirks. Recorded from 1865.

shoe board	a narrow board over the iron bedsteads in College for shoes, etc. (1838).

shoe hole	(1) a small place near the Warden's stables, at the back of Paradise, near Downes' shop, where shoes and boots were cleaned (1838). (2) two small cupboards at the base of toys where shoes and other things were kept (1838). (3) a small room in Gallery in New Commoners in which boots were cleaned (1868).

shop	a College Chamber, upstairs or down (1920).

shops	the shops in College and Kingsgate Streets, which were licet for men in the school: especially School Shop, a visit to which was called going 'down shops' or 'round shops'.

short bat	a wooden bat about 12 ½ inches long by 4 inches wide [about 320 by 100 mm] used by College (1917–22) for batters on Ball Court, and by Commoner juniors in Old Fives Courts. It was also the name of a College competi in which this bat was used.

Short Half	the half-year beginning in September and ending at Christmas: i.e. the Michaelmas or Christmas term. Recorded 1836; still in use. cf. Long Half.

Short Meads	the first part of Cloister Time, when Lock-up was at 7 p.m., and meads were left open until then (1868); extended later to that part of Common Time when Lock-up was at 5 p.m. and Meads were afterwards left open. cf. Long Meads. Obsolete.

Sick House (1670)

Short Roll   a printed booklet published each half, with the names of the whole school grouped in divisions.

Short Stinkers   a College toll (1920); see **toll**.

shot, to take a   to guess at anything at random. Standard slang, but noted as a Notion 1838–84.

shuffle, to   to pretend, feign, act a part fraudulently. e.g. to shuffle a sleep, shuffle continent. It was so used by Shakespeare (1600–1) and used of prevaricating, inconsistency, self-contradiction, by Ben Jonson (1629) and Dryden (c. 1690). Noted as a Notion 1856–1900; obsolete by 1914. It comes from Anglo-Saxon *sceofan*; standard English, scuffle.

shuffler   one who shuffles. Obsolete by 1914.

shut out   locked out of Chapel when bells go down and Chapel doors are shut. Current in 1900; obsolete by 1914.

Sicily   a small triangular patch of turf, about the shape of Sicily, between the south-west corner of Cloisters and Ball Court, where mills (fights) between College men used to take place (1831–43). This patch vanished, and the name was transferred to a similar patch in Grass Court, enclosed by railings (1868), with three shrubs growing in it, or to two small clumps of trees near Walfords and Old Fives Courts. In 1880 the name was assigned to the original position, said to be enclosed by railings. After 1900 it denoted a large triangle of grass between School and Old Fives Courts.

sickers, or **sickness** an umbrage, being offended. In use since 1920.

Sick House (1) an attractive cottage of brick and stone built in 1656 on the west of Meads. It is used by College for all except infectious diseases, and is in effect College's sick-room. Commoners call it College Sick House. (2) an unattractive hospital built in brick in 1886 between Meads and Kingsgate Street, south of College Sick House, for infectious cases and operations: called Sick House by Commoners and Sanatorium by College.

Sick House Meads the meadow in which College Sick House stood, connected with Meads and Grass Court by Sick House Gate and Bangy Gate. These boundaries and gates have long since vanished.

Sid the Dons' nickname for Rev. S. A. McDowall, Don 1906–34.

silver fork a wooden skewer used as a chop-stick in College Hall when forks were scarce. Unsuspecting boys were sometimes sent to Whitesman the butler to ask for a silver fork, to get a rise out of him. Whitesman then lifted the boy off the ground by his ears, and this was called giving him a silver fork. Recorded 1836–8, and repeated 1892, when it is spelt silva, and use as a toasting fork is mentioned. Long obsolete. It was probably a pun: Latin *silva* (wood).

Simmond's a mill (1868): by 1872 Hammond had succeeded Simmond, and it was called Hammond's.

Simon and Jude a double wrought-iron stove in the middle of College Hall, which was taken down in the summer. The flue was conducted under the floor and out through the top of one of the buttresses on the south side of Hall. Praefects and Tolly-keepers used to stand and warm at it while waiting for the Second Master to come up for Hall. At breakfast and tea, Senior Praefects and Tolly-keepers made toast at the eastern hearth, Junior Praefects at the western, for Inferiors in their Chambers, and also for men they had just beaten. Praefects could sweat Queristers to toast for them. On Sunday mornings before 8.30 juniors came up to toast for themselves and other Inferiors in their Chambers (1920). So named from being erected each year on the feast of SS Simon and Jude, 28 October.

Simons W. J. Simons was proprietor of a shop, about no. 73, in Kingsgate Street (1920), where he sold all kinds of athletic outfits, blew up footballs and oiled bats. He could be seen in Short Half coming to or from a Captain of VI with a black bag of footballs.

sines (pronounced sīnēs) a small loaf of unusual shape given to each boy in Old Commoners (i.e. up to 1842) at breakfast. The notion was maintained through New Commoners and on into Houses till about 1890, but is now forgotten. The name is not from Latin *cineres* (cinders), as suggested in 1838: but from

Latin *sĭnĕ* (without), though not (as hinted in 1836) because juniors so often went without them, but because it was without butter or cheese. Dry bread was therefore 'sine', and portions of dry bread were 'sines'. The origin of the word was then forgotten, and a loaf was called 'a sines'.

singing   given two meanings (in the period 1838–43): (1) 'twice a week a man comes down to College to give us lessons in singing by Wilkems method: first begun in Short Half 1842.' ['Wilkem' was the Frenchman Guillaume Louis Bocquillon Wilhem, who developed a monitorial method for group teaching of singing via sight-reading. His method was taken up in England by John Hullah, who in 1841 brought out *Wilhem's Method of Teaching Singing, Adapted to English Use*. See B. Rainbow *Land without Music*, London 1967.] (2) 'on holiday and half-holiday evenings, we sing in School what songs we please.' see also **College** and **Commoner Singing**.

sit in, to   to invigilate a division during an examination.

sitting up   'After evening chapel some boys sit up in bed with a candle on their toys to read novels or mug, as the case may be. We are not allowed to sit up, and when a master comes about we all put out our candles. The masters in general wink at it, it is thought' (1838–43).

Six and Six   see **Sixes**.

Sixes   the triangular contest at Winchester football between College, Commoners and House, played in early December. Before Houses separated from Commoners, it was a straight contest between College and Commoners, and called Six and Six. Recorded from 1836.

Sixes Roll   the list of names of those chosen for College, Commoners and O.T.H. VIs, and dress, brought down by a Don at the request of the Captain of VI a few days before the match, in Hat Place (1900); from Quarter-Deck (1920).

Sixes Week   see **Sealing Week**.

VIth Book   see **books**.

VIth Book copy-book   see **copy-book**.

VIth Book Inferior   a man in VIth Book not a Praefect.

VIth Book note-book   see **note-book**.

VIth Book table   a table to the south of Senior Div table in Mob.Lib., at which only VIth Book men might sit. The library catalogue was on it (1920).

skirmishing on

VIth Chambering   a private bibling administered by the Head or Second Master in VIth Chamber: Long obsolete [and always rare; J. S. Furley, who entered in 1867, remembered only one example in his time at the school (*Winchester in 1867*, 1936)].

Skeleton Island   a spit of land jutting out into Old Barge between Gunner's Hole and Double Hedges, nearly opposite Hochstapler. It was not always an island, but was usually cut off from the rest of Water Meads by marshy ground. There was an overhanging tree on the island named Skeleton Tree. Origin unknown; obsolete by 1914.

Skiers   Porter's Lodge. This was an example of excessive notion-mongering, and considered a very bad notion in College (1920). From Po.Lo., which as Latin polo could mean 'in the sky'.

skimmer   a shallow dive, entering the water just beneath the surface and rising again immediately. Recorded 1836–84; long obsolete.

skin, to   (1) to take off someone else's jersey by pulling it inside-out over his head. Used also as a noun, 'sport me a skin'. Recorded 1836–1907; long obsolete. (2) to draw all the bedclothes off a boy who is in bed. Recorded 1838–84; long obsolete.

Skipper   Captain of a team: especially The Skippers, i.e. the first and second skippers of College VI (1920). National slang since the seventeenth century for the master of a small merchant vessel: a form of 'shipper'.

skirmishing on   running home from Hills when it came on to rain, the boys breaking their ranks as skirmishers do, and not waiting for the Praefect of Hall to call 'On'. Recorded 1831–43; later applied also to running back from Cathedral. A skirmish or scrimmage was an irregular fight, derived from Old German *scherm* (shield).

skiv   one pound; half-a-skiv, 10 shillings (1880).

slab   the board which forms the writing desk in a toys. In the original toys the slab was hinged, and rested on two narrow boards which slid out in the manner of a bureau. When not in use the slab was folded back. When toys were later fixed to the wall, the slab projected below the upper cupboard. Finally, in the cubicle type of toys, the slab rested on supports fixed to the side wall. In 1917 the slab also meant the boarding across the window embrasure in a Praefect's place.

slack-chair   a canvas deck-chair. In 1917–22 every College Praefect had one, with his initials emblazoned on the canvas, and his valet took it downstairs and up, morning and night. All VIth Book Inferiors might have one too: theirs stayed upstairs all the week, and were taken down by the First Junior on Sunday mornings. Inferiors had always to raise leave to sit in a slack-chair in their Chambers, from the owner if present, otherwise from any Praefect. In Cloister Time Praefects sat out in them in Chamber Court, and on Sundays in the Warden's Garden: and all owners of slack-chairs could sit out in Meads in them on Sundays.

Some of these chairs passed from hand to hand and lasted many years, especially one belonging to N. O. W. Steward (Coll. 1913–18): it had broad arm-rests, on which were carved the initials of many previous owners.

slips, or **canvas slips**   pieces of paper distributed to the various Houses, containing the names of the men in each House who were to play in canvas, by the names-docker. A Commoner Notion dating from c. 1900.

slouch hat   a soft khaki hat, like the Australian 'Digger's' hat, turned up and clipped at one side, with a chin-strap, used at Camp from 1919 with the blue patrol jacket as undress uniform.

slow   ignorant of Wiccamical language or customs. In use 1856–1900; now obsolete.

small crockets, or **crockets**   (1836) miniature cricket. It was played with a stump and a fives ball in 1836; with a small plain deal bat 2 inches [50 mm] broad and a small rubber ball (1868); with small-crockets bats (like broomsticks) and tennis balls on Ball Court or in House yards (1892). In 1917 the small-crockets bat (used for small crockets and whiteball game (q.v.) had a round handle and a blade of triangular section. The handle had no binding; it was about the length of a cricket bat, and made by Gradidges.

small porges   see **porges**.

smuggler   a small lead pencil sharpened at both ends, orginally used by men in Senior Part for taking notes surreptitiously, while Praefects construed at pulpiteers. Recorded 1856: still in use 1922. So called because it was smuggled in.

The Rev. R. Quirk (Don 1905–38) was called the Smuggler, his baldness having given rise to the fancy that he was the same at both ends.

snack   a small fives ball, used for bat-fives (1820–8), when it is described as hardly bigger than a large walnut and as hard as wood; used for fives (1831); since 1856 has meant a bat-fives ball, and since 1880 a racquets ball also.

Snack is a fungus growing on trees, used as tinder when dried: in Gloucestershire dialect a snack-ball was a ball made of snack, which was very elastic and bounced well. The name is connected with snag, a knot or protuberance on a tree, or the pruned stump of a branch: so used by Spenser (1589). Either from Norwegian *snag* (a projecting point), or perhaps from Old English *snag* (a snail), derived from Anglo-Saxon *snaca* (a snake).

Snap up, to   (of false quantities) to jockey up by discovering a false quantity made by the man translating. Anyone, however low, could jockey up in this way, but if he himself was wrong, he went down junior. In use 1836–92.

snicks, to go   to go halves. From to go snacks, used by Pope: snack has been in use since c. 1650 for a light meal, bite, or tit-bit, coming later to mean an equal portion: it is another form of snatch. In use 1838–92.

sniggle, to   to smirk, to grin. In use in New Commoners 1868. A variant of snigger, snicker.

soccer on Ball Court   played by senior College men on wet winter afternoons (1920). Goals were made by standing two large fire-irons from the furnace under School against Cloisters wall, and at the other end by sticking two in the grass. The game was played in old fives shoes with a half-sized football.

socius (pronounced so-shuss)   a companion, without whom no junior was allowed to walk to or from Cathedral or Hills (1831), or Chapel (1868): also used as a verb since c. 1850, e.g. 'he sociussed me up Hills', i.e. accompanied. This is straight from Tabula Legum (1561–71): 'neve sine socio, coram magistris incedito: sociati omnes incedunto'. From the outset the authorities preferred boys not to be alone. From Latin *socius* (comrade). The rule no doubt stems from the church tradition that the disciples were sent out two by two.

sock, to   to hit hard at cricket, to win, to defeat (at cricket or in a mill); in the passive, to be beaten. In use 1831–92. Standard slang for defeating, beating, thrashing: e.g. 'give them socks'. The derivation is anybody's guess: (1) the sound of ball on bat; (2) the naval practice of thrashing midshipmen with a sock of wet sand; (3) from 'give suck', or 'sucks to you', used as a coarse taunt; (4) from sockdologer (a decisive blow), a fanciful perversion of doxology, or the end of the service.

sodger, sojer a cross ✕ to call attention to something on paper; a large cross in the margin of an exercise after correction; a percher (q.v.) against a Praefect's name. In use 1839–92. From soldier, either because the cross resembled the two pipe-clayed belts which crossed in the centre of his uniform, or in reference to the fact that soldiers were usually illiterate and signed their names by making a cross.

sog a sovereign. In use 1836–92.

solo a walk without a socius (noun) or alone (adjective or adverb). In use 1856–84.

solus alone, from Latin *solus*; e.g. 'he went solus', 'a solus walk'. In use 1920.

Son see **Pater**

soror sister, from Latin *soror*. In use since 1836.

'Sorry!' means 'I beg your pardon', but with added apology. Though standard English, it is quoted as a Notion 1838–72, and seems to have conveyed a generous apology: 'to knock a boy down and say 'Sorry' is more acceptable than 'I beg your pardon' or anything else of that sort' (1838).

Spanish Poplar a favourite tree, which stood on the north side of Turf in Meads, and was a good place to watch matches from. Recorded 1831; it perished c. 1870.

spank see **beating**.

spec a good thing: 'on spec of' (in consequence of). In use 1856–92. It was not the same as the standard slang 'on spec' (on the off-chance of), which is from 'speculation', but was either an abbreviation of 'special' or (in the phrase 'on spec of') of 'specious', i.e. on the pretext of.

speedy, to take to be a short time doing anything, e.g. washing (1838 only); probably on the analogy of 'to make haste'.

Speedyman the messenger from Oxford who brought the news of a vacancy at New College. Directly he reached Winchester he put up a notice in School to announce that the Posers were on their way. In T. A. Trollope's day (1820–8) Speedyman travelled on foot, bringing news which had already arrived by mail. According to Adams (1831–51) he came in a gig. Hanging on a nail in Porter's Lodge (1922) was an eighteenth-century tricorn hat, and a long jerkin of thick leather, which were reputed to be the uniform either of Speedyman or of 'the Warden's Out-rider' (i.e. a horseman who preceded the Warden's coach when he went on 'progress' through the College estates). In use 1820–80. The nickname sounds ironical, as though the messenger were far too slow: speed was the essence of the Electio ad Oxon, cf. the expression 'sped to New College', of those awarded scholarships there.

speg smart. In use 1831–60. Probably from spick, in the phrase spick-and-span, which means spick-and-span-new, i.e. as fresh as a spike and splinter.

spite, to to dislike a person, or bear him ill-will (not to do something to spite him). In use 1836–90. A survival of the Elizabethan use of the word.

spiting Gabell cutting off your nose to spite your face; or more precisely, denying yourself something in order to annoy another person; or doing something out of spite for somebody and getting punished for it. In each case the person showing spite got the worst of it. Dr Gabell, Headmaster 1809–23, was a man who could not be trifled with.. This notion lingered on many years after his retirement, and arose from an incident quoted by Adams (p. 176): 'the boys, being one day very angry with him, would not ask for a remedy, when they knew he wanted to go out to his farm. He did come into school accordingly, but was so exceptionally severe with them that they repented sorely of their bargain.' In this phrase, 'spite' is in the usual sense of thwart or annoy.

spittoons shallow enamelled bowls, coloured blue on the outside, in which sponges were kept on the top of conduits, in College Chambers (1920). A good example of a kakophemism.

splice, to to throw; also used as a noun, a throw. Senior and Junior Splicing were throwing the cricket ball events in Athla. In use since 1831. This meaning is unique to Winton: possible derivations are: (1) in Cheshire dialect, splice means to beat, or set to energetically, which involves flinging the arms about as when throwing. (2) the obsolete notion 'to splice a pitch-up' meant to scatter a group of men or throw them asunder: from German *spleissen* (to split).

sport, to to display, exhibit, wear, employ, indulge in, provide, give, 'stand'. In continuous use since at least 1780, as is shown in a marginal note to the Statutes about sporting (granting) leave-out, where it is purposely spelt 'support', in imitation of a stammer or the wrong use of a Notion. It is standard English for: making public (Dryden); throwing off epigrams (Addison); expressing an opinion (Newman). At Oxford and the Inns of Court, to 'sport your oak' is to display your outer door as closed. Abbreviated from Latin *disportare* (to disport).

It was widely used at Winton: to sport

an advertisement, an angle, a balk, a blood line, an erection, eyesight, a fringe, a halo, a hiatus, a roll, a tail (1920; see under each word).

action: to act an emotion, or exhibit extravagant movement of body (1856).

a Bin (or hairy Bin): to have an expanse of leg showing between one's trouser-bottoms and socks, as the Bin (C. E. Robinson, Don 1909–45) used to do: this was a bad notion (1920).

a horse: to have a horse (1836).

a line: to walk with two socii: licet, if one of them was a one-year man (1920).

mess: to have mess (1836).

mugging: to translate a man's books lesson for him (1910).

a Quirk (or hairy Quirk): after Rev. R. Quirk (Don 1905–38): identical with a Bin, above.

sport   a meal provided up in Chambers, or downstairs with the Second Master's leave, after Preces, by a man or group of men to celebrate something: e.g. raising a Medal task: thus, a Fifteens or Sixes sport. Anyone in the Chamber who was leaving at the end of the half gave a leaving sport. After refreshments, there were Charades or Steps.

spot   a guess: used particularly of XVs and VIs spot, which Inferiors of less than three years' standing had to make (1900) before the roll came down, to show if they had been taking an intelligent interest in their Canvas. (See **fifteens spot**.)

spot   (adj.) favourite, smart: e.g. 'It is a spot thing to say you slept during the sermon.' In use 1892; now obsolete. For derivation, see below.

spot, to   to take note of, notice, detect, foretell, guess. To 'spot oneself' is to fancy oneself, put on airs, from the idea of spotting oneself as a winner or betting on one's own chances of winning. This is standard slang: to spot a suspicious character was to put a mark against his name; to spot the winner was to mark the expected winner with a dot on a horse-race programme.

spree (also spelt sprea)   (1838: see **Peal**, 5): (1) (of juniors) uppish, bumptious, cheeky, presumptuous: used thus from 1836 to the present day. (2) (of seniors) usurping the privileges of Praefects: thus, a spree man in Commoners was an Inferior to whom, on account of his seniority, the Praefects granted some of their own privileges, e.g. power to sweat (cf. Candle-keepers in College). The term spree man was obsolete by 1870. (3) (of Praefects) domineering, giving oneself airs (see **Peal**, 5). (4) (of things) stylish, smart, neat, tidy, e.g. 'He has spree toys.' Obsolete by 1900. (5) (of food) a **spree mess** was a feast between Toy-time and Chapel of tea, coffee, muffins and cakes, provided either by boys leaving, or from fines inflicted during Toy-time for breaches of etiquette (1836). Such feasts were known (1917) as sports, or leaving sports.

Spree is a variant of spry, which in dialect means clever, lively, jolly, nimble, lithe and (in Hampshire) conceited: and also gay, spruce. In standard English the idea of jollity survives in 'going on the spree'; that of lithe, in 'spry'; and in certain dialects spree can mean smart, trim. For the change of spry to spree, cf.

sly to slee, and Wyke (the village near Winton) to Week. Spree/spry may derive from Irish/Gaelic *spraic* (strength).

squa ra (pronounced squā rā)   squash rackets: played in Old Fives Courts (1920).

square round, to   to move over, or make room, especially round a fire, so as to let another man into the circle. In use 1856–92.

squelch-belch   a 1920 Notion for a paper bag or a sponge-bag full of water, dropped from an upper window on people tolling Chamber Court. It made a delicious thud and is an onomatopoeic word: hence the spurious addition to Tabula Legum, 'Ostiarium ne madefactanto' [The Second Master is not to be soaked].

squish   (1) weak tea. In use 1836–92. (2) an india-rubber ball used from 1880 for kicking in House yards; by 1917 this was a College notion for a squash-rackets ball, which was either red and hollow, or black and solid, the latter being far the livelier.

S.R.O.G.U.S. (pronounced Shrogus)   The Shakespeare Reading and Orpheus Glee United Societies: founded by J. D. Walford and Rev. C. H. Hawkins. By 1917 the glee-singing had quite vanished, and Srogus consisted of readings of Shakespeare's plays in the evening in the Headmaster's house by men with dramatic talent, the Headmaster usually taking the principal part himself.

SS and Trees   an impromptu game of Winchester football, without chosen sides or kicking-in, played in College between 1836 and 1850. So called from the goals, which were, at one end, two iron clamps fixed in the wall of College Mill, in the shape of the letter S: and at the other, two trees.

Stag   in the phrase 'ad Stag', for 'ad Stagnum Log' (towards Log Pond). A Captain winning the toss in Canvas could play either 'ad Coll' (northwards) or 'ad Stag' (southwards) (1920). *Stagnum* is Latin for pond, and Stagnum Log was medieval Latin for Log Pond. This phrase 'ad Stag' is either a revival, or a continuous tradition.

Stalker   Walker (q.v.) (1920). cf. Stalker's Hole, for Walker's Hole.

Standing-up   during the last week of Long Half all boys except VIth Book and Senior Part had to recite in eight lessons a large number of lines which they were supposed to have learned by heart during the year, and if required, construe them (1831). In 1838 the lines were from Latin authors, the highest Part taking up 600 lines each lesson, the lowest 100. They stood to recite, and this was called Standing-up. Marks, given according to performance, had a material effect on the positions of boys in their Parts. The days devoted to these prodigious feats of memory were called Standing-up Week.

By degrees this high standard fell. In 1880 Standing-up was a repetition of all lines learned during the half. In 1907 it was merely a selection of them. In 1917 there was nothing more than a viva-voce lines exam at the end of the half. (Sic transit . . .)

stand round, to   if one were being beaten (1917), the Praefect said 'Stand round', signifying he intended to beat you on the shoulders, and you must get into a convenient position. This was done by taking your gown off from your waistcoat and wrapping it across your neck to protect it: you then stood almost upright, and were beaten. In use from 1880; cf. square round.

Stanley   Mr Stanley Clifton, 'Tailor to the gentlemen of Winchester College' (not Commoners), who came himself or sent a deputy to wait for orders in Trusty Sweater's Hole four mornings a week, with his wares displayed. He was a great friend of College men, and when in 1921 he was elected Mayor of Winton and we asked him to tea in IInd Chamber, it raised a great quill off the Town.

Stanmore Lane   the official name for Blackberry Lane (q.v.).

starcher   a stiff white necktie, so called because it was starched. In use 1868–92.

star in the east   an important trouser-button showing (1920).

starka (pronounced starkā)   naked, especially in the phrase 'tight starka', which has the Wiccamical suffix added to stark (1920).

starva (pronounced starvā)   College lunch, in the dark days of 1917–18, when there was no pudding, soup being added to the menu before the main course, and cheese after it, without appeasing us. Short for starvation.

Steeplecha (pronounced Steeplechā), **Senior** and **Junior**   the school's cross-country running competitions: not a true steeplechase, as there were no streams or other obstacles to jump;.

Steeplecha Lane   the lane beyond Ploughs (1900).

Steps   a rather juvenile game played (1920) up in Chambers instead of Charades after a sport. One man was blindfolded and turned round two or three times: he held out a palm, into which each man put a finger, asking how many steps he was allowed. If it was, say, five, he might not move after taking five steps, and so on. Players climbed over beds, on top of Pot Cupboard and through other hazards, making the steps as elastic as possible.

Sticking-up

stew, to be in a to be afraid, apprehensive. Considered a Notion (1920), but is really standard slang.

Stewart Memorial the gateway erected in 1886 in memory of General Sir Herbert Stewart (Comm. 1855–63, with breaks), who was mortally wounded in 1885 at the battle of Metemneh in the Egyptian campaign of that year. It originally led from School Court to Cloisters, and still did so in 1922, but because it spoiled the view of Chapel Tower was later moved to near Non-Licet Gate.

Sticking-up a custom in Old and New Commoners, recorded 1836–68, occurring on the last three Fridays of each half. An unpopular boy, selected by Commoner Praefects and Course-keeper, was made to climb on to carving table or Middle Desks in Hall, and pelted with pontos by the others. Before the barrage commenced, a Peal was sung: 'Locks and Keys' on the first Friday; 'Boots and Leathers' on the second; 'Gomer Hats' on the last.

Stinks modern sciences. Noted as a Notion 1868, but is standard public-school slang.

Stinks Buildings Science Buildings, south of Sanatorium: erected 1904.

Stinks Cad the name in 1868 for the Lecturer in Physical Science.

Stinks Works the hideous factory and chimney built astride Old Barge and Logie just south of Double Hedges, for the destruction of rubbish and the pumping of sewage up to Hills. It ruined the view down to St Cross.

stoking an important chore in College (1920). It was organised thus: when fires began, the Junior Praefect of each Chamber put up a Stoking Roll showing who had to stoke the fire week by week. New Roll men generally had two weeks each, one-year men had one week. A Foreman was also appointed from among the VIth Book Inferiors to ensure that the stoker had a good fire at certain times: e.g. at Praefects' tea, after College tea, before Toy-time and after breakfast.

stove   (1) a double stove provided in New Commoner Mugging Hall at the end of October, and removed soon after Easter. By 1868 it had disappeared, the name 'stove' being transferred to the fireplace. (2) a fixed stove on Quarter-Deck in School, opposite the door. It was still there in 1868, but was long since removed. (3) a Notion in 1892 for the double stove in College Hall, later known as Simon and Jude.

St   see as if **saint**

straw, clean   clean sheets. In use since 1838, when clean sheets were provided every three weeks. Straw was normal bedding in the middle ages and is mentioned as such in literature of 1607 and 1621. It remained in use at Winton till about 1850. The straw was not loose, but made up into mattresses, with sheets and blankets on top.

'Stro-o-oke!'   quoted in 1892 as the howl of approval uttered when a good stroke was made at fives or racquets, or as an exultant exclamation. It had fallen out of fashion by 1917.

stuckling   a kind of pudding or mince-pie, always served at Election Dinner, and subsequently at Domum Dinner. It consisted of chopped beef or other meat, and green apples (they had to be that year's apples, and were sent up from Devon or Cornwall [1820]), flavoured with caraway seed and enclosed in a pastry turnover. The eating of caraway seeds with apples was recommended by the old physicians, and there are references to it in 1598–9. In south-central England, especially Sussex, a stuckling is an apple pasty or turnover, half-circular in shape and not made in a dish; also called apple-stucklen. It was a harvest pudding, the word probably being derived from stuckle or stook (a sheaf).

studies   the twenty seniors in New Commoners (c. 1868) had small studies, each about 7 feet by 5 [2 by 1.5 m], along one side of Moberly's Court. A study mostly held a table, two chairs and a baking-place or small sofa. The 19th and 20th studies were in one, and shared by the two junior men. Subsequently some Houses had such studies. Study fags were juniors who had to keep Praefects' studies tidy for them.

stump   an 'article' (q.v.) made by knocking off the back of a hard chair: Tolly-keepers had them: they were more comfortable than tug articles (1920).

stumps   wickets. Standard English, but given as a Notion in 1838.

stumpy   short in stature: e.g. 'a stumpy fellow'. Standard English, but given as a Notion in 1838.

Styx   a stream flowing from River through Hell (q.v.). Recorded 1880; obsolete by 1917. The name comes from classical mythology.

subscription-keeper a boy in College appointed to receive the subscription of five shillings or more a month, and take care of the goods bought with it: e.g. cricket and football gear, mustard and pepper (cf. mustard-and-pepper-keeper). The subscription-keeper had leave from games (1838).

suction sweets. In use since 1856. cf. **eyesight**, for good aim.

'Sum' the answer given by a boy at any names-calling. It was an abbreviation for 'Adsum' (I am here), which is quoted as the approved answer in Mathew's poem (1647): possibly as old as the foundation. Not confined to Winton: e.g. at the moment of death, Colonel Newcome says: 'Adsum' (Thackeray, *The Newcomes*).

Sung grace see **Grace**.

superannuate a boy who was obliged to leave at Election because he was over 18 years of age. The only exception were Founder's Kin, who might stay on till they were 25. The story told under Founder's Kin is also given here in word-books, the only differences being that the match was against Eton at Lords, and the child cried: 'Well hit, Papa. Run it out.' This word was in use by 1836, and obsolete by 1892.

Superannuates' Ball see **Domum Ball**.

superjam, to to superannuate. The rule in force in 1892 was that no boy could stay in the school unless he got into Middle Part by the time he was 16: into Senior Part, 17: into VIth Book, 18. The only exceptions to this rule were boys specially favoured with 'leave-on', which had to be obtained from the Headmaster. There were still occasional cases of superjamming in 1917–22.

'Surgite!' see **Grace**.

Surplice Chapel service on Sundays and saints' days when Choir and College wore surplices (1838–84). In 1838 surplices were worn for all full service chapels except Friday morning. By 1892 College had ceased to wear surplices.

sus the remains of College Praefects' tea, left for juniors to finish (1831–1922). The meal was called tea (1831), mess (1838), brew (1856), tea (1917). The sus-eaters were juniors, who 'were glad to get it' (1831) 'and generally drink it in bed out of a pint cup' (1836); valets, brew-cads (1856); washers-up (1917). It comes from Old English *sos*, *soss*, *suss*, used for dogs' meat (1440), and in East Anglian dialect means pigwash, a mess of food, food badly mixed or cooked; also the call to dogs and pigs to come for their food. There was a verb *soss* (to swallow greedily), cf. sozzling: and sosser means guzzler.

sus-bucket   a dustbin, just round the corner of the door Through First, into which tea-leaves were thrown by washers-up (1920).

sweat   hard work, trouble taken over anything, any fagging done by a junior: in use from 1856, if not earlier. These meanings naturally derive from sweat, meaning perspiration, from Anglo-Saxon *swaetan* (to perspire, to toil), and *swat* (perspiration, toil). Common in English literature from the Elizabethan age onwards, the cause (toil) and effect (sweat) being synonymous. In Commoners, 'in sweat' means not yet exempt from fagging.

sweat, to   to work hard, fag: also transitive, to make to toil, engage for fagging, force to any labour: in use from 1856. Shakespeare similarly uses 'toil' transitively. The derivation is as for the noun. The word is standard English, e.g. sweated labour.

sweater   (1) a servant, in College or Commoners. Recorded from 1856. The Trusty Servant is often called Trusty Sweater. Not a standard English usage. (2) a thick woollen jersey worn over an ordinary jersey while kicking at football (1880). Standard English.

sweat roll   a roll made out in Commoners at the end of the first fortnight of the half, when men in sweat (i.e. those who had been in the school less than two years) chose what sweat or duties they would have, the senior men in sweat having first choice (from 1880).

sweaty   (of persons or things) good, efficient, conscientious, superior: i.e. that which has had sweat taken over it. A College notion from 1914.

sweaty hand   an excuse, in almost any context, in College c. 1920: from the phrase used by G. B. Cooke (Coll. 1915–21), who used thus to explain away defeats at fives and squa ra.

sweeping   see **Junior, First**.

swill, to   to wash at a conduit by throwing water over the body, especially after football; to throw any liquid (e.g. tea) over somebody; to spill on the floor. In use c. 1838–1907. Never used for washing out, or drinking. Swill has been standard English since 1280 for washing up or rinsing a vessel, dashing buckets of water on a floor, sousing, flooding. Used by Shakespeare (1599) for a rock being swamped by the sea. From Anglo-Saxon *swillan* (to wash).

Swimming Athla (pronounced Athlā)   swimming sports held in Gunner's Hole (1920) at the end of every Cloister Time, during examinas. Items were senior and junior long races, short races, purling and plunging, and plate diving. A house might send in any number of entries. Individual winners received chits for expenditure at shops up Town. The house with most points got Monty Pot, given by Dr Rendall.

swink, to   to sweat, perspire, work hard. A survival of Anglo-Saxon *swincan* (to toil), appearing as *swuncon* (eighth century), *swanc* (tenth century), *swinken* (c. 1280), swinke (Chaucer), swinck (Spenser, 1579). It was not used by Shakespeare, but Milton uses swinkt (worked out; 1634). Regularly coupled with sweat in Elizabethan literature. Though declared obsolete by Johnson (1755), it continued at Winton till 1884, after which it unfortunately passed out of use. As a noun it meant excessive labour.

swinker   a hard worker, sweater, servant, labourer. Thus swynkere (Chaucer), swincker (1582): it then lapsed from standard English, but survived at Winton till c. 1910: a verse, probably mid-nineteenth-century, survives in the form of an epitaph to a servant in Commoners:

> This is John Browning, a Commoner swinker,
> who lost his life through being a drinker.

sybarite   a woolly waistcoat or cardigan worn under College waistcoat in the cold winters of 1916–22, when it is remarked that 'Commoners have affected highly-coloured ones recently'. From Sybaris, Greek town in southern Italy, famed for luxury.

Tabula Legum *Tabula Legum Paedagogicarum* (Table of the Laws of the Masters): in other words, the school rules in Latin, painted on a board.

This board hung on the east wall of the original school-room (now VIIth Chamber) and is mentioned in Mathew's poem (1647) as the 'requirements of Quintilian' (an orator, rhetorician and teacher in Rome in the first century AD). When School was built (1683–7) the Tabula, or its replica, was erected on its eastern wall, remaining there until the nineteenth century, when it was re-erected over the door, to make room for the organ installed against the east wall. In the 1920s the organ was removed, and the Tabula restored to its rightful place.

The text of the Tabula is given below. In its original form it may have been composed in the sixteenth century by that lively Headmaster, Christopher Johnson, who was bringing up to date a set of rules promulgated by the Founder. At the end of the eighteenth century the Tabula was finally revised and added to by Warden Huntingford, and it is his version of the rules which we read today. Most of them are entirely obsolete, but as a document the Tabula is a remarkable survival of an ancient School Notice.

The text is in Latin. Huntingford's revisions are shown in round brackets: original rules, omitted on revision, in square brackets. An English translation is given in the right-hand column. It is a fascinating exposition of the Latin imperative mood.

TABULA LEGUM PAEDAGOGICARUM	NOTICE OF THE MASTERS' RULES
In Templo.	*In Chapel.*
Deus colitor.	God must be worshipped.
Preces cum devoto (pio) animi affectu peraguntor.	The prayers must be said through in a devout frame of mind.
Oculi non (ne) vagantor.	Your eyes must not wander.
Silentium esto.	There must be silence.
Nihil profanum legitor.	Nothing profane may be read.
In Scola.	*In School.*
Diligentia quisque utitor.	Each boy must observe diligence.

Submisse loquitor secum: clare ad praeceptorem.

He must speak in a whisper to himself: but clearly to the master.

Nemini molestus esto.

He must not be a nuisance to anybody.

Orthographice scribito.

He must spell correctly:

Arma scolastica in promptu semper habeto.

and always have pen, ink and paper ready.

In Aula

In Hall.

Qui mensam (mensas) consecrat, clare pronunciato: caeteri respondento: recti (interim) omnes stanto.

He who says grace at the table (tables) must say it clearly: the remainder will give the response, and all will stand (meanwhile).

Recitationes intelligenter et apte distinguunto.

The readings must be punctuated with intelligence and feeling.

In mensa quies esto (ad mensas sedentibus omnia decora sunto).

There must be silence at table (all must be seemly on the part of those seated at the tables).

(In Atrio.

(In the Court.

Ne quis fenestras saxis pilisve petito.

Nobody may aim stones or balls at the windows:

Aedificium neve inscribendo neve insculpendo deformato:

nor deface the building with writing or carving:

Neve operto capite, neve sine socio, coram Magistris incedito.)

nor approach the Masters with his head covered, nor without a companion.)

In Cubiculis.

In Chambers.

[Noctu dormitor: interdiu studetor.] (Noctu quies esto: vespere studetor.)

[You must sleep at night: study by day.] (At night there must be silence: you must study in the evening.)

[Solum cubiculorum verritor: sternuntor lectuli.] Munda omnia sunto.

[The floor of Chambers must be swept and the beds made.] Everything must be clean.

[Per fenestras nemo in atrium prospicito. Contra qui faxit, piaculum esto.]

[Nobody may look out of the windows into the court. Whoever disobeys must be made an example of.]

In Oppido. Ad Montem.

In Town. Going on Hills.

Sociati omnes incedunto: modestiam prae se ferunto.

All must walk with a companion, and bear themselves with modesty.

Magistris ac obviis honestioribus [gen-
ua flectuntor], capita aperiuntor: vul-
tus, gestus, incessus componuntor.

To Masters and people of quality
they meet [the knee must be bowed],
the head uncovered: their faces, ges-
tures and gait must be orderly.

(Intra terminos ad Montem praescriptos
quisque se contineto.)

(Everybody must keep within the
appointed limits on the Hill.)

In omni loco et tempore.
Qui plebeius est, praefectis obtemper-
ato.
Qui praefectus est (is ordo), legitime
imperato: (vitio careto: caeteris specimen esto).

At all places and times.
He who is an inferior must obey the
praefects.
He who is a praefect (that rank)
must govern according to rule: (be
without fault, and an example to
the rest).

Uterque a mendaciis, ostentationibus,
jurgiis, pugnis et furtis (pravis omnibus verbis factisque) abstineto.
[Togam caeterasque vestes nec disruito
nec lacerato.
Patrium sermonem fugito: Latinum
exerceto.]

Both must refrain from lies, display,
squabbling, fighting and theft (all
bad words and deeds).
[You must not rip or tear your gown
or other garments.
You must eschew your mother tongue
and use Latin.]

Haec aut (et) his similia (qui contra
faxit) si quando deferantur (refer-
antur) judicium damus.
(Feriis exactis, nemo domi impune
moratur.)

These or (and) similar offences, whenever they are reported, we punish.

(When the holidays are over, no one
stays at home with impunity.)

Extra Collegium absque venia exeuntes,
tertia vice expellimus.)

(Boys who go outside College without leave, we expel on the third
offence.)

[See also Through First.]

tag, to   to be offside at Winchester football. A tag is such an event. The word
has been used since 1831 if not earlier. A tag occurs in two ways: (1) A kicks the
ball forward; B, a man on the same side, touches it before anyone on the other
side has done so. (2) A kicks the ball forward; the other side returns it behind him,
and his own side kicks it forward again; if A touches it before he has returned to
where it was kicked, he tags. The penalty for a tag was a hot, one post back.
   In dialect, to tag is to follow closely, and in standard English to tag along has
the same meaning. A similar idea is inherent in the children's game of tag or taw,
mentioned in 1727 and signifying touch: it is called taggy in Hampshire dialect.
In 1838 at Winton, tagging implied hanging back at football when one should be
further forward: in standard English tagging implies following the footsteps of a

leader, as a dog tags its master, the exact opposite. The answer may be found if one regards 'Tag', an exclamation by the players to an individual, not as an accusation of something he has done, but as advice on what to do next, viz. to lag behind into a position of legality. Ultimately the word tag must come from Latin *tangere* (to touch) found in words like attach, take and tack-on: and in the highly technical situations occurring in Winchester football, 'tag' basically means 'tag along behind the rest of your side, unless you want the referee to blow his whistle'.

tagster   one who tags, or lags behind at football (1838); see above.

tail, to sport a   to have your gown hanging down behind you in College Hall, when seated: a bad notion, which new men were inclined to commit (1920), but which was later legalised.

take a div, to   (1) a new man was said to take the classical division into which he was first put (1892). (2) to teach a division.

take up, to   to take a boy's clothès up when he is going to be flogged (1838).

tardy, tardé, tardè   late. Recorded from 1820 onwards: e.g. being tardy for names-calling, or Chapel, which was called being 'tardy Chapel', though by 1892 this had become 'tardy for Chapel'. If a boy showed up his task late he was said to be 'tardy task'.
   Tardy is still standard English: from Latin adverb *tarde* (late). Punctuality was the basis of medieval educational institutions, and the word occurs frequently: e.g. at York Cathedral (1294), or Southwell Minster (1475, 1478).

task   a piece of composition. In 1838, when the word first occurs, each boy had to do two tasks, one prose and the other verse, on a theme given by the master: and the number of lines he had to write were regulated by his position in the school. By 1892 task meant only the composition set for Toy-time on Saturday. It was usually an essay or Latin prose, and had to be showed up on Sunday morning. In 1917–22 VIth Book Senior and Junior Divs had three tasks a week, Latin and Greek prose and verse and occasionally an essay.

Task books   see **books**.

task time   a notion (1917–22) for the time when Div Dons of VIth Book Senior and Junior Div went over each man's tasks for the week with him in private. Frank Carter had them in his div room, Ponto and Platnauer in their houses.

team   when Junior Match was played, and on other occasions when there was a general ascent of Hills, Præfects were pulled up by long lines of juniors, one behind the other, each catching hold of the coat-tails of the man in front (1868).

Te de   the hymn 'Te de profundis, summe Rex'; no. 77 in the Hymnarium. New men had to learn the first and last verses, which were also sung in Sung Grace (1920).

teejay, tégé, tege, or **T.J.**   abbreviation for protégé: a Commoner Notion in use since 1831. (1) original meaning, a new boy who is looked after by a senior during his first weeks. In 1868 the appointment of the senior boy was being made by the Headmaster. (2) later, the word was transposed to the junior appointed to teach a new man his Notions in his first fortnight. Pater was used in College for this, and Son for the new boy. The term was also used as a verb, meaning to protect: thus to teejay (1836) was to look after and tutor a new boy allotted to a Praefect.

Telegraph   (1) a green post on which cricket scores were displayed. There were three rows of figures which slid in grooves (1868). Not peculiar to Winton. (2) Telegraph Hill, 2 ½ miles [1.5 km] out of Winton on the Petersfield Road, not far from Amphitheatre; recorded from 1868. It was the first of a series of beacons between Winton and Portsmouth.

Tempe, or **Vale of Tempe**   a deep ditch full of weeds and nettles on the right (1868), left (1880), as one went to Hills between Black Bridge and Commoner Field (1868), between River and Logie (1892). It was named after the Valley of Tempe, a famous beauty spot in Thessaly in classical times, between Mounts Olympus and Ossa.

temples   small niches carved in the stones of Meads Wall, in which, at Illumina, College juniors had to put lighted tolly-ends which they had saved up during Short Half. There were similar temples in the wall of Grass Court (1868). So called because several of them are carved in the shape of shrines.

ten-shiggers   long football trousers, used until about 1890 when shorts were introduced. They used to cost 10 shillings.

Tent   a cricket pavilion (presumably from the days when tents were used). The word was used by Commoners (1838–72) for a small wooden house in Commoner Field for the convenience of players, where Nevy sold grub. From 1856 it was used for wooden pavilions of early Victorian pattern, viz. Old Tent and Meads Tent: and finally for later and more permanent buildings, such as Webbe (later Hunter) Tent and Frazer Tent.

testis   a witness (Latin). In use 1838–43 in such phrases as 'Testis I was in Chapel this morning' (meaning you are witness that I was). Gordon engagingly adds: 'whether he was or not'. cf. Semper Testis.

'Thank you'   called out when a ball was hit near another boy and one wanted him to 'hand it up' (throw it back) (1838). This is standard English, and an example of what one might call wishful acknowledgement, or payment before delivery.

theme   a given subject to do composition on. Themes were a prominent part of the curriculum in the Elizabethan age, but not used as a Notion after 1843.

thick   (1) very intimate with (1836). This is standard slang; e.g. 'as thick as thieves', etc. (2) stupid, dull, slow (from 1831). cf. *crassus* in Latin: a Shakespearian usage, not standard English today. It also survives in dialect, where it means obstinate.

thick   a dunce, a blockhead; see above. Opposite of 'jig'.

thief   see **Funkey**.

Third Junior   see **Junior, First, Second and Third**

Third Pot   a lock just above Hell. Paters (1920) had to take their Sons to it, and to Amphitheatre, during the first fortnight of the half.

thoke   a rest, an idle time, a lie-in (bed), a long-lie. For derivation see the verb below.

Hatch Thoke (q.v.) was a holiday when boys got up later than usual: so called because names-calling took place and breakfast was served from Buttery Hatch in Hall.

thoke, to   to rest, lie late in bed, have an idle time. One of our most ancient words, recorded as a Notion from 1831: it is not from Greek θῶκος (a seat), but from an Anglo-Saxon root, *thoke* (lying idle): this appears in the fifteenth century as a noun for a fish with soft as distinct from firm flesh, and in East Anglian dialect we have the adjectives thoky or thokish, recorded c. 1682 and signifying slothful, sluggish, idle, slow, dull (of persons and things), and lying idle or fallow (of land).

To **thoke on**, or upon, was to look forward to, or dwell with satisfaction on a future pleasure. cf. to dote on. In use 1831; obsolete by 1917.

thoker   a thick piece of bread soaked in water and toasted or baked in the ashes (1836). So named possibly because it gave the impression of lying there idle while the flames were flickering: cf. toad in the hole (piece of beef baked in batter). Or because a thoker was something to look forward to (see **to thoke**).

thokester   a man who thokes, an idler, a drowsy fellow. Recorded 1838 and still in use (1920).

three at a toys   in Toy-time and books-chambers in College (1920) men might leave their toys to speak to each other in an under-tone, but there might never be more than two men at a toys together. If a third came, the Praefect in course warned: 'Not three at a toys!'

Through First   (i.e. through First Chamber) the foricas in College, reached by a door let into the east wall of Ist, where there was originally a window. It might be used after Lock-up by all; before Lock-up, by Praefects, Tolly-keepers and two-year men. A vulgar parody of Tabula Legum read (1920):

> Per Primam ocius ne ruito.
> Informatorem ne imitanto.
> Ostiarium ne madefactanto.

Thule (pronounced Thulé)   the Chamber in the north-west of Chamber Court: a final addition to the downstairs Chambers in College. Originally they were I, II, III, IV, V and VI, with VII added when School was built. Then I, III and IV became changing and linen rooms, and Thule was added. Thule is the furthest Chamber from the centre of College. The western part of Thule was originally College Bakehouse. Later, the whole Chamber became the abode of Queristers.

Thule had an unusual attraction for sight-seers in the frieze painted on its east wall in the manner of the Bayeux Tapestry, showing personalities of the 1924 period. In origin it was a hot roll (q.v.) for a Chamber Six in 1921, drawn by Christopher Hawkes on paper, but became so famous that in 1925 he was asked to paint it as a frieze: this he did, repainting it in 1959.

The name comes from Vergil (*Georgics* 1.30): 'tibi serviat ultima Thule'. To the ancients, Thule was an inaccessible isle to the north-west, perhaps the Shetlands, Iceland, or Greenland.

Thunderguts   a small, rotund, bald lay-clerk from up Town, with a moustache and a powerful bass voice, who sang in Chapel Choir (1920).

ticket, to take a   a Notion current in 1780 but obsolete by 1900. If a junior rendered a Praefect some service unasked, such as finding something he had lost, or warning him that the Doctor was at hand when he was doing something unlawful, he was told to take a ticket. This meant that next time he came up for punishment by that Praefect, he could plead his ticket and get off it. Dr Gabell himself granted a boy a ticket, the custom being familiar to him from his own schooldays under Dr Warton's headmastership. As Adams says, it was a plenary indulgence, the future offence excused not being defined.

tin gloves

tie   equal (noun or verb). Standard English in sporting results, but used 1838–43 in the form 'to be tie with' for equality in anything.

tight   an adjective and adverb with two meanings: (1) formidable in battle, firm, compact, hard. In standard English we have 'a tight little island'; in dialect tight means irrevocable, unalterable, absolute; at Winton it meant complete, utter: e.g. a tight licking, a tight snob, tight rot. As an abverb it meant absolutely, e.g. tight bowled (188) meant clean bowled; tight junior meant absolutely bottom, tight non-licet entirely forbidden; tight genuine (q.v.) meant praise indeed. Derived from an Old English word *tite* (tyt, tyte, tit), which meant something like ultimate. (2) fast, especially of bowling or a bowler (the sense of hard being also present here). Derived from another old word *tight* or *tite*: an adjective and adverb meaning quickly, soon, fast. It occurs with this meaning in Ben Jonson (1598) and Shakespeare (1600).

tight genuine   downright praise: a glowing testimonial. Recorded 1900. Genuine (q.v.) in the sense of praise was in use from 1831; tight as in (1) above. This notion was not in use in 1917.

tile   a straw hat or boater. Recorded 1838; probably Cockney slang. In 1960 a boater was called a 'strat' in Commoners.

tin gloves   a method of bullying new boys in College, recorded from 1831, but noted as dying out in 1843. A boy was 'fitted with a pair of tin gloves' by having the backs of his hands scored backwards and forwards two or three times with a hot end, so as to burn them a little: the supposed object being to enable him to handle hot ends with impunity. Formerly a red-hot shovel was used instead of a hot end.

tip, to   to give a boy anything, such as money, or a licking (1838). Also used as a noun, meaning a gift of money or anything else. Standard English.

toe-fit-tie

Tired Tim a workman about College (1920). cf. Mate's Mate and Cyclops. This is standard English for a tramp.

tizzie, tizzy, tozzie sixpence. Standard slang, but entered as a Notion 1836–1907. In 1920 Commoners used tozzie.

tizzy Poole an extra large fives-ball, costing sixpence, and sold by Poole, College Head Porter (1836–42).

toad a piece of bread toasted quite black, and put in beer in College to warm it (1838–60).

toasting see Simon and Jude.

toe-can a can of hot water used for filling toe-pan in New Commoners (1868).

toe-fit-tie a practical joke in vogue in College 1831–43. A string was tied round a boy's big toe while he was asleep: the string was pulled, and the boy drawn out of bed to his tormentor's side. Two or three juniors could thus be fetched to the same point from different quarters of the Chamber.

Notion books state that the phrase '-*to fit -ti*' (-to becomes -ti) occurred in a disquisition of the Latin perfect tense in old Latin grammars. This is not understood. But a phrase 'τό fit τι' could have come in a Greek grammar in Latin, in describing how the indefinite article is rendered by changing the definite article to the indefinite pronoun τις: thus, the body is τὸ σῶμα: a body is σῶμά τι: τό has become τι. The notion toe-fit-tie is a pun on this.

toe-pan a large pan or basin of red earthenware placed in each College Chamber for washing the feet in. In use 1836–1897, and in Commoners to 1868; in Houses 1880–4 toe-pan was the foot-bath which everyone had once a week. In 1838 in College 'to have toe-pan' meant to wash the feet in toe-pan, which was used by a different man each night. The name was a pun on the Greek τὸ πᾶν (the all): i.e. (like omnibus) everybody used it.

toe-pan boiler   a tin vessel or kettle for heating water for the toe-pan or other purposes, containing about 3 gallons [13.5 l]. Two such boilers were put on half-faggot each night (1838).

toe-pan roll   originally the list showing which man was to use toe-pan each night: later used for lists showing each man's bath night. In Commoners up to 1868 these lists were made out by the junior in the room and taken down to Linen Gallery, 'so that Gallery Nymphs may know on which nights to put fellows clean towels'. Later, in the Houses these were called tub rolls, and in College bidet rolls, but bidet rolls continued to be headed with the inscription τὸ πᾶν.

toe-pan towel   a towel for drying the feet after using toe-pan. Not recorded after 1842.

toll (pronounced töll), **to**   to run. The noun toll is a run. First recorded 1856. This has been derived from troll, a word with a wide range of meanings, e.g. roll, stroll, bowl along in a coach, allure (in which sense it is also spelt toll). Tool, the word for run at Charterhouse, is also used for bowling along in a coach. There are two arguments against this: the 'o' in troll is long whereas in our toll it is short; and tolling is a gruelling experience, with little bowling along, still less allure about it. Toll is more likely to be a form of 'toil', which can mean, *inter alia*, to travel with weariness or pain. [cf. grind, = walking for exercise.]

toll abs, to   to run away: especially of running away from school (1920).

toll Chamber Court, to   to walk round Chamber Court with a socius (1920). This could be done by Praefects and Tolly-keepers at any time, but not by Inferiors during school hours or before Lock-up. It might only be done clockwise. Nobody could walk up Middle Sands at any time of day except Praefects, Tolly-keepers, or a Praefect and his socius. Chamber Court, twenty minutes before Toy-time, was one mass of people walking round, of all sizes and at varying speeds.

   To **toll round Chamber Court** was to run round Chamber Court for ekker (1920), in shirt and shorts, sometimes done by Praefects after 9.30 p.m.

toll Cloisters, to   to walk round Cloisters, with a socius (1920). This was done anti-clockwise, by men in Chantry before Sunday services in Chantry: and also by College Praefects and VIth Book Inferiors, between the end of Toy-time and Preces. It was quieter than Chamber Court.

   To run Cloisters (q.v.) had a different meaning.

toll Meads, to to walk up and down Meads, from north to south and vice versa (1920). It was licet only for Praefects and their socii.

Tolls (runs), **College** c. 1920 these were:

(1) *Portsmouth Road*
Distance 1 ¾ miles [3.2 km]: time 15–16 minutes (has been done in 12).
Start from Middle Gate: College Walk: across the GWR under the trucks (which have been known to move) at the sidings just north of Jacob's ladder: Portsmouth Road: up to the junction with Double Hedges: west along Double Hedges: up Kingsgate Street: in through Commoner Gate: finish at VIIth Chamber Passage.

(2) *Death Pits*
Distance 3 ¼ miles [5.2 km]: time 21 minutes.
Start as for Portsmouth Road: up to Double Hedges turn: continue on up Portsmouth Road, round the south of Hills through Death Pits: under the GWR: up Towpath: through Delta Field: up College Walk: finish at Outer or Middle Gate.

(3) *Half-Milers*
Distance 3 ½ miles [5.6 km]: time 23 minutes.
Start from VIIth Chamber Passage: out through Commoner Gate: Kingsgate Street: St Cross Road: Half-Milers: Towpath: Delta Field: Middle Gate.

The Praefect of Hall ordered one of the above tolls three or four times a half. All Inferiors had to go unless they had special leave off. Timekeeper ticked off names at the start, and took times at the finish, handling these in to Aul.Prae. Anyone who took far too long had to do it all again.

(4) *Junior Steeplecha Course*
Distance just under 3 miles [4.8 km]: 19 minutes was a good time.
This was run about twice before the event by men of Junior Steeplecha age, under the direction of their house captains, who told off senior men to pace them. The runners walked out in overcoats to the start, and juniors detailed as coat-carriers bicycled back to the finish with the coats.
    Start at Dark Wood: follow the curve of the valley round to a point opposite the second green on the golf-course: up a very steep path at walking-pace to the crest of the ridge: across to the Plough and through it: down Dongas: round the south of Hills: Towpath: Double Hedges: finish at the junction of Double Hedges and Kingsgate Street. In the actual event, the finish was just south of Webbe Tent, having entered Bull's Drove by a gate in the palings.

(5) *Senior Steeplecha Course*
Distance 6 ½ miles [10.5 km] time, never less than 40 minutes (?). This was also run once or twice before the event.
    Start on the north side of Portsmouth Road about a quarter of a mile [0.4 km] from Pseudo-T: up to Pseudo-T: round the left of the flagstaff: down to the right past a cottage: sharp to the right for 120 yards [110 m]: across

the valley: up the other side (very steep, walking): round Parker's Gallop: up Bloody Lane: across to the south of house and north of flagstaff: along Portsmouth Road: round the south of Hills: Towpath: Double Hedges: finish as in Junior Steeplecha.

The following were run for private ekker, or ekker rolls:
(6) *Long Stinkers*
Distance 1 ½ miles (2.4 km): time 10 minutes.
Start, Middle Gate: College Walk: Delta Field: Double Hedges: Kingsgate Street: VIIth Chamber Passage.
(7) *Short Stinkers*
Distance 1 ⅛ miles (1.8 km): time, 7 minutes.
Start, Middle Gate: College Walk: Joel's House: down Logie: up through Meads: VIIth Chamber Passage.

Tolls (runs), **Commoner** c. 1920 these were:
  (1) Bell Inn.
    Time, 10 minutes.
  (2) Tunbridge.
    Time, 10 minutes.
  (3) Round Reach.
    Time, 15 minutes.
  (4) Trainer.
    Time, 17 minutes: to Half-Mile Road and back.
  (5) Round River.
    Time, 23 minutes: Half-Mile Road: Viaduct: Tunbridge: Double Hedges.

tolly a candle; originally of tallow. In use since 1836 if not earlier. The name is a corruption of tallow, which in South Country dialect is sometimes toller: so brolly for umbrella: yolly for yellow.

Tolly-keepers, Candle-keepers, Custodes Candelarum the Inferiors who had been longest in College, and had some of the privileges, but not the powers, of Praefects. The Praefect of Hall fixed their number, which was originally seven, but by 1917 only three. They were exempt from fagging. Praefects in full power had the right to sweat them, but never did. At one time each of them had a breakfast-fag and a valet, while Senior Tolly-keeper had the power to sweat the twenty juniors in Chamber Court. None of these privileges was officially recognised.

The name is derived from the toilies (candles) in each Chamber, over which they once had charge. A relic of this function survived in 1917 in the notion that Tolly-keepers had to blow out Funkey last thing at night in their Chambers. The name might have come from this; or from being in charge of the candle at each End in Hall, where the Candle-keepers sat; or from the control of the enormous stock of candles required in College after sunset, in the days before gas and electricity.

Tom Brown nickname of C. E. Stevens (Coll. 1918–24) who, on arrival, behaved like the proverbial Tom Brown, fresh to school life, and did all the wrong things. In 1969 he was still addressed by this name.

tombstones a Commoner notion for marbles (q.v.).

Tom Cull a small fresh-water fish of the genus Uranidae, known as a Miller's Thumb or a Bullhead. Tom Cull's Day was Good Friday, the end of the close season for Tom Culls.
  This notion crept into the books c. 1892–1907, perhaps at a time when fishing in Water Meads was in fashion. Cull is Gloucestershire dialect for this fish, which cannot have been an intelligent one, for cull also means fool, and tom-cull must therefore mean tomfool.

Tom-Tit Corner, or **Jack Tomtit's Corner** a corner in Meads near Log Pond, so known 1838–1890. In 1838 it was said to be named 'because the boys a long time ago plastered up a live tom-tit in a hole there'.

τò πᾶν, or toe-pan see **bidet roll**.

top-poster a dive from one of the posts which projected from Pot Gate (1868).

tosh mud. Commoner Notion, 1838–43; standard slang for rubbish, nonsense.

Tother, Tother-School in 1836 this meant any school not a public school; in 1868, all schools except Winchester and Eton, but had begun to take on the present meaning of a private or preparatory school. It was also used as an adjective, for totherish (q.v.). Charterhouse uses tother'un for a prep. school.
  Tother is national slang for the other, that other (tother day) and has been adopted in this Notion with the same condescension as when the House of Lords refers to the Commons as 'another place'. Chaucer uses 'that on, that other', and in Scots we have 'the tan (or tane), the tother (or tither)'. 'The tother' occurs from c. 1280: and the couplet 'the tone (or ther tan), the tother' is as old as Wyclif (c. 1360). It also occurs in song no. 35 in John Gay's *Beggar's Opera* (1728): 'How happy could I be with either, / Were tother dear charmer away.' These words are pencilled in Gordon's word-book (1842), perhaps with this notion in mind.

Totherdon (1) the Headmaster of one's prep. school. (2) nickname of R. W. M. Atkin (E 1915–20), who must have resembled one.

totherish a contemptuous adjective, applied to anything which would be done at Tother but not at Winchester: i.e. puerile, silly.

totherite (1) a prep. school boy. (2) a boy from the same Tother as oneself. (3) a boy who does totherish things.

Tout, the   nickname of C. V. Durell, mathma Don 1905–44 and author of mathematical textbooks: College Tutor, then House Don of A. The name stems from his wild and unkempt appearance. [Some three dozen schoolbooks on various branches of mathematics are listed under Clement Vavasor Durell's name in the British Library catalogue.]

Tout Bat   see **College competis**.

Tout Court   the part of Arcadia between Thule and Blue Gate. It was named after the Tout, who as College Tutor used to sit in his window seat above Thule overlooking it.

Towel Tree   the tree nearest Non-Licet Gate on which boys hung towels to dry after bathing (1938-43).

Tower Chairs   rows of chairs under the tower in Chapel, occupied by ladies, and the junior men in Chapel.

tower of Babel   chamber-pots piled on top of each other, upside down, after being washed by Nutley, who inherited this architectural skill from Goodchild (1920). It is now a lost art.

Towpath   runs along River from Second Pot to Tunbridge, on its eastern bank. From Tunbridge to Boat-house there is a narrow bridle-track on both banks. The notion dates from the days of barge traffic.

Towser   Mrs Williams' pedigree King Charles (1918), called 'the little monster' by the Second Man: they were devoted to it.

toy-board   a board fixed on to the seat of a toys to extend its length, thus allowing two men to sit together when going over. A Commoner notion from c. 1890.

Toye's   B House: 69 Kingsgate Street. First House Don, Rev. H. E. Moberly; named after the second House Don, A. J. Toye.

toys   (not toyes, which is a confusion with Toyes above) the tall, narrow cupboard and writing-bureau combined, which stood beside each boy's bed in College, until the mid-nineteenth century. They were 6 feet 3 inches [1.9 m] in height, 1 foot 10 inches [0.55 m] in breadth, 1 foot 8 inches [0.5 m] deep in the lower part. After this, the beds were moved upstairs and the downstairs Chambers became work-rooms, with wooden cubicles, called toys in their turn, round the walls. The modern type of toys in College consisted of a cupboard and shelves fixed to the wall; bracketed to the partition walls is a 'slab' for writing on, and

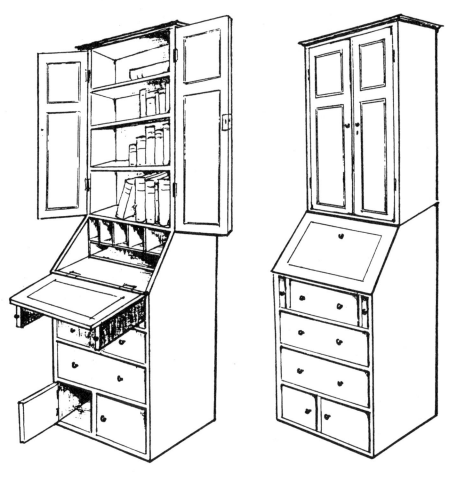

A toys

a seat. There is a photograph of the toys in Porter's Lodge in Leach's *History of Winchester College* (p. 432).

In Old Commoners' Hall (to 1842) each boy had a cupboard for books and papers called a toys, and in New Commoners Mugging Hall (1842–68) the name toys was given to the combined cupboards and desks down each side of the room, occupied by all who did not have a study or 'pigeon-hole'. This kind of toys consisted of an upright cupboard about 5 ½ feet [1.6 m] high and 1 foot [0.3 m] deep, for books and other belongings. It was divided into two parts by a projecting slab about 30 inches [0.7 m] above the floor. The upper half contained three shelves, the top and bottom ones containing books and stationery, the middle one ornaments and photographs. There were folding doors over the shelves, and these and the shelves were usually mugged and otherwise adorned.

Below the slab was another shelf, closed by a flapboard, for holding grub and brewing apparatus. The seat was a board 18 inches [0.45 m] from the

A College toys (1922)

floor, resting on two supports, and quite separate from the toys. In some houses there were also junior toys, of rather different pattern and with less room, but essentially the same. Toys were allotted partly by seniority, partly by position in Short Roll, but everybody had to spend at least one half at a Middle Desk.

When Commoners dispersed into Houses, each mugging hall was fitted with cubicles called toys like those in College. These toys have been copied at many other schools, as far afield as India, and are usually called toys after the Wiccamical original.

Three derivations have been suggested, of which the last is the most likely: (1) that toys originally meant a boy's 'arma scholastica', i.e. his books, paper and pens: and from this the cupboard in which they were kept: and finally the cupboard itself: from the Greek word τεύχεα (equipment). (2) that it comes from French *toise* (a measure of 6 feet [1.8 m]: a fathom). This word, which occurs in a French poem c. 1431, and in Sterne (1760), was said to be the space allotted to each boy in a Chamber; it is in fact the height of the old-style toys. (3) that it is from teye, used in 1440 for a coffer: from French *taie*, Old French *teie*, Latin *theca*, Greek θήκη (a chest, box). It so, teye first underwent the usual Wiccamical change of the vowel to 'o', and became toye, this interim form surviving in Toy-time: then the Wiccamical 's' was added, as in Hills, and the word toys resulted.

Toys   in use 1856–84 in the sense of Toy-time (q.v.).

'Toys!'   backed up by the Praefect in course to signify that Toy-time had begun. By 1917 in College, 'Hour!' was backed up instead by the First Junior in course.

Toy-time, or **toytime**   recorded from 1831 as the evening hours of preparation, called 'prep' elsewhere, when men all had to sit at their toys. In 1836 this was

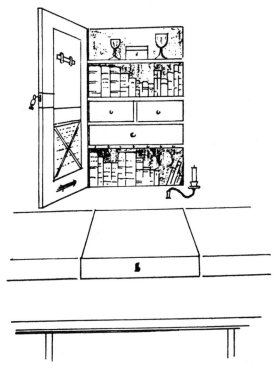

A toys in New Commoners (1868)

between dinner and evening chapel; in 1838, from 7.30 to 9, when the Chamber was 'liable to a visit from the two head masters or Warden to see that all is right'. In Commoners, in 1856, Toy-time could also mean books-chambers, and in 1868 it was from 7 to 8.30 in Short Half and Easter Time. Tutor used to come in, and the two Praefects in course kept order. Leave out of place had to be got from a Praefect in course before anyone might walk about. In 1890 Toy-time was from 7 to 9 in Short Half and Common Time, and 8 to 9 in Cloister Time. In 1920 it was 7 to 8.45 in Short Half and Common Time; 7.45 to 8.45 in Cloister Time.

tozzie sixpence; a corruption of tizzy (q.v.).

tozzy moderately drunk. Recorded in 1838, the author adding: 'the case with a good many boys on the first night of the half year'.

tramp a tie of College XV ribbon, worn until 1915 as a tug tie with a sailor's knot, by men in College XV and dress who were not on VI roll the year before: these wear VI ties, because the striped silk tie, used in College as a VI and dress tie, is used in Commoners and O.T.H. as a XV and dress tie. The tramp was worn on the day of XVs, until night if College won. A **cad** is this same ribbon, worn as a bow-tie by men in College XV and dress.

The ribbon is about an inch [2.5 cm] broad, in alternating bands of white, blue, white, blue, white: small strips of it are worn like a medal ribbon on the coat by supporters of College. Commoners and O.T.H. have the same style of ribbon and also use it on the coat, but not as ties (1920).

Trant   Rev. J. Trant Bramston, called Trant by all who knew him, young and old, including members of his house and his sons. Most of his life was spent in Winchester. Born 1841; in College (Aul.Prae.) 1856–61; Don at Wellington 1865–8; Commoner Tutor 1868–9; took one of the four Commoner Houses in 1869 at the age of 27; House Don of H 1869–1910; retired and lived at St Nicholas, St Cross, where he welcomed dozens of past and present Wykehamists. He edited War Service Rolls. On 24 November 1922, he was 81. He was *the* Old Wykehamist, and a more universal favourite than anyone else in my experience (1922).

Trant's   H House: Culver's Close. First House Don, Trant.

Trees   the line of elms separating Lavender Meads from New Field.

Trench   the early Iron Age trench round the summit of Hills. In the days of going on Hills, it was the boundary beyond which juniors might not pass without leave from a Praefect.

trencher   the wooden platter, 10 inches square [25 cm] and 1 inch [2.5 cm] thick, provided for each man in College Hall at breakfast and tea. Kept in Buttery, and recorded in 1838, trenchers, and the Notion, were still in use in 1922. It is an Old English word of which examples are quoted from 1580: a passage in Ben Jonson (1598) shows that the buttery was the normal place to keep them; a cheese-trencher is mentioned (1607); Pepys (1633) implies that trenchers were changed during meals; Locke (c. 1690) calls them square. The word survives in trencherman (a man of good appetite). It comes from French *tranchoir* (the board for cutting meat and other food to be found in any kitchen), from Latin *truncare* (to cut).

tribunes   large pews behind the screen in Ante-Chapel which were reserved for ladies. The pews and screen were removed c. 1870. Recorded 1856. Derived via French *tribune* (raised seats in church or other meeting places, for musicians and others) from Latin *tribunal* (raised platform for seats of magistrates).

trof   a trifle. Commoner Notion recorded in 1868 only.

Trunk Stream   (1) running from Tunbridge to Waterman's Hut, crossing Adam and Eve in a wooden channel. (2) the continuation of Adam and Eve below Dalma until it joins New Barge again immediately below First Pot (1868–84).

Trusty Servant

Trusty Servant, Trusty Sweater, Trusty Pig picture symbolising the virtues of a perfect College servant, affixed to the west wall of the room called Ante-kitchen (1838), Buttery (1892), Trusty Sweater's Hole (1917), facing the entrance. This emblem first appears in sixteenth-century costume in the manuscript of 'De Collegiata Schola [Wicchamica]'. The picture has been several times repainted, and in 1778 it was altered to eighteenth-century costume in honour of George III's visit.

Aubrey records that the pleasant Latin elegiacs accompanying the picture were composed by a brilliant College boy named John Hoskyns (1566–1638). The English verse translation and the original picture itself may have been done by him while still in College (c. 1580).

An 1880 word-book states that the picture was originally dug up in Chamber Court!

Tub the lidded polygonal chest with metal bindings and lining at the west end of College Hall, into which unwanted dispers and other broken meats were thrown, for distribution to poor women. (See **Jack's Hags**.)

This collection and distribution to poor women were a survival of the medieval way of life, and sufficiently important to justify the creation of a Praefect of Tub (Ollae Prae.), who at one time used to make a good thing out of the sale of mutton dispers. Ben Jonson may have had such chests in mind in 1633 when he mentioned a Hall, Buttery and 'all the tubs about the house'. Tub was replaced by a new one c. 1825. Although Tub is still there, it has not been used for broken meats, nor have Jack's Hags been seen, since 1918.

Tub Mess the Senior Praefects' mess in College, and the table where they sat in Hall (1836).

Tub Roll the roll in each House giving the names of those who are to take baths each night. cf. toe-pan roll.

Tunbridge

tuck, to   to cut one's toenails: a College Notion of 1838. Perhaps related to tuck (to nip with the finger-nail), a word used by Oxford undergraduates c. 1650. The scissors used for this purpose were called **tuckers**.

tuck up a boy's gown, to   to beat him with a stick over the legs (1838). Tuck may here be used in its normal sense, but there may be an echo of an old verb, to tuck (to beat: especially of beating a drum).

tu doces (pronounced tew-do-sees)   a lead-lined chest into which tea-leaves were emptied: the forerunner of sus-bucket, the dustbin provided for this purpose in College (1920). Recorded in this sense in 1836. An additional meaning, of tea-caddy, is given in 1838. Long obsolete, but preserved in Notion books for its amusement value. It was a play upon words: Latin, *tu doces* (thou teachest).

tug   stale, old, common, ordinary, regular, absolute. Recorded from 1831, and still in use. The term eludes confident derivation. At Eton, tug means a Colleger, but we do not know why. At Rugby (c. 1835) toco, from Greek τόκος (interest), meant beating by Praefects. A tug is an iron hoop to which tackle is fixed in mining: hence, to hold tug (stand severe handling or hard work); to hold a person tug (to keep him hard at work). Tuck is English, and tucker Australian, slang for food. There is an obscure word tack, for the lingering taste of certain foods, used by Drayton (1613–22) of cheese: it can also mean bad food, or stale or bad malt liquor: this word, mispronounced, might have survived in College for stale food, especially cheese; food served up a second time, food so familiar as to be unattractive. (See **tuggers** and '**Tugs!**')

tug bun   a currant bun, much in demand, and costing a halfpenny (1892), a penny (1917), and now [1969] probably sixpence.

Tug Bun Concert   a concert given every four years by the Tug Bun Musical Society of Old Wykehamists (1900). The society, concert and Notion are long forgotten.

tund

tug copy-book see **copy-book**.

tuggers a notion on Junior End (1920) for the cheese served in College Hall, but a bad notion on any other End. From tug, either because it was stale, or was a 'commons' of cheese.

tugly ordinarily, generally, usually, absolutely. First recorded 1880: by 1920, one of the commonest words at Winton. We always said 'tugly', never 'ordinarily'. Derived from tug.

'Tugs!' means 'Stale news'; 'I know that already'. In use from 1831 but long obsolete. One writer suggests (*dubia verisimilitudine*) that this is an abbreviation for 'Teach your Grandmother to Suck eggs', but it must be from the 'stale' sense of tug.

Tunbridge the bridge over New Barge at the eastern end of Double Hedges, noted in 1838 as a favourite bathing-place of boys who had not yet learned to swim. The original timber bridge was so narrow that a rowing four could not pass beneath without shipping oars, and a wider iron bridge was built in 1870, to give place to an even better bridge in 1923. Tun is a medieval word, meaning both a wine-cask and a town, so the Tun-bridge might mean the bridge where casks were loaded on barges, or the bridge leading to Town. Another medieval word, tubrigge, means a draw-bridge or tow-bridge, and this is probably the origin of our Tunbridge, signifying that it was a bridge over the tow-path, or fitted with gang-planks at water level to enable a horse to pass beneath.

tund, to to flog a boy across the shoulders with a ground-ash. This was done by a Praefect, and the flogging was called a tunding. A 'tunding on top of Hall' (1836), for a grave offence, was administered by the Praefect of Hall on the dais in Hall. In 1836 a tunding could be from twelve to fifty strokes. All boys were present for a 'tunding on top of Hall'. 'The Tunding Row' was the trouble that arose in the late Victorian period, when corporal punishment at Winton hit the newspaper headlines. Tund was in use from 1831 to 1914, but for some reason vanished completely during the First World War, 'beating' taking its place. It came from Latin *tundere* (to buffet, to bruise).

tu quoque

Tupto   the nickname (1820–8) for Dr G. I. Huntingford (Warden 1789–1832), whose watchword was 'No innovation'. Two derivations were current at the time: (1) the Greek verb τύπτω (I beat), the standard verb for declensions in Greek grammars before λύω (I loose) came into fashion [roughly, in the middle third of the nineteenth century]. (2) for 'tiptoe', in reference to the fact that the Warden's father was a dancing-master.

tu quoque   if A calls B a fool, and B retorts that A is a fool, this is a 'tu quoque', Latin for 'so are you'. It is standard English: but given as a Notion (1838), the writer referring us to 'a very good illustration in *Comic Latin Grammar* page 31' [by Percival Leigh, 1840: see illustration]. Repeated in word-books to 1880.

Turf   the area in a cricket-ground reserved for pitches, as distinct from the out-field, which is 'long grass'. 'Turf' in Meads (1836) was an area of this nature reserved for Praefects and for matches. In 1868 the notion was being applied to such an area in Commoner Field. By 1880 it meant areas of fine grass in Meads and New Field roped off during the winter to preserve them for the cricket season. By 1917 the notion had died, but the areas were still roped off.

Turf-keeper   a College man appointed to ensure that Turf was kept well rolled by juniors, and that nobody walked over it in Easter Time. A notion current in 1868 but obsolete by 1892.

Tutor   in 1917–22 the ten Senior Praefects in College each had two or more 'Pupils' of all the men not in VIth Book. Their duty to their Pupils was to be ready to elucidate difficulties in their mugging, to keep an eye on their place in cuse, and to beat them if exceptionally lazy (this they never did). At the end of the half they gave each Pupil books to the value of ten or fifteen shillings, called Tutor's books. If a Pupil failed to raise a remove through thoking, his tutor should not give him books. If the Pupil raised div books, he should not receive Tutor's books also, but always did.

   Tutors received 'Tutors' Money' from the Aul.Prae. for this purpose: a relic

Turf-keeper

of the Founder's provision that 'every consanguineus was to be in charge of one of the more advanced and discreeter sort of scholars, who was to make him perfect in grammar, and receive 6*s* 8*d* for doing so'.

Tutors were mentioned in 1820–8, when the three or four Senior Praefects had up to seven pupils each, and the Junior Praefects one or two. The Tutors were appointed by the Headmaster, and their duties were to supervise the learning of lessons by the juniors, and their tasks, and to protect them from bullying. Each Tutor received two guineas a year from the Pupil's parents through the Headmaster.

College Tutor was a Don whose original function was to correct the compositions of College men. Latterly he helped College juniors with their work, but this duty also lapsed, and by 1917 he was no more than assistant to the Second Master in the administration of College. In 1885, his rooms were over Middle Gate; in 1917, in the north-west corner of Chamber Court, above Thule.

Commoner Tutors, of whom there were two, until Commoners dispersed in 1869, were in course alternate weeks. They had to be present at meals, toys and names-calling, and go round galleries every night to see that lights were out.

Tutor's collector   each of the two Commoner Tutors chose a man to collect tasks for him, take them into School and distribute them when corrected. Collectors got off watching-out, football and compulsory games in Grass Court.

Tutors' Houses   see **Old Tutors' Houses** or **O.T.H.**

Twenty-two and Twenty-two   a football match, twenty-two to a side, between College and Commoners, played on or about 5 November. After the separation of Houses from Commoners in 1867, Fifteens took the place of Twenty-twos, and this rhyme was composed at the time:

> Says Stephen Herbert, ''Tis a shame,
>   so it to me appears,
> we cannot play the good old game
>   that we have played for years.'

This was Stephen Herbert Gatty (Coll. 1862–8), later a judge, and knighted.

twig, to   to understand anything which is told you (1838). Standard slang: from Gaelic *tuig* (to understand).

twist   a stick spirally indented by the growth of a creeper, with or without the creeper still adhering. Recorded 1856; obsolete by 1900.

This is a medieval word, from Anglo-Saxon *twist* (a rope), meaning something long and pliant which could be plaited. It was used of branches and twigs by Chaucer. In Hampshire and Berkshire, ploughboys who plaited withies into whip-handles called them twists; in Yorkshire, woollen rags bound with spiral threads are called twistes. In standard English, twist can mean a type of shredded tobacco, the arrangement of strands in rope-making, the spiral groove inside a rifle-barrel. So the sense is plain enough: but it is odd that this kind of stick should have been well enough known at Winton to earn a Notion.

Two and Twenty-two   a game played in Junior Game canvas in Short Half between the two Captains of College VI on one side, who took it in turns to play up and kick: and the twenty-two junior men in College on the other. In forming a hot, the twenty-two hotted in a line against one of the Captains. It was a rag-game, but of venerable origin, and conscientiously continued (1921).

two black and one brown   see **black asses**.

Two Guinea Match   played on the first Thursday of Cloister Time between picked-up sides captained by the Captain and second Captain of Lords: the sides being Lords Caps and men likely to get into Lords or 2nd XI. It lasted two days. Originally all players subscribed a sum which totalled two guineas, which was shared out among the winning side, but by 1880 it was given to the Professionals, and by 1922 no money changed hands.

twoster (not pronounced too-ster)   a spirally indented stick. Recorded 1856; obsolete by 1900. A good example of the Wiccamization of a word: the vowel becomes 'o': and -er or -ster is suffixed.

umpires standard English for umpires at cricket and referees at football. Recorded in a Commoner word-book of 1868, as being exempted from compulsory football and watching-out; but in 1880 they had to umpire on half-rems in return for this exemption.

Umslopogaas a workman about College, c. 1920: possibly the same as Cyclops. cf. Mate's Mate and Tired Tim. From a character in Rider Haggard's *Allan Quatermaine*.

underconstumble, to to understand. A ἅπαξ λεγόμενον of c. 1838; probably only in use for a year or two.

Under hatch the shelves for beeswaxers at the foot of the stairs by Hatch in new Commoners (1868).

Underhills another name for Evening Hills. See **Hills**.

under ropes when the ball was under ropes, or between ropes and canvas in Winton football. By 1917 this was called 'in ropes' or 'down ropes'.

Under Sixteen a singles fives competi for men under 16, open to the whole school, played in Common Time (1920).

under the bar in fives doubles as played at Winton (1920), the server having served and the hitter-round having hit-round, both go and crouch against the front wall under the bar, and wait to get up shots that hit the buttress.

Underwood a butler in College Hall (1920): talkative and kindly.

up (noun) a man in the hot at Winchester football.

up up to books.

up-game, or **uppers** a kind of soccer played in House yards and on Ball Court, usually with four a side (1900 on).

up to   in the division of; e.g. 'I shall be up to Mr Bather next half.'

up to books   see **books**.

up to House   a Commoner notion, dating from c. 1860, meaning go back to (e.g. to go up to House) or be at (e.g. he is up to House).

up Town   anywhere in the City of Winchester which was out of bounds: roughly everything north of St Swithun's Street and west of St James' Lane. St Thomas' Street was in bounds for men in A House, when Old Chernocke House was there.

Valet (pronounced vall-it, not vall-ay) a junior attached as body-servant to a Praefect and attending to all his requirements (1820 on). Duties mentioned include making his tea and coffee (1836), and mess (1838); looking after his clothes and washing-drawer (1838), and his toilet and dressing things, taking these last into School if the Praefect had not completed his toilet before Chapel (1831); and taking his desk and books into School in the morning and back to Chambers in the evening. Mansfield (1836) includes among the valet's duties getting water in the morning and making tea or coffee in the evening. Candle-keepers had valets also. By 1917 a valet's main duties were to look after his Praefect's clothes and keep his toys tidy and dusted. As a reward, a Praefect gave his valet a 'Valet's book' at the end of the half, inscribing in it the valet's name and the words: 'Vadletto suo, optime merito'. A *Vadlettus*, the Latin form of varlet (vassal) is provided for the Warden in the Statutes, and Praefects' valets are in imitation of that. Valet in standard English is probably an eighteenth-century importation from the French.

Valet's books see above, and **books**.

Varying a short extempore composition in Latin verse, done by VIth Book during afternoon school without any books. It was always the last item in Election examination. Originally it consisted of turning a piece of Latin verse into some other metre, e.g. an ode of Horace into elegiacs. T. A. Trollope says the compositions (1820–8) had to be epigrammatic, and in the manner of Martial rather than Ovid, and quotes a brilliant example by a boy who wore a wig. Varyings were said to have been introduced by Dr Gabell (1810–24), but were probably even earlier, and inherited by him. Adams remarks that Gabell was a devotee of Horace and is unlikely to have started a fashion for tampering with Horace's metres. The term was still in use in 1856, but obsolete soon after.

velvet, sport see **advertisement**.

verdigris custard served with prunes in College Hall: cf. Ellenberger and Antrobus. It was perfectly wholesome.

Verse Task   a Latin verse composition done once a week. In 1836 all boys did it: by 1922, only VIth Book. Trollope's father, in College under Dr Warton, used to relate how Tom Warton, the Headmaster's brother, sometimes composed boys' verse tasks for them in Chambers in the evening, c. 1755–60.

vessel   half a quarter of a sheet of foolscap (1831–42), of Long Paper (1856–1900). Surviving in College (1920) in a 'half-vessel', one sixteenth of a sheet, measuring about 3 by 2 inches [7.5 by 5 cm], used for putting up a roll in Chambers. Vessel, or fassel, was theme paper at Bury and possibly other schools, and vessel still occurs in dialect for a piece of writing-paper about 7 by 4 ½ inches [17.5 by 11.25 cm]. In Northern Ireland in the early nineteenth century, a vessel was school exercise paper about octavo size. The word is either: (1) a subsidiary use of vessel, from Latin *vascellum*, diminutive of *vas*, meaning a small unit for the reception of a piece of composition; or (2) from Italian *vassiola*, Latin *fasciculus* (a strip of paper used for wrapping a roll of paper).

vice versa   to toll to Meads foricas and back (1920).

viva   a viva-voce examination. Used (1920) for the vivas in the following exams: Election and Monthly (the Headmaster took the viva in both these); new College Scholarships (taken by the Posers: candidates wore white ties). Viva is also a university Notion.

Vivo   an American College yell, popularised by Harry Gordon Selfridge, junr, (Coll. 1913–17), son of Selfridge of London. It was shouted loud, staccato and with stresses, and we found it useful on march-outs for pulling the step together. It ran:

> 'With a Veevo, with a Vyvo, with a Veevo, Vyvo, Vum.
> Bum, get a rat-trap bigger than a cat-trap [twice].
>   Cannibal, cannibal, sis cum bah.
>   Winchester, Winchester [or Harvard, Yale, etc.],
>   Ra, Ra, Ra.'

from the same source we learned a non-collegiate yell:

> 'Down with Harvard, down with Yale.
> Learn your lessons by the mail.
> We ain't asses, we ain't fools.
> Ra, Ra, Ra, the Correspondence Schools.'

The vogue for these yells was doubtless very brief.

voluntary   a copy of verses written occasionally by some of the boys in VIth Book and Senior Part 'ex proprio motu'. Noted 1836 only.

Volt   see **Revolt**.

vulgus a short composition on a set word or subject, done in all parts of the school from the earliest times until c. 1890, when it was discontinued and the notion lapsed. From vulgars, i.e. vulgaria (from Latin *vulgaris*), books of common words and phrases. The best known vulgaria were both written by Wykehamists: viz. John Stanbridge (College 1475; Headmaster of Magdalen College School, then Banbury School), published 1508; and William Horman (College 1468; Headmaster of Eton, then Winchester), published 1519. Christopher Johnson (Headmaster 1560–71) writes: 'Who does not know the excellent vulgaria of Hermanus [Horman]?' In 1529 it is recorded that the IVth, IIIrd and IInd forms at Winchester have a verb set overnight, and next morning have to write vulgaris or vulgares on it, including repetition of lines. At this time Eton also had vulgares. In 1576 Oswestry School had vulgars.

In the Marett papers in Jersey there survives a vulgus on an unusual subject, the death of Daniel Marett, scholar of Winton, at school, on 30 November 1759. It consists of a poem in English, possibly by the Headmaster, Dr Burton, deploring the death, and four different compositions in Latin elegiacs on the same subject, varying from eight to twelve lines.

In 1820–8 at Winton, all Inferiors each night had to do a copy of verses on a given theme, from four to six lines in the upper classes, two lines in the lowest. In 1831 the vulgus was always Latin elegiacs, with a six-line minimum in the higher classes, and four lines in the lower. An example of a vulgus of that period, full of false quantities, on the River Rhine, is preserved:

'Est Rhenus fluvius, rapidus fluit, atque citatus.
Dividit is Galliam ab Allemanne fine.'

In Tom Brown's day at Rugby (c. 1835) the vulgus was believed to have been established by William of Wykeham, and taken to Rugby by the Wykehamist Thomas Arnold. It was a short exercise in Greek or Latin verse on a given subject, the number of lines varying with the form. Hughes thought that the lines learned by heart were of more value than the vulgars.

At Winton in 1838 vulgus was six lines of Latin elegiacs. From 1856 to 1884 it was a Latin epigram of four, five, or six lines, done three times a week. Latterly, vulgus was used of any Latin verse composition.

Walford's (known as New School in 1838) the building which stood on the west side of School. It contained a Mathematical School, a room for IVth Book, and College Praefects' Library. It was built in 1833, and removed in 1870, when the Notion lapsed. Named from John Desborough Walford, Mathematical Don 1834–73.

Walford's Corner the corner where the boundary wall of Grass Court met Walford's. It was once a famous battleground, where boys fought out their grievances.

Walford's water-closets the glass shades to the candles in Chapel. A disreputable Commoner Notion, recorded only in 1868.

Walker senior College Chamberman, 1917–22 (and probably longer). In Hall he waited on Senior Praefects' End. Among his duties was to take up College Tutor's breakfast. He was a keen supporter and critic of College cricket and football. Walker, also known as Stalker, enjoyed his glass of beer. He limped, it was said, because in infancy his mother accidentally dropped him into a vat of boiling beer.

Walker's Hole a horrid little lumber-room, half-way up the stairs from foricas table to 6th Chamber, which stretched under 6th Bidet Room. It could be broken into with ease. Walker often emerged from it, wafting with him an odour of ale.

walking ticket a boy was said (1838) to receive a walking ticket when a master told his parents he was doing no good at school and had better leave.

Wally a nickname shared (1920) between: (1) Major W. S. Cowland, DSO (D 1901–7): Adjutant of the Officers Training Corps and Secretary to Monty Rendall, about whom he had a lively repertoire of tales; (2) John Dolbel Le Couteur, of 7 St Cross Road, and of Jersey extraction. An expert on stained glass, he was engaged in College Mill in 1921 repairing all the glass from the windows of Chapel. A contemporary description of him reads:

'of weird shape, he is one of the seven wonders of the world: nervously
polite: talks quickly in a high-pitched voice: usually carries binoculars,
and his walking-stick with the handle in his pocket: doffs his hat to young
and old with a curious quick motion.'

He died on 13 August 1925 of neuritis and spinal dislocation following a drive
in a Ford car. He became a 'Notion' to College men of his day, on account of
his devotion to antiquarianism, his unusual personality, and his rigid politeness,
which caused him to address even College juniors as 'My dear Sir'. Cowland
was called Wally because his name was Walter; Le Couteur shared the
name through the intricate Wiccamical skein of Le Couteur, Le Touceur,
Whalley-Tooker, Wally.

warden's bibling   a flogging of nine cuts administered by the Warden in
person, but probably not since 1850.

Warden's Child   see **child**.

Warden's Dean   see **Warden's Om**.

Warden's House, Warden's Lodging   on the east side of Outer Court. Begun
by John Harmer (1597), improved and enlarged by Warden Love (1615) and
by John Harris (1633). The garden-front was built by Warden Nicholas (1692).
The gallery facing on Outer Court was added (1833) on designs furnished by
Repton.

Warden's Om   short for 'Custos omnes ad caenam invitat', or the Warden's
bidding for all to attend a feast. This was a momentous occasion, occurring
once a year, when the Warden was moved to provide apple-pies to the
whole community. Vulgarly known as Apple-pie Day, or even Warden's Dean
(pudding). Now remotely obsolete.

Warden's Prog   the Warden's Progress. The annual visitation of College
estates by the Warden, accompanied by the Bursar (1831), by the Fellows
(1836). The visitation may continue, but the Notion is long since dead.

Warden's Stream   a name for Logie, because it runs past the Warden's
Garden.

war in Egypt   the melodious note given out by a chamber-pot when inadvertently kicked (1920). Origin entirely obscure.

warm, to   to stand in front of a Chamber fire with one's back to it; an
important ritual, regulated by privilege (1920). Praefects carried, and Inferiors
docked, their gowns when warming. The favourite times to warm, when most

washing-stool

of the Chamber gathered round Quarter-Deck, were after breakfast, before and after Hall, before Toy-time and before Preces. There was also warming up in Chambers at bedtime, but at 9.30 all below VIth Book had to leave the fireside.

warming-pan   a large watch (1838).

War Scholars   these were admitted to College, at the rate of one or two a year, during and just after the First World War, without any test of their scholarship. Any boy whose father had been killed in the war, especially if he had also been a Wykehamist, was a strong candidate for entry. Boys from the Allied Nations were also admitted. We had two Belgian refugees, Van den Bemden and Prioux, and two Russians, Orloff-Davidoff and Zvegintzov (see **Zogitoff**). The latter distinguished himself by rising nine divs in eight terms (J.P.2 to VIth Book Science Div), and being two years in College VI.

wash butter, to   a method of preparing butter for eating, recorded only in 1838. 'A boy takes a knife and cuts the butter in half, so that one piece sticks to one side of the knife and one piece to the other: he then puts some water on the trencher and pats the butter that is on the knife against the wet trencher, until the butter becomes flat. He then, holding the knife slantways, scrapes the butter off the knife on to the middle of the trencher in two lines.' Mansfield describes butter-washing as battering the butter with a knife against a trencher under a tap at Conduit. See **butter-washer**.

washing-drawer   an oak box or dressing-case in use in College c. 1836–70, for holding toilet requisites. It contained a tray lined with lead paper or tinfoil, and there were partitions in the tray for soap, nail-brush, tooth-brush, comb and clothes-brush. Beneath the tray there was room for hair-brushes, a glass and a towel. Referred to as a washing-box in Commoner word-books, c. 1868 to 1880.

washing-stool   a strong low table with the legs splayed outwards, at which each College Praefect sat in Chambers, wrote and had mess. At washing time it was carried out to Chamber Court Conduit, which only Praefects might use, and his basin and washing apparatus were placed upon it. These tables ceased to be used as wash-stands c. 1850, but the notion, first recorded c. 1831, still clung to the tables, many of which survived in upstairs Chambers in 1922, and were used by Praefects for mugging at night.

washing-up   to wash up Praefects' tea-things was one of juniors' most time-consuming chores in College, c. 1917–22. It was done in the conduits in IVth by juniors (sweated to wash up) from Thule and VIIth: and in the sink (which had taken the place of the conduits) in Ist by juniors from IInd, Vth and VIth. After 1922 juniors washed up for their own Chambers. Previously, the First Junior in course in a Chamber where Praefects had had tea, had to sweat washers-up in other Chambers: one, if one man had had tea: two, for two to four men: three, for more than four (see **mess towel** and **sus-bucket**). The last man to 'finge table' (q.v.) had to clean it with his mess towel. On half-rems washing-up could be begun as soon as tea was finished. On whole-school days it was done between College tea and Toy-time.

watcher-out   a junior who is watching-out. See **watch-out**.

watch-out, to, watching-out   fielding at cricket or football: another substantial chore for juniors at Winton.
  (1) In 1836 it meant fielding (or being on the fielding side) at cricket only, in accordance with the normal parlance of Hampshire cricketers in the eighteenth century. The Hambledon men used to 'watch out' or 'seed out', and in 1786 the Rev. Gilbert White wrote: 'little Tom Clement is visiting Petersfield, where he plays much at cricket. Tom bats: his grandmother bowls: and his great-grandmother watches out.' This meaning was still current at Winton in 1922: and 'watch out' is still a standard English warning, meaning 'look out'.
  Since 1836, watch-out has also meant fielding at cricket practice, at Praefects' games or nets. In 1836 this could be almost a whole-day task, but a junior who made a catch was let off for the rest of the day, and this concession was still being made in 1922.
  In 1900, juniors had to watch-out for one hour twice a week in their first year, and once a week in their second. Watching-out stopped in Cloister Time after Eton Match, after which any watchers-out needed had to be nailed.
  In 1920 there was watching-out on whole-school days for all men still in sweat, from 1.45 to 2.45: 2.45 to 3.45: 6.30 to 7.15. Men who could catch well asked the names-docker to be put at School nets where, if they caught a catch, they might go away. The remainder went to House nets. Dons bowling at School nets also used to send away men who had watched-out well.
  Watching-out still meant being on the fielding side in a game of cricket in 1922.
  (2) It also meant throwing back the football into canvas, or into the field of

play before canvas was installed (1843), by lines of juniors in the early days, and then by fewer juniors stationed at intervals (see **canvas**, and **keep in balls**). This chore continued through Short Half until Sixes were over. In College (1920) it was organised in the following manner.

At the beginning of Short Half the Captain of VI put up a roll of watchers-out on College Notice Board:

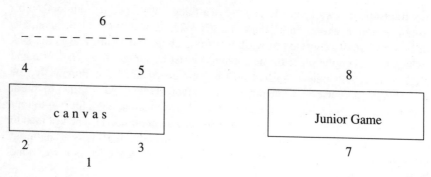

No. 1 was names-docker in canvas. Nos. 2, 3, 4 and 5 stood near the ends. No. 6 was in Mill, with a ladder in Joel's garden so that he could see over the wall. No. 7 was names-docker in Junior Game, and no. 8 the other watcher-out there.

watching-out roll   the roll put up at the beginning of the half, showing when and where juniors were to watch-out. See above.

water-carrier   see **gallery sweat**.

water-closets   a game of cricket played in New Commoners (1868) in Grass Court with a pudding. This notion, of earthy origin, has been emended to Water Assets in the 1892–1907 Notion books.

Waterloo, or **Waterloo boiler**   a funnel-shaped boiler (i.e. vessel for boiling water), much in use (1880) for making egg-flip, and probably similar to an aetna or etna (q.v.).

Waterloo boiler

Waterman's Hut

Waterman's Hut   a cottage between Tunbridge and Hammond's at the end of Double Hedges. Its occupant used to look after hatches and floodgates (1880).

Water Meads   the water meadows of the Itchen valley, south of College: a complex of streams and channels, controlled by hatches. An ancient Notion; still in use 1922.

water someone, to   a College Notion (1920) for pouring water on someone in Chamber Court from an upper window (see **squelch-belch**; and hence the mock Tabula Legum item, 'Ostiarium ne madefactanto'): or on someone on a lower landing from upstairs. A pastime of Praefects and Tolly-keepers. When it had gone too far, the Aul.Prae. intervened and docked the offenders wearing tug coats instead of gowns for a season, a privilege they could exercise between Hall and Preces on half-rems.

Weary Willy   cf. Tired Tim.

Webbe Tent   a two-storeyed, thatched cricket pavilion at the south-west corner of New Field, erected by A. J. Webbe in memory of H. R. Webbe, Captain of Lords 1875. The ground floor was used (1890) as a refreshment room in Cloister Time, the upper storey being reserved for Lords and foreign XIs. By 1917 the whole building was reserved for Lords and their opponents, the ground floor being a dining-room in front and changing-rooms behind. After 1922 Webbe Tent was rebuilt on modern lines as Hunter Tent.

Weirs, the   a school and town Notion for Non-Licet Passage, so called because it might not be used unless one had leave up Town. It was a broad pathway, of great beauty, leading from College Walk along the wall of Wolvesey Palace beside a hurrying stream to the Soke Bridge. So cool and tranquil in summer. But I recall no weirs in the stream.

well   a secret space between the drawers of some toys, 'in which cigars or anything of that sort is kept' (1838).

Weller, the   Miss Agnes Wellsman, the lady who lived in College Sick House (1920) with a maid, Ada, and performed the functions of College matron. She dispensed tonics and medicines after meals, and was generally to be found in or about Sick House chatting with someone in College. She was a close friend of Mrs Williams. Her fault was to over-emphasise her acquaintance with the landed gentry and nobility; her virtue, that she was very kind to men continent, and to new men, whom she used to ask out to tea. Her dog, a Sealyham named Jock, thought nothing of the Kaiser.

Wells   Messrs P. & G. Wells, booksellers to the school, with a shop in College Street which sold all school books, stationery and tollies. They were affiliated to Warren, the printer up Town, who produced the *Wykehamist*, Long and Short Rolls, and lists, etc. See **Phil Wells** and **Elkins**. Previous holders of this valuable monopoly, working backwards, were: J. Wells; D. Nutt; Robbins (c. 1840); Robbins & Wheeler.

welsh, to   to cheat up to books, or in any other circumstance. To 'welsh out of' meant to sconce, take unfairly from. In standard slang, to welch means to abscond from a racecourse without paying one's debts.

West Hall   in New Commoners (1842–69) was over Grubbing Hall. It was converted to classrooms 8 and 9.

Wheeler   a young partner taken on by Robbins, bookseller in College Street, c. 1826: see **Wells**.

Whirlpool   the confluence of Old and New Barge below Second Pot (1880). Obsolete by 1917.

Whisky Corner   a corner south of Webbe Tent, formed by the boundary wall of Dogger's Close. When Dogger's Close was added to New Field in 1894, the corner and the Notion ceased to exist. Nuance unrecorded.

whiteball   like a very large fives ball, about 3 inches [7.5 cm] in diameter and made of similar materials, roughly stitched. It was used in house yards, and also in Whiteball Game, a form of small crockets played on summer evenings (1920) from 6.30 to 7.30 by senior College men. There were wickets at both ends. Play was with a whiteball and a small-crockets bat, on the tip-and-run principle. A player who made 20 had then to go on batting left-handed.

White Bridge   a white bridge over River below First Pot (1880).

White Post   a white post on the right bank of River a little below Tunbridge (1880).

white shoes, to wear   for fives, racquets, etc., in 1920 was in College, a Flannels, XVs Roll, Praefects' and Tolly-keepers' Notion (XVs Roll being included because in the 1880s men in XVs used to play in long white ducks, and could wear their flannels); in Commoners, a Flannels, XVs Roll, Praefects' and three-year Notion.

Whitesman   the butler in College Hall (c. 1838–43) who gave out trenchers, saw to the cleaning of them, 'and in fact superintends all that Purver does'. See **Purver**. In Mansfield's day (1836), trenchers, knives and forks were obtained from Whitesman's Hatch. Mansfield hints that Whitesman and Purver were hereditary nicknames, not the men's real names.

whole rem   see **remedy**.

whole-school day   a day on which there was full afternoon school. Recorded from 1880.

Wickham's   part of the buildings of Old Commoners (see Commoners). Originally the Sustern Chapel (chapel of the Sisters' Hospital), it had 'a narrow spiral staircase, cumbrous timber-work and curiously constructed landing-places', and was occupied for a few years at the end of the eighteenth century by Mr Wickham, the College medical attendant.

Wi.Co.Ri.Co.No.Bo.   Winchester College Rifle Corps Notice Board, on the west side of Hat Place. A facetious Notion of 1920, with all syllables pronounced long: cf. Do.Co.Ro.Fo. [cf. Oxford slang, 'Wagger-pagger-bagger' = wastepaper basket].

William of Wykeham   (1) Fundator noster, Gulielmus de Wykeham, cuius beneficiis hic ad pietatem ac studia literarum alimur. (2) a gross, elongated, mangy and sulky Aberdeen, owned by College Cook, and the predecessor of Roger (q.v.). He used to sit outside Trusty Sweater's Hole in indolence all day, stirring only to bark at people he disliked, which included butchers' boys and most of the men in College, who reciprocated his feelings. He used also to howl at Chapel bells from some lair in the Warden's Lodging. He passed on, to the relief of all, c. 1920.

Willow   the willow tree between Garden Gate and Tunbridge; a Notion c. 1892–1907.

Willows   a line of willows on the right bank of River below Tunbridge (1880).

window-boxes these were placed in all downstairs windows in Chamber Court in Cloister Time, and each stocked by an upstairs Chamber with about 10 shillings' worth of flowers from Hilliers, the choice guided by general consensus of the Chamber. 6th had the window of VIth: Vth, of Vth: 8th, of IInd: 9th, of Ist: 10th, the window between North-West Passage and Chamber Court Conduit: 11th, the window near the door of IIrd: 12th, the two windows of Trusty Sweater's Hole: Ken, the window of IVth. Nasturtia, canary creeper, lobelia and gerania were grown, and in July the Second Master gave a prix for the best window-box. But they looked their best at the end of August, when nobody was there.

window cad a junior whose duty it was to open and shut windows. Obsolete by 1890.

'Windows!' the cry backed up in Hall or Galleries in Houses, on hearing which the junior man present had to close or open the windows complained of.

[**Winton** the old name for Winchester. Winchester College, in full 'St Mary's College at Winchester', was also referred to as 'St Mary Winton'.]

wocket wicket, in all its senses (a stump, the fall of a wicket, a wicket-keeper). In use 1917–22. A good example of the Wiccamical substitution of 'o' for another vowel: cf. crockets (cricket).

woll a 'walk-run', encouraged (1917) by the Headmaster, Monty Rendall, who disapproved of long tolls on a wartime diet. It was constructed from 'walk' and 'toll', and implied that one could break into a walk when tired of running.

word-book a glossary or dictionary of Notions (1850–1900).

work, to to smart, to hurt, to be painful. From Anglo-Saxon *weorc* (pain). In Old English, *work* (pain) occurs as noun and verb in the fourteenth century; tooth-warke (tooth-ache) in the fifteenth century; 'myn hede werches' (my head aches) in 1469. In North Country dialect we have heeadwark (headache), tooth-warch (toothache), belly-work (stomach-ache). In use probably from the foundation, but obsolete by 1917. The word work took a side-track in standard English, to enshrine an idea as old as mankind, that effort is a nuisance or a painful disease. Thus remedy means holiday at Winton: in Latin, *negotium* (activity) is the denial of man's right to *otium* (leisure). Work in standard English usually implies strenuous physical output. In the form irk, it is discomfort or pain; labour, in the sense of travail, is a matter for the hospital; taking trouble over something is called taking pains, as though endeavour were painful.

worker a painful blow on any part of the body with a stick, stone, ball, or fist. In use 1838–84: the use is aligned with 'work' above.

worms   a line cut in the turf at each end of canvas at Winchester football, as goal lines. In use from 1856, if not before. Presumably named from the earth-worms brought to the surface when cutting the lines.

worship   any Chapel service. It was a foible of Monty Rendall, Headmaster 1911–24, so to refer to Chapel services.

worsteders   thick worsted stockings, worn outside the trousers at football to protect the shins. In use c. 1831–1907.

wreck   (also spelt reck) a diving-stage at Gunner's Hole. The highest was Senior Wreck, or Senior Senior. College men also (1917) derisively used the name Senior Wreck for the senior Commoner on Short Roll. The derivation is unknown: reck seems the more correct spelling and may be a form of the word rack, either in the sense of an open framework, such as duck-boarding, or possibly an obscure dialect meaning of rack, a rough narrow footpath.

Wrench Card   a printed calendar of school events during the half, including matches, preachers, etc., and originally compiled by the Aul.Prae. For some reason known as Wrench Ask c. 1917. In 1918 it was discontinued as a war economy, but revived later. It often came out too late to be worth buying. Named from its inventor, R. G. K. ['Piggy'] Wrench (Comm. 1856–60), author of the *Winchester Word-Book*.

Writer   an Officer's valet, who also had certain secretarial duties connected with his Praefect's office: see **Chapel**, **Hall**, **Mob.Lib.** and **School Writers**. In use by 1856.

wurden, to   to throw a thing out of the window of an upstairs Chamber (i.e. 6th, 7th, 8th, 9th, 11th, Ken, or New Chamber) into the Warden's Garden or Logie. Broken china in the river bed beneath these windows indicated that the objects most often wurdened were pint- and chamber-pots. In use by 1910, and after 1922.

Wurden-Gurden, the   the Warden's Garden. A notion of 1916, possibly inspired by hurdy-gurdy.

Wykeham Arms   a public house on the corner of Canon Street and Kingsgate Street, facing School Shop. Strictly out of bounds, of course. Laverty's aged father might be seen tottering across to it (1917).

Wykehamist, or **Wokehamist** (pronounced Wökehamist)   (1) the school magazine, first published in 1866. (2) a present or past member of the school, the latter usually being called an Old Wykehamist or Old Wok. (3) a large spider. To be a Wykehamist (1917), a man had to have (a) spliced a hollis over Mill in a cathedral (i.e. thrown a pebble over College Mill wearing a top-hat). (b) been to Third Pot and Amphitheatre. (c) (i) been beaten three times; or (ii) been hotted into Otterburn by a man in a different div and House (for which purpose College East and West were rated as two Houses). But this last was not always considered a genuine method of becoming a Wykehamist.

Yard   the asphalt court attached to each House, and used for small crockets, uppers and other pastimes.

yolly   yellow. A yolly was a post-chaise, yellow being their usual colour. In use by 1836; obsolete by 1917. Yellow in Lancashire dialect becomes yolla, and elsewhere yolly (cf. tolly, brolly); yolly survives in cockyolly-bird, a nursery name for the yellowhammer, from cock and yolly.

yolly

Young Augustus Passage   this used to lead from Junior Part Cloisters to the div rooms on the west of Moberly Court. A small door led into it from Moberly Court, used by Ponto and Archie Wilson, but not by men in the school. The passage was removed in 1924–5. It was named after the cast of the bust of the young Augustus from the Vatican, which used to stand in a corner of the passage. The inscribed wooden pedestal was still there in 1922, but the cast had vanished.

Zadok   an anthem [by Handel] regularly sung in Chapel (1920), beginning with the words: 'Zadok the priest'.

zephyr   a thin jersey (q.v.) with short sleeves, which were edged (1880) with dark blue, as was the neck: worn by School IV for races. By 1914 it meant a thin vest, white or striped, used for Winchester football, tolling and fives. Zephyr is a trade-name for a fine and light textile fabric, from Latin *Zephyrus* (the West Wind).

Zogitoff, or **Zog**   nickname of a Russian refugee named Michael Zvegintzov, scholar of Winton 1918–23, and then of Corpus: a fine footballer, and a brilliant scientist. When he entered College there was, or had been, a Zog, King of Albania; at the same time a detergent called ZOG was struggling for priority, with the exhortation: 'Zog it off', against VIM and other ancestors of AJAX. Having read thus far in this lexicon, you will perceive that Zogitoff was a ready-made Notion.

Zuyder Zee   the pools which often stood in Meads after the rain. A Notion of 1917.

INDEX TO INTRODUCTION

Adams, H. C. 9, 15
Africa 2, 4
Asquith, A. 13
Asquith, M. 13
Ayer, A. J. 12

Becker, K. F. 14
Bromsgrove School 3
Burge, H. M. 19

Caesar, C. J. 5
Caesarea 5
Callender, J. M. 15
Century Dictionary 5
Christ's Hospital 1
Clarendon Commission 9
Collas, Joan 5
College 7
Colonial Administrative
    Service 4
Commoners 7

De Quincey, T. 10
Diélament 5
Dunchurch Hall School 3

Encyclopedia Britannica 5
English Dialect Dictionary
    11
Eton College 8–9, 12

Farmer, J. S. 11
Fearon, W. A. 8
Firth, J. d'E. 12–13
Fives 3
Fleming, W. 14
Foord, J. 6
Furley, J. S. 8

Gordon, R. 6–7
Great Tunding Row 9
Gwyn, P. 17

Hailey, Lord 4
Harrow School 12
Hawkes, C. F. C. 4
Hegel, G. W. F. 12
Hill, A. D. 11
Hindi 14
Hotten, J. C. 9

Jackson, H. 19
Jersey 5
Joseph, H. W. B. 16

Kennedy, Benjamin 3

Leach, A. F. 11, 15
Liddell, H. G. 1
Lusaka 4

Mansfield, R. B. 9, 15
Maori 14
Mapleton, Dr 10
Markham, F. 19
Marples, M. 1, 11
Mason, C. P. 14
Minerva, owl of 12
Morell, J. D. 14
Morshead, E. D. A. 13
Müller, F. M. 14
Murray, J. A. H. 10
Mushri 13
*Mushri-English Pronounc-
    ing Dictionary* 13–14
Myres, J. N. L. 3–4, 6

New College, Oxford 3
'Nonsense' 2
Northern Rhodesia 4
Notions and Rules 1

Oppidans 17
Oxford 3, 12
Oxford English Dictionary
    10–11, 14

Pali 14
Partridge, E. 10
Philological Society of
    London 10

Rhymes at Random 4
Ridding, G. 7–8, 14–15
Robertson, Major 13
Robeson, P. 4
Robinson, C. E. 13

Scott, R. 1
Sedeman 5
'Sense' 2

Shadwell, L. L. 11
Shrewsbury School 3
Sikololo 4
Skeat, W. W. 10
Société Jersiaise 5
Spectator 8
St Catharine's Hill 4
Stevens, C. G. 2–7
Stone, C. R. 12

'Three Beetleites' 11
Trench, R. C. 10–11
Tuckwell, W. 15
Turner, C. H. 9

Wellington, Duke of 16
Westminster School 1, 12
Whitney, W. D. 15
Wiccamica 15
Winton 5–6, 15
Wrench, R. G. K. 1, 9
Wright, J. 11

Ziff 18
Ziph 10

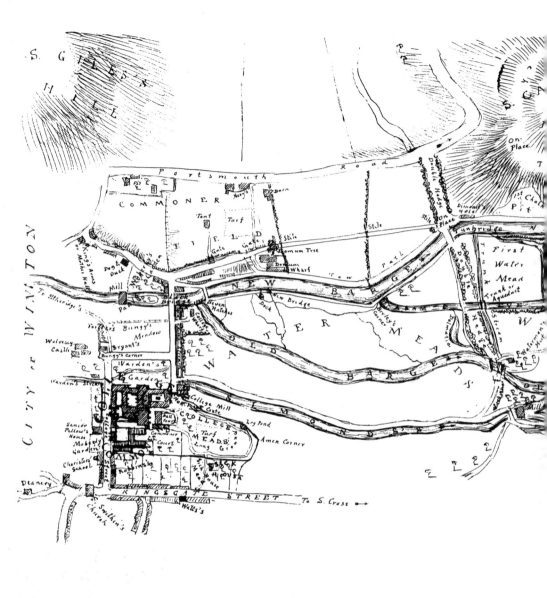

Winchester College and Environs, 1855
(two pages from the word-book of E. R. D. Thomson)